Special Edition
Using
TCP/IP

Second Edition

NIIT

Que Publishing

201 W. 103rd Street

Indianapolis, Indiana 46290

Special Edition Using TCP/IP, Second Edition

Associate Publisher
David Culverwell

Executive Editor
Candace Hall

Acquisitions Editor
Dean Miller

Development Editor
Fran Hatton

Managing Editor
Thomas Hayes

Project Editor
Tricia S. Liebig

Copy Editor
Kate Givens

Indexer
Ken Johnson

Proofreader
Sarah Cisco

Technical Editor
Michelle Truman

Team Coordinator
Cindy Teeters

Interior Designer
Ruth Harvey

Cover Designers
Dan Armstrong
Ruth Harvey

Page Layout
Ayanna Lacey

CONTENTS

ABOUT THE AUTHORS

Ramadas Shanmugam brings with him a rich experience of training and instructional design. He is a computer science student and is passionate about computers and writing. Ramadas is currently working as an instructional designer at NIIT where he designs and authors books on a wide range of subjects. He has co-authored books and instructional training material on Lotus Notes, Windows NT, Mozilla Open Source Browser Programming, and Microsoft Visio. Ramadas is a Microsoft Certified Solutions Developer.

Padmini.R, a graduate in computer science, has been involved in training technical courses on a wide variety of subjects thus gaining extensive exposure in training and instructional design. She has designed and created instructional training material for the Microsoft Windows 2000 Server certification exams, Microsoft Office, and Java Servlets programming.

Nivedita.S, a postgraduate in biochemistry, loves to learn and believes that teaching is the best way to learn. She has designed and developed training material on topics such as StarOffice Suite, FrontPage 2000, and Visual Basic. She has also edited books on C#, Wireless LANs, and Storage Area Networks.

DEDICATION

To Chuchi Amma

—Ramadas Shanmugam

To my family

—Padmini.R

To my beloved family

—Nivedita.S

ACKNOWLEDGMENTS

Looking back from where we started, writing this book has been a gratifying experience. Apart from the long hours and the heated discussions in a language that no one could understand, it was fun writing this book. However, we couldn't have made it happen without the guidance and assistance from:

Kumar, who has been our guiding spirit and source of inspiration.

Sudhir, who flagged off our long journey.

Rajiv, Uma, and Abi, who gave us a helping hand when we needed it the most.

Sindhu, Rashmi, and Parul, who translated the networking imagery with their graphics.

Ranjana and Geetha, who guided our grammar.

Shantanu, who coordinated the reviews for the book.

Fran, Michelle, and Mark, for smoothing the language and technical aspects.

Our family, friends, and colleagues who encouraged us all the way.

TELL US WHAT YOU THINK!

As the reader of this book, *you* are our most important critic and commentator. We value your opinion and want to know what we're doing right, what we could do better, what areas you'd like to see us publish in, and any other words of wisdom you're willing to pass our way.

As Publisher for Que, I welcome your comments. You can fax, e-mail, or write me directly to let me know what you did or didn't like about this book—as well as what we can do to make our books stronger.

Please note that I cannot help you with technical problems related to the topic of this book, and that due to the high volume of mail I receive, I might not be able to reply to every message.

When you write, please be sure to include this book's title and author as well as your name and phone or fax number. I will carefully review your comments and share them with the author and editors who worked on the book.

Fax: 317-581-4666

E-mail: feedback@quepublishing.com

Mail: David Culverwell
          Que
          201 West 103rd Street
          Indianapolis, IN 46290 USA

INTRODUCTION

In this introduction

TCP/IP is a protocol suite that enables reliable, secure, and instant communication over a network or a network of networks, also called an internetwork. With the tremendous growth of networking in the past few decades, TCP/IP has provided a standardized communication and data exchange mechanism that encompasses the hardware and software requirements needed to sustain smooth communication over internetworks.

In its simplest form, TCP/IP can be described as a set of communication standards that has evolved over the past three decades. These standards, documented in the form of Request for Comments, provide instructions and rules for designing network architectures apart from a host of software specifications. With contributions from networking pioneers and experts, the TCP/IP standards have evolved as a premier internetwork communication mechanism that has stood the test of time. Today, the protocol suite provides specifications for implementing mobile communication, realtime multimedia transmission, Quality of Service, and a high degree of data communication security.

THIS BOOK IS FOR YOU

If you are looking to gain thorough knowledge in TCP/IP, this book is for you. A certain degree of exposure to the basics of computing and networking might be required but is not necessary (for an introduction to networking basics, you can read Appendix B, "Local Area Networking Basics"). Network administrators who have been working with TCP/IP implementations on various operating systems might want to know what happens behind the scenes. This book is also targeted at network administrators who want to learn about the fundamental and advanced networking concepts that drive TCP/IP implementations on various operating systems.

HOW THIS BOOK IS ORGANIZED

This book is divided into five sections. The first section introduces you to the concept of internetworking and the core protocols that form the fundamentals of the TCP/IP protocol suite. The next section deals with the software applications and utilities that use TCP/IP for network communication. Third, we delve into subnetting and routing features provided by TCP/IP. Next deals with the security features inherent in the protocol suite. Finally, we delve into some of the advanced TCP/IP technologies with an outlook into the future of TCP/IP.

The first seven chapters introduce basic internetworking concepts and the core protocols that make the fundamentals of TCP/IP for internetworks.

- Chapter 1, "Introduction to Internetworking and TCP/IP," deals with the fundamentals of Internetworking. The chapter also delves into the basics of TCP/IP.

- Chapter 2, "The Network Interface and Link Layers," introduces you to the Network Layer and the Link layer of the TCP/IP reference model.

- Chapter 3, "The Internet Layer Protocol," deals with one of the core TCP/IP protocols called the Internet Protocol.

- Chapter 4, "Internet Control Message Protocol," delves into the error tracking and isolation features offered by TCP/IP using the Internet Control Message Protocol.

- Chapter 5, "Transmission Control and Data Flow," gives you an insight into Transmission Control Protocol, which is another core protocol in the TCP/IP protocol suite.

- Chapter 6, "Timed Data Transmission and Performance Concepts," continues with the exploration of Transmission Control Protocol features. The chapter delves into timed data transmission and performance enhancement features offered by Transmission Control Protocol.

- Chapter 7, "User Datagram Protocol," explores how unreliable data transmission can be implemented using the User Datagram Protocol.

Chapters 8–14 deal with software applications that operate from the Application layer of the TCP/IP reference model.

- Chapter 8, "File Transfer and Access," deals with remote file transfer and access using protocols such as File Transfer Protocol, Trivial File Transfer Protocol, and Network File Access.

- Chapter 9, "Remote Login," deals with protocols such as Telnet and Rlogin that enable remote computer logins.

- Chapter 10, "Messaging Protocols," delves into how TCP/IP implements mailing features using the Simple Mail Transfer Protocol.

- Chapter 11, "Hypertext Transmission," enables you to learn how TCP/IP provides hypertext data transmission using Hypertext Transfer Protocol.

- Chapter 12, "Simple Network Management Protocol (SNMP)," delves into the network management features implemented using TCP/IP's Simple Network Management Protocol.

- Chapter 13, "Domain Name System (DNS)," introduces you to the domain naming and resolving features implemented by TCP/IP using Domain Naming Services.

- Chapter 14, "Bootstrapping Protocols: BOOTP and DHCP," deals with application protocols such as BOOTP and DHCP, which provide bootstrapping and dynamic host configuration features.

Chapters 15–20 delve into the intricacies of the IP addressing scheme and the IP address conversation feature provided by subnetting apart from information on routing architectures and mechanisms provided by TCP/IP.

- Chapter 15, "Subnetting and Classless Addressing," delves into the IP addressing scheme and the classless addressing feature that overcomes the shortage of IP addresses.

- Chapter 16, "IP Routing," introduces routing concepts and routing error handling features implemented in TCP/IP.

- Chapter 17, "Routing Mechanisms," provides an overview of the routing mechanisms implemented by TCP/IP.

- Chapter 18, "Routing on Autonomous Systems," explores the world of autonomous systems and delves into the routing mechanisms implemented within autonomous systems.

- Chapter 19, "Inter-autonomous System Routing Protocol—EGP and BGP," deals with routing between autonomous systems using Exterior Gateway Protocol and Border Gateway Protocol.

- Chapter 20, "Multicasting," introduces you to multicasting and delves into how multicasting can be implemented on a TCP/IP network. The chapter also explores the role played by Internet Group Management Protocol in multicasting datagrams.

The next two chapters are a relatively smaller but highly significant section of the book that delves into the security features provided by the TCP/IP protocol suite.

- In Chapter 21, "Security Concepts and Private Network Connection," you will learn about private networking architectures and security concepts implemented through private internetworking.

- Chapter 22, "IP Security," delves into how TCP/IP addresses fundamental security issues by implementing the IPSec framework.

The last five chapters explore the advanced networking technologies implemented by TCP/IP apart from looking into TCP/IP technologies that will take internetworking into the future.

- Chapter 23, "IP Over Asynchronous Transfer Mode (ATM)," introduces you to asynchronous data transmission using ATM and how IP can be implemented over the ATM framework.

- Chapter 24, "Voice Over IP," delves into the standards and protocols provided by TCP/IP that enable realtime voice transmission.

- In Chapter 25, "Mobile IP," you will learn how mobility support is implemented in IP by using the Mobile IP framework.

- The next generation Internet Protocol implementation, IPv6, is introduced in Chapter 26, "IPv6."

- With the advent of internetworking as a profitable business area, providing Quality of Service has become a vital survival strategy. Chapter 27, "Quality of Service," delves into how TCP/IP implements quality of service on Internetworks.

The appendixes in this book contain a quick reference to

- Networking basics
- TCP application port numbers
- HTTP status codes and header fields

- Request For Comments
- Troubleshooting tips
- Programming structures for data formats

CONVENTIONS USED IN THIS BOOK

This book uses various stylistic and typographic conventions to make it easier to use.

Code snippets and commands that run utilities are specified within a syntax. For example, to show how the `Ping` command must be used, the following code snippet can be provided within syntax.

```
ping xxx.xxx.xxx.xxx
```

The monospace font is used within the syntax to represent code in a different font. When commands or terms appearing in syntax is specified in normal text, it is represented in monospace. For example, the `Ping` command is represented in monospace to ensure that the command is not confused with other terms in normal text.

Note

When you see a note in this book, it indicates additional information that can help you better understand a topic or avoid problems related to the subject at hand.

Tip

Tips introduce techniques applied by experienced developers to simplify a task or to produce a better design. The goal of a tip is to help you apply standard practices that lead to robust and maintainable applications.

Caution

Cautions warn you of hazardous procedures (for example, actions that have the potential to compromise the security of a system).

Cross-references are used throughout the book to help you quickly access related information in other chapters.

→ For an introduction to the terminology associated with transactions, **see** "Understanding Transactions," **p. 100**

CHAPTER 1

INTRODUCTION TO INTERNETWORKING AND TCP/IP

In this chapter

EVOLUTION OF TCP/IP AND THE INTERNET

One of the primal instincts that has contributed to the survival of humankind has been its ability to connect with its environment. This instinct resulted in the creation of primitive family units, tribes, communities, villages, cities, and countries. In the course of time, the human race thrived on its connectivity instinct by linking places with roads, continents with ships, and outerspace with rockets and satellites. The later half of the twentieth century was witness to one of these acts of instinct in the form of linking computers. In the early days of computing, each computer was an island of information that was devoted to processing and providing output to the supplied input. However, when the need to connect computers was realized, a small group of computers were linked together to form a commune of linked computers called a network.

As in any commune, each computer shared the common resources available in the network with other computers in the network. To use these shared resources, the computers are connected to one another by means of hardware equipment such as cables, hubs, and switches. However, computers must first communicate with each other to cohabit in a network. Although the language of zeros and ones is all that it takes for a computer to say "hello" to another computer, certain rules need to be followed. For example, when another person talks to you, it is very important that you listen to that person first and then put forth your opinion. We do this as an unwritten rule to converse easily with others, but a computer needs to be programmed with these rules to enable smooth communication with other computers. Such a set of communication rules came to be known as a protocol.

Typically, a protocol defines the ways and means for establishing, maintaining, and terminating communication with another computer. When the concept of networking started to grow, the need to standardize protocol implementations was felt. All computers must communicate in the same language to ensure uniformity in data exchange. Therefore, a standardized networking protocol called Transmission Control Protocol/Internet Protocol (TCP/IP) was developed.

As the name suggests, TCP/IP is a protocol suite that provides two kinds of services, packaging data and routing the packaged data. Take a scenario where you need to move your house from one city to another. You take the help of a packing and moving service to manage the transit of all your household equipments to your new location. The packing and moving service is responsible for providing secure packaging for all your belongings before transferring them. It is also responsible for transporting your belongings in the shortest possible route to deliver them at your new location within a short period. The TCP/IP protocol suite is similar to the packaging and moving service except for the fact that data is not only packaged and moved to the correct destination but is also unpacked and delivered to the correct application on the destination computer. TCP provides packaging, reassembling, flow control, and error detection services, whereas IP manages the determination of the shortest possible path to the destination computer. An important point to note is that TCP/IP is not a software in itself but a proposed framework with rules and formats that help in the creation of protocol software.

With the implementation of TCP/IP as the standard networking protocol and with the growth in the popularity of networking, a large number of networks started appearing on the networking horizon. This resulted in the creation of a "network of networks" and created the concept of internetworking. Before delving into internetworking, let us take a brief look into the history of internetworking in general and the Internet in particular.

The Internet, the global network of networks, connects millions of computers across the globe. It was born as a result of the need to develop a reliable information exchange system in the United States to enable scientists and administrators to share important data. Defense Advanced Research Projects Agency (DARPA) wanted to create a well-connected network across the United States through which it could monitor and control the functions of all the strategic locations in the United States. The network had to be such that even if parts of the network are affected or disconnected, the functioning of the network should not be disrupted. In addition, the network must not have any central controlling authority because if the control is centralized, any damage to it would throw the network out of gear.

Any node on the network should be able to generate, send, and receive data. Based on these requirements, DARPA envisioned a network in which data would be divided into packets. Each of these packets would be addressed and sent across the network. The packet would move from one machine to another machine on the network until it reached the intended recipient. The routes taken by these packets might be different.

Meanwhile, research on a similar technology, the packet-switching technology, was going on and DARPA was funding the research. It decided to implement this technology on a network that had just four computers. This network was called the *ARPAnet*. It connected academic and military research centers. Slowly, as the need to exchange data increased, more universities joined the network, and from then on, this primitive Internet grew in leaps and bounds. DARPA wanted to create more such networks and interconnect them. Different types of networks started emerging.

After some time, many networks were created that used different technologies and protocols. To enable information exchange across these networks, a common mode of communication, called a protocol, had to be established and followed. This triggered the development of a number of protocols, which were combined to form the ARPAnet protocol suite. This protocol suite was the predecessor of TCP/IP protocol suite, which took shape in 1978. TCP/IP protocol suite is a repertoire of protocols developed for different purposes, the predominant ones being TCP and IP, hence the name. As the Internet began to take shape, DARPA converted machines attached to its research networks to TCP/IP. Thus, the Internet, with ARPANET as the backbone, became the test bed for TCP/IP. In January 1983, the Office of the Secretary of Defense asked all the computers that were connected to networks to use TCP/IP.

Note

Although TCP/IP evolved as a protocol for the Internet, it can be used for any type of an internetwork.

INTERNETWORKING

The concept of networking is more than just connecting two or more computers together. Networks were developed to facilitate sharing resources, such as software or hardware devices, among computers. To communicate with one another, different networks need to be interconnected, just as the computers are linked to form the individual network. For example, if a company has branches spread across a country, the networks in the branch offices should be able to communicate with one another for the most effective functioning of the company. Otherwise, resources, such as files and databases, might become redundant because they will be duplicated across locations. This kind of problem necessitated connecting two or more networks with each other.

However, a couple requirements had to be met before connecting two networks. The networks should use the same protocol for communication. The networks also must use the same or compatible hardware technologies.

But most networks that had to communicate were using different protocols and hardware technologies. This triggered the creation of standards that would bridge the gaps and enable communication between disparate physical networks.

Two or more networks connected to each other form an *internetwork* or *internet*. The networks that are connected to form an internetwork might be dissimilar (see Figure 1.1).

Figure 1.1
Many different network or hardware technologies exist, such as those using token ring, Ethernet, and FDDI.

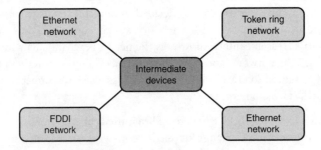

The process of constructing and managing communication among different networks is called *internetworking* or *internetting*. *Internetworking* also refers to the products, concepts, and technologies used to develop the connections among disparate networks. Thus, internetworking enables communication across networks regardless of the underlying network technologies used to build them. The internetwork must also address the problems that could arise in reliability, connectivity, flexibility, and network management. Although internetworking might sound simple, in reality, it is quite complex because the constituent networks might use different protocols, have different topologies, or the underlying technology could be different.

Networks can be classified as circuit-switched networks or packet-switched networks. This classification has been done based on the way in which data is passed between the source and the destination computers. In the case of a circuit-switched network (see Figure 1.2), a direct physical connection is established between the sender and receiver. The data needs to be sent only through the connection that has been established. The other computers cannot use the communication channel until it is released.

> **Note**
>
> An *internet* or an *internetwork* refers to a group of networks that are connected to each other. However, the *Internet* or the *Net* refers to the global network of networks and is the largest internetwork. The Internet uses TCP/IP for connecting the different networks.

In the case of packet-switched networks (see Figure 1.2), data that is to be transmitted, such as a file, is divided into manageable units of data called *packets* or *data packets*. The data packets can take different paths to reach the destination. A connection is not established between the sender and the receiver. Now, a question arises as to how the receiver will recognize all the data packets that belong to a single group and reassemble them together. This problem is solved by adding headers to the packets that are used by the intermediate hosts and the destination to regroup the data packets together. The advantage of packet-switching is that the data transmission will not be affected even if one path is disrupted because the data packets can be transmitted through a different path. In addition, intermediate devices called routers can be used to identify the shortest path to a destination and transmit the data packets through that path.

> **Note**
>
> Packet-switched networks can also be classified according to the distances they cover as a *local area network (LAN)*, *wide area network (WAN)*, and *metropolitan area network (MAN)*. LANs are groups of computers that usually span different floors in a building. MANs span different locations in a city and use high-speed connections, such as fiber-optic cables. WANs operate across different countries and use satellite connections for communication.

ADVANTAGES OF INTERNETWORKING

Internetworking enables networks with dissimilar configurations to communicate with each other. The following are some of the important advantages of internetworking:

1. The design of the networks that form the internetwork need not be changed or, at the most, may require minimal changes to support connectivity with other networks.

2. The network management is distributed and will thus become efficient. Managing smaller networks will be easier and the network administrators will have more control over the network.

3. Internetworks can connect and effectively transmit data even across networks that operate at varying speeds.

Figure 1.2
The data in a circuit-switched connection is transmitted through a predetermined direct physical connection unlike a packet-switched network in which data packets can take different paths to reach the destination.

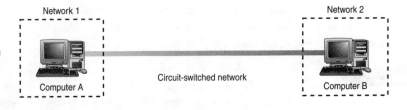

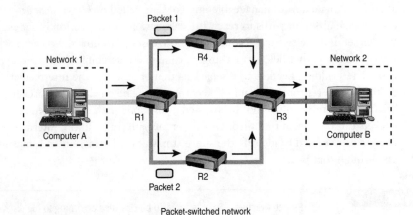

NETWORK TECHNOLOGIES

The Fiber Distributed Data Interconnect (FDDI) can be described as the foremost network technology that was popular in the early days of networking. In the networks of today, Ethernet is the most prevalent network technology. We will discuss some of the features of these technologies in the following sections.

→ For more information on network technologies, **see** "Networking Basics," **p. 425**

ETHERNET

Ethernet is a packet-switched LAN technology that was created by Xerox Corporation to transmit data in a network. It also defines a set of standards, such as the speed of data transmission, the access mechanism of the network, and the maximum amount of data that can be transmitted over the network at any given time. Ethernet uses 10Mbps bus topology because all computers share a single communication channel. One of the access mechanisms used by Ethernet is called *Carrier Sense Multiple Access/Collision Detect (CSMA/CD)*. If a computer on a network that uses Ethernet technology needs to transmit the data to another computer on the same network, it places the data packets in the communication channel. The communication channel is common to all the computers on the network, and so data collision might occur on the network. If a computer is unable to transmit data, it waits for a specific time interval and then retransmits the data.

→ For more information on Ethernet, **see** "Networking Basics," **p. 425**

FIBER DISTRIBUTED DATA INTERCONNECT (FDDI)

FDDI is also a LAN technology that is used to transmit data over optical fiber cables. Therefore, networks that use the FDDI technology transmit data faster than the networks that use the Ethernet technology. The most common access control mechanism that is used by FDDI is token ring. In this technique, data transmission is controlled by a token that is passed on the network. A token is a special data packet that moves on the network. If a computer needs to transmit data, it obtains the token and starts transmitting the data. After the transmission is over, the token is released to the network and the same set of steps is followed again. Data collision is prevented because only one computer can hold the token at a time.

→ For more information on FDDI, **see** "Networking Basics," **p. 425**

INTERMEDIATE DEVICES

To extend a network or connect different networks and form an internetwork, you need networking devices such as repeaters, bridges, routers, LAN Switches, and gateways. These devices are also known as *intermediate devices*. An intermediate device can be used to connect networks using dissimilar network technologies, protocols, and media types.

> **Note**
>
> Sometimes, to ease the administration of large networks, you can divide the large network into smaller networks and connect them by using intermediate devices.

REPEATERS

Electrical signals that represent data to be transmitted might weaken when it passes through the networks if they have to cover long distances. This might lead to loss of data. To overcome this problem, devices called *repeaters*, are used to regenerate the signals. The placement of a repeater on the network, such as Ethernet, plays an important role in network design. Repeaters are not smart devices.

The function of a repeater is to get data from one network, regenerate the signals, and pass it on to the other networks. Repeaters are not smart devices. They cannot perform complex tasks, such as finding the route in which a data packet can be sent. In addition, if data that is passed from one network to the other is corrupted, the corrupted signals are also regenerated. To put it differently, repeaters do not check the data for errors. The advantage of using repeaters is that they have a very simple circuitry and can be implemented easily.

BRIDGES

A bridge is a device that is used to connect two networks, which can be dissimilar or similar. Bridges are independent of the network architecture and the access mechanism of the networks. A bridge is a smart device unlike a repeater. A bridge accepts data from the sender and passes the data to the appropriate destination, whereas repeaters pass data from one network to another mechanically. Using bridges is advantageous because they do not replicate noise. A kind of bridge, called an *adaptive bridge*, is capable of deciding which kind of frames must be forwarded.

Note

A *frame* is the unit of data that can be passed over the physical medium, which is nothing but the cables that connect the computers on a network.

ROUTERS

Routers are used to connect two or more networks that have dissimilar architectures. The data packets on a network can take any path to reach its destination. If a data packet is passed to a router, the router finds the best path and transmits the data packet to the destination. Routers can also be used to connect networks that work with different cabling systems and protocols.

There are a few differences between bridges and routers. They are stated in the following list:

- Although a bridge and a router can determine multiple paths to a destination, a bridge can use only one path between two networks whereas a router can transmit data through multiple paths or routes. A bridge shuts down all paths except one by using a protocol called the spanning tree protocol.

- Bridges are faster than routers because they do not perform complex functions as routers do.

LAN SWITCHES

Switches, like bridges, are used to connect two dissimilar networks. They operate at the hardware level, which makes them operate at higher speeds compared to bridges. The other difference between switches and bridges is that switches can connect two networks with dissimilar bandwidths. Figure 1.3 displays two networks that are connected using switches and routers.

Note

A *hub* is a device that is used to connect hosts on a network that uses the star topology. A star topology describes a physical layout in which all the computers are connected to a central device, which is the hub. The data transmission between computers on the network happens through the hub.

Figure 1.3
Intermediate devices, such as routers and switches, can be used to connect and regulate traffic between two networks.

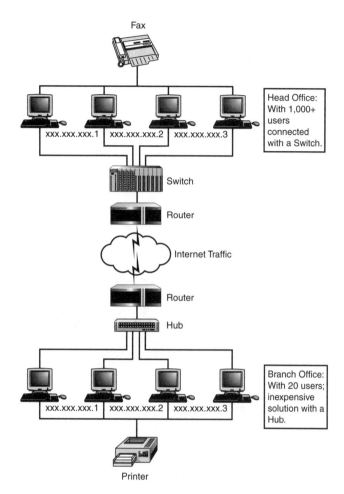

GATEWAYS

Gateways are devices that are used to connect networks working on dissimilar protocols, data formats, and architectures. For example, a gateway can convert data used by one protocol to a format that is compatible with a different protocol. Gateways can be implemented as hardware, software, or a combination of both.

Note

In the context of the Internet, gateways are synonymous with routers.

THE OPEN SYSTEMS INTERCONNECTION MODEL

In a network, all the network components must work in synchronization to enable proper communication over the network. The International Standards Organization (ISO) created a set of specifications called the Open Systems Interconnection (OSI) model for designing a network architecture that would enable applications to function irrespective of the underlying hardware architecture. This reference model describes how the communication system between computers that need to communicate should be designed. The OSI model facilitates the creation of a network architecture that is efficient and supports interoperability among computers of dissimilar configurations.

Note

A *reference model* is a set of specifications that designate how communication should take place on a network. The reference model covers all aspects of communication on a network. The reference model contains layers, which take care of specific processes in the communication. This type of a communication system in which communication happens through a group of layers is called a *layered architecture*. The strength of layered architecture is that it makes communication between computers and networks that work on different technologies possible. Moreover, developers of network applications can concentrate on one aspect of communication. This architecture also ensures that a change to the functionality of one layer does not affect the other layers. If a change has to be implemented, only the relevant layer undergoes a change.

The OSI model has seven layers. Before understanding the different layers of the OSI model, you must understand the different steps involved in the communication between computers. Consider a situation in which Computer A needs to send data to Computer B. The steps that are involved in data transmission are as follows:

1. Computer A sends a data file, which can be an e-mail or an audio file, to Computer B. Depending on the type of information that needs to be transmitted, specific services are invoked. The data files are converted to a standard format and the file is encrypted, if required. Data compression is also done at this stage.

2. After the format of the data is changed, Computer A needs to find the address of the destination computer. In addition, a session is created for data transmission.

3. The data is divided into a group of packets called frames and is sent to the destination. The network system also adds information to the frames called headers, which are used to ensure the security and integrity of data being transferred. This means that if four groups of data are transferred, all of them must be properly received at the other and in the same order. Data loss might occur if the signals are weaker or if there are disturbances in the communication channel. The network architecture must also include provisions to retransmit data, if required.

4. The final step in data transmission is transmitting the data as raw bits over the physical medium. The physical medium of communication could be an optical fiber cable or a coaxial cable.

These different stages of data transmission can be mapped to the different layers of the OSI model.

LAYERS IN THE OSI MODEL

The OSI model, as shown in Figure 1.4, consists of the following layers:

- Application layer
- Presentation layer
- Session layer
- Transport layer
- Network layer
- Data Link layer
- Physical layer

Figure 1.4
The OSI model is a standard reference model for communication on a network.

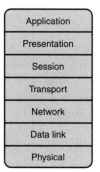

The first five layers in the OSI model are implemented as software, whereas the last two layers are implemented as a combination of hardware and software. The lower layers of the reference model handle data transport and the higher layers take care of connection establishment and data presentation.

The layers of the OSI model play a key role in transmitting data. All these layers must be present at the receiving and sending end of the communication system connecting the computers. Each layer has a well-defined function in transmitting data from one computer to another. The model states what each layer should do to enable data transfer on a network in spite of the hardware constraints. Movement of data across the layers can be categorized as logical movement of data and physical movement of data. The first five layers of the OSI model handle the logical movement of data, whereas the last two layers are responsible for moving the data through the physical medium, which can be a telephone line or an optical fiber cable.

For example, when a computer sends data to another computer on the network, the data from the source computer traverses down the layers starting from the Application layer to the Physical layer. The Physical layer transmits the data to the destination computer. In the receiving computer, the data travels up through these layers starting from the Physical layer.

> **Note**
>
> The layers in the OSI reference model are numbered from 1 to 7 starting with the Physical layer and ending with the Application layer. For example, the Application layer is also referred to as *Layer 7*.

> **Note**
>
> The functionality defined for every layer in the OSI reference model is implemented through one or more protocols. The protocols that operate in a layer communicate only with the protocols in the same layer of the other computer. This type of communication is called *peer-level communication*.

THE APPLICATION LAYER

The Application layer enables a user to access the network by providing a set of services. These services include remote file and directory access, remote login, and e-mail access. In the OSI model, the services that are available in the Application layer are File Transfer, Access, and Management (FTAM), Virtual Terminal Protocol (VTP), and Common Management Information Protocol (CMIP).

THE PRESENTATION LAYER

Taking care of translating data sent by the Application layer is done in the Presentation layer. The functions of the Presentation layer include changing data to a format that is compatible with the destination computer, encrypting and decrypting data, compressing and decompressing data, and so on. The Presentation layer interacts with the file system and the operating system to implement data conversion. Common file formats enable easy exchange of information among computers on a network. The Presentation layer is also responsible for representing data using standard formats, such as ASCII and UNICODE.

THE SESSION LAYER

This layer is responsible for controlling the communication between the two systems by handling dialog control. The role of the Session layer is to establish and terminate connection between the systems. The communication between two computers could be simplex, half-duplex, or full-duplex communication. Communication that can happen in only one direction is called *simplex communication*. In some situations, communication can happen in both the directions, but not simultaneously. This type of communication is called as *half-duplex communication*. Another category of communication is *full-duplex communication*, which enables data transmission in two directions simultaneously. The Session layer controls communication by logically dividing a session into three phases. A *session* is a group of transactions that take place between the source computer and the destination computer. They are connection establishment, data transfer, and connection release. The connection for any communication between two hosts is implemented in these three phases.

THE TRANSPORT LAYER

The Transport layer is responsible for converting data into small packets of information and ensuring that the data reaches the destination properly. There are two main methods used for communication in this layer, the *connectionless service* or the *connection-oriented service*. Sending an e-mail is an example of a connectionless service. This is because when an e-mail is sent, it is not necessary for destination users to have a connection open at their end. To download mail, users can open a connection with the mail server later. However, in the case of online chat services, the sender and the receiver need to establish a connection with the chat server during the chat session. This type of data transfer is known as connection-oriented communication. When an error occurs during data transfer, it is communicated to the receiver through an acknowledgement. The data is then retransmitted to the destination. In a few cases, such as voice and audio transmission, data needs to be transmitted without any delay.

In addition to the connection-related services the Transport layer also enables another type of communication called *request-reply*. Request-reply is used in client/server communication. For example, the client might pass a request to authenticate the username and password of a user to the server and wait for the server to reply. However, it is important to note that, irrespective of the type of communication implemented between the client and the server, the computers would use either a connection-oriented or connectionless mode of data transmission. For example, File Transfer Protocol (FTP) or Telnet clients and servers use a connection-oriented data transmission mode while implementing request-reply for username and password authentication. On the other hand, BOOTP uses a connectionless data transmission mechanism while implementing request-reply for transmitting bootstrap information.

→ For more information on TCP that is a protocol that operates from the Transport layer, **see** "Transmission Control and Data Flow," **p. 73**

→ For more information on UDP that operates from the Transport layer, **see** "UDP," **p. 113**

THE NETWORK LAYER

This layer is responsible for sending the data packets to the correct destination. This layer receives data from the Data Link layer and transmits the data to the destination. The Network layer resolves the address of the destination computer and finds the route through which the data can be sent. If more than one route is found, the Network layer finds the best route through which data can be transmitted. In addition, if a route is affected due to problems on the network, this layer finds an alternative route to send the data. However, the Network layer need not take care of data integrity.

Note

A *route* is defined as the path that is taken by data to reach its destination.

→ For more information on IP that operates from the Network layer, **see** "Internet Protocol: The Internet Layer Protocol," **p. 43**

→ For more information on ICMP that operates from the Network layer, **see** "Internet Layer and Internet Control Message Protocol," **p. 61**

THE DATA LINK LAYER

This layer is responsible for splitting the data that needs to be transmitted into groups called frames. For example, if you need to transmit a file from one computer to another, the Data Link layer divides the contents logically into frames. In addition to this, the Data Link layer needs to ensure that the frames reach their destination properly. If the frames do not reach the destination, this layer must retransmit the frames. The destination computer will acknowledge the receipt of data through special frames called *acknowledgement frames*. However, during data transmission, all the frames of a file that hold data might not be sent in sequence to the destination. To overcome this problem, extra information can be added to the frames to indicate the group to which a particular frame belongs.

The Data Link layer must also avoid duplicate frames being sent to the destination. Furthermore, this layer must synchronize the speed of data transmission between the source computer and the destination computer. If the buffer size of the destination computer is small, the speed of data transmission can be adjusted accordingly.

If the line that is used for data transmission can transmit data in both directions, the Data Link layer needs to take care of problems that might arise due to data congestion. In case of broadcasting, all the computers on the network must be able to share the communication channel. Sharing the communication channel might lead to problems, such as data collision. The medium access sublayer, which is a part of the Data Link layer, is responsible for handling problems related to the sharing of the communication channel.

THE PHYSICAL LAYER

This layer of the OSI model is responsible for transmitting information over the cable, which is the medium of transmission. This layer must ensure that the data transmission speed of the sender and the receiver are the same. If the speed of the receiver is low compared to that of the sender, data packets might not be received properly leading to data loss. On the other hand, if the speed of the receiver is more than that of the sender, the receiver will spend more time waiting for data, which will affect the performance of the computer.

This layer must also ensure that the data sent is received properly at the other end. This layer takes care of handling intricate communication details, such as the voltage that is required to transmit data, initiate connections, and terminate connections. If the distance between the sender and the receiver is more, the signals might weaken leading to data loss. However, intermediate devices, such as repeaters, can be used to amplify the signals and ensure proper data transmission.

Note

> Repeaters operate from the Physical layer of the OSI reference model. Bridges operate from the Data Link layer and the Physical layer of the OSI reference model. Gateways can operate from all seven layers of the OSI reference model.

CH

1

THE TCP/IP REFERENCE MODEL

As the number of networks that were connected to the ARPAnet increased, communication among the computers became a problem. Common standards were required for communication because the hardware and the software that were used were vendor-specific. A common protocol was necessary for communication between the computers. This led to the creation of TCP and IP. With the increase in the number of requirements, several protocols were created to address all the requirements. This also led to the creation of a new reference model, called the TCP/IP reference model. The TCP/IP reference model consists of four layers: Application, Transport, Internet, and Network Interface, as shown in Figure 1.5.

Figure 1.5
The TCP/IP reference model is a standard reference model for communication in the Internet.

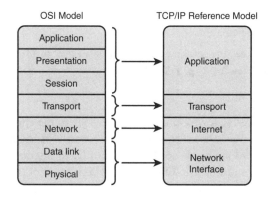

Note

> The TCP/IP specifications are not owned by any single organization or institution. These standards and the changes that are made to the technology are documented as Request for Comments (RFC) for TCP/IP. The area managers of the IETF are responsible for making changes to the RFC documents. The RFCs are numbered chronologically in the order of their release.

Note

> A group of related protocols through which a data packet passes in the OSI and TCP/IP reference models is called a *protocol stack*. When data is transferred from one computer to another, data passes down the protocol stack in every layer. At the destination computer, the data packets travel up the layers in the reference model. The header and the trailer information added by the upper layers are treated as data by the lower layers. Every layer adds its own header information, and sometimes trailer information, to the data and passes it on to the other layers.

THE APPLICATION LAYER

This layer enables users to access the network by providing a few services to the user. Some of the protocols and services available to the user are File Transport Protocol (FTP) for transferring files, Telnet for remote login, and Simple Mail Transfer Protocol (SMTP) for exchanging mail messages. The Application layer interacts with the operating system and the file system for data conversion and encryption. You will learn more about the various protocols of the Application layer in the next part of the book.

THE TRANSPORT LAYER

Communication between computers is handled by the Transport layer, which is comprised of Transmission Control Protocol (TCP) and the User Datagram Protocol (UDP). This layer divides the data into logical units called *packets* before transmitting them. TCP offers a reliable transport of data, whereas UDP does not. TCP is a connection-oriented protocol that ensures that data is transmitted properly to the destination. If there is an error in data transmission, TCP takes the responsibility of transmitting data again to the destination. However, UDP being connectionless, it does not ensure the data packets have reached the destination properly. However, both TCP and UDP seek the help of IP to route the information to the appropriate destination.

→ For more information on TCP, **see** "Transmission Control and Data Flow," **p. 73**

→ For more information on UDP, **see** "UDP," **p. 113**

THE INTERNET LAYER

The Internet layer is responsible for routing the data packets to the appropriate destination. Internet Protocol (IP) is responsible for ensuring that the data reaches the destination properly. However, ensuring data integrity is not a function of IP. IP interacts with Address Resolution Protocol (ARP) and Reverse Address Resolution Protocol (RARP) for address resolution. ARP and RARP operate from a layer called the Link layer. This layer is implemented as a combination of software and hardware and acts as an interface between the Internet layer and the Network Interface layer. The other protocols that operate from the Link layer are Serial Line Internet Protocol (SLIP) and Point-to-Point Protocol (PPP). These two protocols are used for communication over serial lines.

IP interacts with ARP to get the hardware address or the Media Access Control (MAC) address of a computer. The Network Interface layer uses the hardware address to transmit data over the physical medium. The ICMP generates error messages if there are problems in data transmission.

→ For more information on ARP, RARP, PPP, and SLIP, **see** "Network Interface Layer and Link Layers," **p. 25**

→ For more information on IP, **see** "Internet Protocol," **p. 45**

→ For more information on ICMP, **see** "Internet Control Message Protocol," **p. 61**

THE NETWORK INTERFACE LAYER

The functions of the Data Link layer and the Physical layer of the OSI model have been combined into a single layer called the Network Interface layer in the TCP/IP reference model. This layer is responsible for dividing the data sent by the Internet layer into logical groups called *frames*. Depending on the type of connection, which could be connection-oriented or connectionless, this layer adds appropriate headers to the frames. If the session is a connection-oriented session, the headers must indicate the number of frames in the group and the order in which the frames need to be reassembled in the destination. The Network layer at the receiving end then assembles all the constituent frames and sends them to the other layers. This layer ensures that all the frames are received properly by a method called the *Cyclic Redundancy Check* (CRC). Figure 1.6 shows the layers and the constituent protocols specified by the TCP/IP reference model.

Figure 1.6
A wide array of protocols operate from the different layers of the TCP/IP reference model.

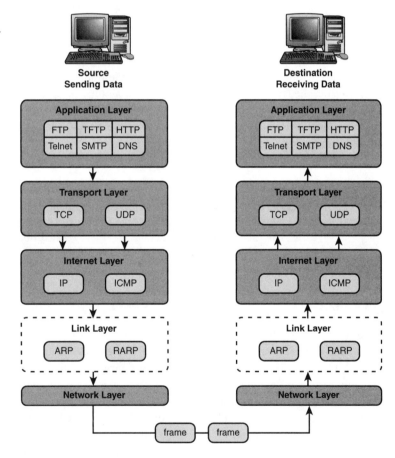

CH
1

INFORMATION EXCHANGE BETWEEN LAYERS IN THE TCP/IP REFERENCE MODEL

The data that needs to be transmitted to a computer is "qualified" with additional information in the form of headers and trailers. These headers and trailers are used by the layers to communicate information to the corresponding layers in the destination computer. For example, IP adds information that is required for routing a data packet as a header, which, in turn, is used by the Internet layer in the destination computer. The message that is sent by the Application layer is encapsulated in an *UDP datagram* or an *IP datagram*, which, in turn, is encapsulated in a frame by the Network Interface layer.

Note

The header part of a datagram or a frame added by a layer is a group of fields used by the protocols in that layer to perform specific tasks. For example, when data needs to be transmitted from one computer to another, the source and destination addresses are required. This information also forms a part of the header information.

A unit of data transfer on the Physical layer is called the frame. The Physical layers between two computers communicate with each other by using frames. At the destination, as the data moves up, the layers read the information sent as a header by their counterparts and pass just the data to upper layers. This data includes header information added by the other layers along with the actual data, which are read at the corresponding layers at the destination. A datagram is the unit of transfer between the Internet layers. The data that is sent by the Application layer is usually referred to as a *message*.

Note

The rest of the book uses the Microsoft implementation of TCP/IP, which conforms to the IETF standards. To enable you to understand the concepts better, some chapters use tools and command references that are Windows-based. However, the concepts and discussions will revolve around the generic TCP/IP standards.

SUMMARY

An internetwork is a group of networks that are connected to one another. The process of constructing and managing internetworks is called internetworking. The International Standards Organization (ISO) created a set of specifications called the Open Systems Interconnection (OSI) model for designing a network architecture that would enable data transfer across networks irrespective of the underlying hardware architecture. The OSI model comprises seven layers and each one of them plays a vital role in communication. The TCP/IP reference model, which is based on the OSI model, acts as a standard for communication on the Internet. The TCP/IP reference model is comprised of four layers.

CHAPTER 2

THE NETWORK INTERFACE AND LINK LAYERS

In this chapter

NETWORK INTERFACE LAYER

You can buy the best of gifts for Christmas, package them in the most beautiful gift wrap, and choose the best mail delivery service to send your gift, but it all depends on the mail carrier to ensure a safe and timely delivery of your gift to your loved ones. The Network Interface layer acts as the mail carrier in the TCP/IP reference model. This layer is responsible for transmitting data over the physical medium. Information is sent over the physical medium in the form of units called frames. The information required by the physical medium for transferring data from the source to the destination is specified in the frame. In addition, the data that is provided by the higher layers of the TCP/IP reference model are encapsulated in a frame before being transmitted over the physical medium. Figure 2.1 shows you how the Link layer manages data encapsulated before transmission and reassembly on receipt at the destination computer.

Figure 2.1
Every layer in the TCP/IP reference adds its own header information, which is finally packed into a frame and sent over the physical medium.

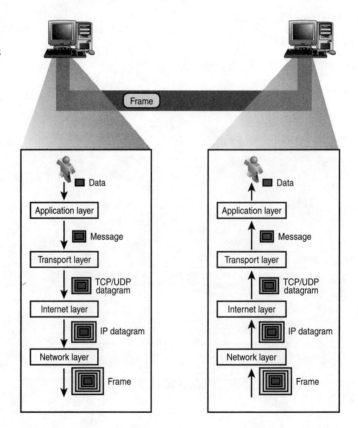

A frame consists of two components, the frame header and data. The data component of the frame consists of data that has been received from the upper layers, such as the Application, Transport, and the Internet layers. However, the components of a frame header differ with the network technology that is used. For example, frames being transmitted over a network implementing Ethernet technology contain fields, such as source address, destination address, type, and cyclic redundancy checksum. On the other hand, frame headers for frames transmitted over an FDDI network contains fields such as preamble, start delimiter, frame control, destination address, source address, frame check sequence, end delimiter, and frame status. Let us analyze the contents of an Ethernet frame header. The following list describes the fields provided by an Ethernet frame header (see Figure 2.2):

- Source Address—This field holds the address of the sending computer. The size of this field is 6 bytes.

- Destination Address—This field holds the address of the destination computer. This field is also 6 bytes in size.

- Type—This field represents the protocol whose data is held in the frame. For example, if the frame contains data that is sent by Internet Protocol (IP), the value in the type field is set to 0800_{16}. A few more values that can be provided in this field are 0806_{16} for an ARP message and 8035_{16} for a RARP message. The size of this field is 2 bytes.

- Cyclic Redundancy Checksum (CRC)—This field is used to store a checksum value that is used to verify the quality of the data. The CRC value can be used to identify whether the data contained in the frame is altered during transit. This field is also referred to as Frame Check Sequence (FCS).

Figure 2.2
The information sent by the upper layer protocols forms the data part of a frame and is sent over the physical medium.

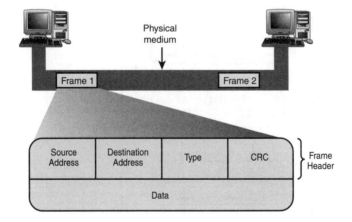

Note

There are different types of frames that can be created for Ethernet. They are Ethernet II, IEEE 802.3, IEEE 802.2, and sub-network access protocol (SNAP). Except for the Type field that is replaced by the Length in certain frame types, the other fields remain the same. The length field is used to indicate the number of bytes that are located following this field in the frame.

THE LINK LAYER

Before data can be sent over the physical medium, the software address that is used by the Internet layer to identify the hosts must be converted to a hardware address that can be recognized by the Network layer. Therefore, an address translation mechanism that translates addresses provided by the Network layer must be implemented. The Link layer, which acts as an interface between the Internet layer and the Network Interface layer performs this vital role (see Figure 2.3). It helps in bridging the gap between the different addressing formats that are used by both the layers. This task of resolving the software address to the corresponding hardware address is performed by a protocol called Address Resolution Protocol (ARP), which operates from the Link layer. In addition, the Link layer also provides the Reverse Address Resolution Protocol (RARP) to translate hardware addresses to the corresponding software addresses.

Address resolution is the process of mapping a software address to the corresponding hardware address and vice versa. The protocols that are used for address resolution are ARP and RARP. The Link layer also contains protocols that are used for transmission of data over serial lines, which are Point-to-Point Protocol (PPP) and Serial Line Internet Protocol (SLIP).

Figure 2.3
The Link layer is used for address resolution and communication over serial lines.

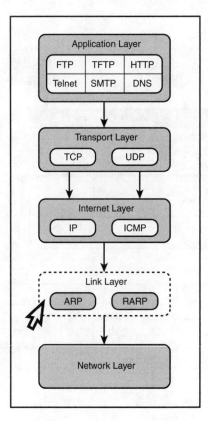

PPP is an Internet standard for transporting data over point-to-point serial connections. It can be used to transport data that is created by multiple protocols, such as TCP/IP or IPX, over the same point-to-point connection. PPP, in turn, interacts with a protocol called the Link Control Protocol (LCP) for establishing and terminating connections. PPP also interacts with a group of protocols called Network Control Protocols (NCPs) to configure the Network layer protocols.

If SLIP is used for communication, the destination and source IP address must be known. However, when a host needs to connect to the Internet by using PPP, all that the application will require to establish the connection is the telephone number of the telephone used for dialing up the ISP, the user ID, and the password. In addition, PPP can be used with protocols other than TCP/IP.

CH
2

Note

Link Control Protocol is used for establishing and testing connections over a telephone line. Both the sender and the receiver must agree upon the format of the LCP packets.

Note

The Internet layer protocols of the TCP/IP reference model or the Network layer protocols of the OSI reference model is associated with an NCP that controls the transmission of data packets created by the protocols over telephone lines. For example, the name of the NCP that is associated with IP is called an IP Control Protocol (IPCP). NCP encapsulates the data sent by the Internet layer protocol or the Network protocol and passes it to the Physical layer for data transmission.

DIFFERENCES BETWEEN SLIP AND PPP

Although SLIP evolved as the first protocol for transmitting data over serial lines, it has a few limitations. PPP is an enhancement of SLIP and offers a few advantages. The differences between SLIP and PPP are discussed in Table 2.1.

TABLE 2.1   SLIP VERSUS PPP

SLIP	PPP
Can be used only with TCP/IP.	Can be used with multiple protocols.
Supports only synchronous transmission of data.	Supports synchronous as well as asynchronous data transmission.

Note

CSLIP (compressed SLIP) is an advanced version of SLIP. CSLIP supports more throughput compared to SLIP because it uses a compressed version of the IP header unlike SLIP, which does not compress the IP header.

ADDRESSING

Addressing is the process of assigning addresses to the hosts on a network. Apart from assigning addresses to the hosts, every network must be identified by a unique address. Communication between computers can happen only if each and every computer on the network is uniquely identified by an address. There are two types of addresses that can be assigned to a computer on a network—the physical or hardware address and the logical or Internet Protocol (IP) address. There are a few rules that are used to assign addresses to the hosts and networks. These rules form the *IP addressing scheme*.

The physical or the hardware address of a computer is the number that is assigned to the Network Interface Unit or the Network Interface Card (NIC) of the computer. *Network Interface Card* (NIC) is a piece of hardware that must be attached to every computer for it to connect to a network. The address that is assigned to the NIC is the one that uniquely identifies the computer on the network. A few computers on a network can contain more than one NIC, each representing an interface to the network to which the computer is connected. A computer that has more than one NIC is also known as a *multihomed computer*.

Note

> A router is an example of a multihomed computer because it has a NIC for every network to which it is connected.

PHYSICAL ADDRESS

The physical address; of a computer is the address that is assigned to its NIC. In an Ethernet network, the physical address is a 48-bit address that is imprinted at the time of manufacturing the card. The Network Interface layer in the TCP/IP reference model can communicate with other computers only by using the physical address (see Figure 2.4).

The physical address of a computer is of two types, fixed and configurable. The addresses of cards, such as proNET and ARCNET, can be changed and are thus called *configurable cards*. However, the addresses of Ethernet cards cannot be changed because they are imprinted during the manufacturing of the cards.

Note

> The hardware address of an Ethernet card is also known as the *Media Access Control* (MAC) address. Thus, in the context of Ethernet, the MAC address and the hardware address can be used interchangeably.

Note

> ARCNET, the Attached Resource Computer Network, was developed by Datapoint Corporation in 1977. The address of an ARCNET NIC is configurable unlike Ethernet addresses, which are imprinted at the time of manufacturing the card.

Figure 2.4
The physical address
of a computer is vital
for communication.

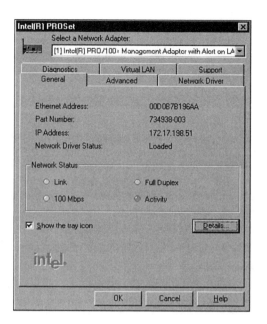

The proNET network is based on the token ring technology developed by the Proteon Technology. Like ARCNET NICs, addresses of the proNET NICs are also configurable. One precaution to be taken by the network administrator while assigning IP addresses is that the same address must not be duplicated.

THE IP ADDRESS

The TCP/IP protocol suite should enable communication between computers irrespective of the underlying hardware technologies. As the hardware address or the physical address of the computer is dependent on the manufacturer and the hardware technology used, a common addressing scheme that is independent of the underlying technology must be used. This common addressing scheme is the *IP addressing scheme*, in which every IP address comprises of 4 bytes. The way in which the IP address is represented is called *dotted-quad*. The network administrator assigns the IP addresses to a computer when installing the operating system.

An address of a computer on a network is identified by two components, the network to which the computer is connected and the number assigned to the computer on the network. These two components are called the network ID and the host ID, respectively.

A *host* is any computer that is connected to a network.

Depending on the number of bytes allotted to the network and host IDs, IP addresses can be classified into five address classes: A, B, C, D, and E. This method of classifying the IP addresses is also known as *classful IP addressing*. The address classes enable easy administration of a network. They are also used to make efficient use of the 4 bytes that can be used for assigning IP addresses.

Note

Classful addressing scheme has a few limitations. First, the number of addresses in the address space is becoming insufficient to cater to the exponential growth of the Internet. Second, it is observed that the addresses that are allotted to the organizations are not being used efficiently. This is due to the allocation of a fixed number of bits for the network number and host number. Due to these limitations, a different scheme called the *classless addressing scheme* was created. This enables network administrators to overcome the limitations of classful addressing by breaking the rigid demarcation between the network number and host numbers. Most of the protocols support classless IP addressing. Rather than referring to an address as a Class C address, it is now commonly referred to as a /24 network. This indicates that 24 bits are allotted for representing the network. Classless IP addressing is also referred to as Classless Interdomain Routing (CIDR).

Note

The range of numbers that can be assigned to every octet is 0–255.

CLASS A ADDRESSING SCHEME

In the class A addressing scheme, the first byte is used for the network ID and the last three bytes are used for the host ID. The format of a class A address is shown in Figure 2.5.

If a company needs to set up a class A network, the network ID is assigned by an organization called the Network Information Center (NIC). The other three bytes are administered locally according to the requirements of the organization.

Figure 2.5
In class A addresses, the first byte is used for the network ID.

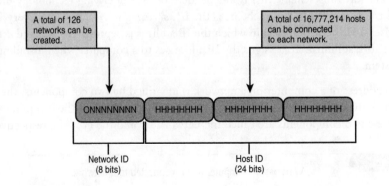

A total of 126 networks can be created.

A total of 16,777,214 hosts can be connected to each network.

ONNNNNNN HHHHHHHH HHHHHHHH HHHHHHHH

Network ID
(8 bits)

Host ID
(24 bits)

In Figure 2.5, N represents the network ID and H represents the host ID. In the 8 bits that are allotted for the network ID, the first bit is set to 0 and only seven bits can be used for the network ID. A maximum of 2^7 class A networks can be set up. However, two addresses, 0.0.0.0 and 127.0.0.0, are reserved for the default route and the loopback address, respectively. Thus, a total of 2^7–2, which is equal to 126, networks can be set up as class A networks. A maximum of 16,777,214 hosts can be connected to each network.

Note

127.0.0.0 is referred to as the *loopback address* and is used for testing the TCP/IP software on the local computer.

CH

2

Note

The default path that is taken by a data packet if there are no entries in the routing table is called the *default route*. In other words, if the sender is not aware of the route through which a data packet needs to be transmitted, the data packets are forwarded to the default gateway.

Note

A *routing table* is a table stored on every host on the network to maintain a list of routes through which a data packet can be sent.

Class A addressing scheme is allotted for large networks that have a limited number of servers and many hosts connected to them. Class A networks are also called /8 networks because the first 8 bits are used to identify the network. Typically, class A addresses are not used by organizations. Instead, a class A network is further subdivided into smaller networks called subnets. This technique is referred to as subnetting. With a single class A address, many small networks can be created. This also avoids unnecessary procurement of class A addresses.

→ For more information on subnetting, **see** "Subnetting and Classless Addressing," **p. 245**

CLASS B ADDRESSING SCHEME

In the class B addressing scheme, 16 bits are used for identifying the network ID and 16 bits for the host ID (see Figure 2.6). In a class B network, the first two bits in the network ID are set to 1 and 0, respectively. Thus, network numbers from 128 to 191 can be used for class B networks.

Class B networks are also called /16 networks because the first 16 bits are used to represent a network. By using the class B addressing scheme, a maximum of 2^{14} networks can be set up and 2^{16}–2 hosts can be connected to each network. Class B networks represent 25% of the IPv4 address space.

Figure 2.6
In class B addresses, the first two bytes are used for the network ID.

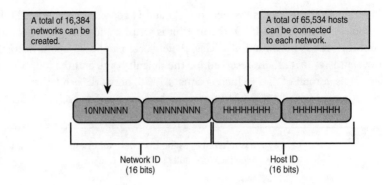

Note

IPv4 address space refers to the total number of networks and hosts that can be created by using IPv4, a version of Internet Protocol.

CLASS C ADDRESSING SCHEME

In the class C addressing scheme, 24 bits are used for the network ID and 8 bits are used for the host ID (see Figure 2.7). In the class C addressing scheme, 2,097,152 networks can be created and each network can have a maximum of 254 hosts connected to it.

Figure 2.7
In class C addresses, the first three bytes are used for the network ID.

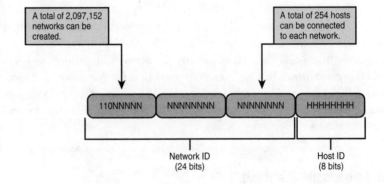

The network ID of a class C address can range between 192 and 223. Class C networks are also called /24 networks because the first 24 bits are used to represent the network ID. Class C networks represent 12.5% of the IPv4 address space.

CLASS D ADDRESSING SCHEME

A multicast address is an address assigned to a group of computers on a network. Class D addresses (see Figure 2.8) are reserved for multicast addresses. In class D addresses, the network number can range between 224 and 239. Class D addresses are used for multicasting.

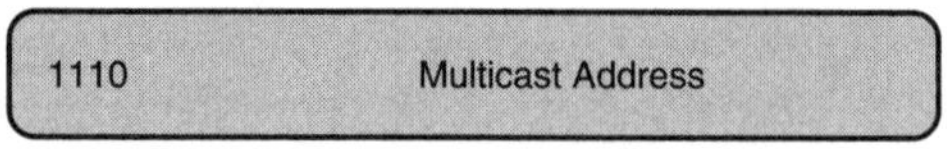

Figure 2.8
Class D addresses are reserved for multicast addresses.

1110	Multicast Address

CH
2

CLASS E ADDRESSING SCHEME

Class E addresses (see Figure 2.9) are reserved for experimental purposes and the network number in this scheme can range from 240 to 255.

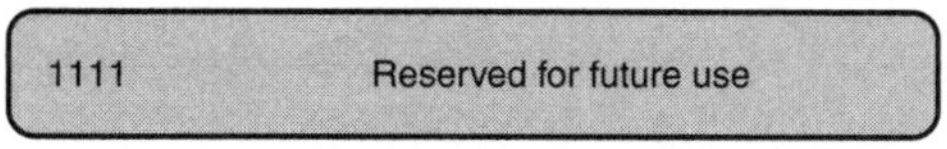

Figure 2.9
Class E addresses are reserved for experimentation.

1111	Reserved for future use

ADDRESS RESOLUTION

The Internet layer and the Network Interface layer follow different ways of addressing a computer and therefore, a method by which you can resolve a software address and get the corresponding hardware address or vice versa is required. This process is called *address resolution*. If on a network, a computer, Computer A, needs to communicate with another computer, Computer B, on the same network, Computer A uses the IP address of Computer B to send data. However, as the Network Interface layer requires the hardware address of Computer B to transmit data over the physical medium, there needs to be a method by which the corresponding hardware address can be found from the IP address. This is done by a Link layer protocol called Address Resolution Protocol (ARP).

ARP is used to resolve IP addresses to the physical address of a computer. It is a generic protocol that can be used to resolve the physical address of any type of network technology. In general, there are two types for resolving IP addresses to the corresponding hardware addresses. They are logical mapping and dynamic binding.

LOGICAL MAPPING

Logical mapping is a technique of mapping an IP address to the corresponding physical address. In this method, information derived from a component of the IP address is used to obtain the physical address of a computer. This technique is used with technologies such as proNET and ARCNET.

DYNAMIC BINDING

Dynamic binding is the process of mapping an Ethernet address to the corresponding software address. This process is implemented by using the ARP. The steps involved in dynamic binding are discussed along with ARP.

ADDRESS RESOLUTION USING ARP

The following are the steps involved in the process of address resolution using ARP:

1. The computer that needs to transmit data broadcasts the IP address of the receiver over the network.
2. The computer whose IP address matches the address sent over the network responds by sending a reply that contains the IP address and the MAC address. The receiving computer sends the reply to the computer that originated the request.
3. The sender uses the MAC address that it received from the receiver to transmit the data packets.
4. The sender obtains the MAC address and stores it in the local cache, which is also called the ARP cache. If data needs to be transmitted to the same IP address, the sender checks the ARP cache for the MAC address. If the ARP cache does not contain the address, steps 1 through 3 are repeated to obtain the physical address.

→ For more information on Ethernet and Address Resolution Protocol, **see** "RFCs," **p. 425**

ARP CACHE

ARP cache is a location on the memory of a host, containing a list of IP addresses and the corresponding physical addresses. The cache is created with a Time to Live (TTL) value or an expiration time value. The cache performs the role of a digital diary which is used to store the names, addresses and other important information about the people with whom you communicate frequently. Every host maintains its own "digital diary" in the form of an ARP cache. The lifetime of the ARP entry is decided by the expiration time. The expiration time for a cache entry is operating system–dependent. There are certain specific situations where the ARP cache timeout value must be modified. For example, it is quite possible that ARP entries related to computers that do not exist on the network are present in the cache. The dynamic nature of any internetwork makes it possible for such redundant entries to be cached. Therefore, ARP cache entries must be cleared from time to time using a predefined timeout value.

When an ARP entry is recorded in the cache, the time at which the entry was created is also recorded. For example, if the timeout interval for the ARP cache entries is five minutes, the entry is deleted five minutes after it was recorded in the cache. However, deletion of ARP cache entries based on the timeout period is not applicable to routers and default gateways. Typically, a Windows 2000 host maintains an unused ARP entry for a maximum of two minutes. If the entry is being used every two minutes, Windows 2000 maintains the entry for a maximum of 10 minutes. This type of cache entry is called a dynamic ARP cache entry. Entries that are recorded using the arp command with an -s option are maintained on the host until the host is rebooted. Such entries are called static ARP cache entries. You will learn more about the arp command in the following sections. ARP cache saves you the cost of broadcasting a request every time a message is to be transmitted. Consider a situation in which Computer A needs to send data to Computer B. The first step in the data transfer is to find the hardware address of Computer B. To do this, Computer A first examines the entries in the ARP cache. If there are matching entries in the ARP cache, the information is picked up from the ARP cache and the broadcast is not sent. By storing entries locally on the ARP cache, broadcast messages that are required for address resolution can be reduced, increasing the efficiency of the network. After the address resolution process is complete, the other phases of data transfer are done as usual.

CH

2

The ARP entries can be displayed using the ARP -a command (see Figure 2.10). The MAC address is displayed as six pairs of hexadecimal numbers separated by a hyphen in Windows.

Note

The format in which the hardware addresses are displayed might depend on the operating system. The command used to display the contents of the ARP cache might vary with the operating system used.

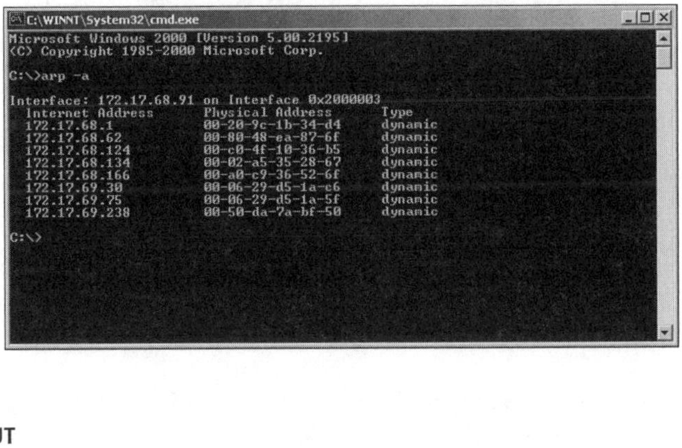

Figure 2.10
The ARP -a command displays the entries in the ARP cache.

CACHE TIMEOUT

Consider a situation in which Computer A needs to transfer data to Computer B. However, Computer B crashed and thus is not connected to the network anymore. Computer A continues to transmit data packets to Computer B, in spite of Computer B not being on the network, by using the ARP cache entries. Transmission of data continues as before because the sending computer does not receive information about computers getting disconnected from the network. The sending computer also does not realize that the ARP cache entries are invalid. However, this problem of invalid cache entries can be overcome with another feature of the ARP cache, the timeout period. After the elapse of the time period specified in timeout period, the entries in the ARP cache are deleted. When Computer A needs to transmit data to Computer B, it checks the cache entries. If there are no matching cache entries, a broadcast is sent to get the MAC address. If the receiver does not send a reply to the broadcast, it means that the broadcast was not successful and data transmission is not carried out at all.

ARP MESSAGE FORMAT

Address resolution is done between two computers by exchanging messages in a specific format. These messages, called ARP messages, are used by the sending computer to broadcast messages in the form of an ARP request to all the computers on the network. The ARP request contains fields that are required by the receiver to process the request. After processing the request, the receiver sends a reply message that is also in the same format as an ARP request message. Figure 2.11 shows you the format of an ARP request/reply message.

Figure 2.11
The values of the fields in an ARP message differ depending on whether the message is used for an ARP request or reply.

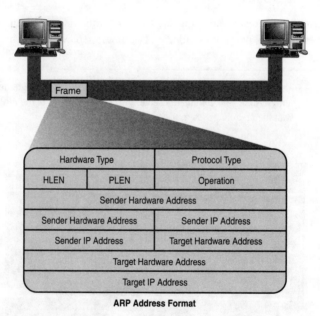

ARP Address Format

The ARP message format contains 28 bytes of information that is used to resolve a hardware address of a computer. The ARP address format shown in Figure 2.11 is a generic form that can be used with any type of hardware address. The length of the message is 28 bytes. An ARP message is encapsulated within a frame.

Table 2.2 lists the fields in an ARP message along with a description of each field.

TABLE 2.2   FIELDS IN THE ARP MESSAGE AND THEIR DESCRIPTION

Field Name	Size (Octets)	Description
Hardware Type	2	Specifies the type of hardware technology used in the network. For example, if the technology used is Ethernet, the value of this field is 1.
Protocol Type	2	Specifies the type of protocol address used. For example, 0800_{16} indicates that the address is an IP address.
HLEN	1	Indicates the length of the hardware address. ARP can be used with any kind of network technology. The hardware addresses used for different network technologies vary. For example, the size of the hardware address in the case of Ethernet is 48 bits.
PLEN	1	Represents the length of the IP address.
Operation	2	Indicates the type of operation that needs to be performed. The operations that could be performed are ARP reply, ARP request, RARP request, or a RARP reply.
Sender Hardware Address	6	Represents the hardware address of the sender. The value of this field depends on the type of operation performed. If an ARP reply is generated, the sender will supply its hardware address by using this field. For example, if Computer A sends a broadcast requesting for the MAC address of Computer B, Computer B responds by filling the sender hardware address field with its hardware address.
Sender IP Address	4	Represents the IP address of the sender.
Target Hardware Address	6	Stores the hardware address of the target computer.
Target IP Address	4	Stores the IP address of the target computer, which is used to generate an ARP request.

➜ To know more about the C/C++ programming structures implementing an ARP message format, **see** "Programming Structures for Data Formats," **p. 447**

REVERSE ADDRESS RESOLUTION PROTOCOL

There are situations where networks are designed with clients that do not have hard disks. Instead, they use the server's hard disk for their software requirements. Take a scenario where an organization is incorporated with a small investment. One of the cost-effective

CH
2

measures that can be implemented in the organization's network is to install a server and link diskless clients on the network to that server. Although the server software would have been purchased with licenses for one or two clients, in effect, an arbitrary number of clients can use the software. In addition, the organization need not purchase hard disks thereby saving money. However, diskless systems will be unable to store their IP addresses because the addresses are stored along with the operating system settings on a hard disk. Now, a question arises as to how these computers communicate with other computers on the network because they do not have their IP addresses stored locally. To solve this problem, Reverse Address Resolution Protocol (RARP) was created. RARP enables a diskless workstation to obtain its IP address from the RARP server by using its physical address. The working of RARP is the reverse of the working of ARP. RARP is a protocol that operates from the Link layer and is used to resolve the physical address of a computer by using its IP address. Like ARP, RARP is a generic protocol that can be used with any type of hardware address format. Hardware address formats refer to the different formats that are used by hardware technologies.

A node that needs its IP address, broadcasts its request to all the computers on the network. The computer that can respond to the request, which is called as the RARP server, sends the IP address in the form of a RARP reply. The IP addresses of all the computers on the network are stored in a configuration file in the RARP server. More than one RARP server can be configured on the network. The configuration details in all the RARP servers will be the same.

Note

A *RARP server* is any computer that stores the configuration details of all the computers on the network. RARP servers can respond only to RARP requests.

More than one RARP server can be present on a network and all of them can respond to a RARP request. Therefore, data collision might occur at anytime on the network. In addition, data collision might cause delay in data transmission. To overcome these problems, you can assign one server as the primary RARP server and the other servers will act as the secondary RARP servers. If the primary server fails to respond to the request, the secondary servers will process the requests. Otherwise, the secondary servers just keep track of the time when the request was received.

Designating one server as the primary RARP server and other servers as secondary RARP servers has an advantage; it prevents a single server from becoming overloaded.

The message format of ARP and RARP are the same. The values in the address fields change with respect to the type of operations performed on the field and are explained in Table 2.3.

TABLE 2.3 FIELDS IN THE RARP MESSAGE AND THEIR DESCRIPTION

Field Name	Size (Octets)	Description
Hardware Type	2	Specifies the type of hardware technology used on the network. For example, if the technology used is Ethernet, the value of this field is 1.
Protocol Type	2	Specifies the type of protocol address used. For example, 0800_{16} indicates that the address format is an IP address.
HLEN	1	Indicates the length of the hardware address used by the network technology. RARP can be used with any network technology and the hardware addresses used in different network technologies differ.
PLEN	1	Represents the length of the IP address.
Operation	2	Indicates the type of operation that needs to be performed. For example, the operation could be an ARP reply, an ARP request, a RARP request, or a RARP reply.
Sender Hardware Address	6	Represents the hardware address of the sender. This field is used when a RARP request is generated. For example, if a computer requires its IP address, it sends a RARP request with its hardware address filled in this field.
Sender IP Address	4	Represents the IP address of the sender.
Target Hardware Address	6	Stores the hardware address of the target computer.
Target IP Address	4	Stores the IP address of the target computer. The RARP server that needs to respond to a RARP request generates a RARP reply with the IP address of the target computer in this field.

CH
2

→ To know more about the C/C++ programming structures implementing a RARP message format, **see** "Programming Structures for Data Formats," **p. 447**

SUMMARY

Addresses are of two types, the physical or hardware address and the logical or IP address. The physical address of a computer is assigned to the network interface unit of the computer and is used by the Network Interface layer of the TCP/IP reference model to transmit data over a network. However, the higher layer protocols need the software address for transmitting data. Address Resolution Protocol (ARP) is used to resolve the physical address of a computer by using the IP address. Reverse Address Resolution Protocol (RARP) is used by diskless workstations to acquire their IP address from the physical address of the computer.

CHAPTER 3

THE INTERNET LAYER PROTOCOL

In this chapter

THE INTERNET LAYER

The Internet layer in the TCP/IP reference model is responsible for transferring data between the source and destination computers. The Internet layer accepts data from the Transport layer and passes the data to the Network Interface layer. The following are the functions of the Internet layer:

- Transmitting data to the Network Interface layer.
- Routing the data to the correct destination. This layer takes care of sending the data through the shortest route if more than one route is available. In addition, if a route through which a datagram is to be sent has problems, the datagram is sent through an alternate route.

Note

The path taken by a datagram to reach the destination is called the *route*.

- Handling errors and fragmentation and reassembling, all of which are discussed in the sections that follow.

The protocols that operate in this layer are Internet Protocol (IP) and Internet Control Message Protocol (ICMP), shown in Figure 3.1. ICMP works with IP to handle errors in data transmission.

Figure 3.1
Internet Protocol and Internet Control Message Protocol operate from the Internet layer of the TCP/IP reference model.

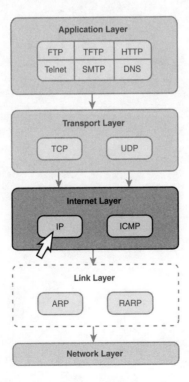

Note

The version of IP that is discussed in this book is called IPv4. IPv4 is the version of IP that was created to provide communication over a TCP/IP-based network. With the growing number of LANs and WANs, the address space that is provided by IPv4 is becoming insufficient. Moreover, requirements due to technological changes led to the creation of a new version of IP called IPv6.

→ To learn more about IPv6, **see** "IPv6," **p. 403**

INTERNET PROTOCOL

Internet Protocol (IP) is a protocol that operates from the Internet layer of the TCP/IP reference model. The specifications of IP are provided in RFC 791. IP is responsible for transmitting data to the correct destination. It also takes care of routing. Irrespective of the protocol used in the Transport layer, all the protocols rely on IP for sending and receiving data. The following are some of the characteristics of IP:

Cʜ

3

- IP provides a connectionless delivery system. This means that every data packet that is sent across the network is treated as an independent unit. IP does not maintain the details of the connection between the server and the client.

- IP does not guarantee a reliable data transfer. However, this does not mean that packets are ignored without a proper rule. Data loss occurs only when there are problems on the network.

- IP provides a *best-effort delivery system*, which means that IP tries to avert data loss as much as possible. Data loss occurs only in exceptional situations, such as problems in the network due to a hardware failure.

Note

The process of delivering data from one computer to another is called *routing*.

→ To learn more about routing, **see** "IP Routing," **p. 259**

DATA TRANSMISSION USING IP

IP takes care of delivering a data packet irrespective of the location of the destination. Location in this context refers to the network on which the computer is located. The sender and the receiver can belong to the same network or might be on different networks. If the receiver is on the same network, the sender transmits the data directly to the destination. This is also called *local delivery* of packets. However, if the destination computer is on a different network, an intermediate device is required. The process of routing a data packet to a computer on a remote network is also called *remote delivery* of packets.

➜ For more information on intermediate devices, **see** "Intermediate Devices," **p. 13**
➜ To know more about how a computer checks whether the destination computer is on the same network, **see** "Routing Concepts," **p. 260**

The sender is ignorant of how the data packets reach the destination. The sender need not be aware of the path taken by the data to reach the destination. This concept is not new to you. For example, in the postal service, if you post a letter, all that you need to do is provide the correct address. You, as a sender, need not be aware of the how the letter is being sent to the destination. Similarly, during the transmission of data, it might pass through a number of intermediate devices before it reaches the final destination without the sender being aware of it. Each intermediate device can decide the best route or path that can be taken by the data.

> **Note**
>
> The data that is sent by the application could be a text file, bitmap file, or an audio file.

FUNCTIONS OF IP

IP defines a set of standards for data transmission. The standards that are defined by IP are as follows:

- IP defines the format of the basic unit of data transmission that can be sent to the Network Interface layer. This basic unit of data transmission is called a *datagram* or an *IP datagram*. The format of a datagram is discussed later in this chapter. A datagram is sent to the Network Interface layer in which it is encapsulated in a frame and transmitted over the physical medium. A *frame* is the basic unit of data transfer defined by the Network Interface layer. A datagram is converted to a frame because the Network Interface layer can transmit data only in the form of frames.

- IP also performs routing. If there are more routes to the same destination, IP determines the best route that a data packet can take to reach the destination and also sends the data packet through the same path.

- IP also defines a set of rules that define the conditions in which a datagram can be discarded. IP works with ICMP, which is responsible for generating error messages when an error occurs during data transmission. The Transport layer protocols, namely TCP and UDP, decide to retransmit data based on the error message that is received.

➜ To know more about how error messages are generated by ICMP, **see** "Internet Control Message Protocol," **p. 61**

IP HOURGLASS MODEL

The data that is created by an application needs to pass through all the layers of the TCP/IP reference model to reach the destination. For example, the Application layer protocol used might be HTTP, FTP, or TFTP. Every application layer protocol is associated with a Transport layer protocol depending on whether it is connection-oriented or connectionless. The Transport layer protocol, in turn, interacts with IP for routing the data packets. It is very important to understand that irrespective of the Application layer protocols and the Transport layer protocols, the only protocol that is used for routing the data packets is IP. When the data transmission through the four layers is visualized, it takes the shape of an hourglass (see Figure 3.2) and thus the model is called the *IP hourglass model.*

Figure 3.2
The IP hourglass model depicts that whatever the path is taken by data, it has to pass through IP.

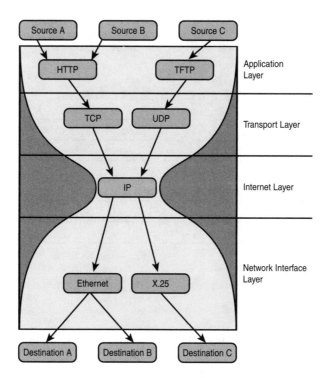

In Figure 3.2, notice that Source A and Source B interact with the HTTP, whereas Source C interacts with TFTP. HTTP interacts with TCP and TFTP interacts with UDP, which are in the Transport layer. TCP and UDP send the data to IP in the Internet layer. IP datagrams are forwarded to the Network Interface layer, which creates the frames based on the network technology used.

→ For information on RFCs, **see** "RFCs," **p. 425**

FORMAT OF AN IP DATAGRAM

The format of data that can be recognized by IP is called an IP datagram. It consists of two components, namely, the header and data, which need to be transmitted. The fields in the datagram, except the data, have specific roles to perform in the transmission of data. Every field in the IP datagram has a fixed size except for the IP Options field, which can be 20–60 bytes in length. The sending computer sends a message to the protocol in the same layer on the destination computer by using the header. The format of an IP datagram is displayed in Figure 3.3.

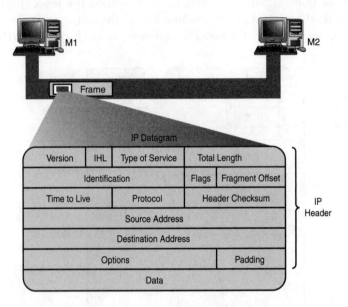

Figure 3.3
The fields in the IP datagram are used for transmitting data.

In the sections that follow, the fields in an IP datagram are discussed in detail.

Version

This field specifies the version of IP used for transferring data. The size of the Version field is 4 bits. Both the sender and the receiver must use the same version of IP to ensure proper interpretation of the fields in the datagram.

Header Length

The size of the Header Length or the IHL field is 4 bits. The Header Length field is used to specify the length of header, which can range from 20 to 60 bytes. You must multiply the value in this field by four to get the length of the IP header. For example, if the value in this field is 3, the length of the header is 3*4, which is 12 bytes.

Total Length

The Total Length field specifies the total length of the datagram. The size of the field is 16 bits. The Total Length field can be calculated as follows:

```
Total length of the datagram = Length of the header + Length of the data
```

If a datagram can be accommodated in a frame, data transmission becomes very simple. However, if the size of the datagram is more than the value that can be accommodated in the frame, the datagram must be divided into logical groups called *fragments*. In few cases, the size of a datagram will be much less than the size of the data that can be passed over the physical medium at one point in time. In that case, padding is done to fill in extra spaces. To find the exact length of the data that is sent over the frame, the Total Length field is used.

Service Type

The Service Type field is used to set priorities or precedence for data transmission. The size of the field is 8 bits. This field is also used to determine the type of service that is required for a particular application. The priority is set using the first three bits and the service type is set using the next three bits. The last two bits are reserved for future use. The Service Type field has two components, Precedence and Types of Service. In the sections that follow, the components of the Service Type field are explained in detail.

Precedence

The component of the Service Type field that is used to set priorities is called Precedence. This component is 3 bits long. Therefore, eight priority values ranging from 0 (000) to 7 (111) can be set. IP specifies the rules for deciding when a packet must be discarded. For example, if congestion occurs on the network, IP identifies the packets that need to be sent immediately and the packets that can be delayed depending on the priority assigned to the packet. If IP is not able to find an alternative, it can discard the packets. If data packets are discarded, ICMP generates an error message and sends it to the Transport layer. The Precedence field was created for programs that were created for the Department of Defense.

Types of Service

The Types of Service (ToS) component is used to determine the type of service that must be provided by the Internet layer depending on the type of application for which the data transfer needs to be done. The types of services that can be provided by IP are maximizing reliability and throughput and minimizing cost and delay. The size of the ToS component is 4 bits. The Transport layer provides the value of this field to the Internet layer. However, the values in these bits are just guidelines and not rules. The devices that operate from the Internet layer use these values to transfer data. The values that can be assigned to this component and a description of each value is provided in Table 3.1. For example, if the application is an Online Transaction Processing (OLTP) system, it will require the delay to be minimized and therefore the value would be 1000_2. However, in a situation where a bulk transfer of data is to be done, maximizing throughput will be appreciated and thus the value will be 0100_2.

Note

Throughput refers to the capacity of a network to transmit data and is measured by recording the total size of data that is transmitted over a network within a fixed time limit. This is also referred to as bandwidth.

TABLE 3.1 VALUES THE Types of Service COMPONENT CAN TAKE

Binary Value	Description
0000	Normal
0001	Minimizing cost
0010	Maximize reliability
0100	Maximize throughput
1000	Minimize delay

Note

0000 is the default value of the Type of Service component.

Note

Only one of the ToS bits can be set at any point of time. A value, such as 11000_2 is invalid. Another important point to be noted is that the TOS bits will be meaningful only if the network devices through which a datagram is routed are programmed to support and provide a quality of service.

Time to Live

The Time to Live (TTL) field is used to specify the time for which a datagram must be retained on the network. This field is 8 bits long. TTL is measured in seconds. The TTL field can be used to improve the performance of a network because it is used to prevent the data packets from remaining indefinitely on the network. TTL values must be set according to the type of service that is required by the network and the speed of the network.

Consider a situation in which a datagram needs to be transmitted over a slow speed network. Considering the fact that the speed of the network is slow, the TTL value must be set to a higher value compared to the one that is set for transmitting the datagram over a high-speed network. If the TTL value is low, the datagram might not reach the intended recipient on time and might eventually be discarded. Another factor that influences the value of the TTL is the type of service that is required by the Application layer.

The TTL value is decremented by every router through which the data packet passes. The TTL value is measured in seconds. The routers decrement the value of the TTL field by 1 second. If the TTL value is 0 before the datagram reaches the destination, the datagram is discarded. After the datagram is discarded, ICMP sends an error message to the Transport layer protocols. The Transport layer then decides whether the data needs to be retransmitted.

Protocol

The Protocol field is used to specify the protocol used to create the data present in the Data field. The size of this field is 8 bits. The values that are assigned to the Protocol field are provided in Table 3.2. IP receives data from all the higher layer protocols. Each layer in the TCP/IP reference model adds information to the data that will be interpreted by the peer protocols to implement certain tasks. Thus, the data part of an IP datagram contains the original data that has to be sent in addition to the headers added by the higher layer protocols. When the datagram is received at the destination, the data needs to be redirected to the appropriate protocol that is operating in the higher layer. For example, IP can interact with TCP or UDP in the higher layers. The protocol plays an important role because messages can be interpreted only by the protocol that created them.

TABLE 3.2 VALUES THE Protocol COMPONENT CAN TAKE

Value (Decimal)	Protocol
1	Internet Control Message Protocol (ICMP)
2	Internet Group Management Protocol (IGMP)
3	Gateway-to-Gateway Protocol (GGP)
4	Internet Protocol (IP)
6	Transmission Control Protocol (TCP)
8	Exterior Gateway Protocol (EGP)
9	Interior Gateway Protocol (IGP)
17	User Datagram Protocol (UDP)
41	Internet Protocol Version 6 (IPv6)
86	Dissimilar Gateway Protocol (DGP)
88	Interior Gateway Routing Protocol (IGRP)
89	Open Shortest Path First (OSPF)

CH
3

Source Address

The Source Address or the Source IP Address field is 32 bits long and is used to identify the sender of the data. This field is used to redirect error messages to the source in case the datagram is discarded before reaching the destination. The error messages are generated by an ICMP, which also operates from the Internet layer. The address that is specified in this field represents the originator of the message.

Destination Address

The Destination Address or the Destination IP Address field is 32 bits long. This field specifies the final destination of a data packet. However, this field does not provide information about the intermediate devices through which a data packet passes.

> **Note**
>
> The details of the intermediate paths that a datagram can take are stored in the local routing table.

→ To know more about routing tables, **see** "Routing Concepts," **p. 260**

Data

The Data field holds the data that needs to be transmitted over the network. The data part of the IP datagram also includes the header information that is sent by the higher layer protocols, such as TCP, HTTP, and so on.

Header Checksum

The Header Checksum field contains the checksum, which is used by the destination to check for the integrity of the transmitted data by applying an algorithm on the IP header. The size of this field is 16 bits. The Header Checksum value is calculated by the sender and is sent along with the IP header. The sender uses a specific algorithm for arriving at the checksum value. When the datagram reaches the destination, the checksum is calculated by the destination by using the same algorithm. If the value that is calculated is not equal to the specified Header Checksum value in the header of the datagram, the packet is discarded. The Header Checksum value is calculated only with the header values and not by using the data. Every intermediate device that receives the data must calculate the Header Checksum value before forwarding it.

> **Note**
>
> The Header Checksum value is not calculated based on the data because every intermediate device through which the datagram passes will require more time to calculate the Header Checksum for all the bits in the data part. Calculating the checksum based on data will also reduce the efficiency of the network because the datagrams will be held by the intermediate device for a long time.
>
> In addition, the data part of an IP datagram consists of headers created by the higher layer protocols. Performing the check on the data will mean that the intermediate devices must understand the data formats of other protocols and calculate the Header Checksum, which will bring down the performance.

→ To know more about the C/C++ programming structures implementing an IP datagram, **see** "Programming Structures For Data Formats," **p. 447**

ALGORITHM TO CALCULATE THE Header Checksum

The sender uses the following steps to calculate the Header Checksum:

1. The header part of the IP datagram is divided into sections of 16 bits each.

2. The values in the sections are added using the one's complement arithmetic. The sum is then complemented and the result forms the Header Checksum.

Note

When the `Header Checksum` is calculated at the sender's end, the value of the `Header Checksum` is taken as 0.

The following are the steps used by the receiver to check whether the `Header Checksum` is correct:

1. The header part of the IP datagram that is received from the sender is divided into sections of 16 bits each.

Note

Normally, the size of each section that is created must be 16 bits.

2. The data in all the sections are added using one's complement arithmetic. The sum obtained is complemented.

Note

At the receiving end, all the sections in the IP header are included, whereas at the sender's end the `Header Checksum` value is taken as 0.

3. If the result is zero, it means that the data is intact and the packet is retained. Otherwise, it means that the data has undergone a change during the transmission and the packet is discarded.

For example, if the header is 48 bytes long, it will first be divided into different sections of 16 bits each. The values in all the sections are added together by using one's complement arithmetic.

Note

One's complement of a binary number can be found by inverting the bits in a binary number. Inversion refers to converting 0s to 1s and vice versa. On the other hand, One's complement arithmetic is a method that specifies the rules for adding two binary numbers. The rules specify that if two 1s are added, the result would be 0 and a carry of 1 would be generated. On the other hand, if three 1s are added, the result would be a 1 and a carry of 1 would be generated. If the addition of the numbers in the last column results in a carry, the sum must be added with 1 to obtain the result.

Calculation of the `Header Checksum` at the sender's might appear as:

```
1111 1110 1001 0110 -------------------------(Section 1)
1101 1111 1001 0001 ------------------------- (Section 2)
0000 0000 0000 0000 ------------------------- (Checksum)
```

Сн

3

Note that the value of the checksum section is taken as zero when the Header Checksum value is calculated at the sender's end. The sum of Section 1, Section 2, and Checksum is

```
11101 1110 0010 0111
```

As the sum that is derived has a carryover of 1, the sum is added to 1 once again.

```
11101 1110 0010 0111 ------------------------- (Sum)
                   1
```

The Header Checksum calculated by the sender is

```
0010 0001 1101 0111
```

The Header Checksum at the receiver's end is calculated as:

```
1111 1110 1001 0110 -----------------------(Section 1)
1101 1111 1001 0001 -----------------------(Section 2)
0010 0001 1101 0111 -----------------------(Checksum)
```

The receiver takes the value of the checksum field from the IP header unlike the sender, which assumes the same to be 0. The sum of Section 1, Section 2, and Checksum is

```
11111 1111 1111 1110
```

The sum obtained has a carryover of 1; therefore, the sum is added to 1 once again.

```
11111 1111 1111 1110 -----------------------(Sum)
                   1
```

The result of the above operation is

```
1111 1111 1111 1111
```

As one's complement of the result, 1111 1111 1111 1111, is performed. If the value that is arrived at is 0, the data packet is retained. Otherwise, the data packet is rejected and an error message is reported to the source.

Note   The complement of a number is obtained by converting all 1s to 0s and vice versa.

An IP datagram has a few more fields that are used for fragmentation. These fields are discussed in the following section.

TRANSMISSION OF DATAGRAMS

Datagrams from the Internet layer are sent to the Network Interface layer where the data is transmitted over the physical medium. The Network Interface layer transmits data in the form of frames. A datagram is packaged into a frame by the Network Interface layer (see Figure 3.4).

Figure 3.4
An IP datagram is encapsulated in a frame and transmitted over the cables.

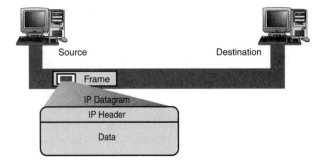

However, there are a few factors that need to be considered while encapsulating a datagram within a frame. They are as follows:

- The amount of data that can be transmitted in a single frame is called *Maximum Transfer Unit* (MTU) and varies with the network technology that is used. MTU size is measured in bytes. For example, the MTU for Ethernet is 1,500 bytes, whereas it is 4,352 bytes for FDDI. If a datagram cannot be accommodated in a single frame, it is divided or fragmented and sent in multiple frames. The process of dividing a datagram into multiple groups called fragments is called *fragmentation*.

  The steps that are followed for fragmenting the datagram is depicted by using the following pseudocode:

```
if (Size of the datagram >= MTU)
{
    if (allowfragmentation==true)
    {
        Fragment data
    }
    else
    {
        Discard data packets
    }
else
{
    Encapsulate the datagram into the frame and start transmission
}
```

> **Note**
>
> IP datagrams have an option, called the Don't Fragment bit, in the `Flags` field that can be used to disallow fragmentation of the transmitted datagram. This can be done by setting the value of the Don't Fragment bit to 1, which is discussed later in this chapter.

- If data needs to be sent across two different networks, each working on a different technology, such as Ethernet or FDDI, encapsulating the datagram within a frame is not possible. This is because of the varying MTU values between each type of network. Therefore, the datagram might have to be fragmented. For example, if data is sent

CH
3

from an Ethernet network to a token ring network, data needs to be fragmented because the MTU for Ethernet is higher than that of token ring.

The process of combining all the fragments at the destination is called *reassembling*.

The fields in the datagram that are used for fragmentation are as follows:

- `Identification`
- `Flags`
- `Fragmentation Offset`

Identification

The `Identification` field is used to identify a datagram. The size of the `Identification` field is 16 bits. A combination of the IP address and the number specified in this field is used to identify the datagram to which a component belongs. An identification number is created for a datagram and the same value is copied to the `Identification` field of all the fragments of the datagram.

The `Identification` field is used to identify all the fragments that are obtained by fragmenting a datagram. For example, if a datagram is split into five fragments, all the five fragments will have the same identification number. This will help the destination computer to reassemble all the fragments that belong to a datagram.

Flags

The `Flag` field has two functions. It helps in determining whether a datagram can be fragmented. It also indicates whether there are any more fragments following the current one. This field is also known as the `More Fragment` field.

The size of this field is 3 bits. The first bit is not used. The second bit is used to indicate whether fragmentation can be done. This field is called the Don't Fragment bit. If the value of this bit is set to `1`, the datagram must not be fragmented. Otherwise, the datagram is fragmented, if necessary. If the datagram must be fragmented, but the value in the second bit is set to `1`, the datagram is discarded.

The last bit in this field is used to indicate whether there are any fragments following the current one. If the value of this field is set to `0`, it indicates that the current fragment is the last fragment in the datagram.

Fragmentation Offset

The `Fragmentation Offset` field is used by the destination to find out the position of a fragment with respect to the entire datagram. The size of the `Fragmentation Offset` field is 13 bits. This field, along with the `Identification` and `Flag` fields, is used by the destination to ensure that all the fragments that belong to a particular datagram are reassembled together. Even if one fragment is not delivered correctly, the entire datagram is discarded. If a datagram is discarded, an error message is sent to the Transport layer by ICMP.

Certain rules need to be followed during the process of fragmentation. They are as follows:

- Only the data part of a datagram can be fragmented. The header occupies 20–60 bytes and the remaining space is allotted for the data that needs to be sent. For example, if the total size of the datagram is 5,000 bytes, a minimum of 20 bytes are used to store the header information. Thus, of the 5,000 bytes allotted for the datagram, only 4,980 bytes are used to store the data. The size of a datagram must be divisible by 8. If the size of a datagram is 300 octets, only 296 bytes can be sent in the fragment and the rest should be sent in another fragment.

- The Fragmentation Offset field is used to indicate the relative position of a fragment with respect to the other fragments of a datagram. The position of the datagram is not represented in terms of the exact position. It contains the number of octets that the fragment contains. The Fragmentation Offset is numbered starting from zero.

Consider a case in which fragments need to be created for a datagram of size 2,500 bytes and are to be sent through an Ethernet network. Assuming that the header size is 20 bytes, the size of data that needs to be fragmented is 2,500–20, which is 2,480 bytes. MTU of an Ethernet network is 1,500, therefore two fragments need to be created for the data. One more point to note is that, in the 1,500 bytes that is provided as MTU, 20 bytes will be required to store the header information for the fragments. That is, only 1,480 bytes can be accommodated in one fragment. The remaining 1,000 bytes must be sent in the next fragment. The fragmentation offset field for the first fragment will be set to 0 and the value for the same in the second fragment will be 185 (1,480÷8). The destination computer also checks for the value in the More Fragment field to check if any more fragments are following the current one.

Note

If the number of bytes that need to be transferred is not in multiples of eight and is a few bytes less than the nearest multiple of eight, extra spaces are included in the data to ensure that the size of the data is divisible by eight. The exact length of the data can be found using the Total Length field and the Padding fields.

Note

Every destination computer has a predefined time by which all the fragments of an IP datagram need to arrive. The fragments received are retained in the memory of the destination computer until all the fragments of a datagram reach it. If all the fragments that belong to a particular datagram do not reach the destination in the time defined, an error message is sent to the sender using ICMP.

→ For more information on the error message sent to the sender, **see** "Internet Control Message Protocol," **p. 61**

ADVANTAGES OF FRAGMENTATION

IP, as mentioned earlier, is used to route data packets to the destination irrespective of the underlying hardware technology. IP implements this by supporting fragmentation. If the MTU is large enough to hold an entire datagram, the network traffic will be low and congestion will also be avoided. The sender can also determine the optimum size for avoiding fragmentation during the transmission of data. This function is carried out by TCP by a mechanism called *path MTU discovery*.

→ To learn more about path MTU discovery and TCP, **see** "Transmission Control and Data Flow," **p. 73**

IP Options

The IP Options field is not a mandatory field. Even without the information provided in this field, data can be transferred from the source to the destination. The IP Options field is only used for providing additional features, such as Record Route, Strict Source Route, and so on, during data transmission. The default size of the IP Options field is zero. The maximum size of this field is 40 bytes. The IP Options field is also responsible for the security of the datagrams. In addition, the field is used for testing and debugging a network. The length of the field is variable and depends on the IP options that are selected.

An IP datagram can consist of more than one IP option. An IP option can be represented in two forms. In the first form only one octet, called Option-Type, is used to represent the option. The second form includes three octets: Option-Type, Option-Length, and Option-Data. The second form requires three octets for each field. The Option-Length field is the sum of the length of the other fields in the option. The Option-Data field is used for storing data related to the Option-Type. The Option-Type is divided into three components: Copy, Option-Class, and Option-Number, which specify the operations that must be performed.

Copy

The Copy field is used to specify whether the option values must be copied to all the fragments. The size of the Copy field is 1 bit. If the value of this bit is set to 0, the option values need to be copied only to the first fragment. If the value in this field is set to 1, the options values must be copied to all the fragments.

Option-Class

The values that can be taken by the Option-Class field are 0 to 3. If the value in this field is 0, the datagram is used for network control. If the value in this field is 2, the datagram is used for debugging the network. Values 1 and 3 are reserved for future use.

Option-Number

The Option-Number field indicates the type of operation to be performed. The size of the Option-Number field is 5 bits. Two most commonly used options are Record Route and Strict Source Route. The values that can be taken by an Option-Type field are listed in Table 3.2.

TABLE 3.2   VARIOUS OPTIONS THAT CAB PROVIDED IN THE IP Options FIELD OF AN IP DATAGRAM

Option-Class	Option-Number	Option-Length	Fields
0	0	-	End of Option
0	1	-	No Operation
0	2	11	Security
0	3	Variable	Loose Source Routing
0	9	Variable	Strict Source Route
0	7	Variable	Record Route
2	4	Variable	Internet Timestamp

Note

The End of Option field marks the end of all the options in an IP datagram.

CH
3

Note

The No Operation field is used for handling the alignment between options in an IP datagram.

Note

The Security field is used to send security-related information.

The value of the Option-Class of the last option is 2, which indicates that it is used for debugging and measuring. However, the other values are used for network control.

In Strict Source Route and Loose Source Routing, the sender specifies the path that must be taken by a datagram. In Strict Source Route, the sender specifies a list of IP addresses that a source must take. There must be no deviation from the path that is specified by the sender. Like Strict Source Route, the sender specifies the list of IP addresses that a datagram must pass through in the case of Loose Source Routing also. The only difference between the former and the later is that in the case of Loose Source Routing, the path taken between two specified IP addresses can vary.

A router can also be made to track the path that is taken by a datagram. Thus, the route taken by a datagram is a dynamically growing route list. This is defined as the Record Route option. The Option-Data field is used to store the dynamically growing route list.

The Internet Timestamp option is used for debugging and measuring. This option is used to record timestamp values in the route taken by a datagram. The timestamp values can be used to find the time taken by a datagram to reach a destination. The values that are obtained can be used to measure the performance of the network.

SUMMARY

The Internet layer in the TCP/IP reference model is responsible for transferring data between the source and destination computers. Routing and data transmission are done by Internet Protocol and error handling is implemented by ICMP. IP provides a connectionless and unreliable data transmission system. IP also specifies the format in which data needs to be transferred, which is also called an IP datagram. The IP datagram, in turn, is encapsulated in a frame and transmitted over the network. The fields in an IP datagram that are used in the transmission of data are Version, Header Length, Types of Service, Total Length, Time to Live, Protocol, Header Checksum, Source Address, and Destination Address. The fields that are used for fragmentation are Flags, Identification, and Fragmentation Offset.

CHAPTER 4

INTERNET CONTROL MESSAGE PROTOCOL

In this chapter

INTRODUCTION TO ICMP

The two main functions of the Internet layer are routing and error handling. Routing data packets to the corresponding destination is the function of IP. IP works with another protocol called Internet Control Message Protocol (ICMP) (see Figure 4.1) to report errors during data transmission. ICMP reports errors to the Transport layer protocol that was involved in the data transmission. That is, ICMP can be used only for fault isolation and not for error correction. ICMP messages can also be used to troubleshoot and optimize the performance of a network. The standards for ICMP are defined in RFC 792.

→ For information on RFCs, **see** "RFCs," **p. 425**

Figure 4.1
ICMP operates along with IP from the Internet layer in the TCP/IP reference model.

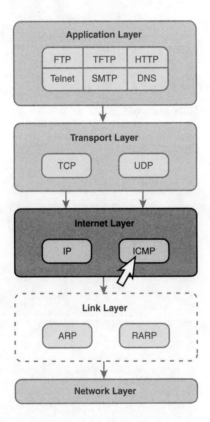

ROLE OF HOSTS AND ROUTERS IN FAULT ISOLATION

The hosts and the routers work together to perform two main functions in data transmission: fault isolation and fault recovery. These are accomplished using ICMP. *Fault isolation* is the process of finding out the problem in the network due to which data transmission is hindered. *Fault recovery* is the process of finding a solution to the problem.

→ To know more about routers and other intermediate devices, **see** "Intermediate Devices," **p. 13**

Every router on an internetwork stores the details about the status of the other routers on the network. Routers, being smart devices, can choose the best route in which a data packet can be sent. This functionality is implemented by virtue of having the details of alternate routes through the other networks. When a router receives a data packet that can be sent through a different route, which would also ensure faster transmission of data, it immediately sends a response to the source about the alternate route as an ICMP message. The host or the source, in turn, must update its routing table with the new route. The host then decides the path to be taken by a data packet by using certain algorithms.

→ To know more about how hosts and routers find the route through which a data packet can be sent, **see** "IP Routing," **p. 259**

Note

Every host on an internetwork, including the router, maintains a list of routes through which a data packet can be routed in the form of a table called the *routing table*. The entries in a routing table are updated when there are changes in the network topology and configurations.

If there is a problem in the network due to which the routes undergo a change, the routing information must be updated in the routing table of the routers. The routers might take some time to update their routing tables. If a host contacts a router in this transient period, the information reported by the router might be incorrect. There might also be situations in which a router that is contacted by the host might not be functioning. In this case, the host might not get any response from the router. The host computer can either choose an alternative route from the routing table to transfer data or try sending information to the same router after some time. When a host sends a datagram to a different computer on the network, it can get two types of error messages. The first type of message is called an *ICMP redirect message*, which informs the host that the data packet can be transmitted through a different route efficiently. The other message is called the *Destination Unreachable* message that is sent by an intermediate device due to network problems.

CH

4

METHODS USED BY A HOST FOR FAULT ISOLATION

There are a few situations in which isolating or finding the exact cause of a problem might be very difficult and time-consuming. To overcome these problems, there are a few algorithms that can be used by a host to isolate the problem. If the exact nature of a problem is not identified, the efficiency of a network will come down drastically. The algorithms that can be used by a host are network level detection and polling.

In network level detection, if the router to which the message is sent is not functioning, an error message is sent to the host indicating that the router is unreachable by the intermediate devices on the network. This message is also referred to as a host dead message. This message is used by the host to decide if it has to continue with data transmission.

Polling is a method used by a host for fault isolation in an internetwork. It is of two types, continuous polling and triggered polling. In *continuous polling*, the host continues sending messages to the router at specific intervals of time to check whether the router is functioning properly. For example, the host will echo requests to the router at regular intervals. If the host does not get a reply from the router, it assumes that a problem exists with the router. However, there is a disadvantage in this method. This method leads to a lot of overhead on the network, thus decreasing the efficiency of the network.

In *triggered polling*, the host also sends a request to the router to check the functioning of the router. However, the difference between the two lies in the fact that in triggered polling this request is sent only if IP receives intimation about inefficient data transmission from the Transport layer protocols.

Routers use a method called triggered updates to stay in synchronization with other routers on an internetwork.

➔ To know more triggered updates, **see** "Routing Mechanisms," **p. 277**

TRANSMISSION OF ICMP MESSAGES

ICMP messages cannot be directly sent to the Network Interface layer for transmission. They are encapsulated in an IP datagram and sent to the next layer. The data part of an IP datagram consists of the ICMP message. The `Protocol` field in the IP header is set to 1 when an ICMP message is transmitted through an IP datagram.

The following are the key facts to remember about ICMP:

- ICMP reports errors that occur during data transmission, but is not responsible for correcting the problems due to the errors. It is the responsibility of the Transport layer protocols to rectify the problems. For example, if a router discards a data packet, the function of ICMP is to report the error to the Transport layer protocols. However, retransmitting data is done by the Transport layer protocols.

- ICMP does not report an error when the problems are encountered by an IP datagram that carries an ICMP message.

- ICMP messages always report problems with fragment zero of a datagram only. *Fragment zero* refers to the first fragment of a datagram. Any problems with the other fragments are not reported by ICMP.

- ICMP messages are always redirected to the host that sent the datagram and not to the intermediate devices. For example, if a datagram originated from a computer named C1 and passed through a router R1 and had problems when it had to pass through a router R3, the ICMP error message is redirected to C1 with the destination address field containing the address of R3.

- ICMP messages are not generated for datagrams that contain multicast addresses or special addresses, such as `127.0.0. 1`. The special address `127.0.0. 1` is also known as the loopback address.

Note

Like IP, ICMP is also a connectionless protocol.

Note

IP is used to transmit ICMP messages. Therefore, there is no guarantee that the IP datagrams that carry the ICMP messages will be delivered to the destination properly. It is the responsibility of the Transport layer to take care of the reliability of data.

ICMP MESSAGE FORMAT

The messages that are reported by ICMP can be classified as errors and queries. *Errors* are used to report problems in the network as *against queries* that are used to troubleshoot networks. The format of an ICMP message (see Figure 4.2) varies depending on the type of error message that is generated. Although certain fields are common to both, there are a few differences. Table 4.1 describes the fields that are used by ICMP for reporting errors.

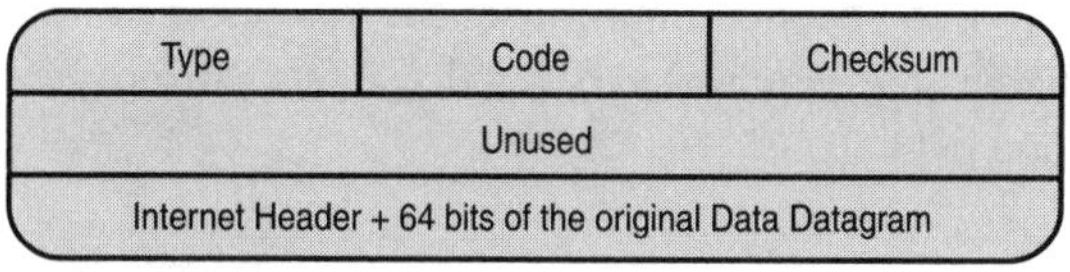

Figure 4.2
The ICMP message format can be used to identify the type of error that is generated.

Type	Code	Checksum
Unused		
Internet Header + 64 bits of the original Data Datagram		

CH

4

TABLE 4.1 FIELDS OF AN IP DATAGRAM

Field	Description
Type	Identifies the error message generated. This is first field in an ICMP message.
Code	Further qualifies the ICMP message that is generated. This field is used to find the cause of the error that is generated.
Checksum	Stores the checksum value used by ICMP. The same algorithm that IP uses for calculating the checksum is used for calculating this checksum. The size of this field is 16 bits.
Unused	Reserved for future use and is set to zero. The computer that receives an ICMP message must not use the value in this field.
Data	Includes the IP header of the datagram that was received and also the first eight bytes of data in the IP datagram. This will be used by the sender to get more details about the error that has occurred.

The Type field in an ICMP message format gives the type of error message that is generated. For example, the Destination Unreachable message indicates that the destination could not be reached. However, the error could have occurred due to many problems, such as hardware failure or a router failure. The exact reason for the failure is given by the Code field. Table 4.2 provides a list of errors that are generated by ICMP.

TABLE 4.2   ERROR MESSAGES GENERATED BY ICMP

Value	Name of the Error
3	Destination Unreachable
4	Source Quench
5	Redirection
11	Time Exceeded
12	Parameter Problem

→ To know more about the errors that are generated by ICMP, **see** "RFCs," **p. 425**

→ To know more about the C/C++ programming structures implementing an ICMP message, **see** "Programming Structures for Data Formats," **p. 447**

DESTINATION UNREACHABLE

The Destination Unreachable message is generated when the destination cannot be contacted. The Code field is used to identify the specific reason for the error. For example, if 3 is the value in the Type field, the host computer uses the Code field to find out why a "Destination Unreachable" message was generated. Table 4.3 lists a few possible values that can be taken by the Code field.

TABLE 4.3   A FEW VALUES TAKEN BY THE Code FIELD

Value	Description
0	Indicates that the entire network is unreachable. Possible causes of this error could be failure of hardware. This problem will be mostly caused by failure of intermediate devices. If an intermediate device fails, the network that is connected to the intermediate device will not be reachable.
1	Indicates that the host is unreachable. This error is generated when there is a hardware failure in the host or the route to the destination host is not available.
2	Indicates that the protocol required to process the datagram is not present in the computer. That is, the protocol that can be used for processing information is not installed properly. The protocol that is required to process the message can be fetched from the Protocol field of the IP header.
3	Indicates that the port is unreachable. For every application that is executed, a logical port is defined in the computer that executes the application. If the application itself is not executing, this error message is generated.
4	Indicates that the destination is unreachable due to fragmentation problems. If the IP datagram is to be fragmented but the Don't Fragment is set, an error is reported. The router sends an error message to the host.
6	Indicates that the router does not know the route to the destination network. This error could be generated in a situation when the router has not updated itself with the latest changes in the topology of the network.

TRANSMISSION OF ICMP MESSAGES 67

SOURCE QUENCH

Errors due to net congestion, also referred to as Source Quench errors, usually occur when the speed of data transmission of the sender and the receiver are not synchronized. If the speed of the sender is high, an intermediate device will have too many data packets to be sent and might not be able to transmit all the data packets. When network congestion occurs, ICMP sends an error to the sender. This enables the sender to adjust the speed of data transmission to match with that of the receiver. This error also informs the source that the data packets have been discarded. The value of the Code field for the Source Quench is taken as 0.

TIME EXCEEDED

The Time Exceeded message is generated when the TTL value in the IP header becomes zero before the datagram is delivered to the destination. This message is generated by the router and sent to the host. This message is also generated by destination hosts that do not receive all the fragments of a datagram within a stipulated time. The value in the Code field for this message can be 0 or 1.

PARAMETER PROBLEM

The Parameter Problem error message is reported when there are problems in the fields in the IP header. Every field in the IP datagram has a few values, which can be assigned only to it. If an invalid value is provided, an ICMP error message is generated.

REDIRECTION

The Redirection message is generated by a router when it finds that a data packet can be sent through a much better route compared to the current one.

> **Note**
> The Redirection messages are used to make data transmission efficient. For example, if a data packet can be sent through two routes, the route that is better can be decided based on a few factors. The factors could be the network technology that is used, the number of routers through which a datagram must pass through, and so on. The routing algorithms are used to decide the route.

The host need not contain information about all the routes that a datagram can take. When a host needs to send a datagram, it refers to a table called the routing table that is present locally to find a route. If it is not able to find an appropriate route, the datagrams are forwarded to the computer that is configured as the default gateway for the host, which, in turn, takes care of forwarding the datagrams to the destination.

→ To know more about how hosts and routers find the route through which a data packet can be sent, **see** "IP Routing," **p. 259**

The routers also take the responsibility of updating the hosts with the changes in the routes at frequent intervals of time. Routes might change if there is a change in the topology of the network. They can also change if a network is restructured. The information that is passed from the routers is accepted as-is by the hosts. In addition, the hosts can also trace the routes by using the Tracert utility. The ICMP query messages are used for this purpose.

QUERY MESSAGES

The Query message can be used to troubleshoot network problems. The commonly used query messages are Echo Request, Echo Reply, Time Stamp Request, and Time Stamp Reply. The different Query messages and the corresponding values are displayed in Table 4.4.

TABLE 4.4   A FEW QUERY MESSAGES GENERATED BY ICMP

Value	Description
8	Echo Request
0	Echo Reply
13	Timestamp Request
14	Timestamp Reply
9	Router Advertisement
10	Router Solicitation

There are also other messages that are generated by ICMP, such as Address Mask Request and Address Mask Reply.

→ To learn about Address Mask Request and Address Mask Reply messages, which are also generated by ICMP, **see** "IP Routing," **p. 259**

ECHO REQUEST AND REPLY

The Echo Request and Echo Reply messages are used to check whether a connection is established between two computers on a network. The sender sends an Echo Request message to the computer for which it needs to check whether the connection is established properly. If the host receives an Echo Reply, the host can proceed with data transmission. However, if a reply is not received, the host needs to select an alternative route. This type of check can be done for computers on the same network or different networks. If an Echo Request is sent to a computer on a different network and an Echo Reply is also received, the host can infer that all the routers in the route are functioning properly.

These messages are used by network management utilities, such as Simple Network Management Protocol (SNMP), to monitor and troubleshoot the network. One of the commonly used utilities called Ping uses these message formats.

The Echo Request and the Echo Reply messages are also used to trace a route by using the Traceroute method. This method is typically implemented as a utility by various operating systems. Now, let us understand how the Traceroute method is used to find a route on an internetwork. When the tracert utility is executed, it sends an Echo Request message with the TTL value set to 1. When the datagram reaches a router, the router will not be able to set the value of the TTL field to 0 and forward the packet. Therefore, the router sends a Destination Unreachable message to the host. The host records the address of the router after the error message is received. Next, the host sends an Echo Request message with the TTL value 2 and the same process is repeated.

TIMESTAMP REQUEST AND REPLY

The source and the destination computers use the Timestamp Request and Reply messages to calculate the time that a data packet takes to reach the destination. The source stores the time at which the datagram leaves the sender and sends a timestamp request to the destination. After the destination receives the datagram, it fills the time at which the datagram was received and also fills the time at which the datagram departed from the destination. This will enable the host to calculate the total round trip time that a datagram has taken to reach the destination.

The values in these messages can be used to improve the performance of the network if the time taken by the data packet to reach the destination is very high.

ROUTER SOLICITATION AND ADVERTISEMENT

When a host needs to send data to a computer on a different network, it must be aware of the address of the router that can pass data to the other computer. If the host does not have the address of the router, it sends a Router Solicitation message to all the computers on the network. The routers respond to the host by sending a Router Advertisement message with a list of addresses. The message also contains the time for which the entries are valid.

CH
4

PING

Ping (Packet Internet Groper) is a tool that is used by network administrators to find problems in connectivity. This utility implements ICMP for checking the connectivity between two systems. It can be used to find the round trip time of a data packet. It can also be used to give statistics about data loss. There might be variations in the options that are provided by the Ping command when it is used with different operating systems.

The Ping command uses the ICMP Echo Request and Echo Reply messages to check the connectivity between two computers. The syntax of the Ping command is

```
Ping IP address
```

For example, if you use the command Ping 128.0.3.4, data packets are sent to the IP address that is specified. If the destination replies by sending a reply, it is assured that the connections are working properly (see Figure 4.3).

Figure 4.3
The Ping command displays the number of packets received, the time, and the TTL values if the connection is established.

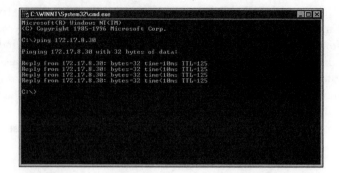

If a reply is not received, the exact nature of the problem should be figured out. The output of the Ping command is shown in Figure 4.4 if the connection is not established.

Figure 4.4
The Ping command displays a message "Request timed out" if a connection cannot be established.

The Ping command can also be used in any of the following situations:

- To check whether TCP/IP is installed properly on a particular computer, you can type the following command at the command prompt:
  ```
  ping loopback address
  ```
- To check for connectivity problems in the network. If a host computer gets an error message indicating that the host is unreachable, the first check made is to check the connectivity between the router and the host. If you find that there are no problems with the network, the next level of checking must be done. The next level of verification is to check the connectivity with the routers.

Note

The Ping command can also be used for checking the validity of a computer name. In case the host name, and not the IP address, causes the problems in connectivity, Domain Naming Service (DNS) must be checked.

→ To know more about DNS, **see** "DNS," **p. 209**

TRACERT

Tracert is also a diagnostic utility that uses the Echo Request and Echo Reply messages to trace the route of a data packet. This can also be used to calculate the round trip time of a data packet. The following is the syntax of this command:

```
Tracert IP address or host name
```

This utility can be used to check if a router is functioning properly or not. One of the fields in the output of the Tracert is the time taken by a data packet to reach the destination. If the value is high, the configuration of the routers must be upgraded or the data packets need to be sent through an alternative route. The output of the Tracert command is displayed in Figure 4.5.

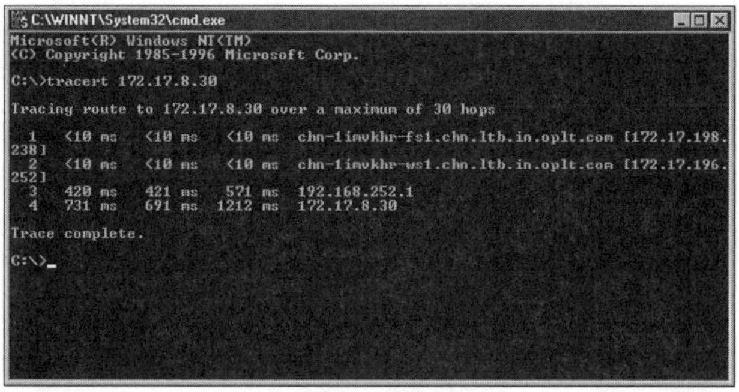

Figure 4.5
The route to reach the destination is displayed by using the Tracert command.

The -w and -h options can be used to specify the timeout period and the number of hops (see Figure 4.6) through which a data packet can be sent.

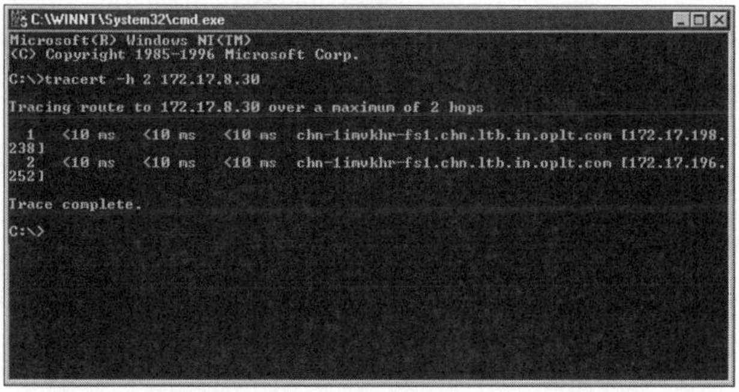

Figure 4.6
The number of hops through which a data packet can pass to reach the target is specified using Tracert.

CH
4

SUMMARY

ICMP is a protocol that operates from the Internet layer of the TCP/IP reference model. It is used for fault isolation and not for error correction. Error correction is the responsibility of the Transport layer protocols. ICMP can also be used for troubleshooting problems in the network. The messages generated by ICMP are classified as errors and queries. Errors, such as Destination Unreachable, Source Quench, Parameter Problem, and so on, are used for reporting errors in data transfer as against queries, which are used to troubleshoot the network. Echo Request, Echo Reply, Timestamp Request, and Timestamp Reply are a few query messages that are generated by ICMP. `Ping` and `Tracert` are diagnostic tools that implement ICMP messages. These tools can be used by network administrators to troubleshoot problems related to network connectivity.

CHAPTER 5

TRANSMISSION CONTROL AND DATA FLOW

In this chapter

INTRODUCTION TO TCP

Exchange of data can be described as one of the primary functions of internetworks. However, to establish a smooth communication mechanism among networks that use diverse hardware and software configurations, a control mechanism that manages modification of data to a format compatible for data transmission must be established. The control mechanism must also manage the actual transfer of data over the diverse networks. The Transport layer, which contains Transmission Control Protocol (TCP) and User Datagram Protocol (UDP), implements such a mechanism. Although data transmission forms the primary goal of the Transport layer protocols, TCP and UDP differ in the way they track data transmission and deliver data. TCP provides a connection-oriented data transfer mechanism in which computers establish a connection between them before the actual data transfer. On the other hand, UDP provides a data transfer facility that manages just the data transfer but does not provide tracking features to ensure successful data delivery. Figure 5.1 indicates the position of the layer from which TCP operates in the TCP/IP reference model.

Figure 5.1
In addition to its role in data transmission, TCP, a Transport layer protocol, provides data tracking features.

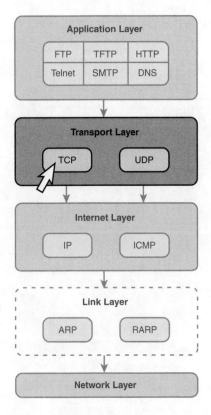

→ To learn more about UDP, **see** "User Datagram Protocol," **p. 113**

From the outset, it is very important to understand that TCP is not a software product but only a set of specifications or standards to build protocol software that enables connection-oriented communication. These specifications were built over the last three decades based on the RFCs contributed to the International Engineering Task Force (IETF) starting from the very first TCP-related RFC being contributed in 1973 by Vint Cerf.

→ For more information on various RFCs, **see** "RFCs," **p. 425**

In simple terms, TCP can be described as a communication standard that breaks down data provided by the Application layer into smaller units called *segments* and tracks the transfer of these data units. The segments transmitted using TCP can be compared to a rocket launched from a rocket launch command center. The rocket is readied for launch in the command center and after it is launched, its progress is closely monitored and tracked by the command center until the mission objectives are met.

Similarly, TCP readies segments for "launch" and tracks the progress of the segment "rocket" until the segment is safely delivered to the destination computer. A rocket launch command center needs to manage only a single rocket, whereas TCP needs to manage the transmission of a multitude of segments across diverse networks, which makes its role all the more vital. The question of how this task is achieved by TCP is answered in the following section.

SERVICES PROVIDED BY TCP

Before delving into the details of how TCP works, have a look at the services provided by the protocol. These services reflect the specifications recommended by TCP-related RFCs and are used to implement certain fundamental concepts of TCP, such as establishing a connection, full-duplex connections, half-duplex connections, acknowledgement, retransmission, piggybacking, and buffered transfer. The services provided by TCP can be broadly divided into connectivity-related services and data transfer-related services.

CH
5

CONNECTIVITY-RELATED SERVICES

The most basic feature provided as part of TCP connectivity services is a connection. A *connection* is a communication channel used for data exchange. When data is transferred from one computer to another, one of the first actions that make the transfer possible is the establishment of a connection between the source and destination computers. The process is as simple as two strangers beginning a conversation where one person initiates the conversation and the other responds, thereby "breaking the ice." When two computers begin communication, the application using TCP on the sending computer informs its OS that a communication with another computer is to be initiated and notifies the receiver that it wants to establish a connection. This process is called an *active open*. The application on the receiving computer, which uses TCP, informs its OS about the commencement of communication with another computer. This process is known as a *passive open*. In response, the OS on the sender and receiver allocate predefined communication channels called ports.

Note

FTP, HTTP, and Telnet are some of the applications that use TCP. The term "application" used to refer to such application protocols is not to be confused with software solutions.

Note

The process of initiating the termination of a connection is called *active close*. The other machine that completes the connection termination process is said to perform a *passive close*.

A *port* is a unique number assigned by the OS to the calling application. Ports are used by the calling application on both machines to communicate and exchange data. Now, if an application needs to communicate with multiple machines, it must use a shared port. Every connection is said to have endpoints. An endpoint is the combination of the port number and the IP address of a machine. Multiple machines can use the same endpoint on a computer to exchange data. Figure 5.2 shows how this concept works.

Figure 5.2
Multiple senders can use the same endpoint on the receiver.

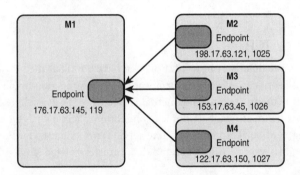

You can see in Figure 5.2 that the endpoint 176.17.63.145, 119 is shared by multiple machines, which have their own endpoints to communicate data.

Note

Every application is provided with a unique port number that is used on all machines irrespective of the OS. For example, when you configure your browser to connect to the Internet, the port number used is always 80 because the World Wide Web service, which is the application in this case, is allocated this unique port number.

Note

Port is not to be confused with the hardware slots used to connect peripheral hardware devices although it bears the same name.

→ To learn about the different port numbers, **see** "TCP Application Ports," **p. 451**

When the sender and the receiver complete the process of initial communication and confirm the establishment of a connection, the connection establishment process is said to be complete. After the connection is established, data transfer can commence. You can compare a connection with a bridge linking an island to the mainland. It is possible to use a connection to conduct a simultaneous exchange of data between the connected machines, like the bridge supporting traffic flowing in both directions. However, the choice of establishing a two-way simultaneous connection depends on the requirements of the calling application on both machines. For example, if the applications on both machines require exchanging data simultaneously, they use the same connection for a simultaneous exchange of data. This type of connection is called *full-duplex connection*. Sometimes, the connection can be used as a one way "bridge" where data travels in one direction at a given point of time. The connection that exhibits this feature is called a *half-duplex connection*. To continue with the bridge metaphor, a half-duplex connection can be described as a bridge that can only support one-way traffic unlike bigger bridges where traffic from both directions is possible. Therefore, computers linked through a half-duplex connection can use the same connection to send and receive data at different points of time but not simultaneously.

DATA TRANSFER SERVICES

Data transfer services are primarily targeted at ensuring a safe and efficient transfer of data between connected machines. Establishing a connection alone does not ensure a safe and complete transfer of data between machines. The vagaries of internetworking, such as lost data segments or duplication of data segments, call for a mechanism by which data transfer can be tracked. When a TCP segment is sent through a connection, the receiver sends a confirmation indicating that the segment has safely reached its destination. This tracking mechanism, called an *acknowledgement*, is sent in the form of a data segment. The sending computer waits until it receives an acknowledgement before sending the next segment.

To manage data segments that are lost during transmission, the sending computer sets a timer, which indicates the time by which an acknowledgement should arrive. If the acknowledgement does not arrive within the specified time limit, the sending computer retransmits the segment.

Note

A mechanism that defines the time limit for retransmitting segments and receiving acknowledgements is called a *timer*.

CH
5

Although it sounds like a nice idea, the issue of duplicate segments and acknowledgements results in other problems. If an acknowledgement arrives late, the sender would have retransmitted a duplicate segment, if the segment sent initially is lost. If the receiver retransmits a duplicate acknowledgement, you will have the problem of duplicate acknowledgments as well. The problem is solved by naming each segment with a sequence number that indicates its position in the sequence of segments being transferred. The acknowledgement number specified in the segment header indicates the sequence number of the next segment that is to arrive from the sender. The sender or receiver then discards duplicate segments and acknowledgements. Figure 5.3 shows how data transfer concepts are implemented using TCP.

Figure 5.3
Acknowledgements, retransmission, and sequence numbers ensure a safe transfer of data between connected machines.

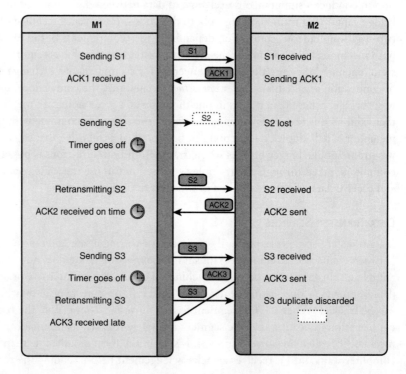

In Figure 5.3, two separate data transmissions are displayed. Note that segments and acknowledgements are named with sequence numbers. The segment S1 has no problem in reaching its destination and its safe receipt is acknowledged with an acknowledgement ACK1 from the receiver computer R1. However, segment S2 is lost during the first transmission and is retransmitted by the sender. The second attempt proves successful and the acknowledgement from the receiving computer is received before the time specified by the timer elapses on the sender. However, for segment S3, the receiver sends a late acknowledgement by which time the sender has already retransmitted S3. However, the duplicate segment is identified by the receiver and is discarded without sending a duplicate acknowledgement.

Data transfer services not only deals with segment tracking but also envisages enhancing the efficiency of data transfer. One method of optimizing existing connection resources is by using a segment bound to another computer for transmitting acknowledgements. Take the example of the acknowledgement ACK1 being sent to the sender M1. If there are any data segments to be sent to M1, you can add the acknowledgement as part of its "baggage" to be delivered to M1. This method of utilizing segments traveling to a particular computer for transmitting miscellaneous data, such as acknowledgments, which are to be sent to the same machine, is called *piggybacking*.

Another efficiency-enhancing mechanism is *buffered transfer*. It is not always necessary that huge volumes of data be transferred at the same time. Sometimes, when small sized data needs to be transferred, instead of wasting precious network traffic, the sending application waits until a bigger chunk of data is ready for transfer. Meanwhile, the application cumulates data segments before implementing the actual transfer. A similar process happens on the receiving computer where the small data segments it receives are cumulated to form a reasonably large chunk before TCP makes the data available to the application requesting the data. A typical example of this feature is your music software that buffers the incoming audio data before playing music.

Note

Buffers are memory resources allocated by the operating system for cumulating data before using the buffered data. Buffers act as temporary storage memory spaces. The size of memory allocated for a buffer varies from computer to computer.

To understand these concepts learned, look at a real-world example by using the netstat utility. This utility, provided by the Windows NT/2000 OS, is a command line tool that enables network administrators to obtain statistical data regarding the state of the connections existing on a network. To take full advantage of netstat, you must use the utility with certain options. For example, when you type the command **netstat -s** at the command prompt, statistical information is displayed pertaining to all the Transport and Internet layer protocols, such as TCP, UDP, ICMP, and IP, which are used by the machines on the network. You can obtain statistical information for a particular protocol by typing **netstat -s -p *protocol name*** at the command prompt. The statistics displayed by this command include active and passive opens, failed connection attempts, connection resets, current connections, and segments received, sent, and retransmitted. Figure 5.4 displays the result of a netstat command that extracts the statistical information for TCP.

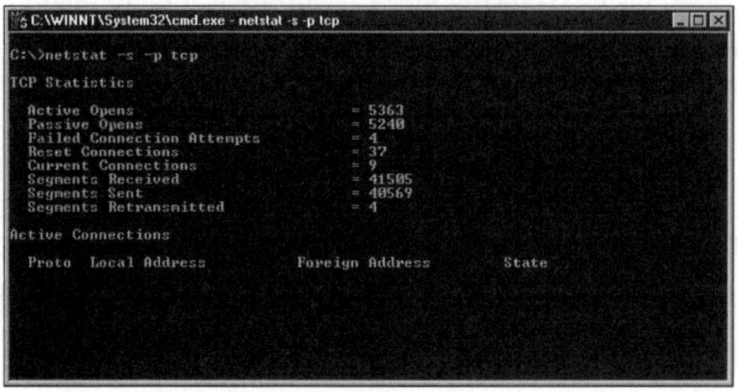

Сн
5

Figure 5.4
The statistics displayed by a netstat command provide an accurate description of TCP performance on the network.

Figure 5.4 displays the number of active and passive opens existing on the network. In addition, the number of segments sent, acknowledged, and retransmitted are also displayed. A low number of retransmitted segments indicate that the network is functioning well.

TCP APPLICATION AREAS

Now that you know how TCP works, it is time to know where and how it is actually used. The following list of application protocols and services use TCP to implement data transfer:

- Domain Naming Service (DNS)—DNS is an IP address translation service that can translate IP addresses into human readable Web site names. DNS uses TCP to transmit zone configuration information that contains large data segments that exceed 512 bytes in size. TCP is essential for reliable replication of zone information across all DNS servers in the internetwork.

- File Transfer Protocol (FTP)—FTP primarily deals with secure exchange of data files. FTP uses TCP to implement a secure user authentication feature before the transmission of data. The connectivity and data tracking features provided by TCP enables FTP to implement the secure file transfer facility.

- Hypertext Transfer Protocol (HTTP)—HTTP can be described as the primary Web page transmission protocol. This protocol depends on TCP to establish a connection with a Web server and to transmit Web pages from the Web server.

- Network File System (NFS)—NFS enables machines to access files stored on other machines. NFS uses TCP to establish a connection with another computer and ensure a reliable transfer of files from the remote machine.

- Rlogin—The Rlogin feature provides the facility to log on to a remote server by using its remote login feature. Rlogin also provides a simpler user authentication feature by using the .rhosts file stored on the server. The file contains the details of usernames, passwords, and client IP addresses. The user need not enter the password after entering the username because the user computer's IP address is verified, and if found valid, the corresponding password contained in the .rhosts file is used to authenticate the username. Rlogin uses TCP to transmit authentication data. TCP is also used to transmit keystrokes entered on client machines to the server and the response provided by the server to the receiver, which is displayed by the receiver.

- Simple Mail Transfer Protocol (SMTP)—SMTP is used to send mail messages to other machines. TCP is used by SMTP to transfer mail message data over the network. SMTP also depends on TCP to ensure the safe delivery of a mail message to the intended recipient.

- Telnet—This protocol provides a remote login feature that enables the transfer of keystrokes typed on a client computer to the server. The result of the keystrokes is echoed back to the client, which displays the typed data on the screen. Telnet uses TCP to implement connectivity and data transfer services to ensure reliable data exchange between the client and server machines.

Although Telnet and Rlogin provide identical remote login features, the login feature implemented by Rlogin is more user-friendly because it automates the process.

To gain a better understanding of how TCP services are implemented by an application protocol, you will now look at how one of application protocols listed earlier, FTP, uses TCP for data transfer. FTP is implemented as a command-line tool, called ftp, on the Windows platform. It is used to transfer and retrieve files from a remote computer. FTP uses TCP for its user authentication and secure file transfer features. To access a remote machine, you must type **ftp** at the command prompt followed by the IP address of the remote machine. Next, enter the username and password to access the remote machine. Figure 5.5 shows you how ftp authenticates user logins.

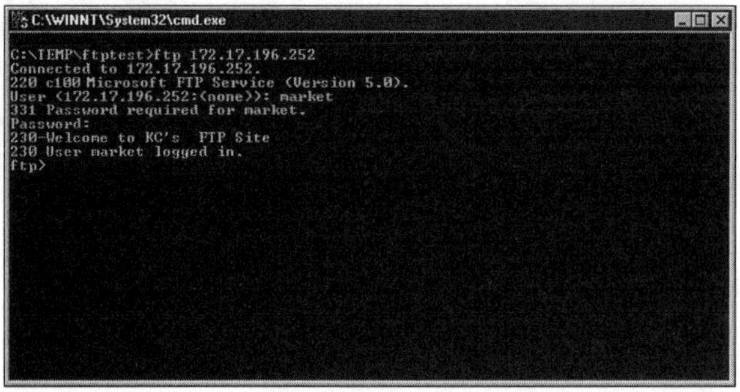

Figure 5.5
The username and password is authenticated by FTP.

In Figure 5.5, the username and password entered by the user is authenticated and acknowledged as valid FTP account information. To transfer files to the remote machine, type **put** *local filename remote filename* at the ftp prompt. To retrieve files from the remote machine, type **get** *remote filename local filename* at the ftp prompt. Figure 5.6 shows you how to transfer and retrieve files using the ftp utility.

CH
5

Figure 5.6
The file transfer and retrieval is acknowledged by ftp.

In Figure 5.6, observe that the file transfer is acknowledged by a `Transfer complete` acknowledgement message. When the `tst3.txt` file is retrieved, observe that the file retrieval is acknowledged by a `Transfer complete` acknowledgement message. These acknowledgement messages indicate that FTP uses TCP to track file transfer and retrieval and provides acknowledgement when the file is successfully transferred or retrieved. However, before initiating a file transfer or retrieval, you must establish a connection with the remote computer. Figure 5.7 shows you what happens if you try a file transfer before establishing a connection.

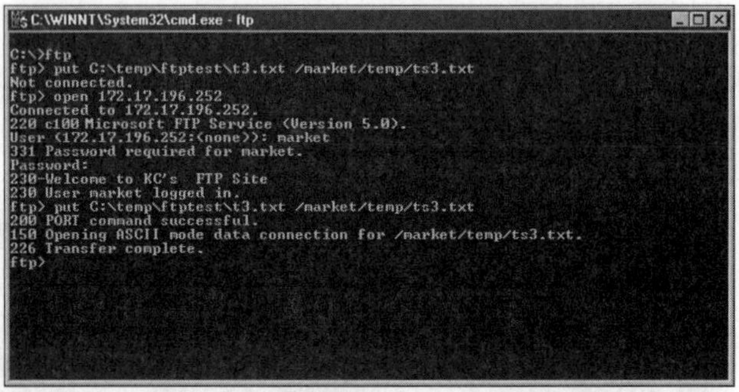

Figure 5.7

File transfer and retrieval operation is not possible without establishing a connection between the sending and receiving machines.

In Figure 5.7, when you use the put command to transfer a file before establishing a connection, the `Not Connected` error is returned. To establish a connection, you use the `open` command. Type **open 172.17.196.252** to open a connection with the remote computer. Next, enter the username and password to log on to the remote machine and then use the put command to transfer files.

TCP SEGMENT HEADER

A data segment is the most important component in the TCP specifications. The entire framework of connections and data transfer services is built around this small, but most significant, component. In addition to the data being transferred, the segment contains important information and instructions stored in the first part of the segment called the *segment header*. This information includes the source and destination ports, sequence and acknowledgement numbers, length of the segment, data to be delivered, and a variety of instructions for the receiver. These instructions are to be used by the application on the receiver to manipulate the additional information present in the segment, verify the authenticity of the data present in the segment, and to manipulate the size of the segment. Figure 5.8 displays the contents of a TCP segment header.

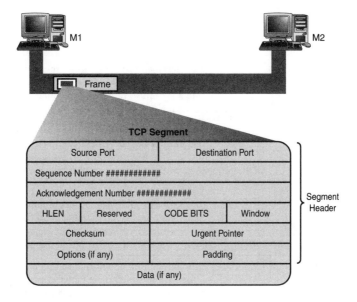

Figure 5.8
The information contained in each of the TCP segment header fields determines how the application on the receiver uses the segment.

Before examining each segment field, it is important to note that the entire TCP segment, with the data and other fields, is contained in the data component of an IP segment. Table 5.1 describes each segment field in detail.

TABLE 5.1   THE FIELDS OF A TCP SEGMENT HEADER

Segment Header Fields	Description
Source Port	Specifies the port number of the sender.
Destination Port	Specifies the port number of the receiver.
Sequence Number	Specifies a unique number that identifies the segment and indicates the position of the segment in the sequence of segments being transferred.
Acknowledgement Number	Specifies the sequence number of a successfully received segment incremented by 1. The number is sent with an acknowledgement segment as a confirmation of the receipt of another segment. The incremented sequence number indicates that the segments with sequence numbers less than the acknowledgment numbers have been successfully received. The number also indicates the sequence number of the next expected segment in the sequence of segments being transmitted from the sender.
HLEN	Specifies the length of the segment header. The length of a header can vary depending on the options set in the Options field of the header. Therefore, the length of the header must be indicated using this field.
Reserved	Specifies a reserved field that is to be used in the future.

CH
5

TABLE 5.1 CONTINUED

Segment Header Fields	Description
CODE BITS	Specifies instructions on using the various fields of the segment header. Instructions are in the form of flags set to indicate a certain setting for a particular field. The flags that can be set include ACK, URG, PSH, RST, SYN, and FIN.
Window	Specifies instructions on the size of segments that can be transmitted next by a sender. This instruction is specified for the sender and is included in the segment header along with the ACK flag when an acknowledgement is sent to the sender.
Checksum	Used as a verification mechanism that contains information on the source and destination computer IP addresses, underlying Transport layer protocol (TCP or UDP), and the length of the entire TCP segment that includes the length of the header and the data part of the segment.
Urgent pointer	Specifies an instruction that the segment contains urgent information, which must be processed immediately instead of adding the segment to the buffer on arrival at the receiver. The URG flag in the CODE BITS field must be set to use this feature.
Options	Specifies the accepted size of the segment, timestamp of the segment, the end of the Options field, and an option that defines the boundaries of an option within the segment header field.

→ To know more about the C/C++ programming structures implementing a segment format, **see** "Programming Structures for Data Formats," **p. 447**

CODE BITS play a very important role in manipulating the segment header. Table 5.2 describes each flag in detail.

TABLE 5.2 THE CODE BITS IN A TCP SEGMENT HEADER

CODE BITS	Description
SYN	Indicates that the sequence number sent with the segment is used to synchronize sequence numbers on the sender and receiver computers. The SYN flag comes into the picture when the initial segments used to establish a connection are exchanged between the sender and receiver. These initial segments are also called SYN segments.
ACK	Instructs the receiver that the Acknowledgement field of the segment header is a valid field that must be used to obtain the Acknowledgement Number because all segments do not use the Acknowledgement Number field for transmitting acknowledgement numbers.

TABLE 5.2   CONTINUED

CODE BITS	Description
PSH	Instructs the receiver to make an incoming segment available to the application immediately without adding the segment to the buffer. In addition, PSH also implements an immediate segment transmission without waiting for building a large data chunk to be transmitted. Therefore, a push action occurs at both the sender and receiver ends of the connection.
RST	Instructs the receiver to terminate the connection with immediate effect and to release the resources, such as buffers, associated with the connection.
URG	Instructs the receiver that the Urgent Pointer field of the segment is valid and that the segment must be directed to the application immediately instead of being buffered because the segment contains urgent information.
FIN	Indicates that the segment is the last segment in the sequence of segments received by the receiver. The last segment that has the FIN flag set is also called the FIN segment.

The Options segment header field plays an important role in the efficient transmission of data. You can set four kinds of options in this field: End of Field, No Operation, Maximum Segment Size, and Timestamp. Table 5.3 describes each of the option types in brief.

TABLE 5.3   THE TYPE OF OPTIONS SET IN THE Options FIELD

Option Types	Description
No Operation	Specifies the end of one option and the beginning of another option in the Options field.
Maximum Segment Size	Specified by the sending to indicate the maximum possible segment size that can be transmitted over a network or networks. This option is the most commonly used option and is sent as part of the first segment that establishes a connection.
Timestamp	Records the time when the segment was first sent to the receiver machine. The option can also be used to record the time of sending an acknowledgment for the successful receipt of a segment. Timestamp values are used to determine the total time taken to complete one send and acknowledgement cycle for a segment.
End of Field	Specifies the end of the Options field in the segment header.

CH
5

Another important field of the TCP header is the Checksum field. This field is used to verify the authenticity of the header and data part of the segment. Checksum contains five components that store the source IP address, the destination IP address, the underlying protocol, the length of the segment header, and a checksum value. These values are stored in the Source Address, Destination Address, Zero, Protocol, and TCP Length components, respectively. In the receiver machine, the checksum value is verified to ensure that the segment has reached without any modification or damage during transit. TCP also creates a checksum for the data part of the segment. Figure 5.9 displays the contents of a TCP Checksum field.

Figure 5.9
TCP Checksum implements the security feature offered by TCP.

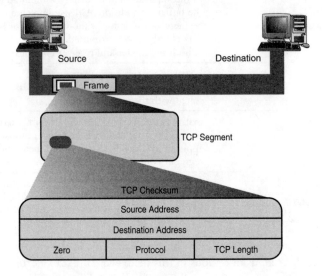

An important point to note is the fact that a TCP segment does not exist as a separate data unit transferred between a sending and receiving computer. The segment goes through two levels of encapsulation before being transmitted to another machine. Each segment is contained in the data part of an IP datagram. The IP datagram is itself encapsulated within a frame. Figure 5.10 shows you how a TCP segment is encapsulated.

Figure 5.10
The frame is the final data unit that is actually transmitted between computers.

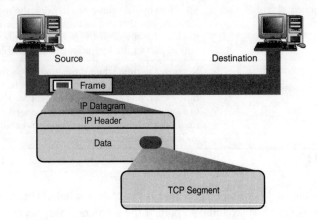

THE CONNECTION PROCESS

Now that you have been introduced to basic concepts of TCP, it is time to go into the actual process behind establishing and terminating connections and transferring data over a network. TCP implements a three-step process for establishing and terminating connections. However, to implement a stable and problem-free connection, you must determine the maximum size of the segments to be transmitted before beginning the actual transmission. You can view the current state of a connection by using the netstat utility provided by Windows.

THE THREE-WAY HANDSHAKE

Establishing a connection between two machines follows a three-step process, called a *three-way handshake*, where the machines exchange sequence numbers and acknowledgments to synchronize the flow of sequential segments before the actual data transfer begins. In the first step, an initiator computer starts the data transfer by instructing the OS that it needs to start a connection. In response, the OS creates endpoints for the application on the sender machine. The initiator uses the endpoint to send an initial segment to the receiver machine. The initial segment is set with the SYN code bit to indicate that the segment is the first in the sequence of segments to arrive. The SYN flag also indicates that the sequence number specified in the segment must be used to synchronize segment sequence numbers that are to be used in the exchange of data.

After receipt of the initial segment, the receiver instructs its OS that it needs to open a connection with another machine. In response, the OS creates an endpoint for the calling application. Next, the receiver uses this endpoint to send a reply segment with its own initial sequence number and an acknowledgement number. The acknowledgement number is calculated by incrementing the received sequence number by one and allocating it to the Acknowledgement Number field. In other words, the reply indicates that the handshake process is being continued and that the initial segment has been received and acknowledged. The SYN and ACK flags need to be set in this second segment to ensure that the sender uses the reply sequence number and the acknowledgement number.

After the reply is received, the connection is almost complete. Now, both machines have recorded the sequence numbers they received from each other. To complete the handshake, the initiator acknowledges the receipt of the segment from the receiver by replying with an acknowledgment segment. A typical example of a three-way handshake is in the status bar of a Web browser window when you try to access a Web site by using the browser. The first message you see is "Connecting to site *Web site name*," after which you see the message "Web site found. Waiting for Reply." These messages indicate that an initial segment has been sent and that the browser is waiting for a reply from the Web server. After the reply arrives, an acknowledgment is sent back from your machine, and data transfer begins by opening the home page of the Web site requested. Figure 5.11 shows how the three-way handshake process is implemented.

CH
5

Figure 5.11
A three-way hand-shake not only establishes a connection between the machines but also serves to synchronize the sequence numbers used during data segment exchange.

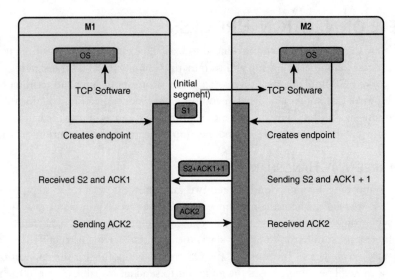

In Figure 5.11, the application using TCP on computer M1 initiates a connection by informing its OS that a connection with another computer needs to be established. The OS responds by creating an endpoint that is used for future data exchanges with the destination machine. Next, an initial segment with a sequence number is sent to computer M2. The TCP software on M2 instructs its OS that a connection needs to be opened with M1. In response, the OS on M2 creates an endpoint that is used by M2 to communicate with M1. In addition, M2 records the sequence number obtained from the initial segment it received. The initial sequence number is used to create an acknowledgement number to confirm the receipt of the initial segment. Next, M2 replies to M1 with a segment containing its own sequence number and an acknowledgment number. On receipt of the reply segment, M1 records the sequence number used by M2 and responds with an acknowledgment to M2. This response indicates that a connection has been established, the sequence numbers have been synchronized, and that data transfer can begin.

TERMINATING A CONNECTION

The process of terminating a full-duplex connection also follows a three-step process. In the first step, the computer sending data, called M1 (see Figure 5.12), completes the transmission of all data segments, and ensures the receipt of acknowledgements for all the data segments. After acknowledgments have been received, M1 sends a closure data segment with the FIN flag turned on (this segment will be called the FIN segment). In addition, M1 informs the OS that the connection is closed and that no more data segments can be transmitted to M2. After receiving the FIN segment, M2 informs its OS that there are no more data segments to arrive from M1. In the second step, M2 acknowledges the FIN segment receipt and completes the termination of data segment flow in one direction (from M1 to M2). However, data segments can be transmitted from M2 to M1 because the second part of the full-duplex connection is still alive, now existing as a half-duplex connection.

The decision to completely sever the connection between M1 and M2 rests with the user input to the OS on M2. If the user instructs the OS to terminate the connection, M2 sends its FIN segment to M1 and waits for the receipt of an acknowledgement. On receipt of the FIN segment from M2, M1 informs its OS that no more data segments are expected from M2. In addition, it replies to the FIN segment with an acknowledgement. This process forms the last step of the three-step process. The OS on both the machines destroys the endpoints to release resources associated with the terminated connection. Figure 5.12 shows how a connection is terminated.

Figure 5.12
After the receipt of the FIN segment from M1, the acknowledgement segment is sent immediately to avoid missing the timer set in M1 though the connection is completely terminated by M2 only after user instructions.

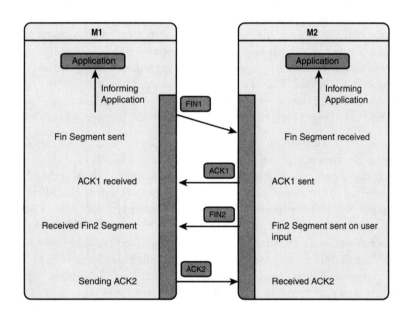

CONFIGURING MAXIMUM SEGMENT SIZE

The initial segment not only contains the sequence number but also instructs the receiver that the segments sent are to be fragmented into fragments of a certain maximum size. This instruction is stored as the Maximum Segment Size option in the Options field of the segment header. A TCP segment is contained in an IP datagram. The need to determine MSS stems from the fact that the size of segments affect the size of the IP datagram and that these datagrams might need to traverse over different kinds of networks. Some networks might transmit datagrams at very high speeds and can support large sized datagrams. If you transmit segments of small sizes over such high-speed networks, you are not utilizing the network resources to their full potential. For example, a segment containing 1 byte of data is packaged into a TCP header with 20 bytes of data and an IP datagram with another 20 bytes. This means that for 1 byte of data to be transmitted, you use 40 additional bytes, which is a gross underutilization of network bandwidth.

CH
5

> **Note**
>
> *Bandwidth* refers to the capacity of a network to transmit data and is measured by recording the total size of data that is transmitted over a network within a fixed time limit.

On the other hand, if you transmit segments of large size over slow networks, the datagrams containing the segment must be fragmented and then transmitted. Fragmenting datagrams reduces the reliability of data transfer because if a datagrams fragment is lost, there is no method for retransmitting fragments to set off the loss. Another factor that determines MSS is the buffer size of the machines involved is the connection. Assume that a computer with a limited buffer size requests data from a computer with a large buffer size. The large data transmission capacity of the sending computer can easily clog the limited buffer on the requesting machine. Therefore, segment size must be optimized to accommodate the requirements of the buffer in both the machines. To overcome these problems, the MSS value is exchanged between the machines when the three-way handshake process occurs.

Each network is configured with a Maximum Transmission Unit (MTU) value that determines its maximum data unit transmission capacity. When machines existing on the same network communicate, the MSS value can be calculated based on the MTU value that is supported by the network. However, if machines existing across different networks need to communicate, the only way to determine the optimum MSS value is by using an initial IP datagram as a probe to discover the MTU of the networks lying in the path between the machines. The probe datagram must be set with the Flag field of the IP header set to 1 to indicate that fragmentation of the datagram is disallowed. If the IP probe reaches its destination without being fragmented, the MSS value used in the probe segment is adopted for future data transmissions. However, if ICMP fires a message indicating that the datagram has been fragmented, the MSS value is reduced to recalculate a new MSS value. Another probe with this new value is then sent to test for fragmentation.

> **Note**
>
> Setting a default MSS value of 536 bytes is another option that you can choose if you want to transmit data over diverse networks.

DETERMINING CONNECTION STATES

Connection states indicate the current state of a connection existing between computers. One of the best methods for determining the status of computers in a connection is by using the netstat utility. The utility lists these connection states for the computers on the network. Table 5.4 describes the various connection states for a TCP connection.

TABLE 5.4 CONNECTION STATES OF A TCP CONNECTION

Connection State	Description
SYN_SEND	Indicates that the local computer has initiated the active open process with another machine.
SYN_RECEIVED	Indicates that the local computer has received a SYN segment from another machine.
ESTABLISHED	Indicates that the local computer has received a SYN segment from another machine, the sequence numbers are synchronized, and a connection is established.
LISTEN	Indicates a state of readiness to accept connection requests.
FIN_WAIT_1	Indicates that an active close process has been initiated. This state forms the first state in the three-step connection termination process.
TIMED_WAIT	Indicates that the local computer is waiting for acknowledgement from another computer after it has initiated an active close process. The wait period is timed by a timer mechanism on the sender's machine.
CLOSE_WAIT	Indicates that a FIN segment has arrived from another computer to begin the process of terminating the connection with that machine.
FIN_WAIT_2	Indicates that the acknowledgement for the FIN segment sent to another computer has arrived. This state forms the second state in the three-step connection termination process.
LAST_ACK	Indicates that user input for terminating a connection is obtained and that a FIN segment can now be sent to complete the connection termination process. This state is the last state in the three-step connection termination process.
CLOSED	Indicates that the acknowledgement for the last FIN segment has arrived and that the connection is terminated.

CH

5

The connection states mentioned in Table 5.4 can be determined by using the netstat utility. You must use the -n option with the netstat command to display the protocol, the local computer endpoint, the remote computer endpoint, and the status of the connection indicated by the connection state. Figure 5.13 shows the connection states that can be obtained by typing the command **netstat -n**.

Figure 5.13
All connection states, except for the LISTEN state, can be obtained using the netstat utility.

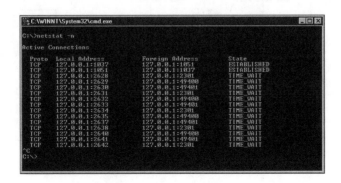

TCP CONNECTION STATE MACHINE

A computer can act as a server and a client while transacting with other computers. Clients request data from the servers while servers respond by providing data or by sending a message stating that data is unavailable. Servers wait for requests from client computers to initiate a connection and to terminate a connection. TCP must manage active and passive opens and closes because a single computer can act as the server and the client. The TCP Connection State Machine is a pictorial representation of how a TCP implementation performs its role as a client, initiating opens and closes and as a server waiting for the client to begin or end a connection. Figure 5.14 shows how the TCP Connection State Machine works.

Figure 5.14
The Connection State Machine is a pictorial representation of how an actual TCP application program manages different connection states.

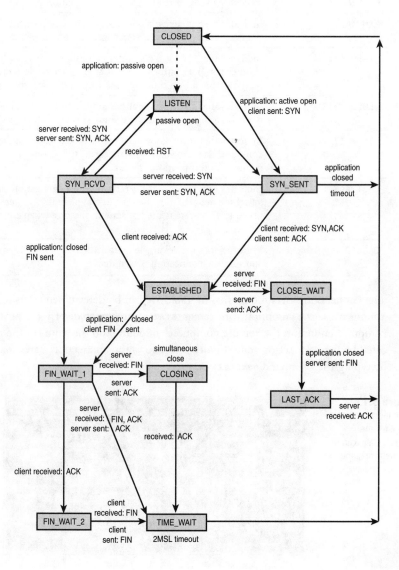

In Figure 5.14, observe that all connection states begin with the CLOSED state. If the computer needs to act as a server, it opens a LISTEN state where it waits for a client to initiate a connection. When a client initiates a connection by sending a SYN segment, the computer responds with a SYN segment and an acknowledgement. This transitions the connection into a SYN_RCVD state. Now, the client acknowledges the server's SYN by sending an acknowledgement. After receiving the client's acknowledgement, a connection is established, indicated by the ESTABLISHED state. Now, when a client wants to terminate the connection, it sends a FIN segment, which is acknowledged by the server. The server moves into a CLOSE_WAIT state where the TCP service on the server waits for its application to decide on terminating the connection. When the server application decides to terminate the connection, it allows TCP to send a FIN segment, which changes the connection state to LAST_ACK. After the acknowledgement for this FIN is received, the connection transits into a CLOSED state once again.

If the computer acts as a client, it initiates a connection by sending a SYN segment. This is indicated by the SYN_SENT state. Once the client receives the acknowledgement and the server's SYN segment, it acknowledges the server SYN and transitions the connection to an ESTABLISHED state. Observe the state transition in the bottom left of Figure 5.14. If the client computer wants to terminate a connection, it sends a FIN and changes the connection state to FIN_WAIT1. Next, the client receives an acknowledgement from the server and transitions into a FIN_WAIT2 state and waits for the server to send its FIN segment for complete termination of the connection. When the server finally sends its FIN segment, the connection transits to a TIME_WAIT state. If the client sends an acknowledgement for the server FIN within a two-minute wait period, the connection is completely terminated and the state transitions to CLOSED. If the two-minute timer expires, the connection is automatically closed.

DATA TRANSFER CONCEPTS

In addition to the connectivity and data transfer services, TCP also tries to enhance the efficiency of data transfer. Establishing a connection between machines does not necessarily mean smooth and efficient transfer of data. Each problem encountered during data transmission has brought forth a number of data transfer concepts aimed at improving data transfer efficiency. Some such data transfer concepts are sliding windows, silly window syndrome, Nagle's algorithm, and delayed acknowledgements.

CH
5

SLIDING WINDOWS

A computer transmits a segment after it receives the acknowledgement for the previous segment. This safe data transfer method has a major disadvantage. At a given point of time, in a full-duplex connection, the machines at both ends of the connection would remain idle waiting for the acknowledgement to arrive before transmitting the next segment. Although this method of data transmission ensures safe delivery of data, the gross underutilization of network resources scores over its reliability advantage. To incorporate efficiency in the existing framework, the concept of sliding windows was introduced.

The concept is quite simple. Instead of transmitting one segment at a time, multiple segments are placed in a group called a window and all segments contained in a window are transmitted as a group without waiting for acknowledgments for each segment. For example, if a window contains five segments to be transmitted, all five are transmitted at the same time. Before learning how the window "slides," you must first learn how a window is designed. All unacknowledged segments are positioned in the left of the window, whereas the segments that can be sent immediately are positioned in the right of the window. When the acknowledgement arrives for the first segment in the window, the window slides to the right to include a segment to the right of the window. This way, the sliding window ensures that a higher number of segments are transmitted from a sender machine. Figure 5.15 shows how the sliding window concept is implemented.

Figure 5.15
The window slides to the right to include a new segment for transmission. When the left of the sliding window reaches the right edge, it is called a zero window and signifies the end of the data transfer.

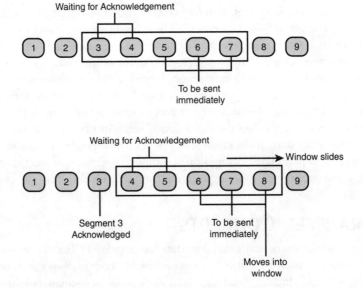

In Figure 5.15, segments 1 and 2 are segments that are sent and acknowledged by the receiver. Segments 3 and 4 are segments that have been sent and are awaiting acknowledgements. Segments 5, 6, and 7 are next in the sequence within the window to be sent immediately. Segments 8 and 9 are segments that will be included into the window when acknowledgments arrive for the segments in the left end of the window. The sliding effect of the window is also shown in Figure 5.15 where the window slides forward and includes segment 8 into the right of the window after releasing the acknowledged segment 3.

It is fine that the sender is able to transmit multiple segments simultaneously but if the receiver is unable to accommodate a large number of segments, it could clog the receiver machine. Therefore, the receiver must control the size of the window on the sender's computer based on the size of data that can be received and buffered. To inform the sender about the window size, the receiver specifies the window size in the Window field of the TCP segment header of acknowledgment segment. This information enables the sender to reduce the size of its window to the size required by the receiver. The process of instructing the receiver about the window size that can be accommodated by the sender is called *window size advertisements*.

A typical example where the sliding window implementation is visible is in your music software that buffers the incoming data before playing the audio.

SENDER SIDE SILLY WINDOW SYNDROME

One of the problems faced by the first implementations of TCP was Silly Window Syndrome. The problem occurs when a sender transmits a large number of segments thereby clogging the buffer of the receiver machine. In response, the receiver advertises a very small window size because its buffer size has been drastically reduced. Now, the sender sends data segments of very small sizes, which results in underutilizing the network resources. The problem can be further categorized as the Sender Side Silly Window Syndrome, where the sender transmits very small data segments, and the Receiver Side Silly Window Syndrome where the receiver advertises a small window size.

The Sender Side Silly Window Syndrome can also occur when the sender transmits small segments supplied by the sending application. To tackle this problem, you must implement an algorithm called the Nagle's algorithm. Named after its inventor, John Nagle, this solution was implemented for the first time on a private TCP/IP network used by Ford Motors. The method he implemented was adopted by other TCP implementations, which were facing the same problem.

Assume a scenario where two people are engrossed in a volatile argument that was getting out of hand. One way of continuing the argument within civilized limits is to cool down the tempers running high on both sides. Nagle's algorithm implements the "cooling down tempers" idea by restricting the instant data transmission by the sender as soon as an acknowledgement is received. Instead of transmitting small segments, the sender accumulates the segments to be sent to form a bigger chunk of data. Now, when an acknowledgement arrives, if the cumulative segments have a combined size close to MSS, the sender transmits all the segments in one go. This method aims at improving network utilization by transmitting larger segments and allowing the receiver some breathing space to clear its buffer before directing the segments to the calling application. After the buffer size improves, the receiver can advertise a larger window size.

CH
5

RECEIVER SIDE SILLY WINDOW SYNDROME

Receiver Side Silly Window Syndrome is tackled by applying a concept similar to the Nagle's algorithm in the receiver machine. This concept, called *delayed acknowledgements*, restricts the instant transmission of acknowledgements when a segment is received from the sender. This delay allows the receiver to clear its buffer, which is overloaded with segments. When 50% of the buffer is cleared, a single acknowledgement for all the segments received can be transmitted. The window size that is advertised is also larger than the window size advertised in an instant acknowledgement transmission because of the improved buffer size. A larger window size also enables the sender to transmit segments of a bigger size.

Caution

An inordinate delay in transmitting acknowledgements can result in the sender retransmitting duplicate segments. In addition, the retransmission timer value that is set by using the Round Trip Time (RTT) calculation is also affected and could result in estimated wrong RTT values. The solution is to set a recommended maximum acknowledgement delay of 500 milliseconds.

→ To learn more about RTT estimation and retransmission time value, **see** "Estimating Round Trip Time," **p. 98**

SUMMARY

The Transport layer of the TCP/IP reference model is responsible for ensuring data transmission between machines on diverse networks. The TCP service, which resides in the Transport layer, implements these services in addition to tracking the delivery of data. TCP offers connectivity services such as establishing connections, full-duplex connections, and half-duplex connections. TCP also provides data transfer services such as acknowledgement, retransmission, buffered transfer, and piggybacking. A wide range of application layer protocols such as DNS, FTP, HTTP, NFS, Rlogin, SMTP, and Telnet use the TCP service to implement connectivity and reliable data transfer features.

TCP concepts are clearly visible when applied on real-world scenarios by using the netstat utility. The utility provides options to obtain statistical information on the protocols implemented in the network. In addition, netstat also provides information on the status of the connections existing in the network. Connection states, such as SYN_SEND, SYN_RECEIVED, and ESTABLISHED, indicate the current status of a connection.

The TCP segment, which is the actual data unit transmitted by TCP, is divided into two parts, the segment header and data part. The segment header is further divided into components, such as Source Port, Destination Port, Sequence Number, Acknowledgement Number, HLEN, Reserved, CODE BITS, Window, Checksum, Urgent Pointer, and Options. You can set flags, such as SYN, ACK, PSH, RST, URG, and FIN in the CODE BITS segment header field. You can also set options, such as MSS, End of Field, No Operation, and Timestamp in the Options segment header field.

TCP provides a three-step process, called a three-way handshake, to establish a connection. A three-way handshake involves exchanging segments containing sequence numbers to synchronize the sequence numbers before actual data transfer commences. A three-way handshake is also used to terminate a connection. The Maximum Segment Size value is also exchanged between communicating computers at the time of establishing a connection.

Data transfer is hindered by problems such as underutilization of network resources and Silly Window Syndrome. TCP provides solutions in the form of Sliding Windows to overcome underutilization of network resources. Silly Window Syndrome is resolved using techniques such as Nagle's algorithm and delayed acknowledgements.

CHAPTER 6

TIMED DATA TRANSMISSION AND PERFORMANCE CONCEPTS

In this chapter

TIMEOUT AND RETRANSMISSION CONCEPTS

The previous lesson introduced you to the basics of TCP. This chapter covers some of the important TCP concepts that enhance data transmission and performance.

Human life revolves around the time of the day. Every aspect of our action is based on the time of the day right from waking up to going to sleep at the end of the day. This human dependency on time has been adopted into the world of TCP connections as well. In fact, time is the essence of the world of TCP connections. When a segment is transmitted, a timer is turned on in the sending computer. If the acknowledgement for the segment does not arrive within the predefined time limit, the timer assumes that the segment is lost and instructs the TCP service on the sender to retransmit.

Note

> A mechanism that defines the time limit for receiving acknowledgements and sending retransmission is called, appropriately, *timer*. The sending computer maintains this mechanism.

While determining this time limit, a number of factors are taken into account. For example, the sender and receiver might be located on the same physical network or on networks located far away, which requires segments to traverse through other networks having different Maximum Transmission Unit (MTU) capacities. In addition, unexpected delays might be caused due to high network traffic or problems in the routers through which the segments need to travel. Therefore, to determine timer setting, also called *timeout*, it is essential to accurately estimate the total time taken by a segment to reach its destination and for the acknowledgment to return. One complete cycle of a send and acknowledgement receipt for a segment is called a *round trip sample time*. The difference between the time of sending a segment and the time of receiving the acknowledgment provides the round trip sample time.

ESTIMATING ROUND TRIP TIME

To determine a timeout value, a weighted average of round trip sample times is calculated. This weighted average method used for determining the timeout value is called *adaptive retransmission algorithm*. The round trip sample time provides the cycle time taken for only a single segment. However, it is possible that the round trip time samples for different segments vary widely. Therefore, it is essential to calculate a weighted average time of a set of round trip sample times calculated by TCP. This weighted average is named *Round Trip Time* (RTT). The RTT value that is determined by using the adaptive retransmission algorithm is set as the timeout value in the sender.

> The weighted average method provides a way of calculating the average of a collection of values taking into account the weightage assigned to each value. For example, if you need to calculate the average money value of a set of products sold in a given period, you need to take into account the number of units of each product sold in the given period. This way an accurate measure of the average sale value can be estimated. The equation that is used to calculate weighted average can be described as
>
> ```
> Weighted average= sum(money value of each product * unit of the
> product sold)/
> total units sold
> ```

In addition to the round trip sample times, another important factor required for RTT calculation is the weightage. In terms of round trip sample times, weightage can be described as the number of segments for which the sample time is calculated. Weightage is set between the values 0 and 1. Assume that you have a few round trip sample times with varying weightage values. The RTT value can be determined by using the following formula:

```
RTT=sum(round trip sample time*weightage)/sum(weightage)
```

This weighted average method ensures a steady change in the RTT value thereby reducing the possibility of wild fluctuations in the timeout value. These fluctuations can result in a drastic increase in retransmission due to small timeouts at one point of time and in the next instant there could be long delays in transmitting the next segment, which results in underutilization of network resources. Now, take the example of a connection where the RTT is currently estimated to be 400ms and the round trip sample times for segments A, B, and C are timed 500ms, 600ms, and 700ms, respectively. The average of these values is 600ms, which is a drastic increase in timeout value if you use a simple average of round trip sample times to calculated RTT. However, when you use the adaptive retransmission algorithm to calculate the new RTT value, RTT is incremented to 571ms, which is a moderate increase in the RTT value. The weightage for segments A, B, and C is taken to be .5, .8, and .1 segments, respectively.

```
(Sum of round trip samples*weightage)=(500*.5)+(600*.8)+(700*.1)
//Sum of round trip samples*weightage comes to 800
Sum of weightage=.5+.8+.1
//Sum of weightage comes to 1.4
Round Trip Sample=(Sum of round trip samples*weightage)/ Sum of weightage
//RTT value comes to 571
```

CH
6

KARN'S ALGORITHM

Although the adaptive retransmission algorithm seems to be definitive by description, there is a shortcoming in its implementation. After a segment is transmitted, due to delays, the time set in the timer elapses resulting in a retransmission. Now, if an acknowledgement arrives, it muddles RTT calculation because the sender has to decide whether the round trip sample time must be based on the time interval between the original transmission and the receipt of acknowledgement or the time interval between the retransmission and the receipt of the acknowledgement. Both ways, the sender might arrive at a wrong round trip sample time estimate.

In the first case, where the round trip sample time is calculated based on the time interval between the original transmission and receipt of the acknowledgement for the last retransmission, if the sender manages to transmit a segment after multiple retransmissions, the round trip sample time will be excessively long. If this method is continued for the transmission or retransmission of consecutive segments, the resulting RTT time might set the timeout value as an excessively long time limit. The longer the timeout, the greater the delay will be in transmitting segments.

However, if you want to adopt the second case, where the round trip sample time is calculated based on the time interval between the last retransmit and the receipt of the acknowledgement, you run the risk of setting an RTT which is too short to manage sudden delays in the connection. If this continues for consecutive segment send operations, the sender needs to retransmit a segment at least twice before receiving an acknowledgement from the receiver.

An easy method for identifying the RTT values for a connection is by using the ping utility provided by an OS such as Windows 2000. This command-line tool transmits four ICMP packets to a destination computer and listens for a reply from the remote computer. The statistics related to the maximum, minimum, and average RTT values calculated for connections existing between the local computer and remote computers are provided by this utility. All that you need to do is type **ping** at the command prompt followed by the target computer's IP address. Figure 6.1 shows the results of this command.

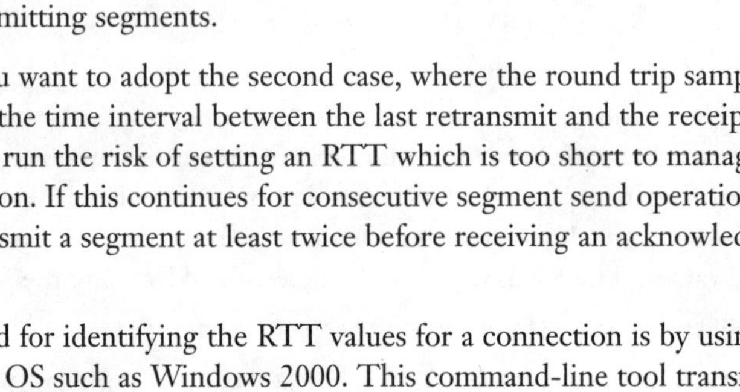

Figure 6.1
The maximum, minimum, and average RTT values are displayed at the end of the transmission or receipt.

```
C:\WINNT\System32\cmd.exe

C:\>ping 172.17.64.251

Pinging 172.17.64.251 with 32 bytes of data:

Reply from 172.17.64.251: bytes=32 time=410ms TTL=122
Reply from 172.17.64.251: bytes=32 time=421ms TTL=122
Reply from 172.17.64.251: bytes=32 time=400ms TTL=122
Reply from 172.17.64.251: bytes=32 time=401ms TTL=122

Ping statistics for 172.17.64.251:
    Packets: Sent = 4, Received = 4, Lost = 0 (0% loss),
Approximate round trip times in milli-seconds:
    Minimum = 400ms, Maximum = 421ms, Average = 408ms

C:\>_
```

You can use the -w option with the ping command to set a timeout value for each packet transmitted by ping. Figure 6.2 shows you the result of entering the command **ping -w 10 172.17.64.251** at the command prompt.

In Figure 6.2, ping reports a 25% loss during transmission because the timeout value specified is small. To avoid such mishaps, you must implement an algorithm called Karn's algorithm. The inventor of this algorithm, Phill Karn, first implemented his solution while transmitting data across a problem prone radio connection by using TCP.

Figure 6.2
A low timeout value results in the loss of the packet during transmission.

```
C:\WINNT\System32\cmd.exe                                    _□×

C:\>ping -w 10 172.17.64.251

Pinging 172.17.64.251 with 32 bytes of data:

Request timed out.
Reply from 172.17.64.251: bytes=32 time=390ms TTL=122
Reply from 172.17.64.251: bytes=32 time=411ms TTL=122
Reply from 172.17.64.251: bytes=32 time=410ms TTL=122

Ping statistics for 172.17.64.251:
      Packets: Sent = 4, Received = 3, Lost = 1 (25% loss),
Approximate round trip times in milli-seconds:
      Minimum = 390ms, Maximum = 411ms, Average = 302ms

C:\>_
```

In its simplest form, Karn's algorithm recommends the computation of RTT values based on segment transmissions that are successfully acknowledged in the very first transmission attempt. However, this strategy could lead to a scenario where segments are never successfully re-sent because the RTT value remains unchanged while resending segments. For example, when a segment is re-sent unsuccessfully and requires another retransmission, instead of implementing an updated timeout or RTT value, if the old RTT value is implemented, the segment never reaches its destination due to the unrealistic timeout value.

Therefore, Karn's algorithm must be implemented after slightly changing the strategy with a technique called *timer backoff*. This technique suggests the creation of separate timeout values for retransmission and first time transmission. The retransmission timeout value can be doubled for every segment requiring retransmission. When a segment is successfully re-sent, the original RTT value is assigned as the timeout value for the next segment. If the segment or any other subsequent segment is transmitted successfully in the very first attempt, the RTT value is recalculated to implement a new timeout value. Figure 6.3 describes how this hybrid technique, called the Karn's algorithm-timer backoff technique, is implemented.

In Figure 6.3, the segment S1 is re-sent with a new timeout value T2. However, S1 needs more time to reach its destination. Therefore, the timeout value for retransmission is doubled. With the new timeout value, S1 is re-sent. Now, for the next segment S2, the original timeout value T1 is implemented. S2 is successfully transmitted and a new RTT value is calculated based on the successful transmission time taken for S2.

PROBE TIMERS

In addition to the transmission timers, TCP provides a specialized set of timers called *probe timers*. These timers are so named because they are used in certain circumstances to define a time limit for sending probe segments. Two examples of probe timers are the Persist timer and the Keepalive timer.

CH
6

Figure 6.3
Karn's algorithm must be implemented with the timer backoff technique to arrive at the correct RTT value.

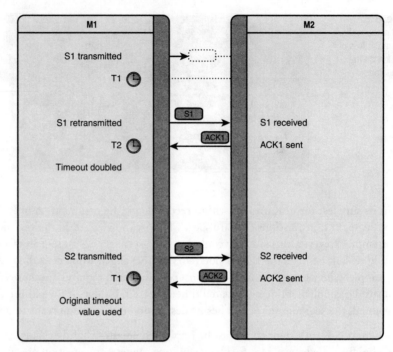

<table>
<tr><td>M1</td><td>M2</td></tr>
<tr><td>S1 transmitted
T1</td><td></td></tr>
<tr><td>S1 retransmitted
T2
Timeout doubled</td><td>S1 received
ACK1 sent</td></tr>
<tr><td>S2 transmitted
T1
Original timeout
value used</td><td>S2 received
ACK2 sent</td></tr>
</table>

Note

In certain special circumstances, a single segment is sent to test the existence of a condition or to return statistical information associated with a connection. Such segments are called probe segments. For example, probes can be sent to verify IP datagram fragmentation or change the window size advertised by the receiver. Probe segments are also sent by a computer to verify if the other computer involved in the connection is accessible and can continue with data exchange.

THE PERSIST TIMER

Sometimes, a receiver advertises a window size of 0 due to the lack of space in its buffer. The 0 sized window advertisement stops subsequent transmissions from the sender, which waits for an acknowledgement segment with a nonzero window size advertisement. If this vital acknowledgement segment is lost during transmission, the sender and the receiver plunge into a stalemate where both computers are waiting to restart data exchange. To avoid such scenarios, the sender queries the receiver on the state of its buffer by sending a probe segment, also called window probe.

Note

A *probe segment* is an exploratory datagram that is transmitted by a sender to a receiver to query for the status of the buffer on the receiver. In response to the probe segment, the receiver sends an acknowledgement segment that provides information on the availability of its buffer.

TCP also defines a time limit for sending subsequent probe segments by creating a Persist timer on the sender as soon as a 0 sized window advertisement is received by the sender. After the elapse of the time specified by the timer, a new window probe is transmitted. If the receiver responds with another 0 sized window advertisement, a new Persist timer is set. This process continues until the receiver or the application on the sender sends a nonzero advertisement or the receiver's computer is closed.

→ To learn more about windows, **see** "Sliding Windows," **p. 93**

THE KEEPALIVE TIMER

Take the case of a situation where you are talking to a friend over the phone and after some-time, there is no reply from the other end. You try to confirm whether your friend is still there on the other end with a "hello." This is exactly what the Keepalive timer does. This probe timer defines the time limit for sending a Keepalive probe segment. The probe deter-mines whether the other computer is reachable and can continue with data exchange. The timer is used in the following three scenarios:

- A timer is set to initiate a probe send action after a two-hour period of inactivity. The inactivity could be due to high network traffic or simply because the user is not present at the terminal and has gone out for lunch. However, the two-hour time limit is set only after receiving a reply from the other computer.

- The other computer might not respond to a probe sent by another computer because it might be rebooting after a crash. In this situation, a Keepalive timer with a 75 second time limit is set. The sender provides 10 probe segments with a 75 second time differ-ence before terminating the connection if there is no response from the receiver.

- A Keepalive timer can be used when the sender is unable to make contact with the receiver due to interruptions in the communication channel, such as problems with the router or any other intermediate device. In this scenario, a maximum of 10 probes with a 75 second interval is sent from the sender. If the receiver does not respond, the con-nection is terminated.

CH
6

PERFORMANCE

Performance is an important factor that determines the success or failure of any object—animate or inanimate. People are rewarded for their efficient performance but what happens to specifications? Specifications that result in successful implementations are adopted as industry standards. However, the performance of an implementation can be maximized only if the specifications are implemented based on certain assumptions.

TCP's performance is limited by three basic assumptions. The most basic assumption is that the speed of the connection is limited by the maximum speed of the slowest intermediate device just as the strength of a chain depends on the strength of its weakest link. For example, the maximum speed of a connection running across a number of high speed links and one slow network is limited by the maximum speed of the network router that manages the slow network. Another limitation is based on an equation called the *bandwidth delay product*. According to the equation, if you multiply the RTT value by the minimum bandwidth available on the receiver, you arrive at a value called the bandwidth delay product. The speed of a connection cannot be greater than this bandwidth delay product value. The minimum bandwidth value must be equal to the buffer size maintained on the receiver. Finally, the speed of your connection is determined by the maximum memory capacity of the slowest computers linking the sender and the receiver.

RECOVERING FROM CONGESTION

The performance of a TCP connection is affected due to a variety of reasons. If an intermediate device, such as a router, which is also another computer, is overloaded with datagrams, a condition known as *congestion* results. If the condition worsens, the intermediate device begins discarding any additional datagram that is on its way to the destination computer. The sending computer interprets congestion as a delay and responds accordingly by resending its segments. Retransmission will further worsen congestion and result in a complete collapse of the network. Therefore, the intermediate device must inform the sender that congestion has occurred at its end. Intermediate devices observe their buffer size and detect the congestion if the buffer is filled to its maximum capacity for buffering datagrams. Next, the intermediate device informs the sender about its congestion status by sending an ICMP message.

After receiving the congestion message, the sender initiates a response at its end to recover from the congestion by reducing its send operations. In addition to the sliding window that is used to send segments, the sender creates another window called the congestion window. The window acts as the sliding window during congestion recovery. When congestion exists, segments are sent based on the congestion window and not on the window size advertised by the receiver. Normally, the congestion window and the advertised window are of equal size. However, during congestion, the congestion window size is halved for every segment lost. In addition, the timeout value is also increased. These remedial steps are collectively called *multiplicative decrease*.

The intermediate device appears to be recovering from the congestion when normal data exchange resumes between the sender and receiver. Now, the sender initiates the second step in the process of congestion remedy by beginning a slow segment send operation. In contrast to the multiplicative decrease measure, a linear increase measure is implemented where the initial size of the congestion window is set to one segment and the size is increased by one segment for every acknowledgement received from the receiver. This measure, also called *slow start*, is very much like the convalescence period recommended for a patient to avoid the relapse of the ailment from which the patient has just recovered.

Though slow start is aimed at a slow recovery process, it is quite possible that slow start might initiate a high rate of segment sends. For example, if an acknowledgement is received for a segment, the window size is increased by 2, which means that for every segment acknowledgement, the congestion window size is doubled. This glitch in the slow start technique could lead to a relapse of the congestion condition. Therefore, slow start must be combined with another control mechanism called congestion avoidance to control the sharp increase in segment sends. *Congestion avoidance* stipulates that the congestion window size be increased by one segment on the receipt of an acknowledgement or acknowledgements for all the segments in the window. A combination of multiplicative decrease, slow start, and congestion avoidance enables a congested intermediate device to recover in a controlled environment. Figure 6.4 shows you how congestion recovery is implemented.

Figure 6.4
To avoid the ill effects of the slow start technique, congestion avoidance measures are adopted.

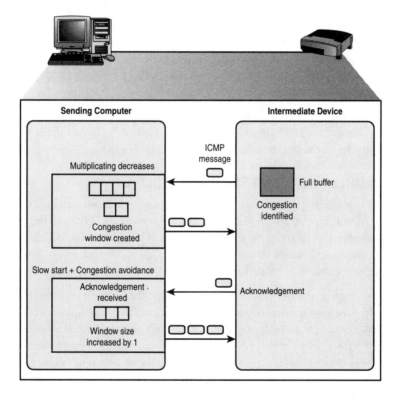

CH
6

DISCOVERING PATH MTU

The size of a segment is an important factor that affects the performance of a connection. The computers involved in a connection might be physically far away or might be on diverse networks. Each of these diverse networks define an upper limit, called Maximum Transmission Unit (MTU), on their capacity for segment transmission. Each network has varying MTU settings. If a large datagram traverses a slow network with a limited MTU capacity, the datagram is bound to get fragmented. Fragmentation introduces an element of unreliability in data transfer because datagram fragments are not tracked. This increases the possibility of the fragment getting lost. To ensure that the segment contained in a datagram is delivered without any loss or damage, you must avoid any possibility of datagram fragmentation due to excessive segment size. This means that the maximum segment size must be determined based on the MTU limits that a datagram might encounter.

To determine the MTU restrictions that consecutive segments might face, the sender launches an IP datagram probing the path MTU. The "Do Not Fragment" bit is turned on in the IP probe datagram. If the probe reaches the receiver without being fragmented during transmission, the MSS set in the probe segment is adopted for future transmissions that will use this connection. If the probe is larger than the MTU set for a network, the intermediate device attempts to fragment the probe. However, the "Do Not Fragment" bit set in the probe prevents fragmentation. In such a scenario, the intermediate device discards the probe datagram and ICMP sends an error message to the receiver. Now, the receiver begins the process of retransmitting the probe after modifying MSS to a size less than the MTU value that caused the problem. This retransmission and MSS modification process continues until a probe successfully reaches its destination. This way the path MTU is discovered.

Path MTU discovery is primarily meant for connections that link computers located in varied networks. The default MTU for sending datagrams to computers located outside the local network is 536 bytes. However, you can use the path MTU discovery mechanism to set a value higher than this default value.

PERFORMANCE ENHANCING SEGMENT HEADER OPTIONS

The capacity to transmit large volumes of data has witnessed a change due to the constant improvements in transmission technology. For example, a transatlantic cable connection has a bandwidth capacity up to several gigabytes. These technological changes have necessitated certain changes to the capacity of a datagram. Now, datagrams can hold a maximum size of data that can be transmitted in a datagram.

In addition to the increase in the bandwidth, network traffic also started increasing exponentially. To derive maximum benefits from the highly trafficked internetworks, performance measures needed to be implemented. One such performance measure is the calculation of RTT values, which you learned earlier in the chapter. To provide for performance monitoring and increased data transmission capacity, the inclusion of two new options called Window Scale and Timestamp, was proposed in RFC 1323. The Window Scale option helps in advertising a segment size that is much higher than the maximum segment size for a datagram. The Timestamp option provides a number of fields that help in the calculation of RTT values to manage performance issues on an internetwork. You will learn about the Window Scale and Timestamp options in the following sections.

Window Scale HEADER OPTION

By default, the receiver can advertise a maximum of 65,535 bytes for a window. However, in certain cases, the receiver might need to advertise a window bigger than the maximum possible limit. For example, segments being transmitted over high-speed networks, which offer a high MTU capacity, need to specify a bigger segment size for the full utilization of network resources. In such scenarios, the window scale option can be used to specify a scaling value that is recorded in the sender and receiver. The scaling option is used to compute the actual window size. For example, if a scaling value of 2 is set for a segment, the receiver computes the actual window size by multiplying 65,535 by 2^2. The resulting number of bytes, which in this case will be 262,140 bytes, is the actual window size for the segment.

This Window Scale option is set as soon as a connection is established when the SYN segment is exchanged between the sender and receiver. The scaling value is determined by TCP based on the buffer capacity. When a SYN segment is sent, the receiver assigns the value 2 to the Window Scale option and transmits the segment. The sender records this value for future segment calculations and computes the correct window size advertised in the SYN segment.

Timestamp HEADER OPTION

The Timestamp header option forms a very important component in the calculation of RTT values. This option, specified in the Options field of the segment header, consists of four fields: kind, len, timestamp value, and timestamp echo reply. The kind field specifies the number of bytes occupied by the timestamp value and timestamp echo reply fields. The len field specifies the total length of the Timestamp option. The timestamp value field specifies a time value that indicates the time of sending the segment. The timestamp echo reply field also contains the time value indicating the time of sending the segment.

To calculate RTT values, the SYN segment is sent with a timestamp indicating the time of sending the segment. The receiver records the timestamp value as soon as it receives the segment. The receiver assigns the recorded timestamp value to the timestamp echo reply field and sends the acknowledgement. After the receipt of the acknowledgement, the sender uses the timestamp echo reply value and the time of receiving acknowledgement to calculate the RTT value for the segment. Remember that the difference between the time of sending the segment and the time of receiving the acknowledgement is used to compute RTT.

Although timestamp echo replies are set for every acknowledgement, if an acknowledgement verifies the receipt of multiple segments received, the timestamp value for the earliest segment received by the receiver is assigned as the timestamp echo reply value in the acknowledgement segment. In addition, the receiver echoes timeout values of lost segments when the segment, presumed lost, finally arrives at the receiver. This way, the receiver echoes the timeout values for almost all segments including retransmitted segments. This feature is especially useful while estimating RTT values for segments transmitted over Long Fat Pipes where the high speed of data transmission makes it difficult to track the round trip sample time for every segment.

CH
6

PERFORMANCE PROBLEMS ON LONG FAT PIPES

Over the years, transmission capacities of networks have improved tremendously. For example, transcontinental telephone lines can transmit data at the rate of 1GB per second. Such networks with huge transmission capacities are called Long Fat Networks or LFNs. When you use a TCP connection over an LFN line, it is termed as a Long Fat Pipe. These gigantic connections with fast transmission times and huge data transmission capacities pose a problem of plenty for TCP. For example, even the maximum window size of 65,535 bytes that can be advertised by the receiver in a Window Header field will lead to underutilization of the network resources on an LFN. However, a solution to this problem comes in the form of the Window Scale option, which can be used to scale the window size to 14 times more than the size allowed for an advertisement in the Window field of the segment header.

On fast LFN networks, it is very difficult to measure RTT values for all transmitted segments because TCP arrives at an RTT value based on the round trip sample times calculated for all the segments in a window. The solution for this problem is offered by the Timestamp option of the Options field in the segment header. This option returns the timestamp for the earliest segment received by the receiver. For example, if an acknowledgement ACK1 acknowledges two segments S1 and S2, the timestamp of segment S1 is echoed to the sender. In the next acknowledgement, the timestamp of segment S2 is returned by the receiver. This way, RTT values can be calculated based on the timestamps for all segments.

Although LFNs provide quick and voluminous data transmission facilities, data loss is also possible. However, on LFNs, data loss of more than one datagram results in huge data losses because at any given point of time, hundreds of datagrams are transmitted over an LFN, and all these datagrams are discarded if multiple datagram losses occur. To recover from such situations, a technique called *fast retransmit and fast recovery* must be adopted. In this method, when a segment with an unexpected sequence number is received indicating that the previous segments were lost, an acknowledgement is returned immediately. The sender receives the acknowledgement and waits for two more acknowledgements that are out of sequence. If the subsequent two acknowledgements are also out of sequence, the segments with the sequence number that have been missed are identified as the lost segments and are retransmitted immediately. Next, instead of initiating a slow start, which might transmit a large number of segments, a congestion avoidance process is initiated where subsequent congestion window sizes are not drastically increased or reduced.

One of the most complicated but interesting problems that occurs in a Long Fat Pipe is the problem of identical segment sequence numbers called *wrapped sequence numbers*. The sequence numbers used in a segment restart their count after the transmitting around 4GB of data. Now, take a scenario where a segment that is assumed lost reappears. The problem here is that the sequence number might be the same as that of another segment because the sequence numbering could have restarted, which means that the receiving computer will receive two segments with the same sequence number.

This condition does not occur in the case of slow networks because each segment is defined with a maximum segment life (MSL) value that destroys the segment after a certain period. On slow networks, the segment sequence numbering restarts after an hour while the recommended MSL value is set at 2 minutes. Therefore, even if a segment is lost, by the time the sequence numbering is restarted from the beginning, the segment is discarded and does not exist. This negates the possibility of identically sequence numbered segments existing at a given point of time.

However, the problem is much more prevalent on high capacity networks, such as LFNs, where the sequence numbering restart time can be a maximum of 34 seconds. Because the MSL value can be set to two minutes, it raises an interesting possibility of having two segments with the same sequence number appearing in the receiver. This problem too is solved using the `Timestamp` option in the `Options` field of the header.

Compare the identically numbered segments with identical twins. Nature provides only two ways of differentiating identical twins. The time of birth is a differentiating factor because the time of birth would certainly differ by a few seconds at the least. Another differentiating factor that nature has bestowed on each twin is the fingerprint, which is unique for each human being. Identically numbered segments too have such a differentiating factor, their `timestamp values`. The `timestamp value` assigned for every segment not only acts as a differentiating "birth" time but also uniquely fingerprints a segment. Now, the segment with an older `timestamp value` is identified as the unwanted segment and is discarded because the older segment, which was assumed lost, would have been retransmitted and probably acknowledged as well. Figure 6.5 describes the process implemented in protecting computers against wrapped sequence numbers.

Figure 6.5
The monotonical increase in the `timestamp value`, which is used to identify a segment in addition to the sequence number, is the most important factor that differentiates segments with identical sequence numbers.

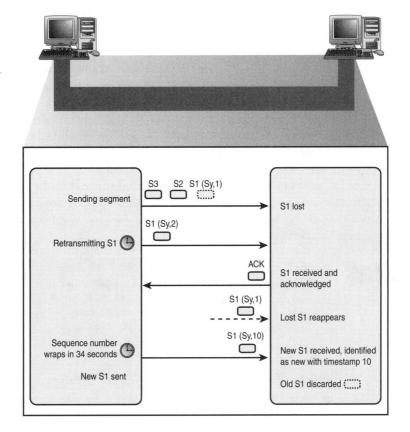

CH

6

In the figure, the segment S1 is lost when it is transmitted the first time. Note that it has a sequence number Sy and a timestamp 1. After the normal timeout period, the segment is retransmitted. However, after the sequence number wraps, another segment with the same sequence number (Sy) is transmitted. The problem arises when the lost segment reappears at the receiver's computer. The only differentiating factor is the timestamp. The older segment has a timestamp of 1 while the new segment is transmitted with the timestamp 10. Therefore, the older segment is discarded.

ENHANCED PERFORMANCE USING T/TCP

Even though TCP provides a number of useful features, such as retransmission, congestion control, and probe timers, inefficiency creeps in when an excessive number of segments are required by TCP to establish a connection. You must exchange seven segments to establish and terminate a connection; three segments to establish a connection (two SYN segments and one Acknowledgement segment) and four segments to terminate the connection (two FIN segments and two Acknowledgement segments). In addition, the maximum segment life recommended by RFC at two minutes severely limits the number of transactions between the sender and receiver computers because if a segment doesn't reach its destination within the MSL limit, it will be discarded en route. Therefore, only a limited number of segments that can reach the receiver within the MSL time limit can be transmitted.

To overcome these problems, you can use the TCP extension for transaction called *T/TCP*. This transaction-oriented TCP extension reduces the number of segments exchanged during connection establishment by using a new connection establishment technique called *accelerated open*. This technique requires the inclusion of an additional header option called *connection count or* CC. This value is a 32-bit number that uniquely identifies a connection from a particular computer. Every time a connection is reestablished between two computers, this number is incremented. The CC field is assigned to the initial SYN segment and is stored by the receiver computer. Before caching the CC value, the CC value is compared with the cached CC values to check if the value is greater than the last valid CC value received from this particular sender. A greater CC value indicates that a new connection is being established in which case, the SYN segment is accepted and the data contained in the segment is passed on to the application.

> **Note**
>
> Data exchanged between two machines that follow the format of a request and a reply is called a *transaction*. This data exchange format is prevalent in situations where a client and a server computer communicate and exchange data through a request initiated by the client and a response provided by the server.

However, if the CC value is less than the last valid cached CC values or if a cache does not exist for connections from that computer, the three-way handshake process is initiated. If the SYN segment is accepted, an acknowledgement is sent to the sending computer. In the acknowledgement, the CC value sent with the SYN segment is assigned to a CCEcho field.

On receipt of this segment, the connection establishment process is complete. Figure 6.6 shows you how the accelerated open technique is implemented.

Figure 6.6
In contrast to the three-way handshake technique, accelerated open avoids the transmission of the last acknowledgment, thereby quickening the connection establishment process.

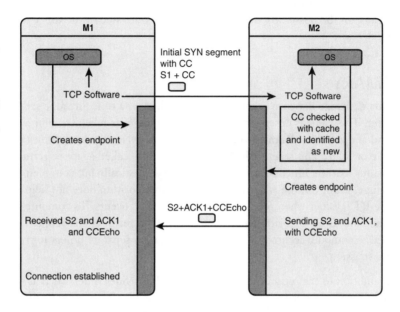

To refresh your memory, the three-way handshake involves sending a SYN segment from the sender, receiving an acknowledgement and a SYN from the receiver, and sending an acknowledgement for the receiver's SYN. This acknowledgement completes the connection establishment process. In contrast, the accelerated open technique avoids the last acknowledgement. Observe that in the figure, the TCP software on the sending computer (M1) does not transmit an acknowledgement on receipt of the SYN segment (SYN2) sent from the receiver (M2). This is because the CCEcho value received in the receiver's SYN indicates that a connection with the number provided in the CCEcho is accepted by the receiver.

The CC value cached on the receiver also enables the receiver to detect any segments generated by the sender using the previous connection by checking the CC value contained in the segment with its cache. If the value is less than the value of the existing connection count, the segment, which is a duplicate segment, is discarded.

Although the accelerated open technique reduces the segment exchange overhead, it breaks a few ground rules and necessitates some operational adjustments on the part of TCP. For example, the sender is allowed to transmit data in the initial SYN segment without the restriction of a window size. A maximum window size of 4KB is recommended for the data contained in the SYN segment to avoid transmitting segments larger than the receiver's buffer. The MSS value is another segment header option that is not calculated while sending data in the SYN segment. T/TCP provides the option of caching the client's MSS value along with the CC value.

CH
6

In an accelerated open, the segment that carries the acknowledgement and the receiver's SYN value is not transmitted immediately. Instead, it waits for any data to be transmitted along with the segment. However, it must be ensured that the wait period does not take too long because of the possibility of exceeding the timeout value of the timer set on the sender computer.

SUMMARY

Data exchange between computers is controlled by a timeout value set on the sending computer. This value is determined by measuring the time taken to complete one full cycle of send and acknowledgement receipt. A weighted average of cycle times is called a round trip time or RTT. This weighted average method, also called adaptive retransmission algorithm, ensures that the timeout value is not modified drastically but is implemented as a slight change. However, the adaptive retransmission algorithm does not help in calculating accurate RTT values when retransmission of segments occurs. To compute an accurate RTT value, the Karn's algorithm and the timer backoff technique is adopted. This strategy can be used to compute accurate RTT values by creating separate timers for retransmission and transmission.

In addition to the retransmission timers, TCP provides timers such as the Persist timer and the Keepalive timer for timing probe segments. The Persist timer times the probes used to check for the availability of a nonzero window advertisement on the receiver. The Keepalive timer times the probes used for checking the availability of the sender or receiver after a long period of inactivity.

TCP Performance depends on certain assumptions, which stipulate that the speed of a network connection depends on the bandwidth delay product, performance of an intermediate computer, and the window size advertised by the receiver. Performance of a connection can be affected by a number of other factors, such as congestion and path MTU, and segment header options, such as Window Scale and Timestamp options. These options are used to overcome performance problems that arise in a high-speed network such as Long Fat Pipes. In addition, you can use the T/TCP service to manage performance overheads caused in a typical TCP connection. T/TCP reduces the number of segments exchanged during the connection establishment process by implementing cached connection counters and accelerated opens.

CHAPTER **7**

USER DATAGRAM PROTOCOL

In this chapter

INTRODUCTION TO UDP

The exchange of data in the world of computers primarily involves two computers that send and receive data to and from each other. This data exchange can happen as a one-time send operation or a simultaneous exchange of data. In either case, the Transport layer protocols such as TCP and UDP, specified by the TCP/IP reference model, come into the picture. TCP is used to transfer IP datagrams among host computers. TCP transfers data as streams to destination computers based on the computer's IP address. Unlike TCP, the User Datagram Protocol (UDP) does not send data as a stream of bytes. In addition, this protocol does not establish a connection with another application to exchange information. Applications using UDP exchange data in discrete units called datagrams, which are similar to IP datagrams. A *datagram* is essentially a single unit of binary data. The first eight bytes of a datagram contain the header information and the remaining bytes contain data.

In the TCP/IP protocol suite, User Datagram Protocol allows an application program to send datagrams to other application programs on remote computers. In the TCP/IP reference model, UDP lies in the Transport layer, above the Network layer and below the Application layer. UDP uses IP to transport a message between two computers because the Internet layer is responsible for transferring data between computers. Figure 7.1 shows the position of the layer from which UDP operates in the TCP/IP reference model.

Figure 7.1
UDP provides a connectionless data transmission.

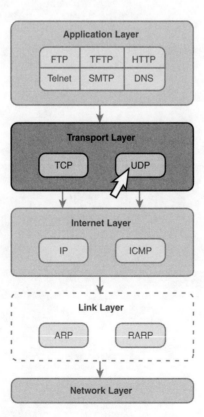

Typically, UDP is implemented on networking environments where reliable data transmission is not required. Such environments also demand fewer overheads on data transmission and cannot afford the reliability measures, such as establishing connections and acknowledging each datagram, that are typical in a connection-oriented Transport layer protocol. For example, when real-time audio transmission must be implemented, datagrams that hold the sound data must be transmitted quickly without the need to establish a reliable connection between the communicating computers. Therefore, sound datagrams cannot be acknowledged or transmitted over an established connection. The Real-time Transport Protocol (RTP) that implements real-time transmission of sound and video images is an example of an application protocol that uses UDP.

→ To learn more about RTP, **see** "Real-Time Transport Protocol," **p. 384**

FEATURES OF UDP

UDP can be compared to the mail service where mail is delivered to a person by using the address on the envelope. The sender has to rely on the underlying system, in this case the mail delivery system, to deliver the mail. The mail might go via various countries and continents, with each country having its own postal system, stamps, and charges. In the mail service, the sender merely drops the mail in the mailbox and relies on the mail service to ensure safe delivery. Similarly, UDP drops the datagram received from the Application layer onto the underlying layer, the Transport layer, and assumes that the message will be delivered to the intended recipient.

When an application sends a UDP datagram over the network, it has no way of finding whether the datagram reached its destination. UDP does not do any error checking and cannot recover data that was incorrectly delivered. The sender and receiver must typically implement their own application protocol on top of UDP to ensure secured delivery of data packets because of this unreliability.

UDP does not maintain a connection with the remote UDP layer on the destination computer. While transferring data packets generated by the application implementing UDP, outgoing datagrams are pushed by UDP. It also accepts the incoming datagrams. Therefore, an application program implementing UDP must deal directly with connection-related communication problems that a connection-oriented protocol like TCP would have handled.

Note

The application program implementing UDP should handle some of the communication problems to ensure reliable delivery of datagrams. They are retransmission of lost packets, packetization and reassembly, flow control, congestion avoidance, generating checksums, and acknowledging the receipt of packets.

CH
7

UDP provides two services to the user's network applications. It provides port numbers to distinguish different user requests. Multiplexing information between applications is based on the UDP port numbers. The other service provided by UDP is a checksum field located in the UPD datagram header to verify the integrity of the data.

A host computer requires both the IP address and the protocol port number to communicate with a remote computer. The protocol port number of both the source and the destination computers are required in every message for successful communication on a network. UDP is responsible for identifying the source or destination ports within a host. The path of communication between an application and UDP is through UDP ports. These ports are numbered beginning from zero.

Note

There are scenarios where different streams of data must be transmitted in a single data unit. To transmit such a data unit, all data streams are combined into a single data unit and transmitted over the network. This process is defined as multiplexing. A good example of multiplexing is the transmission of varying frequencies of analog signals across a telephone line. The signals with varying frequencies are multiplexed into an analog signal before being transmitted over the telephone line. When the signal arrives on the other end, the individual signals contained in the transmitted signal are unpacked. This process is called *demultiplexing*.

UDP ports allow different applications to maintain their own channels for data. These port numbers enable multiple applications to send and receive data concurrently. An application that is offering service, also known as the server, waits for messages to come through a specific port dedicated to that service. Some applications use static port numbers that are reserved for or registered to the application. Other applications use dynamic (unregistered) port numbers. The sending application sends UDP datagrams through the source port, and the receiving application accepts this datagram through the destination port. The UDP port headers are two bytes long and therefore, valid port numbers range from 0 to 65,535. By convention, values above 49,151 represent dynamic ports.

UDP lacks any form of congestion control. Congestion control is needed to prevent overloading and congestion in a network. Congestion control also enables you to optimize the network bandwidth, performance, and throughput. For example, if multimedia applications stream high bit-rate video data simultaneously, without using any congestion control, intermediate devices such as routers would be clogged with datagrams. This would prevent display of video images on the user's terminal. Thus, the lack of congestion control in UDP is a potential serious problem. Many researchers have proposed new mechanisms to force all sources, including UDP sources, to perform adaptive congestion control.

UDP preserves the message size defined by the application. It never combines two application messages together, or divides a single application message into parts. When a computer sends data through UDP, the data arrives at the remote computer as a single unit. For example, if the sender sends five datagrams to the UDP port, the destination will read five datagrams from the UDP port. In addition, the size of each datagram sent matches the size of each datagram received. The following list summarizes the features of UDP:

- UDP is transaction-oriented, and provides a procedure for applications to send messages to other programs with a minimal transport service. For example, TFTP is a file transfer application that uses UDP in the Transport layer. It merely provides the remote host name that is used for file uploads and downloads. Figure 7.2 illustrates that TFTP provides minimal transport services and does not implement connection or handshake mechanisms to transfer data.

Figure 7.2
Username or password authentication is not required for transferring files by using TFTP because it does not use connection-oriented protocols to transfer files.

- UDP is a connectionless and unreliable delivery mechanism. UDP does not establish a connection between the sending and receiving computers before sending a datagram.
- Encapsulation and reverse encapsulation of data packets are based on the protocol ports used by UDP. Each UDP datagram includes a well-known port number. For example, TFTP that deploys UDP uses the port number 69 for data transfer. This port number is encapsulated in all the communication between the sender and the receiver and in addition, both the TFTP server and TFTP client will communicate by using this predefined UDP port number.
- UDP gives applications direct access to the datagram service of the Internet layer. For example, the datagram services provided by the Internet layer, such as fragmentation and reassembling, are also provided by the UDP application. Details on the datagram services provided by UDP are covered in the section "Implementing UDP in an Application."
- User Datagram Protocol uses Internet Protocol (IP) as the underlying protocol for data transfer mechanisms.
- The UDP header and data are delivered to the final destination in the same form as originally transmitted.
- UDP does not provide acknowledgements, or does not control the order of arrival of data packets. Therefore, UDP messages can be lost.

CH
7

- Delivery and duplicate detection of data packets are not implemented.

- UDP cannot report errors when the packets are not delivered. However, when UDP packets are delivered, valid data are passed to the appropriate application identified by the source and destination port numbers.

ANALYZING THE UDP DATAGRAM STRUCTURE

Data transferred using UDP is incorporated in the UDP datagram, which is the most important component of the UDP specification. In addition to the data part, a UDP datagram contains important information required to deliver the datagram at a particular destination. This information is stored in the header component of the datagram. The UDP header consists of four fields: Source port, Destination port, Length, and Checksum. Table 7.1 describes the four fields of datagram headers in detail. All these fields are 2 bytes long. Figure 7.3 shows you the structure of a UDP datagram header.

Figure 7.3
The four fields contained in the UDP header provide the required information to ensure safe delivery of datagrams.

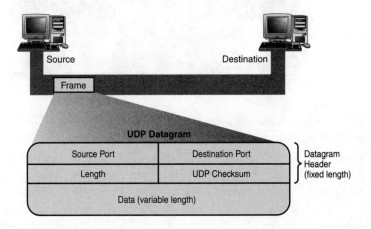

Table 7.1 describes each of the datagram fields in detail.

TABLE 7.1   DATAGRAM HEADER FIELDS AND THEIR DESCRIPTION

Field	Definition
Source Port	Indicates the port of the sending process and the port to which a reply should be addressed. If the source port is not used, a value specified for this field is 0. This is an optional field. The length of this field is 16 bits.
Destination Port	Indicates the port to which the packet is addressed.
Length	Indicates the length of the user datagram, including the header and the data, in bytes. The minimum value for this field is 8. The UDP datagram size is a simple count of the number of bytes of information contained in the header and data components. This field refers to the length of the variable-sized data portion and the length of the fixed sized header. The maximum size of a datagram varies depending on the operating system.

TABLE 7.1	CONTINUED
Field	**Definition**
	With a two-byte field, the theoretical maximum datagram size is 65,535 bytes. However, some implementations of UDP restrict the datagram size to as low as 8,192 bytes.
Checksum	Indicates a value that is computed from the values stored in the IP header, the UDP header, and the data. To derive a 16-bit value from the computed sum, zeroes are padded at the end. This field is computed based on an algorithm and is optional. Figure 7.4 shows the structure of a UDP checksum pseudo header.

Note

The *pseudo header*, which is conceptually prefixed to the UDP header, contains the source address, the destination address, the protocol, and the UDP length. The information provided in the pseudo header gives protection against misrouted datagrams.

Figure 7.4
The psuedoheader is used by UDP to calculate the checksum value of the UDP datagram.

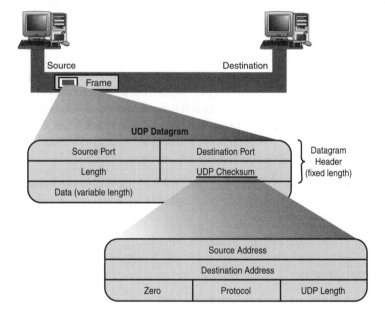

UNDERSTANDING UDP CHECKSUM

The UDP checksum enables error detection while transporting data packets on a network. UDP at the sender's computer performs the one's complement of the sum of all the 16-bit fields in the UDP header. The checksum is also calculated for a few of the fields in the IP header in addition to the UDP header. The computed result is stored in the checksum field of the UDP header. If the computed checksum is zero, this field must be set to 0xFFFF, which is the one's compliment of zero. If this value is not computed, the value 0x0000 is stored in this field. This indicates that the value of the transmitted checksum is 000000 and that the sender computer has not calculated the checksum. Checksum is not calculated if the datagram does not contain any data to be delivered.

In the destination computer, the Internet layer passes an incoming IP datagram to UDP if the value in the Type field of the IP header is UDP. When the UDP implementation receives the datagram from IP, it examines the UDP checksum. All 16-bit fields in the UDP header are added together, including the checksum. If this sum equals 1111111111111111, the datagram has no errors. If one of the bits in the computed sum is zero, it indicates that the datagram was inadvertently altered during transmission and thus has some errors. If the checksum field in the UDP header is zero, it means that the sender did not calculate checksum and the field can be ignored. If the checksum is valid or nonzero, UDP at the destination computer examines the destination port number and if an application is bound to that port, the datagram is transferred to an application message queue to buffer the incoming datagrams before transferring them to the application. If the checksum is not valid, the destination computer discards the UDP datagram. If the incoming UDP datagrams arrive faster and the application message queue is full, UDP datagrams are discarded by the destination computer. At the destination computer, UDP will continue to discard the datagrams until there is space in the application message queue.

A network application must implement the programming routines to generate and validate UDP checksums. In addition, it may be able to decide whether UDP datagrams without checksums should be discarded or passed to that application. Sometimes, checksum generation can be disabled if Ethernet is the only network between the two UDP implementations in the communicating machines. This is because the Ethernet cable is more widely used in secured Local Area Networks in which there is no datagram loss. However, it is recommended that checksum generation be enabled always to reduce undetected errors because the data might be sent across less reliable media.

For example, if a UDP header has three fields that contains the following 16-bit values: 0110011001100101, 0101010101010110, and 0000111100001111, the checksum can be calculated as follows:

The first two 16-bit data are added:

0110011001100101
0101010101010110

The sum of first and second 16-bit data is:

1011101110111011

Adding the third 16 bit data to the above sum gives:

1011101110111011
0000111100001111

The sum of these two values is:

1100101011001010

The 1's complement of the sum `1100101011001010` is `0011010100110101`. Now the checksum computed by the sender's UDP is `0011010100110101`. At the destination computer, the values of all the four 16-bit fields, `source port`, `destination port`, `length`, and `checksum` are added. If no errors were introduced in the datagram, the sum at the receiver will be `1111111111111111`. If one of the bits is a zero, it indicates that errors were introduced in the datagram.

You may wonder why UDP provides a checksum in the first place because many Link layer protocols also provide error checking. The reason is that there is no guarantee that all the protocols between the source and destination computers provide error checking. One of the layers might use a protocol that does not provide error checking. IP being a protocol that is supposed to operate from any Link layer protocol, it is better that the Transport layer protocols provide error checking as a safety measure. Although UDP provides error checking, it does not take care of error recovery. Some implementations of UDP simply discard the damaged datagram, whereas others pass the damaged segment to the application with a warning.

The UDP checksum value represents an encoding of the datagram data that is calculated first by the sender and later by the receiver. If an individual datagram is altered or corrupted during transmission due to a hacker or due to disruptions during transmission, the calculated checksums of the sender and receiver will not match and UDP will detect this error. The checksum algorithm is not foolproof, but is used as a safety measure in many cases. Checksum generation by UDP is optional as opposed to the checksum calculation by TCP, which is mandatory.

WORKING WITH UDP

In UDP-based applications, data passes between the application and the UDP implementation on the sending and receiving computers. For example, Simple Network Management Protocol (SNMP) is an application that uses UDP. Its protocol layering scheme in the TCP/IP reference model is SNMP, UDP, IP, and Ethernet. Data passing out from the applications through UDP converges in the Internet layer and is pushed to the network through the network interface driver. The TCP module, UDP module, and the Ethernet driver multiplex different types of data into a single frame format. They also de-multiplex an incoming frame into an appropriate datagram or segment according to the `type` field in the protocol header. If a frame or data packet arrives at the Internet layer, this unit of data is passed upward to either TCP or UDP, as determined by the value of the `Protocol` field in the IP header. If the UDP datagram reaches a UDP implementation, it is passed upward to the network application based on the value of the `Port` field in the UDP header.

A computer might send UDP packets without establishing a connection to the recipient. UDP takes messages from the application and attaches `source` and `destination port` `number` fields for the multiplexing/demultiplexing service. UDP computes the UDP checksum, stores it in the `Checksum` field, and encapsulates UDP messages within an IP datagram. It stores values in appropriate fields in the UDP header and forwards the data together with

CH
7

the header for transmission to the Internet layer. The Network layer stores values in the rest of the header fields in the IP datagram, encapsulates it, and then delivers the IP datagram to the receiving host. The UDP header and data are not processed by the routers on the network and are delivered to the final destination in the same form as originally transmitted.

The frames are demultiplexed at the destination computer. At the final destination, the UDP protocol layer receives datagrams from the Network layer. These datagrams are validated using the checksum and all invalid datagrams with incorrect checksum are discarded by UDP. UDP uses the port numbers and the IP source and destination addresses to deliver the data in the UDP datagram to the correct application process.

IMPLEMENTING UDP IN AN APPLICATION

The application interface of UDP must manage all the services related to the Internet and Network layers. Some of the basic programming requirements for a network application deploying UDP are explained as follows:

1. The application that deploys UDP needs the functions that determine the effective datagram size to be used by a particular interface implementing IP, remote host, or TOS.

2. The application must be able to set the TTL and TOS values to send a UDP datagram and these values must be passed transparently to the Internet layer. UDP can pass the received TOS to the Application layer.

3. The application based on UDP must be able to obtain the route to the destination computer from the datagram being sent and must be able to supply the route to the sending computer from the reversed route for sending the corresponding reply.

4. A few values must be provided by the Application layer to IP. The application that deploys UDP must be able to specify these values so that UDP can pass these values to IP through the UDP datagram.

Note

At present, the IP options that must be passed by UDP are source route, record route, and time stamp. However, new options might be defined in the future. UDP does not process the format or content of options it passes to or from the application.

5. The application must be able to return the complete IP datagram including the entire IP header in response to a receive operation. Such an interface would also allow UDP to pass a full IP datagram complete with header to IP to send data packets.

6. An application must be able to either specify or ignore the sending computer IP address, also called IP source address, which is used by the UDP datagram. If the IP source address is not specified, the application implementing UDP must be able to choose an appropriate source address.

Now, you will learn about other considerations in deploying UDP as the Transport layer protocol. When a computer sends a UDP datagram, the source address must be the IP address of the host computer. A UDP datagram received with an invalid IP source address, such as a broadcast or multicast address, must be discarded by UDP or by the Internet layer. Broadcast or multicast addresses are invalid addresses in UDP because they do not conform to any of the class A, B, C, D and E addressing schemes used in Transport layer protocols as these broadcast and multicast addresses do not have port numbers or they do not have a valid IP address scheme of host.domain:port. UDP must be able to determine the source and destination IP addresses and the protocol field from the IP header.

UDP must pass all ICMP error messages that it receives from the Internet layer to the Application layer. If a datagram arrives addressed to a nonexistent UDP port, UDP should send a Port Unreachable ICMP message. ICMP error messages resulting from sending a UDP datagram are not received in the same sequence as they were sent. Hence, a UDP-based application that wants to receive ICMP error messages is responsible for implementing the necessary actions to demultiplex these messages when they arrive. The application is also responsible for avoiding confusion that might be caused if it receives a delayed ICMP error message corresponding to the port used earlier.

UDP VERSUS TCP

When a client needs to request certain data from a database server, it takes at least three datagrams to establish a TCP connection, another three to send and confirm a small amount of data each way, and another three to close the connection. However, if UDP is used, it uses only two datagrams to achieve almost the same result. UDP does not require the client to establish and close a connection with the server. The client simply puts the data into a datagram and sends it to the server. The server formulates its reply, puts the data into a datagram addressed to the client, and transmits it back to the client. Although this method of data transfer is both faster and more efficient than TCP for simple transactions, UDP cannot deal with datagram loss. UDP allows an application to contact a service on a certain port on the remote computer. However, it does not establish a connection with the remote computer.

UDP is an alternative to TCP and, together with IP, is sometimes referred to as UDP/IP. Like TCP, UDP uses IP to actually send a datagram from one computer to another. However, UDP does not provide the feature of dividing a message into packets and reassembling it at the other end.

The primary difference between UDP and TCP lies in the way they implement data transfer. TCP includes support for guaranteed delivery, in which the recipient automatically acknowledges the sender when a message is received. In addition, the sender waits and retransmits the data if the receiver does not respond within a specified time limit. The reliability features built into TCP can be expensive in terms of the overhead during execution. UDP, on the other hand, does not implement guaranteed message delivery. A UDP datagram can get lost during transmission and the protocol will not be able to detect or report

CH

7

this. However, UDP does not prevent reliable message delivery; it merely defers those details to a higher level of the TCP/IP reference model.

UDP has the advantage over TCP in one critical area, packet overhead. Because TCP is a reliable protocol, it ensures that data arrives at its destination intact. As a result, it exchanges a relatively high number of packets over the network. UDP does not have this overhead and is considerably faster than TCP. UDP further minimizes the overhead associated with message transfers because no connection is established before transmission.

TCP uses a three-way handshake before it starts the data transfer process. UDP just starts the data transmission without any formal preliminaries. TCP maintains connection state in the computers involved in the connection. This connection state includes sliding window and the buffer size on the receiver computer, congestion control parameters, and sequence and acknowledgment number parameters. UDP, on the other hand, does not maintain a connection state and does not track any of these parameters. A server devoted to a particular application can typically support many clients that are more active when the application implements UDP rather than TCP. For example, an SNMP management system implementing UDP can support multiple SNMP agents.

The size of the header in a TCP segment has 20 bytes, whereas the size of UDP is just 8 bytes. TCP has a congestion control mechanism that reduces data transmission from the sender when one or more links between the sender and receiver becomes excessively congested. This reduction can have a severe impact on real-time applications, which can tolerate some packet loss but require a minimum send rate. On the other hand, the speed at which UDP sends data is constrained by the rate at which the application generates data, the processing power, clock speed of the source computer, and the bandwidth of the connection. However, the receiving host does not necessarily receive all the data. When the network is congested, a significant fraction of the UDP-transmitted data can be lost when the router buffers are clogged with a large number of datagrams. In the case of UDP, the receiving rate is limited by possible network congestion even if the sending rate is not restricted.

Unlike TCP, UDP cannot ensure that the datagrams reach the destination in the proper order. For example, if a client sends four datagrams to a server in the order D1, D2, D3, D4, UDP may send the datagrams to the server in the order D3, D1, D4, D2.

The application that implements UDP must ensure that the entire message has arrived and is in the correct order because UDP does sequence the data packets reaching it. However, UDP datagrams do not always arrive out-of-order. It happens only under heavy traffic conditions or in scenarios where multiple paths exist between the source and the destination computer and each path has a different delay characteristic, also called a *jitter*.

CONSIDERATIONS FOR CHOOSING UDP

Now you might be wondering why an application developer will ever choose to build an application implementing UDP rather than implementing TCP. Although TCP is preferred to UDP because TCP provides a reliable data transfer service, many applications are better suited for UDP for the following reasons.

Both UDP and TCP provide different services. Most applications are implemented to use only one of the protocols. You can choose the protocol that best suits your needs. If you need a reliable streamed delivery service, TCP is the best. If you need a connectionless datagram service, UDP is the best. If you need efficiency for data transmission over long-haul circuits, TCP is the best. If you need efficiency for data transmission over fast networks with short latency, UDP is the best. However, applications can be developed such that it makes up for services not provided by the protocol chosen. For instance if you choose UDP and you need reliability in data transfer, the application must be developed to take care of reliability. If you choose TCP and you need to transfer data in the form of rows, the application must insert markers in the byte stream to delimit records.

UDP is useful for applications that do not require TCP's sequencing or flow control. Primarily, UDP's services will be of use in situations where the sender issues a single request query and needs to obtain a reply message from the server. In such situations, prompt data transmission is important. UDP is the solution in situations where speed is of paramount importance or the number of packets sent over the network must be kept minimum.

Applications requiring ordered reliable delivery of streams of data must use TCP. UDP is used by applications that do not require the services provided by TCP or that need to use communications services, such as multicast or broadcast delivery, not provided by TCP. Finally, multicast applications implement UDP because TCP cannot be employed with multicast.

Network applications that want to save processing time because they have very small data units to exchange may prefer UDP to TCP. For example, the Trivial File Transfer Protocol (TFTP) uses UDP instead of TCP.

APPLICATIONS IMPLEMENTING UDP

Some routing protocols, such as RIP, implement UDP as its Transport layer protocol. UDP is also commonly used with multimedia applications, such as Internet phone, real-time video conferencing, and streaming of stored audio and video. Some applications that use UDP are explained in the following sections.

REMOTE SHELL

Remote shell (rsh or remsh) is one the remote UNIX style commands. The remote Unix-style commands are also known as *r* commands*. The r* commands are primarily used between Unix systems and are designed for interaction between trusted hosts. These commands use UDP because data security is not an issue.

NFS

Network File System, first developed by Sun Microsystems Inc, uses UDP and is excellent for booting UNIX file systems on multiple computers. A diskless workstation can access its server's hard disk as if the disk were local to the workstation. NFS adds significant data transmission load to the network and is not efficient when used on slow links. The NFS

CH

7

client is implemented in the kernel allowing all applications and commands on the client computers to use the NFS booted disk as if it were a local disk. UDP is used as the Transport layer protocol by NFS to download and install file systems on NFS clients from NFS server.

→ To learn more about NFS, **see** "NFS," **p. 143**

SNMP

Simple Network Management Protocol (SNMP) uses UDP and is designed for use by central network management computers. SNMP is not actually a protocol. It is a client/server application that runs on UDP. It was developed to be an efficient means of sending network management information over a UDP connection, using port 161 for SNMP messages and 162 for SNMP traps.

> **Note**
>
> The message sent by an SNMP agent to an SNMP management system when the agent software detects a certain type of event locally on the agent computer is called an SNMP trap message. These events are usually error events.

→ To learn more about NFS, **see** "Network Management Basics and SNMP," **p. 194**

For instance, the SNMP management server, called an SNMP agent, always listens for incoming datagrams on port 161. If an SNMP agent wants to use the SNMP management service, it sends its request to port number 161 on the destination computer.

NTP

Network Time Protocol (NTP) is used to synchronize a set of network clocks by using a set of distributed clients and servers. NTP is built on UDP and uses the UPD port 123 for data transmission. NTP uses UDP to pass the server time values across various client computers so that the time is synchronized across the network.

DNS

DNS is an example of an Application layer protocol that uses UDP and uses port 53 for transmitting data. DNS can also be implemented on TCP with the same port number. When the DNS application in a host wants to make a query, it constructs a DNS query message and passes the message to a UDP socket. Without the handshake operation, UDP adds header fields to the message and passes the resulting segment to the Network layer. The Network layer encapsulates the UDP datagram into a frame and sends the datagram to the DNS server. The DNS application at the querying host then waits for a reply to its query from the DNS server. If it does not receive a reply, it either tries sending the query to another DNS server, or it informs the invoking application that the DNS query failed.

→ To learn more about DNS, **see** "DNS Basics," **p. 209**

TFTP

Trivial File Transfer Protocol (TFTP) is a simple UDP-based protocol used for transferring files between computers. It is simpler to use but it does not match the file transfer capabilities of FTP. TFTP is used in cases where user authentication and the need to view directories on remote computers are not required. Its two major uses are to bootstrap diskless machines that are being installed over the network and to install images that reside in firmware. TFTP is widely used to download bootcode on diskless workstations.

A computer only needs to run a TFTP server if it is acting as a boot server for other computer's diskless clients, or for remote installations. The server provides access only to a fraction of the files on a system because TFTP has no built-in access control. The TFTP file interface is very simple, providing no access control or security. TFTP provides its own reliable delivery by using a simple stop-and-wait acknowledgment system. In this system, the file transfer is delayed until an acknowledgement is received from the destination computer. On Unix systems, the TFTP service is provided by tftpd or in.tftpd utilities.

Figures 7.5 and 7.6 show a file transfer between the TFTP client and the TFTP server. The TFTP client uploads a file named `overview.html` to the TFTP server. The IP address of the TFTP client is `172.17.199.115`. The IP address of the TFTP server is `172.17.198.51`.

Figure 7.5
The TFTP client computer uses the PUT command to upload a file named `overview.html` to the TFTP server.

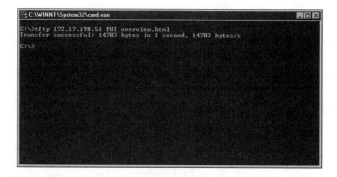

Figure 7.6
The receipt status of the `overview.html` file is displayed by the TFTP server.

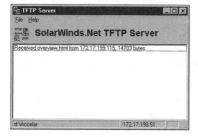

CH
7

To download the same file, `overview.html` from the TFTP server to the TFTP client, you use the GET command on the client computer TFTP prompt. Figures 7.7 and 7.8 illustrate this transaction between the TFTP client and the TFTP server.

Figure 7.7
The TFTP client computer has used the `GET` command to download a file named `overview.html` from the TFTP server.

Figure 7.8
The sent status of the `overview.html` file is displayed on the TFTP server console.

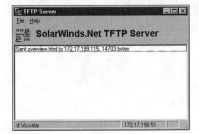

As can be seen from Figures 7.7 and 7.8, TFTP uses UDP as the Transport layer protocol. The TFTP client does not establish a connection with the TFTP server. There is no acknowledgement, connection, or handshake between the TFTP server and the TFTP client. Both the TFTP client and server use the well-defined UDP port number 69 for file transfer. In this example, the TFTP client initiates a PUT request to the TFTP server. This request is encapsulated in the UDP datagram along with sender's port number, which is 69. UDP transports this request datagram to the TFTP server by using the IP address of the TFTP server, which is 172.17.198.51, and the port number 69. At the receiving end, the TFTP server sends a message to the TFTP client by using the same well-defined TFTP port number 69 and the TFTP client's IP address of 172.17.199.115.

SUMMARY

UDP is a Transport layer protocol that operates from the layer above the Internet layer and below the Application layer protocol. UDP is connectionless, unreliable, and less secure. UDP messages can be lost, duplicated, or delivered out of order. The UDP header and data are delivered to the final destination in the same form as originally transmitted. The UDP checksum enables error detection while transporting data packets on a network. However, generation of checksum values is not mandatory in UDP. UDP is widely used in many network applications such as SNMP, TFTP, NFS, DNS, video-conferencing, Internet telephony, and other multimedia and streaming applications for its speed.

CHAPTER **8**

FILE TRANSFER AND ACCESS

In this chapter

INTRODUCTION TO FTP

Data exchange as a concept has existed right from the early days of humankind. The evolution of human languages and methods of communication, such as cave drawings, pictures, and the written script, stemmed from the need to exchange data. In the modern age, one of the popular means of data exchange is through computers connected to one another to form a network. In a network, the need for exchanging data has taken a number of diverse forms based on the requirements of a computer requesting data, called the client, and the capability of the computer providing that service, called the server. For example, the client might request a copy of the files stored on the server or might require a remote server-based bootstrap service. The client can also request the server to configure IP addresses for clients, name clients based on their IP address, and provide e-mail services, hypertext Web content transmission services, and client management services on a network.

These services provided by the server are implemented as applications on various operating systems. Any software that needs to connect and communicate with other computers uses the appropriate applications. In the TCP/IP reference model, these applications operate from the Application layer. This layer acts as the interface between the software installed on an operating system (OS) and the lower level protocols that implement data transmission tracking, routing, and physical transfer of data. Some of the Application layer protocols include

- File Transfer Protocol (FTP)
- Trivial File Transfer Protocol (TFTP)
- Network File System (NFS)
- Simple Mail Transfer Protocol (SMTP)
- Simple Network Management Protocol (SNMP)
- Hypertext Transfer Protocol (HTTP)
- Telnet
- Rlogin
- Domain Naming Service (DNS)
- Dynamic Host Configuration Protocol (DHCP)
- Bootstrap Protocol (BOOTP)

→ To learn more about SMTP, **see** "Messaging Concepts and SMTP," **p. 164**
→ To learn more about SNMP, **see** "Network Management," **p. 194**
→ To learn more about HTTP, **see** "Web Fundamentals and HTTP Basics," **p. 176**
→ To learn more about Telnet, **see** "Telnet Protocol," **p. 150**
→ To learn more about Rlogin, **see** "Rlogin," **p. 160**
→ To learn more about DNS, **see** "The Need for DNS," **p. 210**
→ To learn more about DHCP, **see** "Dynamic Host Configuration Protocol," **p. 236**
→ To learn more about BOOTP, **see** "Bootstrap Protocol—An Overview," **p. 230**

The file transfer services are implemented using the FTP, TFTP, and NFS Application layer protocols. Figure 8.1 shows the position of the Application layer from which FTP, TFTP, and NFS operate in the TCP/IP reference model.

Figure 8.1
File transfer and access are the most fundamental services provided by the Application layer.

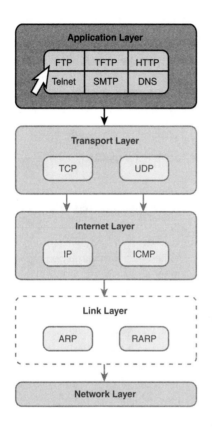

File access is a service that is essential in a number of internetworking environments. For example, a marketing manager might need to access files stored on a remote server that contain the sales figures of a particular division. The information stored on internetworks is not the only transferable material though. The network of networks that form internetworks is a storehouse of software and hardware resources, which can be shared by other computers on the internetwork. To use software resources, you must access and transfer the software installation files available on the various computers on the internetwork. To use shared hardware devices, such as printers, you need to install hardware device drivers before connecting to the hardware resources.

FTP is the primary specification used for implementing file transfer services. FTP specifies a protocol that can be used by software to share and transfer files between remote computers, implement safe file transfers by providing user authentication services, and implement a common file format between computers using varied file storage formats.

Note

A number of RFC contributions have been made for FTP starting from RFC 114, which provided the seed for implementing file transfer. RFC 114, proposed by Abhay Bhushan in 1971, was the result of a file transfer implementation on GE645/Multics and PDP-10/DM/CG-ITS computers at Massachusetts Institute of Technology (MIT). Over the next four years, a number of RFCs were raised to improve the original implementation. By 1975, all the existing RFCs related to file transfer on Macintosh machines were officially combined and released as RFC 686. Further revisions were introduced as RFCs 691 and 765. RFC 959 is the currently available specification on FTP. To learn more about the history of FTP and view the chronological details of its development, access
`http://www.ietf.org/rfc/rfc0959.txt?number=959`.

→ To learn more about the RFCs related to FTP, **see** "RFCs," **p. 425**

THE FILE TRANSFER PROCESS

FTP implementation is based on a command-execution model where two types of connections are established, one that "commands" the transfer of files and another that implements the actual transfer. This command-execution connection mechanism can be compared to the implementation of a military ceasefire. When two warring nations agree on peace, they sign a treaty to terminate the war and implement a ceasefire. However, to implement the ceasefire, the commands from the governments must be executed by the troops in the battlefield.

The command type of FTP connection is called the *control connection*. When a client wants to obtain files stored on a server, it initiates a request to establish a connection with the server. This request, also called an *active open* in TCP/IP terminology, is used to establish a connection with the server on port 21, which is the predefined port used to establish a control connection. The server, which is waiting for clients to initiate such connections, accepts the request and completes the connection establishment process.

After the control connection is established, the file transfer process can begin. However, it is the client that needs the files and the client who must open another connection, which executes the commands supplied by the control connection. This type of connection is called a *data connection*. After the client issues a file transfer command through the control connection, it waits for the server to send the required files. The server then initiates an active open for the data connection through the predefined port 20. The client receives the required files through a temporary port, also called ephemeral port, created for this purpose. Data connections are temporary connections that are created as and when a file transfer process is executed. Figure 8.2 shows how the files are transferred using FTP.

Note

In addition to the well-defined ports assigned for various applications, a client might need a temporary port to communicate with a server. Such ports created for a temporary need as and when required by the client are called *ephemeral ports*. The specifications for some of these ports, numbered between 1024 and 49151, are maintained by an organization called Internet Assigned Numbers Authority (IANA). Ports numbered between 1024 and 5000 can be used as temporary ports as and when required.

Figure 8.2
The client data connection port used to transfer files from the server is also called an ephemeral port due to its temporary nature.

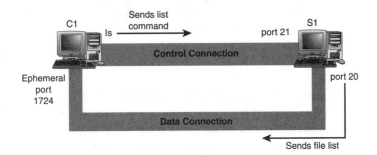

In Figure 8.2, the client C1 establishes a control connection to the server S1, which is listening on port 21 for such a request from clients. Next, it commands the server through the control connection to list the files on the server. In response, the client creates a list of files and sends the list to the client through the data connection. The server opens the connection through its port number 20. The client computer listens for the incoming file list through its ephemeral port.

FILE TRANSFER DATA FORMATS

In addition to the connections required for file transfer, the data format of the files transferred among computers is an important factor that must be taken into account while implementing FTP. For example, files can be transferred in NVT ASCII, EBCDIC, or binary formats. Files can be transferred in the form of streamed bytes, compressed data, or blocks. You can change the file structure to send files as records, pages, or bytes. In addition, you can also control the format of the transferred files.

By default, the *Network Virtual Terminal American Standard Code for Information Interchange ASCII (NVT ASCII)* format is used to transfer files. This format is an ASCII format type that is defined in the Telnet specification. This data format requires the implementation of a translator on the client and the server. This translator converts data contained in the transferred files to the local file formats used in the connected computers.

The Extended Binary-Coded Decimal Interchange Code (EBCDIC) file format is an ASCII-like specification that is implemented on IBM computers for transferring files. The client and the server involved in file transfer must use this file format specification. Binary file formats are used in file transfer when the client needs to transfer binary files from the server. It is possible that the size of a binary file stored on the client and the server are different. For example, the binary file size on the server can be larger than the binary file sizes on the client. In such cases, the server must specify the file size before sending the files over the network.

Note

A method of representing the alphabets in English with numbers ranging from 0 to 127 is called *ASCII*, in short for American Standard Code for Information Interchange. The ASCII code corresponding to each character is allocated 7 bits of memory. This method allows keystrokes to be translated into binary data before being stored in text files or transferred between computers. The extended ASCII format used by DOS and the NVT ASCII format used by Telnet are the variants of ASCII. The standard format for ASCII is ISO Latin 1.

If a large file is transferred over a traffic-clogged network, it might result in data loss and increased network traffic. This is because an intermediate device, which is unable to accommodate additional packets due to an overflowing buffer, might discard large files. Moreover, large file sizes might result in fragmentation of the IP datagram, which increases the possibility of data loss. Fragmentation, in turn, increases network traffic. To avoid data loss, you can transfer files in a compressed format.

Another data transfer mode specified by FTP is the block mode in which the file is transferred as blocks of data. Each block of data contains a header part that specifies the length of the block and describes the data contained in the block. The description is used to identify the last block to be received, identify potentially damaged data blocks, or reset markers to indicate that the block needs to be retransmitted. You can also transfer files as a stream of bytes. This transmission mode is called *stream mode*, where a file is transferred in the form of contiguous bytes.

The structure of files being transferred also varies depending on the file format. For example, text files are structured in the form of records with each line of data in the text file forming a record. Files can be transferred in the form of pages as well, with each page numbered sequentially to arrange the file in the correct sequence of pages when the client receives a page of the file. Binary files are structured in the most basic binary data format.

To control the display of transferred text files on the client computer, you can transfer files with certain settings. For example, to control printer output, you can set the Telnet format control settings. This setting ensures that the contents are printed line by line because of the carriage return and line feed options provided by the Telnet protocol. By default, carriage return or line feed settings are ignored while printing data contained in a text file. You can also set FORTRAN language type carriage returns for your text where the first character of a line being displayed or printed is a special character. This character instructs the printer or display device to indicate that the characters that follow must be displayed or printed in a new line.

CH
8

FILE TRANSFER COMMANDS

FTP commands are the prime "movers" in the file transfer service specified by FTP. These commands are used to log on to the FTP server, browse through the contents of the server's shared file structure, obtain a list of files available on the server, and manage the transfer of files to and from the server. A multitude of FTP commands are used on operating systems, such as Unix or Windows. Table 8.1 describes the features provided by some of the common commands used with the ftp command line utility provided by Windows.

TABLE 8.1   COMMONLY USED FTP COMMANDS

Command	Description
USER *username*	Implements user authentication after a control connection has been established. This command is also used to log on with a different username by resetting the current user account information.
PASS *password*	Supplies the password for the username provided as parameter for the USER command.
open *computer name/ IP address port*	Establishes a connection with an FTP server. The *computer name* parameter can be the human readable name assigned to the computer or an IP address. The client port on which the connection is being initiated can also be supplied as a parameter, although this parameter is optional. The open command automatically initiates the USER and the PASS commands to start the user authentication process after a connection is established.
ls *dirname filename*	Lists the files available in the directory on the remote server. The directory name is specified using the *dirname* parameter. If you do not want the files to be listed on the client computer's monitor, the output can be redirected to a file by using the *filename* parameter.
dir *dirname filename*	Lists the files available in the directory on the remote server. The directory name is specified using the *dirname* parameter. This command is similar to the ls command but provides detailed information on the listed files. The details include permission settings, time of creation, and size. The output provided by this command can be redirected to a file, which is indicated by the *filename* parameter, if you do not want the files to be displayed on the client computer's monitor.
cd *dirname*	Changes the current working directory on the server to the directory name indicated by the *dirname* parameter.
mkdir *dirname*	Creates a new directory on the server. The term *mkdir* indicates that a "make directory" operation can be performed using this command. The directory name is indicated by the *dirname* parameter that must be specified with the command. To use this command, you must have directory creation permissions on the server.

TABLE 8.1   CONTINUED

Command	Description
rmdir *dirname*	Deletes an existing directory on the server. The term *rmdir* indicates that a "remove directory" action can be performed by using this command. The directory to be deleted is indicated by the *dirname* parameter. To use this command, you must have directory deletion permissions on the server.
get *remotefilename* *localfilename*	Copies a file on the server to a location on the hard disk of the client. The path to the remote file is specified using the *remotefilename* parameter. The path to the location where the file is to be stored on the client is specified using the *localfilename* parameter.
put *localfilename* *remotefilename*	Copies a file that is on the client hard disk and store it in a directory located on the server. The path to the local file is indicated by the *localfilename* parameter. The directory on the server where the local file must be copied is indicated by the *remotefilename* parameter.
mget *remotefilename1* *remotefilename2* *localdirname*	Copies multiple files that are located on the server into a directory on the client hard disk. The term *mget* indicates that this command can be used to perform a "multiple get" operation. This command is similar to the get command but transfers multiple files. The files on the remote server must be specified consecutively, without any delimiters such as commas. However, you must provide spaces between the file names. The directory name on the client hard disk where the files must be copied is indicated by the *localdirname* parameter.
mput *localfilename1* *localfilename2* *remotedirname*	Transfers multiple files located on the client to a directory located on the server. The term *mput* indicates that a "multiple put" operation can be performed. This command is similar to the put command. However, unlike the put command, this command enables you to transfer multiple files from the client to the server. The local filenames must be specified consecutively without any delimiters followed by the server directory name where the files must be copied.
close	Terminates the control connection established with the server.
bye	Closes the ftp utility and returns to the command prompt.

After the server processes a command, a response is sent to the client and includes a number code (also called *FTP reply code*), a human readable message in the form of a string of characters that describes the success or failure of the command, and the output of the command if the command is executed successfully. The FTP software on the client computer uses the FTP reply code to display user-friendly status messages describing file transfer processes. Sometimes, the user might directly use the commands from the command prompt instead of using FTP software. In such cases, the human readable message, provided as part of the response, would be enough to denote the status of the file transfer process. The number 200 indicates that the command was successfully executed. The number code is a three-digit number. The first and the second digits indicate the meaning of the number code displayed on the client's terminal. The following list describes the possible meaning of the FTP reply code when a specific number occurs as the first or second digit.

Note

The characters *x*, *y*, and *z* in the number codes provided in the list can be replaced by any number that can be combined with the first or second digit.

- 1yz—Indicates that a response to the command is successfully initiated. However, this does not mean that the command was completely successful. You can expect another reply indicating the status of the command.
- 2yz—Indicates that the command was successfully executed. This reply is followed by the result of the command.
- 3yz—Indicates that the command was processed but requires another command to successfully complete the client request.
- 4yz—Indicates that an error occurred while executing the command. However, this error is temporary. This number code also means that the client can specify this command once again.
- 5yz—Indicates that the server failed to execute the command.
- x0z—Indicates that the client specified a syntactically erroneous command.
- x1z—Indicates that the server is responding with a message intended for the user of the client software.
- x2z—Indicates that the response is related to the status of the data connection or control connection that exists between the client and the server.
- x3z—Indicates that the response contains user account information. Typically, reply codes with 3 as the second digit relate to responses for user login or user account–related commands.
- x4z—Reply code of this type has not been used as of yet.
- x5z—Indicates the status of the file system on the server in response to any client command that deals with the server file system. For example, the server responds with the number 250 if the cd command, which deals with the file system on the server, is successful.

Note

Each operating system uses a particular format for organizing and maintaining files. This organizational structure defines the method of storing files, directories, and subdirectories in an OS. Such an organizational structure is called a *file system*. An example of a file system is the hierarchical file system where files are stored in directories and subdirectories positioned as nodes and branches of a tree structure.

Table 8.2 describes a few FTP reply codes and highlights the significance of the occurrence of numbers as the first and second digits in the codes.

TABLE 8.2   FTP REPLY CODES

Reply Code	Description
125	Indicates that a data connection already exists and the connection can be used to continue data transmission.
200	Indicates that the command was successfully executed.
331	Indicates that the username provided by the client is valid and that the password needs to be specified by the client.
425	Indicates that the server is unable to open a data connection. The client can issue the command once again for the server to attempt opening the data connection.
530	Indicates that the client has not established a control connection with the server.
500	Indicates that there are syntactical errors in the command issued by the client.
213	Indicates that the response contains information on the status of the file or files being transferred from the server.
225	Indicates that a data connection is established. The reply code also indicates that there are no file transfer operations currently in progress.
332	Indicates that a user account is required for logging on to the server.
452	Indicates that the command issued by the client was not executed due to nonavailability of file space on the client or server.

In a typical file transfer operation between a client and a server, the client logs on to the server, changes the current working directory on the server, retrieves files, and transfers them. Figures 8.3, 8.4, and 8.5 show you how you can use ftp commands to log on and transfer files from an FTP server.

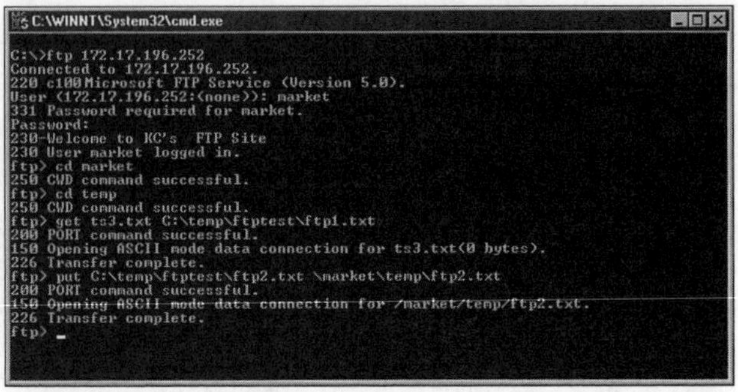

Figure 8.3
The user named market logs on to the FTP server and retrieves a file from the server and transfers another to the server.

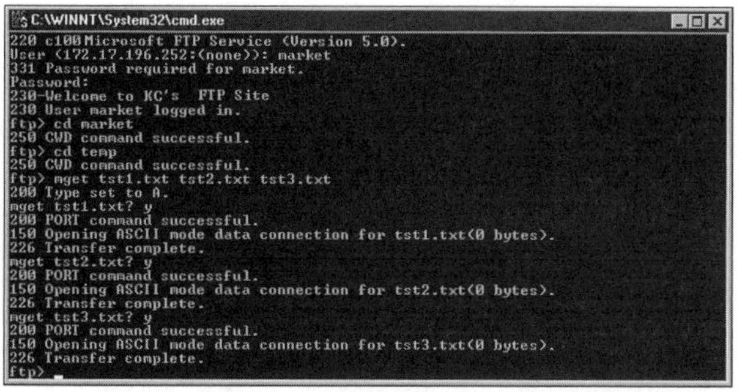

Figure 8.4
Multiple files are transferred to the local hard disk from the server.

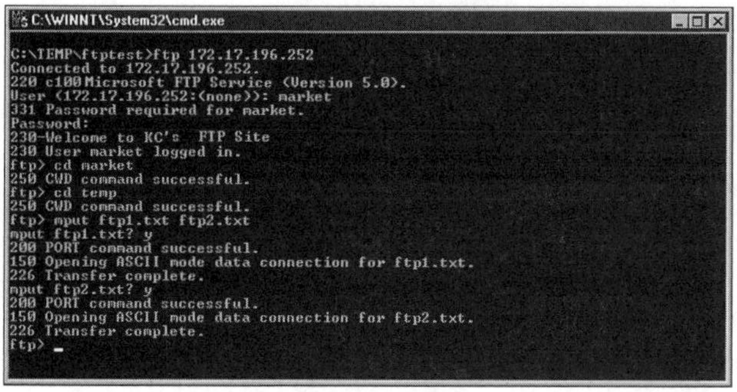

Figure 8.5
Multiple files are transferred to the FTP server from the local directory.

Some FTP sites allow you to log on with a generic user account and password. You can use these sites to perform file transfer operations called *anonymous FTP* where the user account you specify is **anonymous**. However, you must specify a valid e-mail address as the password for the anonymous account (see Figure 8.6).

Figure 8.6
The e-mail address entered as the password must be a complete e-mail address following the emailname@mail serviceprovider. com notation.

Some sites allow you to log on if you type the password **guest**. Anonymous logins provide restricted access to the files on the server. For example, you cannot create a new directory on the server with an anonymous login. Figure 8.7 shows you how permissions are restricted for an anonymous login.

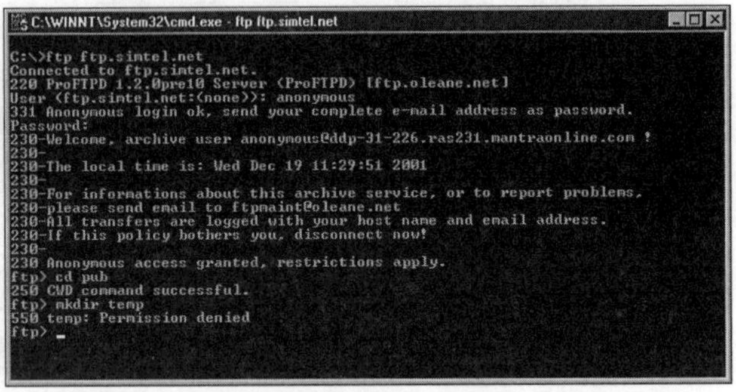

Figure 8.7

A Permission denied response is displayed when the client issues an mkdir command to create a directory named temp on the server because guest users are restricted by the site administrator from creating directories.

TRIVIAL FILE TRANSFER

Computers, network devices, or peripheral devices, such as printers, might need to transfer small files without establishing control or data connections as implemented by FTP. For example, hardware devices, such as printers, hubs, or switches, might need to download firmware information from the server at the time of starting the device. Diskless computers might need to download bootstrap system files from a server. In such situations, a simple file transfer protocol that is implemented on the connectionless UDP protocol is the best choice. Trivial File Transfer Protocol (TFTP) provides such a simple file transfer mechanism.

Note

The TFTP specification was first proposed and designed in an RFC contributed by Noel Chiappa and was revised by a number of others, such as Bob Baldwin, Dave Clark, and Steve Szymanski. In addition, a revision necessitated by a bug in the implementation called the Sorcerer's Apprentice bug was adopted from the conclusions of research conducted by Advanced Research Projects Agency (ARPA). Currently, the official specification on TFTP is available in RFC 1350.

Before studying the actual implementation of the protocol, it is important to understand the structure of a TFTP packet, which is the basic data unit transferred using the protocol. A TFTP packet can be classified in five different ways based on its structure, which depends on the nature of the data transferred. The first two types of packets are a read request and a write request packet. Read request or write request packets form the initial packets to be sent in a stream of consecutive packets. A *read request packet* is sent to the server when the client needs to download files from the server. A *write request packet* is sent to the server when the client needs to transfer files to the server. The third type of packet, also called *data packet*, holds the actual data that is required by the client computer or device. The connected devices also exchange *acknowledgement packets*, which is the fourth type of packet. To indicate the occurrence of an error, the fifth packet type called an *error packet* can be exchanged between the devices.

All packet types have an Opcode field that contains a number value indicating the nature of the packet. For example, the number code of 0 indicates that the packet is a read request packet. Request packets also contain fields to describe the filename and the mode of transmission. Data packets contain an additional field called Block number that uniquely identifies a packet by specifying a block number. In addition to the Block number field, data packets contain the Data field that store the required data being transmitted. An acknowledgement packet also contains a Block number field to indicate that a particular data packet with the same block number is acknowledged. The Opcode field in an acknowledgement packet indicates the nature of the packet. Error message packets contain an ErrorCode field and an ErrorMessage field in addition to the Opcode field. Figure 8.8 shows the structure of the different types of TFTP packets.

Figure 8.8
Different types of TFTP packets are used during the process of file transfer.

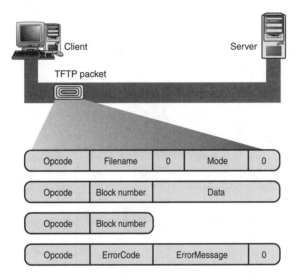

The file transfer process implemented in TFTP is a very simple process. Initially, a read or write request packet is sent by a client device to the server to indicate that the client needs to read or write a particular file. Next, the actual data transfer process is implemented by exchanging data packets. Each packet is acknowledged on receipt. The timers on the server and the client control the retransmission of packets if the acknowledgement for a packet does not arrive within a specified period of time. If errors occur during file transfer, an error message is communicated through the error message packet.

PROBLEMS IN THE TFTP SPECIFICATION

Although the file transfer process is a simple implementation, complications arise when duplicate data packets and acknowledgements are retransmitted due to a delay in acknowledgements. For example, if an acknowledgement from a client is delayed, the server retransmits a duplicate packet. In addition, the client retransmits another acknowledgement for the previous packet if the next packet to be received does not arrive within its timer specified limit because it is possible that the acknowledgement previously sent did not reach the server. Now, the duplicate packet sent by the server is also acknowledged by the client resulting in the receipt of two acknowledgements by the server. For each acknowledgement received by the server, it transmits the next packet twice and starts a cycle of incremental duplicate packet transmission. This implementation bug, called the *Sorcerer's Apprentice* bug, can be solved by turning off the timer mechanism on the client to ensure that the retransmission does not occur if acknowledgements are delayed. Figure 8.9 shows you how the Sorcerer's Apprentice bug occurs.

Figure 8.9
The Sorcerer's Apprentice bug was resolved from the findings of a research conducted by ARPA under the supervision of the Office of Naval Research.

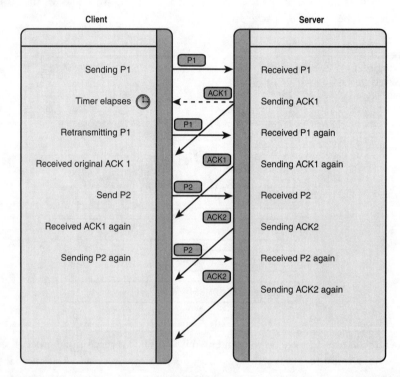

In addition to this bug, security issues are a major concern of TFTP implementation. User authentication or passwords are not provided in TFTP because of its simple implementation process. If the information being stored on a TFTP server contains sensitive data, such as company account numbers or passwords for accessing important files, the possibility of security leaks is high. To avoid security problems, ensure that files related to bootstrap processes or firmware information alone is stored on servers. Other files that contain restricted information must not be transferred using TFTP.

NETWORK FILE ACCESS

In a world where diverse operating systems, file systems, and standards and specifications have become common, a standard file access mechanism is essential for sharing and transferring files between computers on an internetwork. Network File System (NFS) protocol is one such common file access mechanism provided by Sun Microsystems, Inc. NFS provides specifications for implementing a seamless environment where computers operating on varied operating systems can access files. The official specification for this protocol is available in RFC 1094. NFS version 3, which aims at implementing a Web-based file access mechanism, is proposed in RFC 1813.

NFS was primarily implemented to establish connectivity between computers running on Unix OS and other operating systems such as mainframes or Windows. NFS is built on a number of component protocols, such as NFS core protocol, External Data Representation (XDR), and Remote Procedure Calls (RPC).

When a computer needs to access the files on another machine, it uses the NFS client to send a request in the form of an RPC data packet contained in a TCP segment or UDP datagram. An *RPC packet* is the data unit provided by an NFS application to the Transport layer protocols. Before packaging the request into the RPC packet, the client obtains a port for communicating with the remote computer through a request to the server. Next, the data format of the request is converted by XDR to standardize the request data into a format compatible for transmission.

On the server side, the reverse of this process is implemented. The request is reformatted to a format compatible with the data format implemented on the server. Next, the NFS server locates the required file on the hard disk of the server and returns a file handle to the file system on the server. The client uses this file handle to access the files on the server. When a user tries to access a file on a remote computer running on a different operating system, the underlying NFS implementation is invisible and the user is able to access and use the remote file as though it were located on the local hard disk. Figure 8.10 shows an implementation of the NFS specification.

> **Note**
>
> A *file handle* is an opaque software object that represents the file system on the server.

NFS CORE PROTOCOLS

In the process of providing file access, the Mount protocol plays a very important role along with other NFS components, such as port mapper and file handle. The *Mount protocol* functions as a management mechanism that uses the port mapper and the file handle to access a remote computer's file system. Port mapper is a port registration mechanism that enables the server to register its ephemeral ports. This registration process is essential to allow the access of the server file system from the client computer.

Figure 8.10
A typical implementation of NFS can be described as file access provided by a Windows client to the files on computers running Unix.

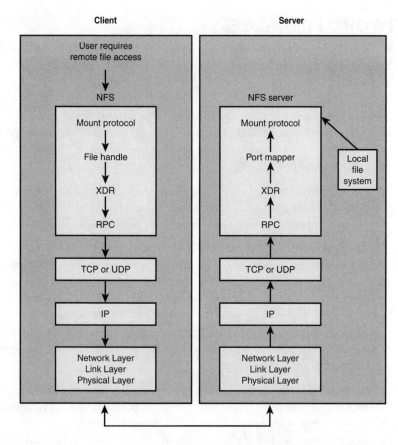

The file handle can be described as a pointer used by the client to access the remote server file system. The handle represents the file system of the server on the client computer. The Mount protocol on the client computer obtains the server port number and the server file handle to gain access to the server file system. This process is a simple transaction implemented using UDP.

The port mapper on the server registers a port on the server that must be used for file access. When the user on the client computer needs to access a file on the remote computer, the NFS's Mount protocol requests a port number to the server to obtain the port number registered on the server. The server responds by sending the port number to the requesting client. Next, the client Mount protocol requests a file handle that will be used as a representation of the server file system. When the server returns the file handle, the client begins accessing files through the port by using the file handle. Figure 8.11 shows how the Mount protocol uses the port mapper and file handle to access remote files.

Figure 8.11
Mount protocol gains access to the remote server file system by using the port mapper and file handle.

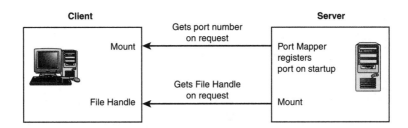

Before beginning the actual process of file transfer, the data formats in the connected computers need to be taken into account. To manage diverse data formats, XDR provided by NFS converts the data exchanged between the computers. XDR converts data into a standard format before transmitting it over the network. XDR on the respective computers ensure the conversion of incoming data into a format compatible with the local file system.

REMOTE PROCEDURE CALLS

The actual process of file access is implemented through a specification of Sun Microsystems, Inc. called Remote Procedure Calls (RPC). When a client needs to access a remote file through the file handler, an RPC program, called the stub, packages the client request into an RPC packet and transfers the package to the Transport layer protocol, which could be TCP or UDP. On the server side, another stub unpacks the message and redirects the contents to the NFS server application, which acquires the required results and supplies it to the server stub. Now, the server stub packages the results into a reply RPC message and transmits it over the network through a Transport layer protocol. The client stub receives the packaged reply message, unpacks the message, and redirects it to the requesting client application.

The RPC message forms the crux around which the elaborate NFS framework is built. There are two types of RPC messages, an RPC reply and request message. An RPC request message contains fields, such as `transaction ID`, `program number`, and `version number`. Table 8.3 describes each field in detail.

TABLE 8.3   FIELDS IN AN RPC REQUEST MESSAGE

Fields	Description
Transaction ID	Specifies an identifier that uniquely identifies the request and reply messages exchanged between the client and the server. The request and reply RPC messages have identical transaction IDs.
Call	Indicates whether the message is a request or a reply.
RPC version	Authenticates the client and is used by the server to determine whether it can proceed with the execution of the reply for the request.
Program number	Indicates the program that must be called to search for the required data.

CH
8

TABLE 8.3 CONTINUED

Fields	Description
Version number	Indicates the version of the program that must be called to search for the required data.
Procedure number	Indicates the procedure that must be called to launch the data search program.
Credentials	Specifies the version of RPC being used for file access. Currently, RPC version 2 is used for this process.
Verifier	Used to add security features such as encryption to scramble the data sent over the network.
Procedure Parameters	Specifies the actual request data sent to the server.

The reply RPC message contains only a few fields. Fields such as transaction ID and verifier implement similar features as in the request message. The other fields included in the reply message are reply, status, accept status, and procedure results. The reply field indicates that the message is an RPC reply message. The status field with a value 0 indicates that the server has accepted the request sent by the client. The accept status field also indicates the success of the request sent to the server. The results that are to be transmitted to the client are contained in the procedure results field of the reply RPC message. Figure 8.12 shows the structure of the request and reply RPC messages.

Figure 8.12
RPC is now being implemented in a number of operating systems such as Windows NT and Linux.

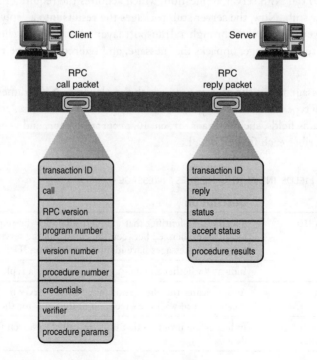

SUMMARY

File transfer and access has become one of the fundamental requirements of internetworking. The Application layer of the TCP/IP reference model provides three protocols to implement file transfer and access: FTP, TFTP, and NFS.

FTP can be described as the primary Application layer protocol being implemented for file transfer. FTP provides user authentication services in addition to its file transfer features. TFTP is typically used in scenarios where a small number of files need to be transferred without any user authentication or security. File access across disparate operating systems is possible by using NFS. This protocol uses its core component protocols, such as Mount protocol, port mapper, and file handle, to establish a connection between the file systems of the connected computers. Remote Procedure Calls are used to manage the actual file access process. XDR is specified as part of the NSF specification to standardize data formats being used between the client and the server during file access.

CHAPTER

REMOTE LOGIN

In this chapter

TELNET PROTOCOL

A number of breakthroughs that contributed to the development of e-mail, file transfer, and remote file access were developed during the early days of the IT industry. One such "ancient" application is the Telecommunications Network (Telnet) protocol, initially developed by the Advanced Research Projects Agent (ARPA), which was established in 1956 by the US Department of Defense (DOD) to conduct scientific and technological research. ARPA established a link between four computers located in four different universities across America, thereby creating a primitive network called the ARPAnet. This primitive network, linking computers in the University of Utah, the Stanford Research Institute, University of California, Los Angeles, and the University of California, Santa Barbara, was the predecessor of the Internet that we use nowadays.

One of the original aims of ARPAnet was to use the software and hardware resources available on remote computers. Telnet was created to achieve this goal. When a user logs on to another computer using Telnet, a terminal that represents the remote computer is displayed on the user's computer. Now, the user can create and store files on the remote computer or use other peripheral services provided by the remote computer. In effect, the remote computer acts as a server that manages all resource requirements of the Telnet users on a network. This type of centralized computing environment is called a *time-sharing environment* where a single server manages the processing requirements of a number of user computers on a network.

Note

Time-sharing environment was the dominant network management system in many networks before the advent of Windows NT server's load-sharing environment that provided services, such as user authentication and permission. Although the load-sharing environment did not take care of managing the processing requirements of every user computer on the network, it successfully replaced the time-sharing environment as the primary network management system in use in many networks nowadays.

Telnet was first implemented by a Massachusetts-based company called Bolt, Beranek, and Newman (BB&N) in 1974 and was documented as a specification in the RFC 764 contributed by John Postel. The specification was further improved on by RFC 854 and is currently defined by RFC 855. Although the use of Telnet has declined over the years, it is still used as a remote login facility to access library catalogs, databases on legacy systems, and to use software for implementing e-mail or any other service provided by remote computers.

Some of the most important applications that implement services, such as connectivity, data exchange, and file transfer are provided by the various application protocols in the Application layer of the TCP/IP reference model. One such feature provided by the Application layer is remote login, which is specified by the Telnet and Rlogin protocols. Figure 9.1 indicates the position of the layer from which Telnet and Rlogin operate in the TCP/IP reference model.

Figure 9.1
Although both Telnet and Rlogin are remote login services operating from the same layer, Rlogin provides simple remote login implementation, whereas Telnet provides greater interoperability between computers implementing diverse Telnet implementations.

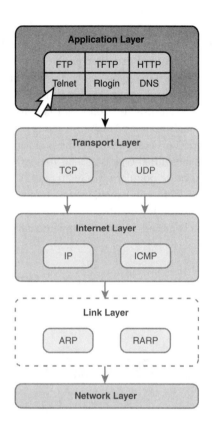

TYPICAL TELNET PROTOCOL IMPLEMENTATION

By definition, remote login is a mechanism for providing an environment where the characters typed at the user's computer (the Telnet client) are processed by the remote computer (the Telnet server) and output is displayed on the user's console. The characters are sent back to the client where it is displayed. Sometimes, the user might also be required to enter commands that are to be executed by the software on the Telnet server. The output of these commands is also displayed on the client console. Multiple users can access the server and use its resources. The server is responsible for managing the requests from multiple users by providing a separate program thread for each user.

> **Note**
>
> A *thread* is a unit of program code in an application that is independent of the program code in the rest of the application. An application can implement any number of threads to manage multiple independent requirements.

The Telnet protocol implements such an environment by using a Telnet client software and a Telnet server software, in addition to the terminal drivers that emulate the client and server terminals. Terminals can be classified into various types based on their processing capabilities. For example, the intelligent terminal type can perform special display operations such as support for high-resolution graphics images. Smart terminals are terminals with limited processing capabilities that can provide support for cursors and darker character displays like boldface. Dumb terminals do not possess processing capability and are totally controlled by the local computer's processor. One of the popular terminal implementations is the vt100 terminal type. This terminal type is used as the default type for terminal emulation software, such as Telnet. Another popular terminal type is ANSI, defined by the American National Standards Institute. Before moving ahead with our learning on the process of communication implemented on Telnet, observe Figure 9.2, which shows how the process of communication between a client and a server is implemented by using the Telnet protocol.

Figure 9.2
A Telnet implementation creates the illusion of working with software on the local computer for a user, whereas the actual processes take place on the remote Telnet server.

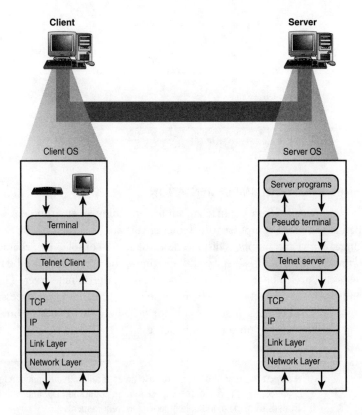

Note

To enable a user to work with the software and the hardware resources on a computer, software called the *terminal driver* manages the keyboard and hardware device drivers that control monitor display.

The Telnet client software is responsible for converting user input into a standardized character format called Network Virtual Terminal ASCII (NVT). The Telnet server software located on the remote computer converts the incoming NVT characters into a format compatible with the character set supported on the remote computer.

When a user presses any keys or enters commands on the client computer, the keystrokes are directed to the Telnet client software by the terminal driver. The Telnet client software translates the keystrokes into NVT ASCII character set before directing the data containing the characters to the underlying protocols. The need for standardizing the characters arises from the fact that the operating systems installed on the client and the server can use different character sets for transmitting data. For example, DOS-based computers use the extended ASCII character set, whereas Unix-based computers might use the ISO Latin 1 ASCII character set to process and display data. Therefore, the NVT ASCII character set is adopted as the common ASCII format used for transmitting data.

CH
9

The data is first packaged within a TCP datagram and then within an IP packet and finally within a frame. The frame is then transferred over the network to the target computer. After reaching the destination computer, the characters are extracted from the frame-IP-TCP encapsulation and then directed to the Telnet server software. Now, the Telnet server software translates the data from the NVT ASCII character set to a format that is compatible with the character set used by the server. Next, the characters are directed to the terminal driver on the server. This is because the OS on the server cannot process the characters unless a terminal driver issues the characters. This terminal driver is called the *pseudoterminal driver*. Now the psuedoterminal driver redirects the characters to the appropriate hardware or software on the server OS.

Every keystroke entered by the user is processed by the server and also redirected or "echoed" back to the client computer through the same route taken to send the keystrokes to the server. A single connection is used to transmit the packets between the client and the server. However, the need for establishing a half-duplex or a full-duplex connection depends on the mode of data transmission that is being implemented between the client and the server. For example, the client and the server can establish a character-by-character data transmission and echo or choose to transmit and echo data line-by-line.

In addition to data, certain commands are exchanged between the client and the server. These commands control the data transmission between the connected computers and also help in the process of establishing a mutually acceptable mode of transmission between the client and the server. This process is called *option negotiation*. The various modes of data transmission include half duplex, character, kludge line, and real line modes. You will learn more about these modes in the section "Telnet Modes" later in this chapter.

TELNET COMMANDS

After the TCP connection is established between the client and the server, a number of instructions are exchanged between the client and the server in the form of packets. The connected computers use these instruction packets to establish certain ground rules for communication based on the features they support. For example, the client might decide to display all the characters typed by the user before transmitting the characters to the server. In this case, the client and the server must instruct each other that the echo feature must be turned off on the server. Such instructions are called *Telnet commands*. Depending on the communication needs of the client or the server, both computers can use most of these commands. Each command is supplied by the client or the server as a code number. This code number is the decimal representation of its binary equivalent, which is the actual form in which the command is transmitted. Table 9.1 provides a description of the various commands exchanged between the client and the server.

TABLE 9.1   COMMON TELNET COMMANDS

Commands	Description
EOF (End of File)	Indicates that the end of the file being transmitted to the destination computer is reached. When the data contained in a file is transmitted over Telnet, this command is sent as the last packet after the data contained in the file has been completely transmitted. The code number of this command is 236.
EOR (End of Record)	Indicates that the last line of a file has been transmitted. If the contents of a file are being transmitted line by line, after the last line in the file has been transmitted, this packet is sent to indicate the completion of the transmission. The code number of the command is 239.
SUSP (Suspend Current Process)	Indicates that the client is instructing the server to suspend the operation currently being performed by the server. Code number 237 represents this command.
BRK (Break)	Indicates a break in data transmission. The code number 243 represents the command.
IP (Interrupt Process)	Indicates that the client wants to abort a program running on the server. For example, if the remote program launched by the client over a Telnet connection crashes, the user will be unable to obtain any output or response from the remote program. The only possible action that can be taken by the user is to terminate the program. If the user uses the Ctrl+C key combination, which terminates the server program, the keystrokes are converted into the code number 244. This number code represents the IP command. When this command reaches the server, it terminates the malfunctioning server program.
AO (Abort Output)	Indicates that the output provided by the server program must be disabled. For example, if a client program needs to verify whether a server program is currently running, all that the client needs to do is check for the exit code provided by the server program when it is terminated. The client does not require the output provided by the server program. Here, the client can send the AO command to disable output from the server program and obtain the exit code alone when the server program is terminated. The code number 245 represents the AO command.

TABLE 9.1   CONTINUED

Commands	Description
NOP (No Operation)	Indicates a blank command, which does not contain or signify any instruction to the client or the server. The command has a code number 241.
AYT (Are You There)	Indicates a command from the client to the server to verify whether the server is still running. The response to the AYT command is provided by the server in the form of a visible or audible reply if it is still running. The code number 246 represents this command.
GA (Go Ahead)	Represents an instruction to the client from the server to allow user input. When the server has processed a line of data contained in a packet received from the client, the server allows the client to accept user input by sending the GA command. The code number 249 represents this command.
EC (Escape Character)	Indicates an instruction to the server that the character preceding this command is not to be transmitted to the server and must be erased. For example, to delete a character that has been entered by mistake, the user might need to use the Backspace key. To indicate that the user has pressed the Backspace key the EC command is sent by the client to the server. This command is represented by the code number 247.
EL (Erase Line)	Indicates to the server that the line being processed by the server must be erased. This command is represented by the code number 248.
DM (Data Mark)	Indicates that the server must ignore all the packets containing characters received by the server before receiving the packet containing this command. Only subsequent packets containing commands must be processed and the data packets must be ignored. Data Mark commands are used in circumstances where the client needs to instruct the server to terminate a crashed server program. For example, when a server program malfunctions, the server is unable to process the commands being received from the client. The incoming data packets fill up the server buffer, which results in the server advertising a zero sized window. Now, the client is not able to send any data packets nor is it able to terminate the server program by sending an IP command. To resolve this situation, a TCP datagram set with the Urgent bit is sent to the server. The Urgent bit ensures that the subsequent packets containing commands are processed immediately without being discarded by the flow control mechanisms, such as Nagle's Algorithm or delayed acknowledgement, on the server. Packets containing data are ignored. The packet containing the IP command is processed immediately, thereby terminating the crashed server program. Next, when the packet containing the DM command is received, the server switches back to the normal mode where data packets are also processed. The DM command is represented by the code number 242 and is also called a *synch signal*.

CH
9

TABLE 9.1 CONTINUED	
Commands	**Description**
IAC (Interpret As Command)	Indicates that the data following this command must be interpreted as commands. For example, this command is used when the user types a set of characters and then presses Backspace to delete a character before typing the correct character. When the user presses the Backspace key, the EC command is generated. However, to distinguish the EC command from the set of characters, the IAC command is sent before the EC command to instruct the server that the data in the packet received after the IAC command must be interpreted as a command and not as data. However, the data contained in the subsequent packets will not be interpreted as commands. The code number 255 represents the IAC command.
WILL option	Indicates to the destination computer (server or client) receiving this command that the request to enable the option, specified by the option parameter, is accepted. The WILL command can also be used to indicate that the computer sending the command is offering to enable an option. For example, if the client requests the server to enable the ECHO option and if the server accepts the request, the server responds to the client request by replying with the WILL command. The command is used to negotiate option settings between the client and the server after establishing a preliminary TCP connection. The code number 251 represents this command.
WONT option	Indicates to the destination computer that the request to enable the option, specified by the option parameter, is refused. The WONT command can also be used to indicate the acceptance of a request from another computer to disable an option. If a computer needs to indicate that it offers to disable an option, it can use the WONT command. The WONT command is used in the process of option negotiation between a client and a server. The code number 252 represents this command.
DO option	Indicates that a request sent by a computer for enabling the option, specified by the option parameter, is accepted by the receiving computer. In addition, if the sending computer offers to enable a particular option, the computer receiving this offer can indicate its acceptance of the offer by using the DO command. This command is represented by the code number 253 and is used during the process of option negotiation to establish the options that are to be used for communicating between a client and a server.
DONT option	Indicates that a request to enable the option, specified by the option parameter, is refused by the receiving computer. The receiving computer can also use this command to accept an offer from the sending computer to disable a particular option. The receiving computer can also make a request to

TABLE 9.1   CONTINUED

Commands	Description
	disable an option on the sending computer by using the DONT command. The client and the server use this command during the process of option negotiation.
SB (Suboption Begin) and SE (Suboption End)	Indicate that the commands specified between these commands form the suboptions for an option enabled on the sending computer. A typical example for describing an option with suboptions is the TERMINAL TYPE option. If the client accepts a request from the server to send its terminal type after enabling this Telnet option, the client responds with a set of characters providing the name of the terminal type. These characters form the suboption for the TERMINAL TYPE option. To distinguish between the option and the suboptions, the characters indicating the name of the terminal type is specified between the SB and SE commands.

Сн
9

Note

In addition to the output in the form of data, some application programs return a number value to indicate the reason or meaning of the output. These number values are called *exit codes*. For example, a program that returns data stored on another computer based on a request also returns an exit code that indicates the success or failure of the operation.

→ To learn more about flow control mechanisms and window size, **see** "Data Transfer Concepts," **p. 93**

Note

Options are certain features provided by the client and the server to control the communication between the computers. Commands such as WILL, WONT, DO, and DONT are used to enable or disable these options. You will learn more about options in the section "Telnet Options."

Note

Some options have suboptions, which are sent only on request after the option is enabled. Suboptions can be described as the information required to describe an option. After the receiving computer gets a request, the requesting computer sends the suboptions.

TELNET MODES

When a user enters characters on the client computer, the characters are transmitted to the server in many different modes although the user does not realize these backend operations.

For example, the default mode of data transmission is called half-duplex mode. In this mode, the client displays the characters typed by the user before transmitting the characters to the server. However, before accepting any further user input, the client waits for a GA command from the server. Data or commands are not exchanged simultaneously over the connection. A half-duplex connection is enough to implement this transmission mode. However, most Telnet implementations run over full-duplex connections, which results in the underutilization of resources when this mode is implemented. Therefore, the half-duplex mode is rarely used nowadays.

→ To learn more about full-duplex and half-duplex connections, **see** "Services Provided by TCP," **p. 75**

When user input is transmitted character-by-character and then echoed back by the server to be displayed on the client, the transmission mode used is called *Character* mode. The client must respond to the echoed character by acknowledging the receipt of the echo. The SUPRESS GO AHEAD option on the server must be enabled to prevent the GA command from being transmitted from the server. This is done to ensure that the client waits for an echoed character from the server instead of displaying the character immediately after the user types them on the client. In addition, the ECHO option must be enabled on the server to enable the reflection of each character received by the server. On slow networks, the character-by-character transmission followed by a character-by-character echo followed by an acknowledgement for each echo will result in a lot of transmission problems, such as data loss, delayed acknowledgement, and underutilization of resources.

To overcome the problems posed by the half-duplex mode and the character mode, the *kludge line* mode was adopted. In this mode, the client displays a line entered by the user before transmitting the line to the server. However, unlike in the half-duplex mode, the client does not wait for the GA command before accepting user input. Instead, the client continues to accept user input and transmits data, line by line. To implement the kludge line mode, either the SUPRESS GO AHEAD option or the ECHO option must be disabled on the server. This is to ensure that the client displays user input before being sent to the server.

TELNET OPTIONS

One of the earliest communications that takes place between a client and a server after establishing a TCP connection is the exchange of packets to agree on certain options that control how data is transmitted between the Telnet client and server. These options provide a mechanism for exchanging information on the terminal type and the environmental settings, such as the home directory or path to the executable files, implemented on the client and the server OS. Information on the type of terminal supported on the client and the server is essential to set options that determine data transfer. Table 9.2 describes some of the common options negotiated between a Telnet client and server.

TABLE 9.2 COMMON TELNET OPTIONS

Option	Description
ECHO	Indicates whether the computer will reflect the data received from the sending computer. This action ensures that the data is displayed on the sending computer. The ECHO option is usually enabled on the server.
SUPRESS GO AHEAD	Indicates whether the GA command must not be sent to the client. By enabling this option, the GA command is prevented from being sent to the client.
TERMINAL TYPE	Signifies information about the terminal driver supported by the client or the server.
TSPEED	Indicates the speed of data transmission supported by the terminal driver on the client. This option contains suboptions, such as transmit speed and receive speed. The suboptions are sent as packets during option negotiation.
NAWS	Signifies an instruction to negotiate the window size of the client terminal driver. The client sends suboptions, such as the number of rows and columns, to indicate the size of a terminal window if this option is enabled.
LFLOW	Indicates that the client needs to perform data flow control. This option is usually enabled on the client to ensure greater control of data transmitted to the server.
LINEMODE	Indicates that a real line mode is operating between the client and the server. In this mode, the client processes each character before a complete line of perfectly edited characters is sent to the server.
ENVIRON	Signifies the environmental variable settings on a client or server that has enabled this option.
STATUS	Signifies the current status of any option defined on a client or a server. The status of an option describes whether the option is enabled or disabled. For example, if a computer needs to verify whether an option is enabled, the STATUS option and its suboptions are used. The suboptions provide complete information on the status of options being verified and is sent to the receiving computer.

To enable or disable these options, the client and the server instruct each other by using the DO, DONT, WILL, and WONT commands. This exchange of instructions between the client and the server is called *option negotiation*. A computer (client or server) can offer to enable an option or request another computer to enable the option on that computer. To indicate an offer to enable an option, the computer sends a WILL option. To request another computer to enable the option, the computer sends a DO option command.

Disabling options is a process similar to enabling options. To negotiate the disabling of options, an offer or a request can be transmitted between the client and the server. A computer can disable an option by offering to do so as indicated by the WONT option command. The receiving computer can accept this offer by responding with a DONT option reply. If a computer requests another computer to disable an option, it must send the DONT option

CH
9

command to the receiving computer. In response, if the receiving computer accepts the request, it sends a WONT option command to the sending computer.

One of the facilities offered by Telnet is its capability to establish communication between a client implementing any OS and a server running on a Unix platform. One such implementation of the Telnet client is the Telnet utility provided by the Windows OS. You can use this utility to connect to remote Unix servers. Figure 9.3 shows you how to log on to a Unix server from a Window client by using Telnet.

Note

Typically, Telnet servers are provided as a service on any Unix-based OS. However, Telnet clients can be installed on different operating systems, such as Windows or Linux.

Figure 9.3
Listing files and directory content using the ls command, creating files and directories using applications, such as vi and mkdir, and working with software available on the Unix server are some of the features provided by the Telnet utility.

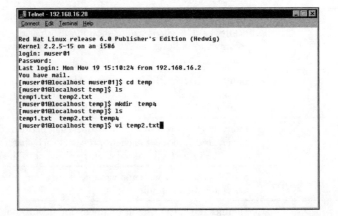

RLOGIN

The Rlogin application is another application that provides remote login. Rlogin was primarily designed to provide remote login features between Unix clients and servers. The very first Rlogin application was implemented on version 4.2 of the BSD Unix OS. Rlogin has been documented as a specification in RFC 1282.

The primary difference between Rlogin and Telnet is the fact that Rlogin provides a simple remote login feature whereas Telnet implements a much more sophisticated feature that manages remote login on diverse computers. However, the process of data transmission is similar in Telnet and Rlogin. In addition to remote login, Rlogin provides an automatic user recognition feature implemented through the .rhosts file. This file contains information on the IP address of computers that log on to the Rlogin server and user account information, such as usernames and passwords related to the IP address. The next time when a user tries to log on from a computer listed in the .rhosts file, the user need not enter the password and is logged on automatically to the server. However, due to the security lapses posed by this feature, the implementation of .rhosts is not recommended.

Rlogin does not require the negotiation of options immediately after establishing a preliminary connection between a client and server. Instead, the client transmits four null terminated character strings to the Rlogin server. The first data transmission contains a string containing no data except for the null terminator. Next, the login name used by the client to work on the client operating system is provided in the second string. The third string contains the user account name entered by the user to log on to the Rlogin server. The fourth string consists of the client terminal information, such as the terminal name and the speed supported by the terminal driver. In response, the server acknowledges the receipt of the strings by replying with an empty null terminated string.

RLOGIN CONTROL COMMANDS

The Rlogin control commands manage a number of issues for the application ranging from displaying characters on the client monitor, interrupting a program launched using Rlogin on the server, and requesting the window size of the client. Rlogin provides the user with the feature of controlling the display of characters on the client monitor by using the Ctrl+S key combinations (indicating Stop) and the Ctrl+Q key combinations (indicating Start). The Stop key combination prevents the display of characters by redirecting the characters into a buffer. The Start key combination releases the buffered characters and redirects these characters to the client monitor. This type of display control is called *local flow control*.

The Stop and Start combinations are also used to restrict the server from sending data. Instead, the server data is redirected to its buffer and is released only when the user types the Start keystroke combination. This server-based data transmission control is called *remote flow control*. The flow control keystrokes entered by the user are translated into control commands that must be interpreted by the Rlogin client and server software. For example, if a local flow control operation needs to be implemented, a control command instructing the Rlogin client software is embedded within the data. On the other hand, if a remote flow control operation needs to be implemented, control commands that instruct the Rlogin server are embedded within the data sent to the server. However, to distinguish control commands from data, the client sets a TCP segment header option called Urgent bit in the packets containing the data.

→ To learn more about TCP segment header options, **see** "TCP Segment Header," **p. 82**

In addition to flow control commands, the client might send interrupt requests to the server in the form of a control command if the server does not respond due to a server program crash or due to an overflowing buffer. The interrupt request control command instructs the server to process the command alone and to ignore the data part of the packet received by the server. A server also uses control commands to request the window size of the terminal driver being implemented on the client. In response, the client uses the screen size command to send the window size used to transmit data.

To use the remote login features of Rlogin, you must enter **Rlogin** at the command prompt along with a set of options. The following list describes these options in detail:

- ■ -l *username*—Specifies a username other than the one used to log on to the Unix client OS. If this option is not specified, the client username is used as the default login name for Rlogin.

- ■ -t *terminal type*—Specifies the type of terminal supported by the client computer. You can specify the terminal type as ansi or dumb. The ansi terminal type is taken as the default terminal type.

- ■ -e *character*—Specifies the character that must be used to indicate an escape character. By default, the ~ (tilde) symbol signifies an escape character in Rlogin.

- ■ -E—Indicates that no character must be recognized as an escape character.

- ■ -D—Displays the username used for remote login and local login. This option is also used as a diagnostic tool to check for problems in the TCP connection.

Figure 9.4 shows you how to log on to an Rlogin server.

Figure 9.4
The login name muser01 is used to log on to the Rlogin server. The exclamation character (!) is specified as the escape character using the -e option.

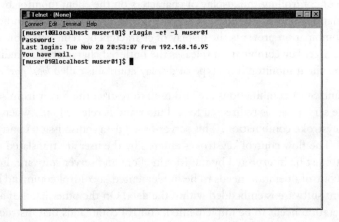

SUMMARY

The Telnet and the Rlogin applications implement the remote login feature as part of the Application layer in the TCP/IP reference model. The Telnet protocol is based on five components: Network Virtual Terminal, Commands, Modes, Options, and the Option Negotiation process. Rlogin is also based on the components that are used to build the Telnet application. However, Rlogin provides a simpler implementation and does not cater to a diverse collection of clients. Rlogin also implements commands to control character display, interrupt a process, and advertise window size.

CHAPTER **10**

MESSAGING PROTOCOLS

In this chapter

MESSAGING CONCEPTS AND SMTP

The most commonly used service on the Internet is the mailing service. Users connected to an internetwork use e-mails to exchange information with each other. Using the mail services that are available on a TCP/IP internetwork are advantageous because they provide platform independent communication. Simple Mail Transfer Protocol (SMTP) is a protocol that is present in the TCP/IP protocol suite for transferring mail in an internetwork. SMTP is an Application layer protocol (see Figure 10.1) that uses TCP for sending mail.

Figure 10.1
SMTP is a protocol that operates from the Application layer of the TCP/IP reference model and is used for sending mail on an internetwork.

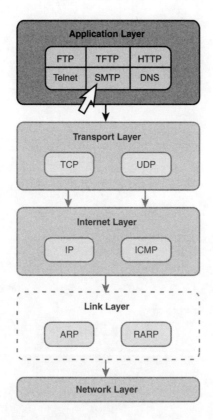

SMTP provides a reliable transfer of mail by interacting with TCP in the Transport layer. Mail messages can be sent in ASCII and non-ASCII formats. However, SMTP can be used to send only those messages that are in the NVT ASCII format. To send mails that contain binary data, video, image, or audio files, an extension to SMTP called Multimedia Internet Mail Extensions (MIME) is used. SMTP also operates with two other protocols called Post Office Protocol (POP) and Internet Message Access Protocol (IMAP), which are used for receiving mails. They are explained later in this chapter.

The specifications for SMTP are detailed in RFC 821 and the format of the messages that can be sent is defined in RFC 822.

→ To know more about RFCs that define the protocols in the TCP/IP protocol suite, **see** "RFCs," **p. 425**

→ To know more NVT ASCII, **see** "File Transfer and Access," **p. 129**

COMPONENTS USED FOR MESSAGING

Sending and receiving mail consist of different stages. Each stage is handled by one or more components of the mailing system. The different components of the mailing system are the user agent (UA), the mail transfer agent (MTA), and the mail server.

When you need to send mail, you need to provide the message that is to be sent, your mail address, and the recipient's mail address. A mail transfer agent (MTA) coordinates the transfer of mail among users who might be in the same network or different networks. If the sender and receiver of the messages are on different networks, there will be an MTA on each side. The MTA at the sender's end that tries to establish a connection with the receiver to transfer mail is referred to as a *client MTA* or *client SMTP*. The MTA at the receiver's end that accepts the request from the client MTA is called the *server MTA* or *server SMTP*.

The component of the mailing system that is used to compose messages and send them to the MTA is called a *user agent (UA)*. Microsoft Outlook and Pegasus are two examples of software that are commonly used as user agents. The UA takes care of all the interactions with the user. To send the messages to an MTA, the UA needs to establish connection with the MTA. The connection between the UA and the MTA is established using SMTP commands, which are dealt with later in this chapter. The mails that are sent are stored on a computer called a mail server. The location on the mail server in which the mails are stored is called the *mail queue*. A mail server has software installed on it that can handle messaging. One of the common mail server software programs used is Microsoft Exchange Server. In the case of large networks, individual computers can function as dedicated mail servers. Otherwise, if the mail traffic is considerably low, a server that already exists on the network can also function as the mail server.

The MTA checks the status of the mail queues frequently. If there are any messages that need to be delivered, the client MTA tries to establish a connection with the server MTA. After a connection is established, the messages are sent to the server MTA, which, in turn, stores the mail in the mailbox of the recipient. The server MTA then tries to establish a connection with the receiver.

If server MTA is able to establish a connection, the messages are delivered to the recipient through the UA. The mechanism used by the user to access mail from the mailbox is determined by message access protocols, such as POP and IMAP. The interaction between UAs and the MTAs is displayed in Figure 10.2.

You can set the time duration for which a mail can be stored in the mail server before the MTA transfers it to the recipient. This duration is dependent on the mail server software that is used. In addition, network administrators can also limit the size of the mailbox, which is the sum of the sizes of all the messages for a particular user. For example, the network administrator can place a restriction of 5MB size on the mailboxes of all the users on a network. If the mailbox size crosses this limit, the mailbox is said to be overflowing and an error message is sent to the originator of the message.

Figure 10.2
Two or more MTAs communicate with each other to transfer mail.

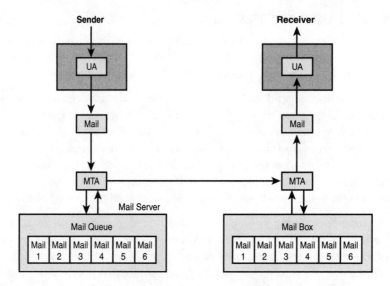

In the case of mail transfer it is possible that the recipient might not be online. In such a case, the mails are not delivered to the user. They are stored in the mail queue on the mail server and this process is called *spooling*. The server MTA keeps checking the mail queue at frequent intervals of time. If it finds that the mail queue has messages for a particular user who is now online, the messages are delivered to the user. The details about how a recipient accesses a message are dealt with in detail later in this chapter.

Note

The way in which an MTA is implemented in messaging software depends on the product that is using it. In the case of a Windows-based system, the MTA is integrated with the mail server. A common example is Eudora WorldMail. However, a few MTAs that are Unix-based have the MTAs operating as a separate unit.

Note

In the case of a mail server that has Microsoft Exchange Server installed on it, the MTA runs as a service.

MAILBOX

Mail is delivered to specific locations on the hard disk, called *mailboxes*, of the mail server. Every user is identified by a unique address called the *mail address*. The mail address comprises of two components, the local part and the domain name. The local part identifies the user and the domain name identifies the name of the computer in which the mailbox is located. The IP address is required for sending and receiving data over a network. To resolve the domain name to the corresponding IP address, Domain Naming Service (DNS), which also operates from the Application layer of the TCP/IP reference model, is used.

→ To know more Domain Naming Service, **see** "DNS," **p. 209**

Note

The mail for all the users are stored in a single file, called mailbox, on the hard disk of the mail server. The mailbox names, such as abc.com, are used by the messaging system to control access to the mail server.

ALIAS EXPANSION

Sometimes, you might send mail to more than one recipient. Mail can be sent to more than one recipient by mentioning the addresses of all the recipients separately or identifying them with a single name, which is called an *electronic mailing list* or an *address group*. If an electronic mailing list is specified as the recipient address, the agent refers to a database called the alias expansion database and sends the message to the intended recipients. This process is called *alias expansion*.

FUNCTIONING OF SMTP

The mail transfer process works in three phases: connection establishment, data transfer, and connection termination. RFC 821 specifies the commands that are used to transfer mail through these phases. The steps performed to establish a connection are as follows:

1. The client MTA establishes a connection with the server MTA through port number 25.

2. After the connection is established, the client sends a HELO message to pass the domain address of the client to the server MTA. For establishing a connection between the server MTA and the client MTA by using TCP, the IP address of both computers is used.

3. If the server MTA accepts the connection request, it sends a request command completed message to the client MTA indicating that the message transfer can be initiated.

4. The client uses the MAIL command to send the name of the user sending the message to the server.

5. If the server MTA is ready to accept mail, it responds by sending an OK command.

6. The client MTA now sends the address of the recipient through the RCPT command. If the server MTA recognizes the recipient, it sends an OK command. Otherwise, it rejects the request.

Note

> If the mail is comprised of multiple clients, the MAIL command is sent to all the recipients separately. For example, if you have to send a message to three users, the RCPT command is executed three times to inform the server MTA about the address of all the recipients.

7. The client MTA starts sending the mail data by using the DATA command after the server MTA is informed about the address of the mail recipients. The server MTA acknowledges the receipt of data by sending message number 354, which is denoted as Start Mail input. The end of the mail message is indicated by a period, which is also called an *end of mail data indicator*. After the end of the mail data indicator is detected by the server MTA, the server sends an OK command.

8. After the message transfer is complete, the client sends a QUIT command to terminate the connection.

Note

> The address of the sender and the receiver is also referred to as the *envelope*.

SMTP COMMANDS

The server and client MTAs communicate with each other through a set of commands that are defined in RFC 821. The response to the messages can be in the form of commands or numbers called *response codes*.

Note

> The SMTP commands are not case-sensitive.

HELO COMMAND

The HELO command is used by the sender MTA to initiate a mail transfer with the receiver. To do this, the sender MTA sends its mail address to the receiver. The receiver, in turn, acknowledges the request by sending its address.

HELO *sender's address*

MAIL COMMAND

The MAIL command is used by the sender to identify itself with the receiver.

MAIL FROM:*reverse path/reverse address*

The *reverse path* indicates the route to be taken to reach the sender of the mail. If the reverse path includes just the address of the sender it is called the *reverse address*. If there are problems during mail transfer, error messages are redirected to the address specified in the reverse path or as the reverse address.

RCPT COMMAND

The RCPT command is used to send the address of the recipients to the server MTA.

RCPT TO:*forward path/forward address*

The *forward path* is the route to be taken to reach the recipient to which the mail must be sent. Sometimes, just the address of the receiver, called the *forward address*, is specified instead of the complete path. If the server MTA does not recognize the address of the recipient, a failure reply with a code 550 is sent to the client MTA.

Note

The server MTA uses the alias expansion database for checking the validity of the mail addresses.

DATA COMMAND

The DATA command is used to send the mail message to the server MTA. The end of the mail message is indicated by a period. When the message is received by the final destination, it adds the details of the sender and the receiver and the time at which the message was received.

CH

10

SEND COMMAND

The terms mailing and sending are different in the context of SMTP. The process of delivering mail to a user's mailbox is called *mailing*. The process of delivering mail to the computer in which the user works is known as *sending*. The MAIL command is used for mailing, whereas the SEND command is used for sending mail to the user. The SEND command requires the user to be online for receiving messages. If the SEND command is not successful, an error message is sent to the sender.

Note

Mailing and sending are also referred to as the delivery methods.

SEND OR MAIL (SOML) COMMAND

The SOML command is also used for sending messages. Unlike the SEND command, which returns an error message if the user is not online on the network, the SOML command does not return an error message. Instead it transfers the mail to the mailbox of the user.

SEND AND MAIL (SAML) COMMAND

The SAML command is used both for mailing and sending. This command is successful only if both the tasks, sending and mailing, succeed unlike SOML, which expects only one task to succeed.

> **Note**
>
> The SEND, SOML, and SAML commands can be used only with computers that accept terminal messages.

QUIT COMMAND

The QUIT command is used to terminate the connection between the client MTA and the server MTA. The QUIT message is sent to the user after the mail is transferred completely.

RSET COMMAND

The RSET command is used to cancel the current transaction between the client MTA and the server MTA. After the RSET command is executed, the memory associated with the current transaction is released.

EXPN COMMAND

Mail could be sent to one or more recipients. A set of mail recipients can also be grouped as an electronic mailing list. If the name of the electronic mailing list is specified, the server MTA sends a message to the client to expand the mailing list to get the corresponding addresses in the mailing list by using the EXPN command.

RELAYING MAIL USING SMTP

Mail might have to pass through more than one host to reach the final destination. The process of transferring mail through more than one destination is called *relaying*. When messages have to be relayed, the route to the destination must be specified instead of just the address of the final destination.

The reverse path specified along with the MAIL command, being the route to the originator, has the address of the sender as the first address. On the other hand, the forward path that is specified along with the RCPT command has the address of the destination as the first address. When an MTA receives mail that needs to be forwarded to a different MTA, the reverse path and forward path are changed. For example, if an MTA named M1 sends mail to another MTA named M2, the first address in the reverse path, which is M1, will be the address of the sender and the first address in the reverse path, which is M2, will be the address of the destination. If M2 has to relay the mail to M3, the values in the forward and the reverse path must be changed accordingly.

Error messages are generated if the path that is specified is incorrect. The error messages are redirected to the sender's address by using the addresses in the reverse path.

> **Note**
>
> SMTP can be used to send mail across systems that do not use the same protocol or connection mechanism. This is made possible through devices called *mail gateways* or *mail bridges*. These devices get messages in a format that is not supported by SMTP and convert the same to a format that is recognized by SMTP and vice versa.

FORMAT OF A MAIL ADDRESS

Mail addresses are used to identify the location on the mail server on which a message needs to be stored. In other words, mail addresses are used to identify the mailbox of a user. Every mail address is made up of two components, the user ID and the domain name. The domain name specifies the domain to which the user ID belongs. The user ID is also called the *local part*. An example of a mail address is dianne@abc.com. In this example, *dianne* is used to represents the user and *abc.com* refers to the domain name. The mail of more than one user can be stored on a mail server. The user ID is used to uniquely identify the mail for a particular user on the same server.

SMTP interacts with a service that operates from the Application layer called the Domain Naming Service (DNS) for resolving host names to the corresponding IP addresses. For example, if the address of the recipient is abc@xyz.com, MTA interacts with DNS to find the IP address of the host named xyz.com. The name resolution information is stored on a computer called the DNS server. Name resolution information stored on the DNS server includes the IP addresses and the corresponding computer names. DNS stores information that is required for mail transfer in the records called the Mail Exchange (MX) records.

→ To know more MX records, **see** "DNS," **p. 209**

CH
10

> **Note**
>
> Extended Simple Mail Transfer Protocol (ESMTP) is an advanced version of SMTP that has built-in support for transferring messages that are in the non-ASCII format unlike SMTP, which uses an extension called MIME to transfer video files, audio files, and other data that are in the non-ASCII format. ESMTP also supports message pipelining in which more than one SMTP message can be sent in the same data packet, thus reducing the network traffic.

> **Note**
>
> When a message is not delivered to the destination, an error is reported to the computer that sent the message. The originator of the message can be found by using the reverse path. The first address in the reverse path is the address of the computer that sent the messages. Error messages are generated and sent only for mail which did not reach the destination successfully. The error messages that are sent to the sender do not provide sufficient information for troubleshooting. ESMTP enables the sender to get a delivery status notification (DSN) for mail that is sent over the Internet.

POP

SMTP is used as a standard for transferring mail to a recipient. *Transferring* mail is the process of sending mail to the mailbox of the user. *Accessing* mail refers to the process of reading and manipulating mail from the mail server. Accessing mail is not a functionality of SMTP. The protocols that are used for accessing mail from a mail server are Post Office Protocol (POP) and Internet Message Access Protocol (IMAP). SMTP needs a connection to be active for transferring mail. This will be a constraint on the users because they cannot be expected to be online all the time. Mailboxes are accessed only when required and not otherwise. Thus, to make the process of accessing mail user-friendly, POP and IMAP have been created to support mail access from the mail server. When you compose a message and click the Send button, the SMTP protocol is used to transfer the mail to the recipients. When you read a message from a mailbox, you might be using either POP or IMAP to access them. The advantages and disadvantages of POP and IMAP are discussed later in this chapter.

Note The port number that is used by POP is 110.

Mail from a mail server can be accessed in three modes: offline, disconnected, and online. However, POP supports only the offline mode of working. In the offline mode, when a user needs to access mail, the first step is establishing a connection between the client and the server. After the connection is established, the mail for the user is transferred to the user's computer and thus a copy of the mail does not exist on the mail server. The downloaded messages can then be accessed and manipulated from the local computer at any point in time. POP is a message access protocol that is used for accessing mail in the offline mode.

However, there is a limitation when mail is accessed in the offline mode. In the offline mode, it will be better if the user accesses the messages from the same computer because messages are transferred to a client computer. Although it is possible to download different messages to different computers, the mail that belongs to a user will be scattered across different computers.

Although there is a limitation in implementing POP, the offline mode of operation that is supported by POP makes minimal use of the resources of the server. This also helps reduce the overload on the network because the network resources are not locked for a long time when messages are accessed using POP. The latest version of POP that is in use is POP3.

IMAP

Consider a situation in which a user needs to access mail from many computers. If the user is working in the offline mode, the messages would have to be downloaded to these different locations. If the user needs to access messages that were downloaded earlier, it might not be possible because the mail would have been saved on different computers. To overcome these problems with POP, a more efficient protocol called the IMAP is used. IMAP provides two modes of accessing mail, online and disconnected. In the online mode, after establishing a connection with the mail server, the user can access and work with the messages directly on the server.

IMAP enables remote management of mail. In addition, it enables users to fetch mail that satisfies a particular condition. Downloading just the required messages helps reduce the overhead on the network and the mail server. This feature of IMAP is very useful for users who need to download the required messages to manage the limited mailbox size allocated to them.

The following are the advantages of using IMAP:

- A user can access the mailbox from any computer.
- A mailbox can be accessed simultaneously by more than one user by using shared folders. The state of the mailbox is reflected correctly to the users accessing the mailbox. In other words, any additions or modifications to the mailbox will be reflected correctly.
- IMAP also supports the offline mode of operations for compatibility with POP. For example, if you are using Microsoft Outlook as your mail client, you have an option of creating a folder called the Personal Folders, which can store the mail that you receive on the local machine. When you transfer all your mail to Personal Folders, copies of the mail do not exist on the server. However, you can choose to retain all the messages on the server and access your mail from any computer.
- In disconnected mode, the user is allowed to make a local copy of the mail and terminate the connection. Unlike the offline mode, the messages are not deleted from the mailbox on the server. If the user has made any changes to the local copies of the messages, the changes can be synchronized when the connection is established once again.

CH

10

> **Note**
>
> The difference between POP and IMAP is that because IMAP supports more features than POP, it is more difficult to implement than POP.

> **Note**
>
> The latest version of IMAP that is in use is IMAP4.

The similarities between IMAP and POP are

- Both POP and IMAP are message access protocols and use SMTP for sending mails.
- Both the protocols support offline operations.
- Both the protocols enable mailboxes to be accessed from any computer.

MIME

SMTP is used for transferring messages that use the ASCII format. To transfer mail that does not use this format, an extension of SMTP called Multimedia Mail Extensions (MIME) is used. MIME is used to convert data in a non-ASCII format to the format that is used by SMTP. The files that do not store data in the standard ASCII format are image files, such as JPEG, and video files. MIME can also be used to send application-specific data.

> **Note**
>
> For example, MIME needs to be used for mailing a Microsoft Word document that is present in the rich text format. Another application that makes use of MIME frequently is a browser. A browser receives data in various formats that have to be interpreted into a format that can be displayed to the user. For proper interpretation and display of such files, a browser must implement a MIME-type interpretation component.

The information about MIME is included as a header along with the header information that is sent by default along with messages. The MIME information that is included in the header is as follows:

- The address of the sender.
- The address of the receiver.
- The version of MIME used. The current version of MIME that is used is MIME-Version 1.1.
- The type of content that is transferred, such as video, audio, or an image.
- The encoding scheme that is used to convert the data from non-ASCII format to the ASCII format. The various encoding schemes that are used are 7bit, 8bit, binary, base64, and quoted-printable.

SUMMARY

SMTP is an Application layer protocol that is used for sending mail in an internetwork. SMTP uses TCP for communication between two computers. SMTP provides a reliable data transfer mechanism because it uses TCP for connection management. The different components that are used for transferring messages are the user agent (UA) and the mail transfer agent (MTA). MTA uses the SMTP commands that are defined in RFC 821 to transfer mail. The format in which the messages need to be transferred are defined in RFC 822. POP and IMAP are message access protocols and are used for accessing mail from the mailboxes. The different modes in which the mail can be accessed from a mail server are online, offline, and disconnected. MIME is an extension of SMTP that is used to transfer messages that are in the non-ASCII format.

CHAPTER 11

HYPERTEXT TRANSMISSION

In this chapter

WEB FUNDAMENTALS AND HTTP BASICS

The Internet is a storehouse of volumes of diverse information and resources ranging from software executables and services to information in the form of graphics images or text. A presentation medium that is able to encompass the inherent diversity in these resources is essential for easy data exchange. The World Wide Web, simply called the Web, provides such a medium. Although the Web is commonly perceived to be synonymous with the Internet, it is not. The Web only acts as a presentation medium through which you can explore the vast landscape of the Internet.

Think of the Web as a vast public library with books organized in clearly named shelves. Now, if you want to borrow a book on Buddhism, you need to search the books on the shelf named World Religions and find the book you want. Similarly, Web servers are then the library containing a number of shelves for making the information in the books available. Web servers are merely computers that run an Internet Web hosting software, such as Microsoft Internet Information Server or Apache Server. Web servers host a number of Web sites, which are like the books stored in the shelves of the library. Web sites present the information itself in an accessible format. Coincidentally, as with books, information is contained in the form of *pages*. Web pages are made with files containing instructions on how to display the information, as well as the end result viewable to the one seeking the information.

Before borrowing a book, you would want to look through or "browse" the index or the back cover of the book and read a few pages. Although this action is as simple as reading a book on the shelf in a public library, when it comes to browsing through the contents of a Web site hosted on a remote Web server, you need a utility that emulates your hands. Such a tool is called a browser. This tool displays the contents of a Web page based on the instructions contained in the code of the Web page. These instructions are coded in a language called Hypertext Markup Language (HTML).

Note

> *HTML* defines the structure and layout of the contents in a Web page by providing instructions to the browser. These instructions are specified using placeholders called tags and the parameters contained in a tag called attributes. The actual content that must be displayed is specified between tags. For example, to display the link to another Web page the `<A></A>` tag pair is used. The text displayed between the `<A>` and the `</A>` tags are displayed with an underline to signify that the text is a link to another page. The `HREF` attribute specified within the `<A>` tag as `<A HREF=www.mcp.com>` indicates the URL of the target Web page to which the text acts as a link. HTML has been further improved to define a new extensible language called Extensible Markup Language (XML) that provides greater flexibility and programming power for creating Web pages.

Note

Hypertext is a method of linking objects, such as Web pages, software executables, graphics, and documents. For example, when object A displayed in a document is linked to an object B, you can click object A to access object B. Hypertext was invented by Ted Nelson as a database system to access heterogeneous data from databases. The linking object that you click is called a *hyperlink* and appears as an underlined text or button on the document. Web pages coded using HTML primarily use hypertext to present the heterogeneous data available on the Internet.

The browser located on the client computer and the Web server software running on a remote computer need to establish certain ground rules for communication. These communication rules define how a browser can request data and how the requested data must be transferred from the Web server to the client before being displayed by the browser. The Application layer of the TCP/IP reference model provides such a specification in the form of the Hypertext Transfer Protocol (HTTP). Figure 11.1 shows the position of the layer from which HTTP operates in the TCP/IP reference model.

Figure 11.1
In recent years, HTTP has become one of the most dominant and popular Application layer protocols specified by the TCP/IP reference model.

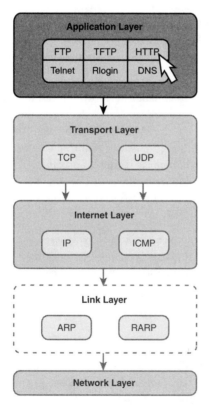

CH
11

The most significant development that fuelled the transformation of the Net from a CUI-based data exchange medium to the GUI-based data exchange medium is the invention of the protocol called HTTP. The credit for this development is attributed to Tim Berners-Lee, who wanted to ease communication of data by providing a method of accessing documents through links. While working in the European Laboratory for Particle Physics, Tim Berners-Lee developed a protocol for enabling easy access of research material by presenting documents by using links that display the required document when selected. The protocol underwent a number of changes right from its inception in 1990. HTTP 0.9, the first version of the protocol, implemented primitive data transfer features and was improved upon by the specification proposed in RFC 1945. The latest version of the protocol is documented in RFC 2616 that includes specification on a number of concepts implemented by version 1.1 of HTTP, such as caching, persistent connections, and virtual Web site hosting features provided by Web server software.

→ For more information on various RFCs, **see** "RFCs," **p. 425**

Although HTTP can be described as the primary Internet protocol being used today, it has certain restrictions. For instance, HTTP needs to transfer data by using a connection-oriented transfer protocol, such as TCP, and depends on TCP to ensure safe and secure transmission of data. HTTP works on a system of requests and responses where the browser requests data and the server responds with the data or a message indicating nonavailability of data. However, data transmission can also happen from the client to the server when user input needs to be communicated to the server.

HTTP provides a number of features to enhance performance and to enable the client and server to exchange information on the features supported by each other. For example, the caching feature provides a method of storing Web content obtained from a previous transaction. This enables the client that caches the first successful response to provide a quicker response the next time the same Web content is requested by the user. Another performance enhancer is the use of intermediate computers called proxies. A proxy acts as an intermediary between a local network and the Internet to provide security to the resources provided by the local network. Proxies also maintain Web content caches from previous transactions.

One of the most important reasons for the explosion of Web usage is the ease of information access it provides. To access a Web page containing the information you want, all that you need to do is type the name of the Web site in the address bar of your browser. The name is specified in the form of a Uniform Resource Locator (URL) that is resolved into an IP address to identify a remote Web server.

Note

To access a particular Web page on the server directly, you must enter the path to the location where the Web page is stored on the server. For example, to access the legal disclaimer details provided by Pearson Education, you must type /legal.cfm after typing www.mcp.com. This complete URL is called a *relative URL*. Another method of specifying the location of a particular Web page is to specify the file path starting from the root directory on the hard disk. This file path is called an *absolute URL*.

In addition to the name of the Web site, a URL contains information on the port number, additional parameters, and query information to the server. These details are optional and are specified by the browser only in specific situations. For example, the port number is specified by the browser only when the browser does not use port number 80, which is the port that is usually used for HTTP connections. In certain situations, the browser needs to query for information from the server. For example, a user might enter search strings to search for information using a *search engine*. Such information is passed to the server in the form of a query. Parameters are additional information provided by the client regarding the version number of HTTP implemented by the client, encoding information used to encrypt the transferred data, and the format of the data transferred. However, parameters are optional information.

The information contained in the URL is extracted by the browser and packaged into an HTTP message. This message is of two types, request and response. The browser creates an HTTP request containing the information required by the user and transfers it to the underlying Transport, Link, and Network layer protocols. The request message is received by the destination computer running the Web server software and is extracted from its frame-IP-TCP segment encapsulation before being directed to the Web server software. The server processes the request message and obtains the required information. Next, it creates an HTTP response message and packages the message into a frame-IP datagram-TCP segment encapsulation before transmitting it over the network. The response is received by the client, interpreted by the browser, and displayed to the user. Figure 11.2 shows the process of data exchange between the browser on a client and the Web server on a remote server.

CH
11

CONNECTIONS

An HTTP message is the most important component around which the entire HTTP framework is built. However, before learning about the components of an HTTP message, it is essential to understand how connectivity between an HTTP client and a Web server is maintained. One of the major drawbacks in version 1.0 of HTTP is the need to establish a fresh TCP connection every time the user requests to download Web content from the server.

Consider a scenario where you are talking over the phone with your friend and after every line you speak, the connection is terminated and then re-established. In addition to the fact that it would be virtually impossible to communicate with your friend, the process of constantly terminating and re-establishing a connection would be a tremendous drain on resources used to maintain the phone link. When you translate this situation to the TCP connection mechanism between a browser and a Web server that was used by HTTP 1.0, you can understand the tremendous load on the Web servers and the Internet in general while responding to a number of user requests from a single computer and the multitude of requests from different clients.

Figure 11.2
A request message sent to the Web server might include requests for displaying graphics images and textual information and for downloading software executables, audio files, and video files.

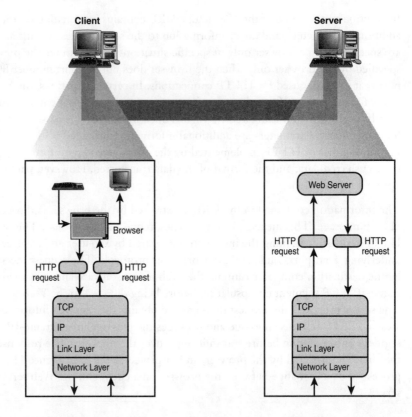

This inefficient mechanism was dropped while implementing HTTP 1.1 where a connection is maintained between the communicating computers until one of the connected computers indicates that it wants to close the connection. The indication is provided as an instruction in the header field of a message by setting the value of the Connection Header method to Close. This type of continuously maintained TCP connection is called *persistent connection*.

Although the persistent connection mechanism provides a number of benefits, as in the case of most solutions, it throws up a new problem. When a request or response is sent over the persistent connection in the form of a sequence of messages, it is difficult to identify the beginning or end of the message sequence. To overcome this problem, it is imperative that the information on the length of all the messages in the sequence is specified in each message. If the client or server is not able to determine the length before sending a request or a response sequence, that particular message is sent with the Connection Header field set to Close. This indicates that the message is the last in the message sequence thereby delimiting one message sequence from another. You will learn more about the header fields in the section "The HTTP Request" later in this chapter.

One of the major advantages that accrue from a persistent connection is a feature called *pipeline*. Using this feature, the client can transmit a sequence of messages without waiting for a response from the server for each request. However, there are certain ground rules stipulated by the HTTP specification that need to be followed while the client implements a pipeline. For example, if a client pipelines request messages without verifying whether the TCP connection implemented between the client and the server is persistent, the client must be programmed to resend the pipeline requests in the event of not receiving the corresponding response messages.

PERSISTENT CONNECTION GROUND RULES

When the client and the server implement a persistent connection, there are certain ground rules that must be followed. The following list details these ground rules:

- Graceful Timeout—Although TCP implements timeout values for the receipt of acknowledgements, persistent connections do not specify any time restrictions for the receipt of response or request messages. This might result in a situation where the client or the Web server might await a response for an indefinite period. Therefore, proxy servers and Web servers implement a timeout value, which ensures that a connection is terminated if there is no exchange of responses or requests between the client and server. When a timeout value is set on the proxy (which always represents a client) or a Web server, if a connection is idle for a period greater than the timeout value, the client or the server implementing the timeout must terminate the connection. The computers can terminate the connection by sending a message with the Connection Header field value set to Close. The client and the server must always look out for any "close" message from either computer and terminate the connection as soon as it is received. This is necessary to avoid any unnecessary wastage of network resources that might occur if one end of a connection remains open while the other end has been closed.

- Asynchronous Close Recovery—There are situations when a server terminates a connection on timeout while the client might have transmitted a message sequence under the assumption that the connection is still alive. The same situation can occur when a client terminates a connection on timeout while the server has transmitted a sequence of responses. These are highly probable on slow networks where delays in transmission of data are high. In such situations, the client or the server that transmits messages over a terminated connection must be programmed to re-establish a new connection and then retransmit the messages.

- Limited Number of Connections—At any given point of time, the number of persistent connections used by a client to connect to a server must be limited to two. If clients are connected to a server through a proxy, the proxy must not implement more than 2*N number of connections where N signifies the number of proxy users. For example, if three users access www.mcp.com through a proxy, the proxy can open a maximum of six connections to the www.mcp.com Web server.

CH
11

In addition to the rules specified in the list, the server must be programmed to ensure that the connection is not terminated during the process of transmitting a response. However, the server can terminate the connection in the event of network failure or if the client computer crashes wherein the client does not respond for a period more than the server timeout value. It is also essential that for every connection established with a client, the server must respond to at least one request sent by the client. If there is no response, the client can terminate the connection after its timeout value has elapsed.

ADVANTAGES OF A PERSISTENT CONNECTION

Persistent connection implementations offer a number of performance gains of which the most visible being the improved efficiency in the time taken to transmit data. This is made possible by implementing the pipeline where a sequence of request messages is transmitted without waiting for a response for each message. Clients that need to access and display dynamic Web content need to implement a pipeline over a persistent connection. For example, Web sites that host news channels provide up-to-date information on a variety of events happening around the world including information on sports, politics, and share prices. To access and display such dynamic information, clients must implement a pipelined persistent connection without which the Web content updated on the server is not transmitted to the client immediately.

Another important performance gain is the avoidance of excessive packet exchange between the client and the server due to multiple TCP connection opens required by HTTP 1.0. A typical TCP connection follows the process of a three-way handshake to establish a connection. Although the three-way handshake process cannot be done away with, the need to open a new connection for every message does not exist thereby reducing the number of three-way handshakes to one common three-way handshake process for a number of message sequences. Due to a lesser number of packets being exchanged between the client and server, network congestion is drastically reduced. Moreover, the time it takes to transmit subsequent packets (containing a request or response message) is also reduced as there is no need to perform fresh connection opens for every packet transmitted.

The cumulative gain from all these features is the fact that the load on the processing capabilities of clients, Web servers, and intermediate devices is drastically reduced. Now, these computers can cater to other processing requirements instead of allocating processing time for opening and terminating TCP connections for each message. In addition, the memory needed by each computer involved in the transaction to maintain buffers and windows is also reduced.

➔ To learn more about windows, **see** "Data Transfer Concepts," **p. 93**

COMPONENTS OF AN HTTP MESSAGE

The role of an HTTP message includes much more than a simple transfer of data. The message forms the lifeblood of the entire HTTP implementation. In addition to the actual data, a message contains information related to the nature of the message, the version of

HTTP used, the target URL, the preferences of the client and the server, the connection, and a host of other essential instructions to the client and the server. Based on the source, a message can be classified into a request message or a response message with each type having varying components. Each component is further divided into subcomponents. Although the message components might vary based on its type, a common component called the Header is present in both the request and the response. Subcomponents present in the Header component are called fields. You will learn more about these components in the following sections.

THE HTTP REQUEST

The idea behind sending a request message from a client is to query for the availability of a Web page and retrieve it from the Web server. Therefore, a request message has four components that contain information pertaining to a request for a Web page. These components are Request Line, Header, Blank Line, and the Body component. Internally, the Blank Line component is represented as the CR LF pair, which is the ASCII code of the carriage return (CR) and line feed (LF) characters. The CR LF pair indicates the end of the Header component. The Body component is either left blank or it contains encoding information or data to be delivered to the destination computer. Encoding information is specified while transferring sensitive data that needs to be encrypted for secure transfer and delivery. Figure 11.3 shows you the components of an HTTP request message.

CH

11

Figure 11.3
Each component of the request message contains subcomponents that contain the actual information stored in the components.

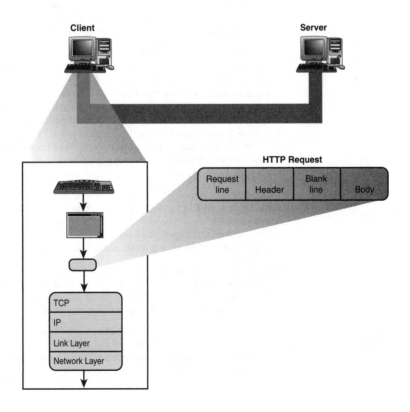

The Request Line component forms one of the most important components in a request message. It contains subcomponents such as request type, URL of the destination computer (which is the Web server), and the version of the HTTP implementation. The request type, which is also called a *method*, contains instructions to the server on the action that must be performed by the server to satisfy the client request. The method carries the actual "message" sent by the client to the server. A particular method is specified for each message. Each method uniquely identifies the type of message based on the instruction it provides. Table 11.1 describes the various methods that can be specified in a Request Line component.

TABLE 11.1 COMMON TELNET COMMANDS

Methods	Description
GET	Indicates that the document indicated in the URL specified in the Request Line component must be retrieved by the server and sent in the Body component of the response to this request message.
PUT	Indicates that the document contained in the Body component of the message must be placed on the server at the location indicated by the URL specified in the Request Line component. If the document already exists, the old document is overwritten with the contents of the new document.
PATCH	Indicates that the contents of the document that is contained in the Body component of the message must be used to update the contents of another document existing on the server. The URL specified in the Request Line component of the request message indicates the target document.
POST	Indicates that the server must accept the data contained in the Body component of the message as the user input sent by the client. Some examples of user input include entries specified in a form on a Web page or user input to add new entries to a database maintained by the Web server. The POST method is also used to indicate that data is sent in the form of messages sent by the user to mailing lists, newsgroups, bulletin boards, or discussion forums. In addition, this method is used to append a new child object to an existing parent object on the Web page hosted by the server. The location of the resource is specified in the URL contained in the Request Line component.
HEAD	Requests additional information on the document indicated by the URL. In response to this request type, the server must specify information about the document in the header fields of the corresponding response message. The information returned in the response header is used to verify the validity of hyperlinks and whether the hyperlinks have been recently modified.
COPY	Indicates that the contents of the file specified in the URL of the Request Line component must be transferred to a location on the server. The target location on the server is specified in the header fields of the Header component.
MOVE	Indicates that the file specified by the URL of the Request Line component must be moved to another location on the server. The target location on the server is specified in the header fields.

TABLE 11.1   CONTINUED

Methods	Description
DELETE	Indicates that the file specified in the URL of the Request Line component must be deleted from the server.
LINK	Indicates that a link must be created from a file located on the server to another file. The URL specifies the path to the source file on the server while the path to the target file to which the link must be created is specified in the header fields. The target file can be located on the same Web server or on other Web servers.
UNLINK	Indicates that an existing link must be deleted from the file located on the server. The URL specified in the Request Line component provides the file path.
OPTION	Indicates a request for information on the communication options set on the server. Primarily, this method is used to obtain the communication capabilities of the server and information on the requirements to retrieve a resource available on the server.

Note

Document Object Model Level 1 (DOM Level 1) is a programming API for defining the structure of a Web page and its elements. The API provides language and platform-neutral functions that enable programs and scripts to dynamically modify the content, structure, and display format of the content in a document or a Web page. To use these functions, DOM defines the elements of a Web page in a parent-child format. For example, the browser window will be the grandparent, the Web page will be the parent, and the elements in the Web page, such as frames, images, buttons, or text boxes, will be child objects. The DOM structure will not be the same for all Web pages and entirely depends on the instructions given by the markup language used to create the Web page.

CH

11

THE HTTP RESPONSE

The structure of an HTTP response is quite similar to an HTTP request. The vital difference between the two message types is in the contents of the header fields and in the absence of a Request Line component. Instead of the Request Line component, a component called the Status Line is provided in a response. As in a request, the response also contains a Body component, which is used to transfer the encoding information or the data requested by the client. Figure 11.4 shows the components of an HTTP response message.

The Status Line component contains information on the version of HTTP implemented on the server, the status code indicating the status of the corresponding request for the response, and the description of the status code. The status codes are classified into informational, success, redirection, client error, and server error. More than 35 status codes have been specified in RFC 2616 for specifying the status of the request sent to a client. Table 11.2 describes the different types of status codes.

Figure 11.4
Apart from Web pages, the response contains information on server capabilities, documents stored on the server, or error codes.

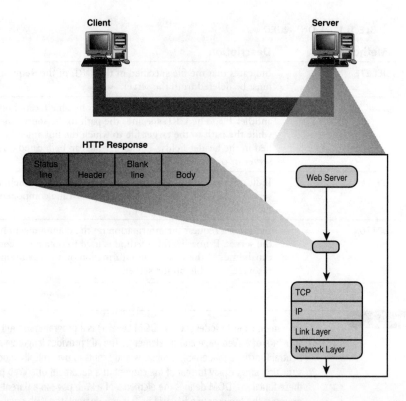

TABLE 11.2 TYPES OF HTTP STATUS CODES

Status Code	Description
Information	Indicates that the server is processing the request.
Success	Indicates that the request sent by the client has been accepted by the server and has been successfully processed.
Redirection	Indicates that the client needs to supply additional information to obtain a successful response from the server for the original requests. The client might need to obtain additional information from the user if the requirement for such information is indicated by the redirection status code. For example, if the user fails to enter the password while logging on to a Web site, a redirection status code is sent as a response to the logon request sent by the client. This redirection status code indicates that the user needs to provide the password in addition to the username.
Client Error	Indicates that the client has transmitted erroneous information in the request.
Server Error	Indicates that an internal error has occurred on the server when the request was being processed. This error status code also indicates if the error is permanent or temporary. This error code, indicated by the number 404, is a common occurrence while browsing the Net.

➜ To learn more about status codes, **see** "HTTP Status Codes and Header Fields," **p. 443**

THE HEADER COMPONENT

A Header component provides additional information that is not specified in the Request Line or Status Line component of a message. It is a common component present in a request and a response message. In a request, the Header component is used in combination with the method specified in the Request Line component to instruct the server on how to process the request sent by the client. The Header component contains more than 45 header fields for a message. Header components are classified into three groups: request header, response header, and entity header.

A request header usually contains information on the format of data that must be supplied by the server, the permissions held by the client, user's e-mail address, client port number, and the identity and version of the browser sending the request from the client. A request header can also contain instructions to the server to process a request based on certain conditions. For example, the server can be instructed to send only those Web pages that have been created later than a specific date.

Response headers are used to convey information regarding the response. It includes information on the age of the Web page, in the form of a date or delta second value, returned by server, the identity of the server, and the methods supported by the server. In addition, entity headers also contain the retry time, which indicates the period for which the server is available to entertain a repeat request for the same Web page.

> **Note**
>
> The time specified in a header field as an integer is called delta seconds. The value is provided in a decimal format.

Entity headers are used to provide information on the Web page being transmitted to a destination computer (client or server). It contains information on the length of the message, date of expiry for the Web page, language used in the Web page, the location of the Web page on the client or the server, and the last date on which the contents of the Web page was modified.

→ To learn more about header fields, **see** "HTTP Status Codes and Header Fields," **p. 443**

NEGOTIATING CLIENT/SERVER CAPABILITIES

The Header component in an HTTP message holds vital information related to the data contained in the message and the connection implemented between the client and the server. In addition, the Header component also contains information on certain capabilities of the client and the server. For example, information on the data formats supported by the client is contained in the Accept header field. The client and the server must reach an agreement on the data being transferred, the method of transferring data that is supplied in the connection information, and the validity of the data being transferred. Therefore, a process of negotiation between the client and the server is conducted before exchange of requests or responses.

The negotiation process can be classified into three types: server-driven, agent-driven, and transparent. The process of *server-driven negotiation* requires the Web server to determine the best possible response for a request received from the client, which will cater to the client's preferences. The client assists the server in this process by specifying some of its preferences in its request header fields. For example, the character set implemented by the client is specified in the Accept-Charset request header. Based on this information, the server translates data to be returned by the response message in the character set indicated. However, all client preferences are not specified in its request header. Therefore, the server tries to "guess" the client requirements before transmitting a response.

There are several disadvantages in this type of negotiation. For example, if this method of negotiation must be successful, the server must accurately determine the requirements of the client. However, it is highly unlikely that the server can guess all the preferences of the client although the client can supply some of its preferences through the request header fields. Moreover, implementing this preference determination feature on the Web server increases the complexity of programming the Web server software.

Another flaw in the server-driven negotiation is the fact that a cache, which stores successful responses, cannot use a cached response to respond to multiple requests that require the same response because each request might need a different guess by the Web server. Most of these problems are resolved when you implement the agent-driven negotiation. An *agent-driven negotiation* requires the user agent (which is the browser) to send a request to the server, which verifies its capabilities and sends a response indicating all the possible features it can support. For example, a client might request the server to send information on the languages it supports. The server might then send the details of the languages it supports and the preferred language used in the response. This preferred language is the default language used by the server. Now, the client makes a selection of preferences from this response and uses these preferences while making future requests to the server.

If the client is not satisfied with the preferences provided by the server, it sends another request with alternative requirements. For example, if the client needs French language support, which is not indicated by the server response, the client requests support for an alternative language by resending another request for German language support. The re-sent request requires another response from the server. The server analyzes its capabilities based on the new requirements of the client before providing the response. The need for a second response is the only disadvantage in the agent-driven negotiation model.

The *transparent negotiation* model resolves all problems associated with the server-driven and agent-driven negotiations. In this process, the server sends a list of all possible features it can support to the cache maintained on a proxy server. Now, the proxy server uses its cache to provide an appropriate response to client requests based on the list of supported features indicated to it by the Web server. This process eliminates the need for a second request from the client and ensures that all possible features needed by a client or multiple clients are supported by the proxy server using its cache.

One example of how a Web server implements server-driven negotiation is the File Type option that can be set in Microsoft Internet Information Server (IIS). To set this option, you need to work with the Default Web Site Properties dialog box. This dialog box is displayed when you select the Properties option from the context-sensitive menu of a Web site listed in the IIS console. Next, select the HTTP Headers tab and click the File Types button. From the File Types dialog box, click the New Type button to open the File Type dialog box. Here, enter the extension of a file type and the associated content type. For example, you can enter the file extension as .xml and the content type as text/xml. IIS uses these settings to determine the best possible response it can provide for a client HTTP request. File type settings are also used to indicate all possible content types supported by a server to a proxy for enabling transparent negotiation. Figure 11.5 shows you how to specify the content type supported by IIS for a particular Web site.

Figure 11.5
File type settings can be specified for each Web site maintained on the Web server.

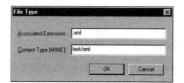

HTTP PERFORMANCE

Data transmission and exchange performance plays a vital role in the efficient functioning of an HTTP implementation on the client and the Web server. One of the performance enhancers provided by the HTTP specification is the concept of cache. The sections that follow analyze the performance specifications provided by HTTP.

CACHING

The primary goal of a cache implemented on a proxy server and a Web server is to ensure that a request is handled by a cache instead of being handled by a server. For example, the cache maintained on a proxy server handles a client request if a response for the request is available. Similarly, if the cache on the Web server contains a response for a request received from the client, it does not process the request. Instead, the Web server automatically sends the cached response, thereby saving time and processing effort. On the client end, by avoiding the need to send requests to the server, the client saves on opening a TCP connection. In addition, the client increases the speed of providing the required information to the user by providing the cached response obtained from the proxy. There are two types of caches that can be implemented: shared and nonshared caches. Shared caches allow other computers to access cached data. Nonshared caches, on the other hand, restrict access to cached data and allow only one computer to access the cache.

When a successful response is obtained from a server, the response is stored in the cache. This can be used whenever the same client makes the same request in the future. However, if the response deals with dynamic data, the risk of obsolescence of data contained in the response is high. To ensure that the response provided from the cache is not obsolete, two methods of updating the cache can be implemented, namely, the expiration model and the validation model.

The *expiration model* specifies that the responses stored in a cache be set with a certain time value. The *time value* specifies a date of expiry for the cached content within which the responses remain "fresh." This time value can be specified by the server the first time a successful response is sent to the client. However, it is not always essential that the server determines or sets this time value. In situations where the server does not specify the expiration time, the cache calculates it. This value is computed by using algorithms that use header field information such as Age or Last-Modified time.

To determine the time when the cache needs to be updated, the current age of the responses needs to be calculated. For this, formulas that take into account the current date, the expiration date, Age header field, corrected initial value, and request time values are used. To determine the current age of a response, the cache uses the following formulas:

```
corrected_received_age=max(now-expiration date, Age_value)
corrected_initial_age=corrected_received_age+(now-request_time
resident_time=now-response_time
current_age=corrected_initial_age+resident_time
```

In the preceding syntax, now signifies the current time in the local computer and request_time signifies the time on the local computer when the request was sent to the server. In the first formula, max(now-expiration date, Age_value) means that between the time values provided by now-expiration_date and Age_value, the greater of the two values is used as the corrected_received_age value.

A cache might need to verify if an obsolete response can be used to respond to requests. The cache needs to use certain header fields to verify with the server the validity of the cached response. This model is called the *validation model*. One of the header fields used to validate a response is the Last-Modified field. If the contents on the server have not been updated since the date specified in the field, the response is declared valid. Otherwise, an updated response needs to be obtained from the server.

Another field used to validate a response is the Etag field. This field acts as a placeholder that can be assigned any entity value. *Entity values* point to a resource existing in a Web page. For example, if a button or an image exists on a Web page, the object is called an *entity*. If there are any differences between the value stored in the field and the entity value on the server, the cached response is declared as invalid and needs an update.

Despite the use of models for updating caches, they can store incomplete responses. For instance, if a server returns a response with incomplete data, the response is still stored in the cache as a partial response. However, these responses are provided to the requesting client only after marking it as a partial response by using the Partial Content status code.

Summary

The HTTP application protocol implements Web content data transfer features in the TCP/IP reference model. HTTP implements this feature by sending a request from the client and obtaining a response from the server. Unlike previous HTTP versions, in version 1.1 of the protocol, the request and response are transmitted over a persistent connection that is kept alive until the client or server terminates the connection. To determine the capabilities supported by the client and the server, the computers exchange information in header fields of a request message or a response message. The components of an HTTP message vary slightly according to the type of the message. The HTTP request is structured in the form of a Request Line, Header, Blank Line, and Body. The HTTP response is structured in the form of a Status Line, Header, Blank Line, and a Body. The header can be further classified as request, response, and entity. To enhance the performance of an HTTP implementation, the HTTP specification proposes caching the responses obtained from the server and verifying the validity of the cached responses by using the expiration model or the validation model.

Ch

11

CHAPTER 12

SIMPLE NETWORK MANAGEMENT PROTOCOL (SNMP)

In this chapter

NETWORK MANAGEMENT

Simple Network Management Protocol (SNMP) is a protocol that belongs to the TCP/IP protocol suite and is used for network management. SNMP operates from the Application layer (see Figure 12.1) of the TCP/IP reference model. SNMP, being an Application layer protocol, can be used for any hardware and software technology and is adopted as the standard for network management on the Internet.

Figure 12.1
SNMP operates from the Application layer of the TCP/IP reference model and is used as the standard for network management.

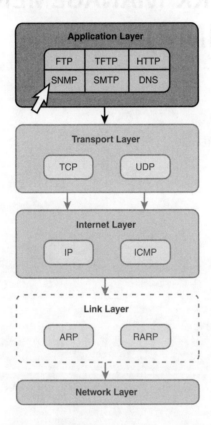

Network management is the process of monitoring a network to ensure the smooth functioning of various network components. It is also used to ensure that the policies laid down by the manager are implemented in the network. Network management also involves maintenance of the network components. Network administrators can use network management tools to find performance bottlenecks in the network and make the required changes to the network. Network management also involves making decisions on software and hardware upgrades if the network administrator finds out that the software or the hardware configuration of a computer must be upgraded to overcome the problems.

Consider a scenario where the network administrator needs to manage and troubleshoot a medium-sized network by using SNMP. Typically, the network administrator needs to monitor the occurrence of any performance bottleneck and identify the root cause of the bottleneck. The factors that cause bottlenecks include faulty hardware devices (hubs, switches), slow processing capabilities on the computers in the network, and low bandwidth available on the network. SNMP enables the network manager to pinpoint the factors that have caused bottlenecks apart from the specific hardware devices that are responsible for the problem. Now, the network administrator can decide on the best performance enhancing strategy to employ based on the vital information provided by SNMP. In this way, SNMP eases network monitoring and administration enabling the network administrators to maximize the performance capabilities of their networks.

Note

System management is a subset of network management, which is used to monitor individual devices such as a computer, router, and printer.

Apart from local networks, SNMP is the de facto standard for managing TCP/IP Internetworks. All the devices connected to a network have an impact on the performance of the network. In addition, the performances of a few devices are also interrelated. For example, the performance of a router is affected by factors such as the ports, the cables, and speed of the computers en route. Router performance can be affected by factors such as router processor capability or buffer overflows. To find the exact cause of the problem, all the components of the network that might influence the speed of the router must be monitored. The network management system must enable a network administrator to monitor all the devices that are connected to the network. For example, if the speed of the network is found to be low, one of the reasons for the problem could be the router. The number of packets that reach and leave the router at a particular point of time must be monitored. To collect information about devices, SNMP enables devices such as computers, routers, printers, and hubs to be monitored from a computer called the SNMP manager. SNMP uses a distributed architecture for network management.

CH

12

Two components are used for network management using SNMP, SNMP managers and SNMP agents. The SNMP managers and agents interact with each other to exchange data. The *SNMP manager* is a computer that controls the functioning of SNMP agents. The SNMP manager, SNMP agents, and other components that are used with SNMP for network management are discussed in the section "Components of the SNMP Architecture."

Note

The SNMP manager is a computer on which the SNMP manager software is installed. A computer need not be dedicated to function as an SNMP manager. A server that already exists on the network can act as an SNMP manager.

SNMP interacts with UDP in the Transport layer for transferring data over the network. SNMP transmits data to the Transport layer in the form of SNMP messages. These messages are, in turn, encapsulated in an UDP datagram and sent to the lower layers. The SNMP manager and the agents use a set of commands for interaction. The values that are to be passed along with the command and the code used to identify the commands, also called PDU numbers, comprise the SNMP message.

SNMP provides a connectionless service because the underlying Transport layer protocol that is used for communication is UDP. The well-defined UDP ports that are used by SNMP are 161 and 162. The SNMP manager receives responses and traps from the agent through port number 161 and the SNMP agent receives requests from the SNMP manager at port number 162. The advantage of providing a connectionless service is that the managers and the agents do not depend on each other for their functioning. That is, an agent or manager need not wait for a connection to be established at the other end to send or receive messages. Similarly, if the agents have to send alert signals to the manager, they need not wait for a connection to be established. This would also not be preferred by the agent because the severity of the alert also needs to be considered.

Note

The alert signals that are sent from the agent to the manager are also known as traps.

Note

The terms *managers* and *SNMP managers* can be used interchangeably. The terms *agents* and *SNMP agents* can also be used interchangeably.

A connectionless service also enables the network traffic to be reduced because the receipt of data packets need not be acknowledged and network resources are not utilized for retransmission of data packets. UDP port numbers 161 and 162 are used for transmitting and receiving SNMP messages.

→ For more information on User Datagram Protocol, **see** "User Datagram Protocol," **p. 113**

COMPONENTS OF THE SNMP ARCHITECTURE

The SNMP architecture comprises two main components, managers and agents, apart from a set of standards that are used for controlling the interaction between the components. The SNMP managers and agents communicate with each other by using SNMP commands. These commands are defined in RFC 1157. The managers control the functioning of the agents. The agents provide the information required by the managers by interacting with devices such as computers and routers. These devices are also called managed devices. The protocol that is used for communication between the managers and the agents is SNMP and is also referred to as the management protocol.

→ For more information on RFCs, **see** "RFCs," **p. 425**

MANAGED DEVICES

The performances of the devices that need to be managed are routers, bridges, gateways, printers, the computers, and so on. All these devices are also known as managed devices, network elements, or managed nodes. For example, the details that need to be recorded about a router can be the number of packets sent and received at a point of time.

SNMP AGENTS

An *SNMP agent*, generally called an *agent*, is a component of the network management system. It is used to obtain information about the functioning of the managed device as requested by the SNMP manager. The agents act as the interface between the SNMP manager and the managed devices. If you need to monitor a computer, you must install the agent software on it. In case the device you want to monitor is not a computer, you can install the agent software on the computer that can thus communicate with it, such as a computer connected to the device. An SNMP agent is a passive component in the SNMP architecture. It does not communicate with the SNMP managers unless a request is received from the manager. However, it can use a set of messages called traps when it needs to gain the attention of the processor, such as when unusual errors occur. The SNMP agents perform the following functions:

- Store and retrieve values according to the commands that are received from the manager. The values related to the managed device are stored in a database called the Management Information Base (MIB).
- Send alerts to the manager in the form of trap messages.

Every computer running the agent software contains an MIB for maintaining the details related to the managed devices. However, in the case of a diskless workstation in which a hard disk is not available, a different computer that runs the agent can be used to store information about the managed devices. Such agents are called *proxy agents*. A proxy agent can be used to interact with more than one computer that is not capable of storing the details about the managed devices.

SNMP MANAGER

An *SNMP manager* is a computer that is used to coordinate with the agents to collect information about the managed devices. This component of the network management system remains passive until it receives requests from the manager. An SNMP manager is also referred to as a *Network Management Workstation (NMS)*. A computer on a network can be assigned as the SNMP manager by installing the SNMP management software. The SNMP manager performs the following functions:

- Sends queries to the agents and also accepts values from the agents.
- Sets values in the agents to control few functions.
- Accepts alerts from the agents called traps.

Note

The SNMP manager can also be called a network manager.

MANAGED OBJECTS

A managed object is a part of a managed device that can be monitored separately. For example, a processor is one of the objects of a managed device that can be monitored separately.

MANAGEMENT INFORMATION BASE

A Management Information Base (MIB) is a repository of information about the managed objects that can be used by the SNMP manager. The information stored in an MIB can be related to performance of the managed device, such as the number of data packets that have been sent and received, or information related to the configuration of the managed device.

An MIB is used to represent data in a format that is independent of the intricacies of the hardware and software. Collections of related managed objects are defined in specific MIB modules or MIB groups. For example, an MIB group is called ip, which is used to store information about the transactions related to IP in the Internet layer.

STRUCTURE OF MANAGEMENT INFORMATION

Structure of Management Information (SMI) defines the rules for identifying and accessing information about the managed objects in the MIB. It states that every managed object must conform to the following standards:

- Every managed object must have a unique identifier, which is called an object identifier (OID).

- The format and the syntax in which the managed objects must be defined are defined in a language called the Abstract Syntax Notation 1 (ASN.1). ASN.1 is a standard used for defining data that needs to be transmitted over a network. ASN.1 is independent of the languages that are used or the applications that are used to create the data. The data formats that are defined by ASN.1 can be used to send any form of data, such as text files, audio, or video. ASN.1 is supported by almost all the operating systems.

- The encoding scheme used for representing the managed objects is called *Basic Encoding Rules (BER)*. This is one of the standard encoding schemes that is implemented universally. The advantage with BER is that it supports applications that would operate with low bandwidths.

Note

The way in which the managed objects are to be encoded during transmission is called the *encoding scheme*.

OBJECT IDENTIFIERS

Object identifiers (OID) follow a hierarchy defined by the IETF. This is done to ensure standardization of OIDs. The OIDs can be represented as numbers in the MIB separated by periods or can be represented as a group of names separated by periods. The representation of an OID by using names eases readability. For example, the OID of the ip group is `iso.org.dod.internet.mgmt.mib.ip`, which is also represented in the number form as `1.3.6.1.2.1.4`.

The structure of the OID hierarchy is similar to a directory structure that is used to store files on a hard disk. The node at the top level of the hierarchy is called the root node. Figure 12.2 represents the hierarchy of names that is used to identify objects in the MIB. The subtree in the hierarchy that is relevant to SNMP is mib and is represented by the number 1. The nodes in the hierarchy are commonly represented along with their corresponding number representation in parentheses. For example, the MIB subtree is represented as `mib(1)`. All the OIDs that are used to represent MIB objects must start with the number `1.3.6.1.2.1`.

Figure 12.2
The OIDs must be defined by the hierarchy that is specified by IETF.

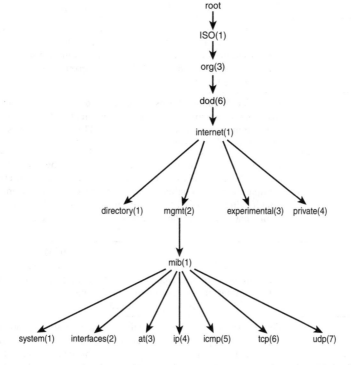

CH
12

The MIB subtree is further divided into various groups. They are listed in Table 12.1. The group used for storing information in the MIB depends on the managed device. For example, values related to IP can be stored only using the ip group. Each group contains a list of identifiers that are used to identify specific problems with the group or the managed device. Figure 12.3 displays the values that belong to the ip group of the object hierarchy.

Figure 12.3
The ip subtree or the ip group of the mib group is used to store information about IP in the MIB.

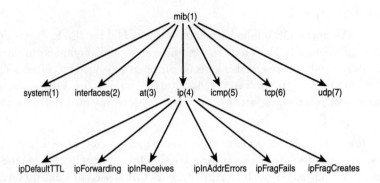

TABLE 12.1   GROUPS THAT BELONG TO THE mib(1) SUBTREE

Group Name	Description
System(1)	Maintains system-related information such as system uptime and system location. This group consists of seven variables. One of the variables available in this group is sysLocation, which can be referred to get the physical location of the computer. The OID of the system group is 1.3.6.1.2.1.1.
interfaces(2)	Maintains details about the interfaces. Ethernet and PPP are examples of an interface. This group contains only a single variable that is used to keep track of the total number of interfaces open at a point of time. The OID of the interfaces group is 1.3.6.1.2.1.2. This group also defines a table, which is a data type used to store the details about an interface.
at(3)	Stores details about address resolution and defines three variables. The at group is now a deprecated group because its functions are implemented by the ip group in the latest version of SNMP. This group defines three variables. The OID of the at group is 1.3.6.1.2.1.3.
ip(4)	The ip group is used to store the details of IP. The network administrators can use these details to monitor the functioning of the Internet layer. For example, this group defines variables that store information, such as the default value of the TTL field of the IP header and the number of IP datagrams that were discarded due to various reasons. The OID of the ip group is 1.3.6.1.2.1.4.
icmp(5)	The icmp group is used to store the details of ICMP. This group defines variables that can be used to store the value of the number of ICMP messages that were sent and received. For instance, this group can be used to keep track of the number of destination unreachable messages that were generated. The OID of this group is 1.3.6.1.2.1.5.
tcp(6)	The tcp group is used to maintain information about problems related to TCP. For example, the details about the state of a connection can be maintained by using this group. The OID of this group is 1.3.6.1.2.1.6.
udp(7)	This group is used to maintain details about the functioning of UDP. For example, this group defines a variable that can be used to store the value of the number of UDP datagrams that were received. The OID of this group is 1.3.6.1.2.1.7.

➜ For more information on Internet Protocol, **see** "Internet Protocol: The Internet Layer Protocol," **p. 45**

DATA TYPES DEFINED IN MIB

SMI allows the creation of two types of data in an MIB, the basic or simple data type and the structured data type. *Simple data types* are used to represent the smallest unit of data in the MIB. They cannot be broken down further. *Structured data types* are built using simple data types. Simple data types are also called *atomic data types*. Table 12.2 displays a list of simple data types. The values that are created in the groups specified should be defined with any of the data types stated earlier.

TABLE 12.2 SIMPLE DATA TYPES USED IN AN MIB

Data Type	Description
Integer	A 32-bit number that can be used to represent the operational status of a managed device. For example, the variable `ipDefaultTTL` of the ip group is used to store the value that will be assigned to the `TTL` field in the IP header if no value is provided by the higher layers.
Octet String	A data type used for storing text values. The size of this data type is not a constant. For example, `sysLocation` of the system group is a text that is used to provide the location of the node.
Counter	This data type is used to keep track of the variables that act as counters in the MIB. For example, the variable that is used to store the number of ICMP messages that are received is a counter. The size of this data type is four bytes. It is represented as `icmpInErrors` in the icmp group. The minimum value of this field is `0` and the maximum value that can be taken is 2^{32}-1. After the counter value reaches the maximum value, the value is set to `0` automatically. A few more examples of variables that belong to the Counter data type in the ip group are `ipInAddrErrors`, `ipForwDatagrams`, and `ipFragFails`.
IpAddress	A data type used to store an IP address. The size of this field is four bytes.
Gauge	A data type that is similar to the Counter data type. The only difference is that after it reaches the maximum value, it is not set back to zero unless it is done explicitly. The maximum and the minimum values that are set for the Counter data type are applicable to the Gauge data type too.
Timeticks	A data type used to store time in 1/100 of a second. The size of this data type is also four bytes.

CH
12

Note

The IpAddress data type is used to represent an IPv4 address and not an IPv6 address.

The structured data types used in MIB are Sequence and Sequence of. A *Sequence* data type is created by a combination of different simple data types. An example of a sequence data type is a table. However, the *Sequence of* data type is created using the same simple data type. For example, if the simple data type used is Integer, all the component data types that form the sequence of data type must be of type Integer.

SNMP COMMUNITIES

The interaction between the SNMP managers and agents must be secure because they exchange vital information between each other. Apart from sending requests to the agents for obtaining vital information, managers can also change values in the MIB through the agents. Modifications of values must be done in a secure manner. Before allowing a manager to change the value in the MIB, a check needs to be done to ensure that the manager is authenticated to perform this operation. To implement such security measures, the SNMP managers and agents are grouped into communities. There are three types of communities: read-only, read-write, and trap.

The *read-only* community signifies that the manager can access the MIB but cannot modify the values in it. However, the *read-write* community *enables* the manager to change the values in the MIB, in addition to being able to read the content. The *trap* community enables the SNMP manager to receive trap messages, which are alert signals sent to indicate that a critical error has occurred. The community name is specified in the second field of the SNMP message. The fields in SNMP messages are covered in detail in the section "Format of an SNMP Message," later in this chapter. The default value of this field is public, which stands for the read-only community. If the value of the field is private, it denotes that the community type is read-write. The SNMP agents can be used to send traps when an unauthorized SNMP manager tries to access values in the SNMP agent.

The community names play a very important role in managing the security of the managed devices. Measures must be taken to avoid unauthorized access to the information on the managed devices because the functioning of the devices can be affected.

In Windows 2000 Server, SNMP is installed as a service on the operating system. The SNMP manager software is installed on the computer that acts as the SNMP manager and the agent software is installed on the agents. Logical groups are created with descriptive names called communities. Agents will accept requests from managers that belong to the same community. However, an agent can be configured to accept requests from managers that belong to different communities. In that case, an agent will accept a request only from an authenticated list of managers. By default, a community named public is created by the Windows 2000 Server operating system. Figure 12.4 displays the default SNMP community that is assigned in Windows 2000 Server and the corresponding access right. The access right assigned to this community is read-only. However, the network administrator can create other communities and assign appropriate access rights to them. A community name that is created can be any name that is valid in the context of the operating system and must be descriptive. For example, you can create a community called managers and assign read-write access rights to them.

Figure 12.4
The default community name that is created in Windows 2000 Server is public and the access right that is assigned to the community is read-only.

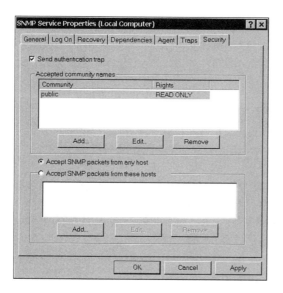

COMMANDS USED BY MANAGERS AND AGENTS

The SNMP managers and agents interact with each other using a set of commands called the SNMP commands. The SNMP managers and the agents use SNMP messages to send commands. The details required by the SNMP managers and agents to process the commands are also included in the SNMP message. The get request and the get next request commands are sent by the SNMP manager to the agents. The agents respond to the managers through get response. The SNMP managers and the agents communicate with each other through UDP ports 161 and 162.

> **Note**
>
> The SNMP managers and the agent can run on the same computer. However, the port numbers that are used by the SNMP manager and the agent must be different.

CH

12

THE get request COMMAND

The SNMP manager uses the get request command to obtain MIB information from the agent. This command can be used to obtain a value for a single MIB object from the SNMP agent. To provide the requested information, the SNMP agent requires some information. This information is provided by the SNMP manager through specific fields in the SNMP message.

THE get next request COMMAND

The get next request command is used by the SNMP manager to obtain a group of values from the SNMP agent. For example, the SNMP manager can request the information in a routing table.

THE get response COMMAND

The SNMP agents use the get response command to respond to the get request and the get next request commands that are sent by the SNMP manager.

THE set request COMMAND

The SNMP manager uses the set request command to assign values to the MIB object in the SNMP agent. This command will be successful only if the manager has read-write access rights. Otherwise, an error is reported.

THE trap COMMAND

Agents do not initiate communication with the SNMP manager. However, in exceptional cases when the agent comes across errors or network problems, it sends an alert signal to the SNMP manager in the form of trap messages.

> **Note**
> In the context of SNMP, traps and trap messages are the same.

Trap messages are sent to the SNMP agent when an illegal access is performed on a computer, an error occurs at a router, or when an agent is shut down or restarted. Table 12.3 displays the various trap messages that can be generated by the agent.

TABLE 12.3   TRAP MESSAGES GENERATED BY THE SNMP AGENT

Trap Code	Value	Description
0	ColdStart	Indicates that the agent is restarting and represents a hard boot.
1	WarmStart	Indicates that the agent is restarting and represents a soft boot.
2	LinkDown	Indicates that a device is not functioning properly. For example, if a computer or a router is malfunctioning, this message is sent.
3	Linkup	Indicates that a device that was malfunctioning has resumed function.
4	AuthenticationFailure	Indicates that an unauthorized access has occurred. This trap is generated because of an invalid community name.

TABLE 12.3 CONTINUED

Trap Code	Value	Description
5	`EgpNeighborLoss`	Indicates that an EGP device is not functional.
6	`EnterpriseSpecific`	This is used to indicate the other types of error messages that are generated, which do not belong to the any of the categories mentioned. More information about this trap can be found from the specific code in the SNMP message format.

➔ For more information on User Datagram Protocol, **see** "InterAutonomous System Routing Protocol—EGP and BGP," **p. 311**

FORMAT OF AN SNMP MESSAGE

The SNMP messages are encapsulated in a UDP datagram (see Figure 12.5) and passed over the network.

Source
Destination
Frame
IP Datagram
IP Header
UDP Header
SNMP Message

Figure 12.5
SNMP messages are encapsulated in an UDP datagram. IP in the Internet layer is responsible for routing the SNMP message to the appropriate destination.

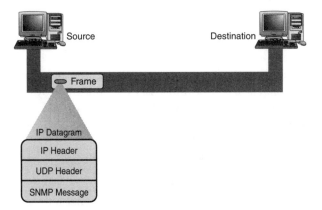

The SNMP message format is used by the managers and the agents to exchange information with each other. Figure 12.6 displays the format of an SNMP message.

version
Community name
PDU code
request number
error status
error index
values

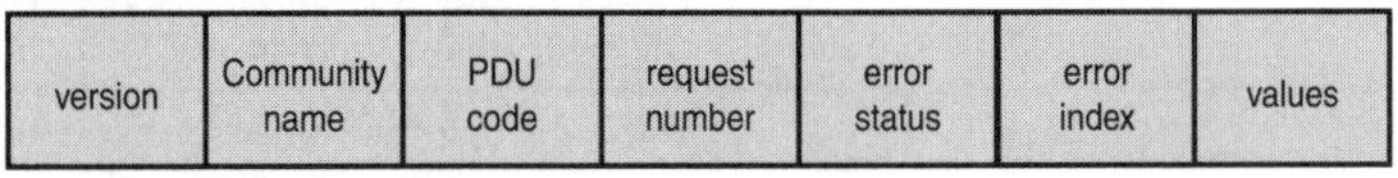

Figure 12.6
The information required by the managers and the agents is exchanged using the fields in an SNMP message.

Every SNMP message consists of the following information:

- The version of SNMP used to send the message. The first version of SNMP, called SNMPv1, is represented by the value 0.

- The second field in the SNMP message is the name of the SNMP community to which the agent belongs.

- The third field in the SNMP message is the Protocol Data Unit (PDU) number. This is used to represent the code of the command used. The value of this field can range between 0 and 4. The values of the PDU field and the corresponding SNMP commands are displayed in Table 12.4.

TABLE 12.4   PDU VALUES AND THE COMMANDS THEY REPRESENT

Value	Command
0	get request
1	get next request
2	get response
3	set request
4	Trap

- The field next to the PDU is used to represent the error messages that are generated by the agent. Each one of the error messages is represented by a code. This field is also referred as the error status field. Table 12.5 lists the error messages that can be generated by an agent.

TABLE 12.5   ERROR MESSAGES GENERATED BY AN AGENT

Code	Error Message	Description
0	NoError	Indicates that the operation was error free.
1	TooBig	Indicates that the reply to the get request or the get next request command could not be sent in a single SNMP message.
2	NoSuchName	Indicates that the value requested through the get request and get next request commands sent by the manager do not exist in the MIB.
3	BadValue	Indicates that the values specified in the set request command sent by the manager is invalid and thus cannot be modified in the MIB.
4	ReadOnly	Indicates that the community is read-only and not read-write.
5	GenErr	Indicates other types of errors.

- The field next to the error status field is used to find the variable in the SNMP message that has caused the error.

- The values of variables that are required by the SNMP manager and the values that are sent by the agent to the manager follow the error index field in the SNMP message. The values are sent in the form of OID and the corresponding value. If a request is sent from the SNMP manager to the agent, only the OID is specified and the value is left blank. When the agent responds to the request, it fills the values for the OIDs in the SNMP message and sends it back to the SNMP manager.

Note

The get request, get next request, and the set commands can be used to obtain the values of more than one variable at a point of time.

Note

In SNMPv1, if the agent is not able to provide a value to a variable that is requested by the manager, the entire request fails.

SUMMARY

Network administrators need to constantly monitor their networks to identify performance bottlenecks and to resolve performance issues caused by these bottlenecks. Simple Network Management Protocol (SNMP) can be used by network administrators to identify and pin-point the root cause of any performance bottleneck encountered on local networks or on a TCP/IP internetwork. The SNMP architecture consists of components, such as SNMP manager and SNMP agent, which communicate with each other through SNMP messages. An agent acts as an interface between the SNMP manager and a Management Information Base that stores information about the managed devices. The manager sends commands to read information from the MIB through the agent or control the functioning of a device by setting certain values in the MIB. Agents and managers ensure authenticated access by using community names. Agents remain passive unless the managers request information from the MIB. However, agents can initiate a transaction by sending traps to the managers.

CH
12

CHAPTER 13

DOMAIN NAME SYSTEM (DNS)

In this chapter

THE NEED FOR DNS

Computers that are connected to a network are identified by a unique address called the MAC address or the hardware address of the computer. However, because the hardware address is dependent on the hardware technology used, an addressing scheme, called the IP addressing scheme, was created. This can be used independent of the hardware technology. The IP address is also called the *software address* of a computer.

The Network layer requires the hardware addresses for transferring data over the physical medium. To convert IP addresses to hardware addresses, Address Resolution Protocol (ARP) is used. In spite of providing access to computers irrespective of the underlying hardware technology, IP addresses have a limitation. Users cannot be expected to remember the IP address to access a computer on the network. It's easier to use descriptive names to access a computer rather than using the IP address of the same. *Domain Name System (DNS)* is used for enabling users to provide descriptive names to identify and access a computer. However, IP of the Internet layer requires IP addresses to route data. Therefore, a technique by which the name of a computer, called the *host name*, can be mapped to the corresponding IP address is required. This is achieved by maintaining a distributed database called the Domain Name System (DNS) that contains the mapping between the host names and the IP addresses. Figure 13.1 indicates the position of the layer from which DNS operates in the TCP/IP reference model.

Note

DNS is also called *DNS database*.

Note

The DNS database is called a distributed database because the contents of the database are stored in multiple computers.

→ For more information on Address Resolution Protocol (ARP), **see** "The Network Interface and Link Layers," **p. 25**

Note

The *host name* is also referred to as a *computer name*.

DNS also provides the set of standards that are required for communication between two computers. DNS operates from the Application layer of the TCP/IP reference model. Application layer protocols, such as HTTP and FTP, use DNS to resolve computer names and IP addresses and vice versa. The specifications of DNS are provided in RFCs 1034 and 1035.

Note

DNS is also referred to as *Domain Naming Service*. In the context of DNS providing a set of standards for communication between two computers for resolving computer names, it is referred to as a service that operates from the Application layer of the TCP/IP reference model. However, the expansion of DNS according to RFCs 1034 and 1035 is Domain Name System. The RFC also defines a set of standards that need to be followed to use DNS.

→ For information on RFCs, **see** "RFCs," **p. 425**

Figure 13.1
DNS operates from the Application layer of the TCP/IP reference model and is used to resolve host names to IP addresses.

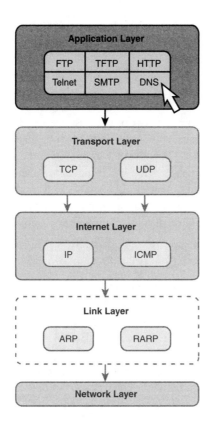

CH

13

For example, in Windows 2000 Server, name resolution is implemented by installing DNS as a networking service (see Figure 13.2).

Figure 13.2
DNS can be installed only on computers installed with the Windows 2000 Server operating system.

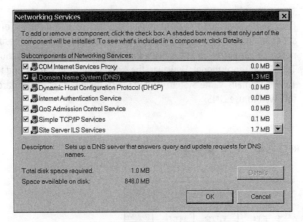

ADVANTAGES OF USING DNS

Before the evolution of DNS, the mapping between the host names and the IP addresses was maintained by the Network Information Center (NIC) in a file called hosts.txt. A copy of the hosts.txt file had to be maintained on all the computers on the network. As computers were added to the network, the hosts.txt file had to be updated and the new copy had to be replicated on the other computers. This mechanism became cumbersome with the increase in the number of computers that were to be connected to the Internet. The limitations of maintaining the DNS database on a single computer are as follows:

- As the number of computers increases, the size of the database would become too large and managing the database would become very difficult.

- The search time that will be taken for processing a single query will be too long because the complete database needs to be browsed.

- Storing the database on a single computer would also not be fault tolerant because if the database is damaged, the entire network will be affected.

DNS solves these problems by maintaining a distributed database and uses different techniques to update it with changes in the network. DNS is independent of the underlying mechanism that is used for communication between the hosts.

Note

DNS was created for standardizing the names used for computers that were connected to the Internet. Moreover, the host naming conventions specified by DNS enables communication between computers irrespective of the underlying architecture. DNS can also be used for administering host names and domains in an intranet. NetBIOS is the communications standard that is used by Windows for a network that consists of computers running only on the Windows operating system. The name resolution in a pure Windows network is done by a name resolution service called Windows Internet Naming Service (WINS). However, if the network is heterogeneous and uses TCP/IP as the communication protocol, DNS must be used for name resolution.

Note

InterNIC (Internet Network Information Center) or the NIC was the organization responsible for administering registration to top-level domains. These days a nonprofit organization called Internet Corporation of Assigned Names and Numbers (ICANN) is taking care of accrediting registrars of domain names. In turn, the registrars manage the process of registering domain names, which is done for a fee. This comes in the wake of some changes in government policies.

NAMING CONVENTIONS USED IN DNS

The host names or the computer names that are used in DNS must follow the hierarchical structure of assigning names to hosts as defined by the NIC. In the hierarchy that is defined by NIC, computers are grouped into smaller manageable units called domains. The hierarchy starts with the root node. The label of the root node is left blank. Under the root node is a standard set of domains (see Figure 13.3), which have been created based on the type of the organization.

These domains are represented by a three-letter code. An example of a three letter is .com, which is used to represent commercial organizations. The domains that come under the root node can also be based on the country in which the domain exists and is represented as a two-letter code. For example, us represents the United States. The domains that come under the root node are called *top-level domains* and the next level of domains is called the *second-level domains*. A domain can consist of a group of computers called hosts or could be further subdivided into subdomains. Table 13.1 displays a list of standard domains defined by NIC.

Figure 13.3
All the internetworks that are created must follow the naming conventions defined in the domain naming hierarchy specified by NIC.

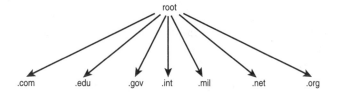

Cн
13

TABLE 13.1	STANDARD DOMAINS DEFINED BY NIC	
Serial Number	**Domain Name**	**Description**
1	com	Represents commercial organizations.
2	edu	Represents educational institutions.
3	gov	Represents government organizations.
4	int	Represents international organizations.

TABLE 13.1   CONTINUED

Serial Number	Domain Name	Description
5	mil	Represents military organizations in the U.S.
6	net	Represents a commercial network.
7	org	Represents other types of organizations.

In addition to the top-level domain names specified in Table 13.1, new domain names, such as .biz, .info, and .name have been approved by ICANN. Businesses can use .biz as a domain name for their Web sites. Individuals creating Web sites of their own can use the .name domain name to add their names to their Web site. The .info domain name can be used for any Web site that provides information. To obtain more information on the new top-level domain names approved by ICANN, access http://www.internic.net/faqs/new-tlds.html.

Like the classful addressing scheme used for assigning IP addresses in which a part of the IP address is provided by the NIC depending on the type of address class used, a domain name is also partly provided by the NIC. That is, if a domain needs to be created for a commercial organization, a domain other than the top-level domains specified in the domain naming hierarchy cannot be created. The standard top-level domain for commercial organizations, .com, must be used. However, the NIC enables the organization to administer a local set of domains, which will be the subdomains of .com. For example, if a commercial organization called BlueValley Computers wants to host a Web site for its company, it cannot use any other top-level domain name but .com. However, the name of the second-level domain can be created as per the requirements of the organization after the approval of the NIC. If Bluevalley.com has been approved as the Web site name for the organization, creation of subdomains for BlueValley.com is left to the discretion of the organization. Examples of subdomains that can be created are Department1.BlueValley.com and Department2.BlueValley.com. An important point to note is that the name Bluevalley.com must not be in use already.

→ For more information on classful addressing scheme, **see** "The Network Interface and Link Layers," **p. 25**

Note

Before the evolution of the hierarchical system of filenames, a flat namespace, which is also a naming convention, was used to name the domains and computers. There were no standards to generalize the naming of computers. This prevented standardization of domain names across the Internet. Moreover, the process of adding a new computer or a domain was cumbersome. When a new computer is added to a network, the host name must be validated by the authority responsible. Moreover, the flat namespace cannot be used for generalizing all types of networks.

The rules for naming domains are as follows:

- The name of each node in the hierarchy can be a maximum of 62 characters long.
- The total size of the domain name can be a maximum of 256 characters only.

In DNS, the process of referring to a domain name is different from the way in which the path of files and directories are specified in the operating system. In the case of DNS, the domain names start with the node, which is at the bottom of the hierarchy, and ends with the root node, which is internally represented by a period. For example, if you are accessing the Web site www.quepublishing.com, the complete path of the Web site will be www.quepublishing.com., where . at the end of the name represents the root node, com represents the top-level domain, and quepublishing represents the domain that is administered by the organization, and so on.

After a computer is connected to the network, the network administrator provides it an IP address and a computer name. The network administrator also updates the DNS database with the corresponding entries. The process of resolving the computer names to the corresponding IP addresses and vice versa is called name resolution in DNS, which is discussed in detail later in this chapter.

Note

DNS interacts with Dynamic Host Configuration Protocol (DHCP) for keeping track of additions and modifications to the IP addresses. This feature can be configured while installing a DHCP server on Windows 2000 Server. However, if the IP addresses are assigned manually, the network administrator must manually update the mapping between the host names and the IP addresses.

Transfer of DNS Messages

DNS operates from the Application layer of the TCP/IP reference model. Application protocols such as HTTP interact with DNS for name resolution. For example, if you access the Web site named www.que.com, the application that is using HTTP, which in this case is a Web browser, forwards a query to a computer called the DNS server requesting the corresponding IP address. If the request cannot be resolved locally, a DNS message is created and passed over the network to the DNS server that can answer the queries. DNS relies on the underlying Transport layer protocol to transfer the messages to other computers. The Transport layer protocol that is used by DNS is most commonly UDP. There are a few situations in which TCP is used by DNS, which is discussed later in this chapter.

CH

13

Note

A network consists of at least one computer that acts as the DNS server. All the queries for name resolution are directed to the DNS server.

The format in which DNS messages or queries are sent over the network is called the DNS message format. DNS messages are encapsulated in a UDP datagram (see Figure 13.4) or a TCP segment and passed over the network. In any case, the protocol that is used for delivering the DNS messages is IP.

> **Note**
>
> DNS uses the well-defined port 53 for interacting with UDP and TCP.

→ For more information on IP, **see** "Internet Protocol: The Internet Layer Protocol," **p. 44**

→ For more information on TCP, **see** "TCP—Introduction and Data Flow," **p. 74**

→ For more information on UDP, **see** "User Datagram Protocol," **p. 113**

Figure 13.4
The queries to a DNS server are sent as a DNS message that is encapsulated in a UDP datagram.

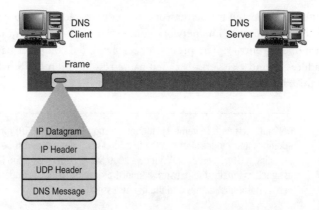

COMPONENTS AND STEPS INVOLVED IN NAME RESOLUTION

Name resolution is the process of resolving the IP address to the corresponding host name and vice versa. There are different components, such as the resolver, the DNS servers, and zone files, which form a part of this process. The database is distributed across different computers and thus is distributed across a network. Dividing a database into logical groups makes it easy for administrators to maintain the database. In addition, the load of the DNS servers will be balanced. Moreover, if all the records are stored in a single database, searching for data would take a long time.

RESOLVER

All the applications that require name resolution forward their request to a component in the client called the resolver (see Figure 13.5), which acts as an interface between the applications and the DNS servers. Web browsers or a mail client, such as Microsoft Outlook, are applications that require name resolution. The requests to the resolver are sent in the form of DNS messages. The applications invoke the resolver through functions or methods that are implemented in the application. The methods that are used to contact the resolver are `getHostByAddr()` and `getHostByName()`.

> **Note**
>
> The resolver and the application that requires name resolution function from the same computer.

> **Note**
>
> The networking services that are required to build a TCP/IP network are built into the operating system. A few of the networking services are installed with the operating system by default and the rest can be installed as and when required. The functionality of a resolver will be built into the network services.

The resolver sends the request to the DNS server. If the DNS server is able to find the corresponding IP address, it sends the details to the resolver. Otherwise, the DNS server intimates the resolver on what needs to be done by the resolver to get the name resolved.

Figure 13.5
The resolver is used to accept queries from the application and forward them to a name server.

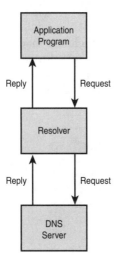

ZONES

DNS databases contain the mapping between names and IP addresses. However, if the number of computers that are connected to an internetwork is very large, it will be difficult and inefficient to manage the database on a single computer. As a solution, the details required for name resolution are distributed across DNS servers to balance the load of the DNS servers and also facilitate efficient management of the databases.

CH
13

A domain in the domain names hierarchy that can be administered separately is called a *zone*. For example, if the name of a domain is www.abc.com, a zone can be created for the domain named abc, which is a subdomain of the domain.com. The zone will contain the details of all the computers that belong to that domain. If the number of computers connected to a domain managed as a single zone becomes too large to be administered as a single unit, the domain can be further subdivided into subdomains and each domain can be mapped to a zone that will hold the details of all the computers in the zone.

The server that contains the details for a zone is called the *name server* or the *DNS server*. For name resolution, the queries that are received from the resolver are answered by the name server for the zone. The name server that needs to be contacted to resolve the names details of a particular domain is said to be authoritative for that domain. The TCP/IP implementation on the DNS client computer takes care of redirecting the queries to the appropriate DNS server. For example, if a name server contains the zone files for the domain named abc, name resolution queries for the domain can be answered only by that name server and thus makes it authoritative for that domain. If the name server receives a query about a name that is not part of its zone, it cannot answer the query because its not authoritative for the domain. In that case, the query is redirected to a different name server. The network administrator must take care of configuring and administering the DNS servers.

If the number of computers present in the zone is too high, the zone can be further divided into *subzones*. The number of name servers for the zones will also increase accordingly. Each subzone will have a name server that can resolve the DNS queries for that subzone. Figure 13.6 shows the options that are available in Windows 2000 Server for initiating a zone transfer.

Figure 13.6
A zone transfer can be initiated to all the DNS servers that are present on the network or to a specific set of servers by specifying their IP addresses.

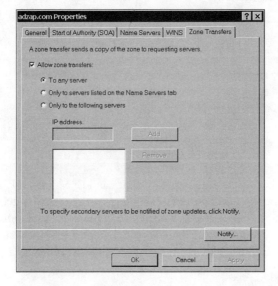

PRIMARY AND SECONDARY NAME SERVERS

DNS implements fault tolerance by enabling the network administrators to configure more than one name server for a domain. Configuring more than one name server on the network helps balance the load on the servers. This also ensures that minimum inconvenience is caused to users if a name server fails because the other name servers can be used for name resolution.

Note

Fault tolerance is the ability of an OS to handle exceptional situations, such as a hard disk failure. It refers to the set of measures taken by the OS to overcome the problem at the earliest.

The name servers are of two types, primary and secondary. *Primary name servers* are the name servers that contain the databases, which are also called *zone files*. The zone files are loaded from the hard disk of the primary name server. The secondary name servers get the information about the zone from the primary name servers. That is, the information present in the primary name servers is replicated in the secondary name servers for the zone. There can be more than one secondary name server for a zone.

ZONE TRANSFER

Any additions or modifications to the network must be updated in the zone files. This must be done in the zone file that exists on the primary name server. The secondary servers keep contacting the primary server to check for changes in the zone files. If there are changes in the zone files, a replication is initiated to update the zone files in the secondary name servers. This process of replicating zone file's data from the primary name servers in the secondary name servers is called *zone transfer*.

Note

The primary name server is also referred to as the primary zone or primary master and the secondary name server is also referred to as secondary zone or secondary master.

CH

13

NAME RESOLUTION PROCESS

Any application program that requires an IP address or a computer name passes its query to the resolver. The resolver checks the cache to find any matching entries. If the resolver is not able to find any matching entries, it passes the request to the name server of the zone. If the zone server is authoritative, it sends a required reply to the resolver. However, if the name server is not authoritative, it passes the query to the name server that can provide the required information.

For example, if a computer named c1.companyX.com needs to send a message to a computer named c10.companyX.com, the sender passes the query to the resolver. The resolver checks the cache for matching entries. If there are no matching entries in the cache, the resolver passes the query to the name server for the domain companyx.com. The name server for the domain being responsible for the name of the destination computer answers the query from the resolver. As stated earlier, the name server must be contacted to resolve the name details of a particular domain. This name server is said to be responsible for that domain.

Consider a situation wherein a computer named c1.abc.companyX.com needs to communicate with a computer named c10.def.companyY.com. The sender passes the request to the resolver. The resolver checks the cache to find matching entries. If there are no matching entries, the resolver passes the query to the local DNS server of the name server of the domain companyX.com. Because the local DNS server is responsible for all the computers in the domain companyX.com alone, it cannot resolve the host name being queried. Therefore, this DNS server in turn passes the query to the name server for .com, which is a root server. The root server in turn passes the query to one of the name servers that form a part of the .com domain hierarchy. Redirection of requests from one server to the other happens until the name server for the domain def.companyY.com is reached.

The lifetime of the cache entries is decided by the Time to Live (TTL) value that is present in the resource records. The cache entries that are recorded by the resolver might not be up-to-date with the changes made to the domain names and the IP addresses. Therefore, the entries in the cache are deleted after the TTL period expires. If a query that is received does not have matching entries in the cache, the complete name resolution process is repeated. Therefore, the answers to the queries that are received from the authoritative name server are accurate compared to the entries in the cache. This is because, when a change is made to the entries in the DNS database, the changes are not propagated to all the domains, except for the secondary DNS servers for the same domain.

Two methods can be followed if a name server is not able to resolve the queries that are sent by the client. They are iteration and recursion. In the case of *iteration*, the name server sends a reply back to the client if it is not able to resolve the query and refers the name of other name servers to be contacted by the client to get the query resolved. Iteration is also referred to as *iterative resolution*.

In the case of *recursive resolution*, if the name server is not authoritative of the host name requested, it passes the request to other name servers, which can resolve the query. An authoritative name server must know the address of the root servers in the domain name hierarchy. Examples of root servers include the servers for .edu and .com. Name servers and the clients exchange information between each other in the form of DNS messages.

Note

The servers that contain the details of the zone of the top-level domains are also known as root servers. All the DNS servers must contain the IP addresses of the root servers. If a name server receives a query that cannot be answered, it needs to redirect the query to a name server that can answer the query. However, if it does not find a server that can answer the request, it can direct the query to the root server. The root server can then take care of forwarding the query to the appropriate name server.

DNS CACHING

DNS enables faster name resolution by a process called *DNS caching*. In this process, the name servers on the network store the information about the answers to the name resolution queries locally. The name servers store all the responses received from the other name servers. Caching DNS queries helps reduce the time taken for name resolution and thus helps optimize the cost involved in resolving host names.

A name server checks the DNS cache only if it is not authoritative of the domain about which the query is posted. One important factor that needs to be considered for storing entries in the cache is the time for which the cache entries need to be held. The entries that are stored in the DNS cache must be valid. To ensure that the entries in the DNS cache are valid, the name servers set a time period for which the cache entries are to be held. This time period, called the *Time to Live (TTL)* period, is set when the name servers respond to the queries. After the elapse of the duration specified as TTL, the cache entries are deleted.

Note

The definition of TTL in the context of DNS is different from the one that is defined in the context of IP.

Note

DNS does not impose any restriction on the size of the DNS cache. However, the amount of memory that can be allocated for the DNS cache is limited by the memory available in the name server.

Note

The name servers can prevent the caching by setting the TTL value as 0.

CH

13

DNS MESSAGE FORMAT

The clients can request various categories of information from the server. For example, a Web server can request a domain name and a mail client can request details required for mail exchange. The type of reply that is required by the application is indicated through the query type field that is present in the DNS message. The details that are required by the client are conveyed to the server through a DNS message, which is in the format shown in

Figure 13.7. The name server, in turn, responds to the request by filling the required details in the message and routes it back to the client. Answers to the queries of the client are returned in the form of special types of records called *resource records (RR)* that are a part of the DNS message.

Figure 13.7
The format of the DNS reply and request messages are similar.

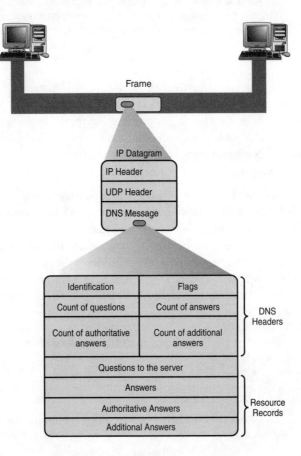

The following are the fields in a DNS message:

- Identification—Used to match the request sent by the client with the response sent by the server through the number in this field.

- Flags—Is a group of bits used to indicate various operations. Table 13.2 displays the different subfields of the Flags field.

TABLE 13.2   SUBFIELDS THAT CONSTITUTE THE Flags FIELD

Field Name	Description
Query/Response (QR)	Indicates the purpose of the DNS message. If set to 1, this indicates that the message is a response. If the value is 0, this indicates that the message is a query. This is a 1-bit field.

	TABLE 13.2 CONTINUED
Field Name	**Description**
Query Type (QT)	Indicates the type of query that is to be processed. The values that can be taken by this field are 0 and 1. 0 indicates a Standard query and 1 indicates an Inverse query. The size of this field is four bits. Standard and Inverse queries are discussed later in this chapter.
Authoritative Answer (AA)	Indicates that the name server that is being queried is authoritative of the domain being queried if the value in this field is set to 1. If the value in this field is 0, it indicates that the name server is not authoritative of the domain being queried. This field is 1 bit in size.
Truncated (TC)	When a DNS message is sent using UDP, the maximum size of the message must be 512 bytes. If the value of this field is set to 1, it indicates that the reply to the DNS query exceeded 512 bytes and thus got truncated because the Transport layer protocol used is UDP. However, the entire reply is not ignored. If the Truncated bit is set, a connection is established between the name server and client using TCP and the query processing is redone by the server so that the client receives the complete message.
Recursion Desired (RD)	If the name server being queried is not authoritative of the domain being queried, the name server performs an iterative resolution unless the value of this subfield is set to 1. To put it in simple terms, the client requests a recursive resolution from the name server through this bit.
Recursion Available (RA)	The name server uses this field to indicate that it is ready to accept recursive queries from the client.
Unused	The three bits that follow the Recursion Available field is reserved for future use. The value of this field must always be set to 0.
Error Code or Return Code (RCODE)	The name server uses this field to indicate errors caused while processing the query. The size of this field is 4 bits. If the value of this field is set to 0, it indicates that the query processing was successful. If there is a problem in the format of the DNS message, the error value 1 is returned to the client. If the domain name that is being queried for does not exist, the error value 3 is generated. Error value 4 is reported when the name server does not support a query type. A name server can also be configured to decline queries from certain clients. Error value 5 is returned to the client if the type of query sent is declined by the server. Error values 6–15 are reserved for future use.

CH

13

Note

UDP cannot be used as the Transport layer protocol in situations where the size of the DNS messages exceeds 512 bytes because UDP imposes this restriction on the size of the message. In such cases, TCP must be used as the underlying transport protocol. If TCP is used as the Transport layer protocol and the size of the DNS message exceeds 512 bytes, the message portion is divided into TCP segments by TCP before it is transmitted over the network. Another situation in which TCP is used with DNS is in the case of zone transfers where reliable transmission of data is required.

Note

The size of the DNS message header is 12 bytes. The other fields in the message format are variable in length.

- Number of Questions—Stores the number of questions that are sent to the name server. By default, the value in this field is set to 1 because a query must have at least one question.
- Number of Answers—Indicates the number of answers that have been returned.
- Authority—This field contains the name servers that can be used for resolving the queries. This field will be used if recursive resolution is used.

QUERIES

The Queries component of the DNS message provides the details about the queries. This field provides information that is required to process the queries, such as query name, query type, and query class. The Query Name subfield holds the name of the domain being queried. The query name sent along with the query must follow the label naming conventions defined by DNS for the size of the domain names.

The Query Type subfield indicates the type of information being requested from the servers. Table 13.3 displays a few commonly used query types.

TABLE 13.3   COMMONLY USED QUERY TYPES

Query Type	Description
A	Indicates that the IP address corresponding to the domain name provided in the query name field is required by the client.
NS	Indicates the name server that is authoritative of the domain being queried.
CNAME	Indicates the canonical name, which is an alias name, for a name server.
PTR	Indicates that the name server must send the domain name corresponding to the IP address provided. This field is also called pointer records. The functionality implemented for this query is the reverse as that of the one implemented for query type A.

TABLE 13.3   CONTINUED

Query Type	Description
HINFO	Is used to get the configuration of the host.
MX	Is used for mail exchange by SMTP.
AXFR	Is used by the secondary name servers to initiate zone transfers.

Figure 13.8 displays a CNAME record in Windows 2000 Server.

Figure 13.8
A CNAME record is also called an Alias record in Windows 2000 Server.

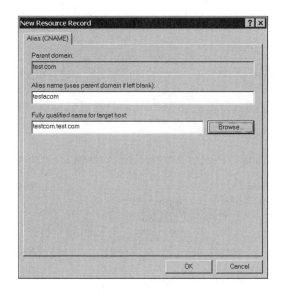

Figure 13.9 displays a sample MX record in Windows 2000 Server.

The query class that is commonly used is called *Internet Address* class and is also referred to as *IN*. The other query classes available are CS, CSNET, and HS.

RESOURCE RECORDS

The DNS database is organized in the form of special type of records called resource records (RRs). The components of a RR include the domain name, query type, query class, TTL, the length of the resource data, and finally, the resource data. The length of the resource data sent as response depends on the query type. When a name server responds to a client's query, the contents of the resource records are returned as a response to the query. Figure 13.10 displays the contents of a resource record. The value in the domain name field, which is a part of the RR, consists of the domain name being queried and is the same as the value specified in the query name field. To avoid redundant values, the domain name field in the RR contains a pointer to the query name field in the DNS message. If the name server being queried is not authoritative of the domain name being queried, it can refer to a

CH
13

list of name servers, which can be queried, to the client. These values are sent through the `domain name` field of a resource record.

Figure 13.9
A MX record is used by SMTP to forward mail to the mail server.

Figure 13.10
The values in the resource record depend on the type of query from the client.

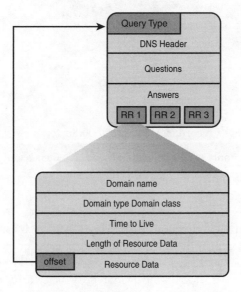

The other fields that are part of the RR are as follows:

- `Domain Type`—Placed after the `domain name` field in a DNS message. The value in this field and the query field are the same.

- Domain Class—Placed next to the Domain Type field. This field contains the same value as that of the Query Class field.

- TTL—Specifies the time for which the reply can be cached by a name server. The size of this field is 32 bits.

- Data Length—Present next to the TTL field in a RR. This field holds the length of the RR.

- Resource Data—Contains answers to the queries of the client. The first part of the Resource Data field is a number that provides the IP address of a computer. The size of this field depends on the version of IP used. The domain name is stored after the number field in a resource record. An offset pointer can contain a pointer to the Query Name field if the values in the Query Name field and the domain name field are the same.

STANDARD QUERIES   DNS can be used to resolve IP addresses to host names and vice versa. A standard query is used to resolve host names to IP addresses. In a standard query, the domain name, query type, and query class fields are specified. The response is returned in the form of RRs. If the name server is not authoritative of the domain being queried and if recursive resolution is supported, the relevant RRs are returned.

INVERSE QUERIES   The functionality of inverse queries is the reverse of standard queries. The inverse queries resolve IP addresses to host names. These queries are used to map RRs to the corresponding domain names. These queries are used for maintenance activities in the DNS servers. Figure 13.11 provides an example of how inverse queries are recorded as entries in a DNS database installed on a Windows 2000 Server.

Figure 13.11
Apart from inverse lookup database entries found in the Reverse Lookup Zones folder, forward lookup database entries are stored in the Forward Lookup Zones folder.

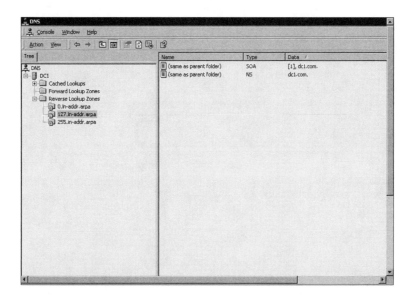

CH
13

SUMMARY

Domain Name System (DNS) enables users to provide descriptive names to identify and access a computer on a network. DNS is a distributed database that contains the details about the mapping between the host names and the corresponding IP addresses. For easy administration of host names or computer names, a standard is followed when creating host names and domain names. This standard is called the domain name hierarchy. The process of resolving host names to IP addresses is called name resolution. The components involved in name resolution are the resolver and the name servers. An application program that wants name resolution to be done passes its query to the resolver. The resolver passes the query to a computer designated as the name server or the DNS server. It holds the details required for name resolution in its hard disk. If the name server is authoritative of the queried domain, a reply is sent to the client. If not, the names of other servers that can answer the query are provided to the client. The client and the servers interact with each other by exchanging DNS messages. The answers to the queries of the client are provided through a component of the DNS message called the resource record.

CHAPTER **14**

BOOTSTRAPPING PROTOCOLS: BOOTP AND DHCP

In this chapter

BOOTSTRAP PROTOCOL—AN OVERVIEW

Bootstrapping is the process of loading the operating system, which is essential for running all the other programs. During the bootstrap process, the configuration information, the operating system images, and the file system are obtained. The protocols that are used to obtain the configuration information are referred to as *bootstrapping protocols*. Bootstrapping protocols enable a client to automatically obtain configuration information, such as an IP address, from a server on the network. This chapter deals with two commonly used bootstrapping protocols, BOOTP and DHCP.

Before a computer can form a part of a TCP/IP network, it needs to know certain information about its identity and location. For example, it needs configuration details such as its IP address and subnet mask, the address of the router, and the address of a name server. Usually, such details are stored in a configuration file that is accessed from a storage medium during the bootstrap process.

In the case of computers that do not have a disk and computers that boot for the first time, the configuration details are obtained from a server by using bootstrapping protocols. However, the common startup program, which is also required for system boot, is stored in the ROM of the diskless workstations. The commonly used bootstrapping protocols are RARP, BOOTP, and DHCP.

➔ To learn more about RARP, **see** "The Network Interface and Link Layers," **p. 25**

RARP is a bootstrapping protocol that can be used to obtain the IP address from a RARP server. The disadvantage with RARP is that it can be used to obtain only the IP address. The rest of the configuration information required can be obtained with the help of bootstrap protocols such as BOOTP and DHCP.

RARP has other disadvantages too. RARP is a Link Layer protocol unlike BOOTP and DHCP, which operate at the Application layer, as shown in Figure 14.1. RARP can be implemented only on computers that allow direct access to the frames because it is a lower layer protocol. RARP uses the computer's physical address to find the corresponding IP address. It is not useful in networks where hardware addresses are dynamically allocated to computers that contain configurable network cards.

➔ To learn more about configurable network cards, **see** "The Network Interface and Link Layers," **p. 25**

To overcome these shortcomings of RARP, BOOTP was designed and developed. As an extension to BOOTP, dynamic host configuration protocol (DHCP) was also developed. BOOTP and DHCP are discussed in detail in the sections that follow.

Figure 14.1
BOOTP and DHCP
operate in the
Application layer.

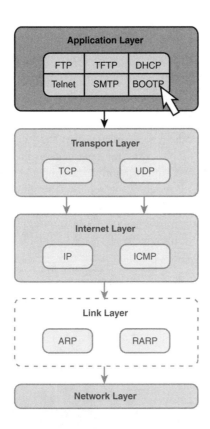

BOOTP PERFORMANCE

Loading the configuration information from the BOOTP server is done in two phases: obtaining the path to the boot file (the file containing configuration information) and obtaining the boot file itself. BOOTP is used to carry out the first phase. This phase involves obtaining the IP addresses of the server and client and the path to the boot file containing other configuration information. The second phase, which involves a file transfer, can be carried out by using protocols such as trivial file transfer protocol (TFTP), file transfer protocol (FTP), or simple file transfer protocol (SFTP).

→ To learn more about FTP, and TFTP, **see** "File Transfer and Access," **p. 129**

> **Note**
>
> Simple File Transfer Protocol (SFTP) is a protocol specification that combines the best features provided by TFTP and FTP. The specifications for SFTP have been proposed in RFC 913. SFTP provides less complexity than FTP and uses a comparatively less number of TCP connections than FTP to implement file transfer and access. However, unlike TFTP, SFTP implements certain advanced features such as user authentication, listing of directories on the server, directory structure modification, and file-related services such as renaming and delete. SFTP also implements command-execution model to control

CH
14

file transfer and access from the client. However, it uses a single TCP connection to issue commands from the client and to transfer files. SFTP uses the ASCII character set to issue control commands unlike FTP, which implements the NVT ASCII character set for transmitting control commands.

BOOTP operates in a client/server mode, where the computer that requests for bootstrap information is referred to as *the BOOTP client*, and the one that provides the BOOTP information is referred to as *the BOOTP server*. Information is exchanged between the BOOTP server and client in the form of BOOTP requests and replies. A single packet is exchanged between the BOOTP server and the client to transfer bootstrapping information. The format that is used by the client and server for exchanging bootstrapping information is in the form of a BOOTP message. A BOOTP message is encapsulated in a UDP datagram and sent to the Internet layer.

The BOOTP requests and replies, which are UDP datagrams, are encapsulated in IP datagrams. Figure 14.2 shows a BOOTP message that is encoded in a UDP datagram, which is also encoded within an IP datagram.

Figure 14.2
The UDP datagram, which contains the BOOTP message, is encapsulated within an IP datagram.

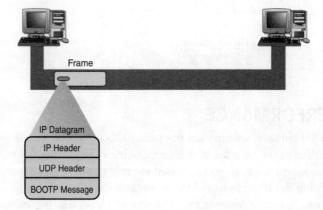

To understand how a computer can send its messages using an IP datagram before it even knows its IP address, consider the scenario in which a diskless workstation wants bootstrap information from a BOOTP server. The following steps illustrate the process of exchange of bootstrap information.

1. The diskless computer (the client) uses the limited broadcast IP address to broadcast its request on the network because it does not know its own IP address or the network's ID. The request will contain a transaction ID that will uniquely identify the BOOTP request.

2. After receiving the request, the BOOTP server refers to the configuration table to match the hardware address to the IP address. The configuration table is a database that contains hardware addresses and corresponding IP addresses and is manually entered by a system administrator.

3. The server also uses the limited broadcast IP address to send the reply. Even though the server knows the address of the diskless computer, it cannot send its reply using an IP datagram because the diskless computer cannot recognize its own IP address.

4. The client uses the transaction ID to recognize the broadcasted reply.

> **Note**
>
> A limited broadcast IP address has all 1s as its destination address and is used to broadcast the message to all the computers on the same network.

BOOTP uses IP for packet transfer. As is the case with any packet on IP networks, these packets are subject to damage, loss, and duplication. To prevent damage of the packets, the BOOTP protocol requires that a BOOTP packet is sent with the "do not fragment" bit so that computers with insufficient memory need not face the trouble of reassembling the datagrams.

To prevent loss of BOOTP packets, BOOTP uses the timeout and retransmission technique. When a client sends a request packet, it starts a timer. If the client does not receive a reply before the timer expires, the client retransmits the request packet. To prevent the collision of this packet with other request packets, the client retransmits after a random period of delay.

→ To learn more about timeout and retransmission technique, **see** "Introduction to TCP," **p. 74**

THE BOOTP MESSAGE FORMAT

The message format is the same for both the BOOTP request and reply messages. Figure 14.3 shows the structure of a BOOTP message.

Table 14.1 describes the fields in a BOOTP message.

TABLE 14.1 FIELDS IN A BOOTP MESSAGE	
Fields	**Description**
Operation Code	Specifies if the message is a request packet or a reply packet. A request packet holds the value 1 and a reply packet holds the value 2 in this field.
Hardware Type	Denotes the type of hardware technology being used. For example, if the hardware type is Ethernet, this field holds the value 1.

CH
14

TABLE 14.1   CONTINUED

Fields	Description
Hardware Length	Specifies the length of the hardware address in bytes. For example, in Ethernet networks, this field holds the value 6.
Hop Count	Specifies the maximum number of hops that a message can pass through. Initially, the client fills the value 0 in this field. However, the gateways that are configured to accept BOOTP requests can modify this field to hold the value of the number of hops. A BOOTP request has 0 in this field. Depending on the number of routers the packet has to hop through, the BOOTP server fills the Hop Count field in the reply. ■ To learn more about routing concepts, **see** "IP Routing," **p. 259**
Transaction ID	Carries an integer that is used by the client to match the responses to the requests. The value is set by the client and the server returns the same value in its response to the client. The Transaction ID is a random integer that is generated by the client. When a client examines a request packet and finds a discrepancy in the Transaction ID that is sent, the hardware address of the client can be used to ensure that the reply is meant for that particular client.
Seconds	Denotes the number of seconds elapsed after starting the client boot process. If the value in this field is high, the servers assign high priority to that client.
Client IP Address	Contains the IP address of the client in the BOOTP request, if the client is aware of its IP address and needs other configuration details such as the subnet mask and the address of name server.
Client IP Address	Contains the IP address of the client in the BOOTP reply, if the client is not aware of its IP address. The server fills this field in its response to the client's request.
Server IP Address	Contains the IP address of the server in the BOOTP reply and is usually filled by the server. If the client fills the IP address or hostname of the server, the request is directed to the specified server instead of being broadcast. In case the client does not know the IP address of the server and needs to broadcast the request, this field contains the limited broadcast address.
Gateway IP Address	Contains the IP address of a router and is filled by the server in the reply message. A typical BOOTP request contains a 0 in this field. If the client and the server are not located in the same network, the gateway fills this field with its own address and forwards the request to other networks.
Client Hardware Address	Holds the physical address of the client.
Server Name	Specifies the domain name of the server. This is an optional field and is present in the reply message.
Boot Filename	Contains the path to the boot file on the server. This field is filled by the server.

TABLE 14.1	CONTINUED
Fields	**Description**
Options	Contains vendor-specific information or additional information, such as network mask. The total size of this field is 64 bytes. The first four bytes of this field contains the IP address referred to as the magic cookie. This cookie suggests the way in which the client should interpret the data that follows. The value of the magic cookie is 99.130.83.99 in network byte order. The Options field contains both fixed length and variable length subfields. The subfields are described in the following section.

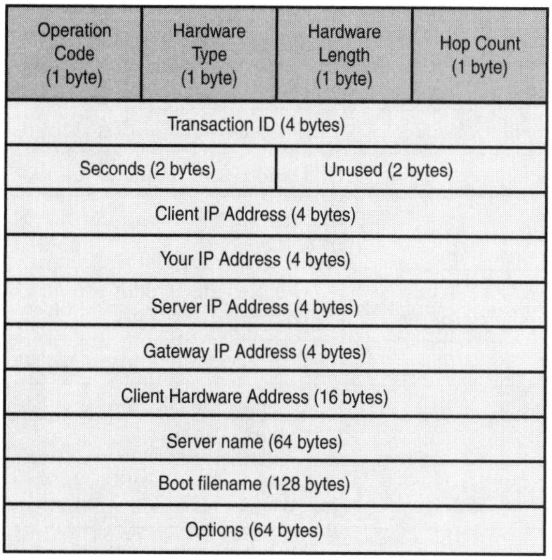

Figure 14.3
All the fields in a BOOTP message are of fixed length.

SUBFIELDS IN THE Options FIELD

The Options field contains two types of subfields, fixed length and variable length. Certain fixed length subfields do not have any data associated with them and are comprised of a single tag octet. The subfields with data have a single-tag octet, an octet indicating the length, and the data octets.

Table 14.2 describes the fixed length subfields in the Options field.

TABLE 14.2	THE FIXED LENGTH SUBFIELDS OF THE Options FIELD		
Subfield	**Tag**	**Length**	**Description**
Pad	0	1	Carries no data. It forces the following fields to limit to the preferred boundaries.
Subnet mask	1	4	Denotes the local and network subnet mask.

CH

14

TABLE 14.2 CONTINUED

Subfield	Tag	Length	Description
Time offset	2	4	Indicates the time offset of the subnet from the coordinated universal time (CUT).
End	255	1	Specifies the end of data.

Table 14.3 describes the variable length subfields in the Options field.

TABLE 14.3 THE VARIABLE LENGTH SUBFIELDS OF THE Options FIELD

Subfield	Tag	Description
Gateway field	3	Stores the IP addresses of gateways.
Time server field	4	Denotes the IP addresses of time servers.
IEN-116 name server field	5	Denotes the IP addresses of name servers.
Domain name server field	6	Denotes the IP addresses of domain name servers.
Log server field	7	Denotes the IP addresses of MIT-LCS UDP log servers.
Cookie/quote server field	8	Denotes the IP addresses of Quote of the Day servers.
LPR server field	9	Denotes the IP addresses of Print servers.
Impress server field	10	Denotes the IP addresses of Impress Network Image servers.
RLP server field	11	Denotes the IP addresses of Resource Location Protocol servers.
Hostname	12	Specifies the client name.
Boot file size	13	Specifies the size of the boot file. Usually, it is a two-octet value.
Reserved fields	128-254	Specifies data that is dependent on the kind of implementation.

DYNAMIC HOST CONFIGURATION PROTOCOL

DHCP is another bootstrap protocol that helps computers to obtain their configuration information from servers designated as DHCP servers. DHCP, an extension of BOOTP, scores over the latter in two ways. The first advantage is that DHCP provides all the configuration information required by the client in a single packet. For example, a DHCP message contains information about the subnet mask along with the IP address. The second advantage is that DHCP allows dynamic allocation of IP addresses to the client.

DHCP allows three ways of assigning addresses to the client: manual configuration, automatic configuration, and dynamic configuration.

For handling the requests from diskless workstations, a DHCP server contains a database that comprises a configuration table, which is similar to the one present in BOOTP servers. This configuration table is used to statically bind a hardware address to an IP address of the client. This method of assigning permanent addresses based on the configuration table is referred as *manual configuration*.

In the case of computers that contain their own hard disks, the configuration information can be stored locally. That is, the IP address of the computer is static and must be manually assigned by the network administrator when the operating system is installed. The disadvantage of this method is that the network administrator must ensure that the IP address of each computer is unique. If the IP addresses are not unique, communication between the computers will be hindered. To overcome the disadvantages of assigning static IP addresses, DHCP enables dynamic allocation of IP addresses to the clients. To perform dynamic allocation, DHCP maintains a database that contains a pool of IP addresses. The address pool is a range of IP addresses that is configured by the network administrator. When a client boots, it sends a DHCP request to the server to get an IP address. The DHCP server must ensure that the IP address assigned to computers are unique. This method of dynamic allocation of IP addresses is referred to as *automatic configuration*. Permanent IP addresses are allocated to the clients using this method.

When a computer is moved from one subnet to another or when a portable computer requires a temporary connection, BOOTP cannot be used because of the static binding between the hardware and IP addresses. To handle such situations, DHCP dynamically allocates IP addresses for a certain time period. This method of dynamic allocation of IP addresses for a specified time period is called *dynamic configuration*.

System administrators can decide to set static addresses for certain groups of systems and dynamic addresses for others. For example, administrators might decide to assign dynamic addresses to computers that want to belong to a particular group. Depending on the hardware or physical address of the client and the network to which it belongs, the DHCP server chooses a particular method of assigning addresses.

Similar to BOOTP, DHCP uses the client/server mode, where the computer that requests the configuration information is called the *DHCP client* and the one that provides the information is called the *DHCP server*.

DHCP is backwards-compatible with BOOTP. In other words, a computer can send a BOOTP request to a DHCP server and obtain the IP address corresponding to its hardware address.

CH

14

DHCP PERFORMANCE

The most significant feature of DHCP is the dynamic address assignment. Apart from the IP address, the DHCP packet also provides other configuration information such as the subnet mask to the client. This enables the client to automatically configure itself to connect to the network without any user intervention. This significantly reduces the workload of the system administrator.

Note

The system administrator can configure the settings for TCP/IP so as to enable a system to automatically configure itself or to force manual configuration of the settings.

Figure 14.4 shows a dialog box that allows a system administrator to configure DHCP settings in a Windows environment.

Figure 14.4
The Microsoft TCP/IP Properties dialog box enables automatic or dynamic configuration in a Windows environment.

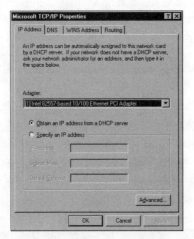

When a client sends a request to the DHCP server, the server assigns an IP address from the pool of addresses provided by the administrator. After receiving the response, the client accepts the address and sends an acknowledgment back to the server.

DHCP leases temporary addresses for a specified period of time. The server decides the lease period during the allocation of the address. When the lease period elapses, the client has to either renew the lease or terminate the usage of this address.

The system administrator determines the lease period depending on the needs of the environment. For example, for mobile users who need connection to the network for about an hour, the lease time can be set to an hour. A system administrator can also assign infinity as the lease time to allow clients to permanently hold the IP address.

During the process of obtaining configuration information from the DHCP server, a DHCP client can be in any one of the following six states:

- INITIALIZE
- SELECT
- REQUEST
- BOUND
- RENEW
- REBIND

Figure 14.5 shows the various states attained by a DHCP client and the various messages exchanged during the allocation of address by the DHCP server.

Figure 14.5
During the dynamic allocation of addresses, the DHCP client changes six states.

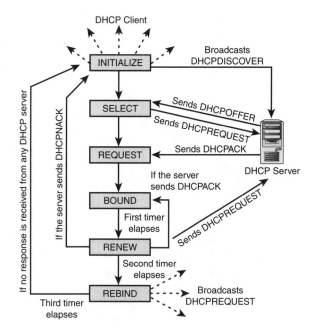

To reduce the load on a single DHCP server in large networks, multiple computers might be assigned as DHCP servers. To use DHCP, a client broadcasts a message to contact all the DHCP servers. After receiving replies from the DHCP servers, the client selects one of the servers and sends a request to the selected server. The server acknowledges the request, and the lease time period begins.

A client enters the INITIALIZE state when it boots for the first time. To send datagrams over the network, it requires an IP address. To acquire its IP address, it first needs to contact any one of the DHCP servers on the network. To do so, it broadcasts a DHCPDISCOVER message on the network and then enters the SELECT state. Although all the DHCP servers

CH
14

on the network receive the broadcasted DHCPDISCOVER message, only the servers that have been programmed to respond to this request can respond. The responses are in the form of DHCPOFFER messages. A client can receive DHCPOFFER messages or none at all depending on whether the DHCP server is functioning properly. The DHCPOFFER messages contain an IP address along with the configuration information required for the client. The client selects one of the offers and sends back a DHCPREQUEST message to the client. The main purpose of a DHCPREQUEST message is to negotiate the lease time with the DHCP server. After sending the DHCPREQUEST message, the client enters the REQUEST state.

The DHCP server sends a DHCPACK message to acknowledge the receipt of the DHCPREQUEST message and to begin the lease period. After receiving the DHCPACK message, the client enters the BOUND state. The client remains in the BOUND state until the lease period elapses.

> **Note**
>
> After receiving an IP address, the client stores it in its hard disk, if it has any.

When a client enters the BOUND state, it starts three timers. The DHCP server assigns values to the timers during address allocation. If any value is not assigned by the server, the client uses the default values for the timers. For example, the default value of the first timer is half the total lease time. The first timer controls the renewal of the lease. The expiry of the first timer indicates that the client needs to renew the lease. To renew the lease, the client sends a DHCPREQUEST message to the DHCP server that issued the address. Using the DHCPREQUEST message, the client requests the server to extend the lease time period.

The server can decide whether the client can use the IP address. It sends a DHCPACK (DHCP acknowledgement) message to the client if it decides to let the client continue using the IP address. The client then returns to the BOUND state. The DHCPACK message may or may not contain a new value for the lease time. If the server disapproves the use of the IP address by the client, it sends a DHCPNACK (DHCP negative acknowledgement) message to the client. The client then stops using the IP address and returns to the INITIALIZE state.

If the client does not receive any response after sending the DHCPREQUEST message for extension of lease period, it means that the specified server is not reachable or is down. In such cases, DHCP uses the second timer, which expires after 87.5% of the lease time. The client then enters into the REBIND state. In this state, the client broadcasts a DHCPRE-QUEST message, which can be accepted by any DHCP server that is programmed to accept the request from this particular client. The server that accepts the request can choose to either extend or terminate the lease period. If the server extends the lease, the client enters the BOUND state. If the server denies the client a lease, the client returns to the INITIALIZE state and begins to send DHCPREQUEST messages for fresh IP addresses.

If a client in its REBIND state does not receive any response from any of the DHCP servers, and the third timer also expires, the client has to release the IP address and move to the INITIALIZE state.

DHCP allows a client to terminate the lease prematurely when it is not required any longer. For example, a mobile user with a network connection might decide to move to a different network and might want to disconnect the current session. In such cases, DHCP does not require the client to wait until the end of the lease period. This property of DHCP is useful in situations where the exact lease period cannot be determined by either the client or the server. It is also useful in networks where servers do not have adequate IP addresses that can be allocated. The IP addresses released by the clients can be allocated to other clients who are waiting for the connection. To terminate the lease, the client (in the BOUND state) sends a DHCPRELEASE message to the server and returns to the INITIALIZE stage.

THE DHCP MESSAGE FORMAT

The DHCP message format is similar to that of BOOTP message format. That is why DHCP is backward compatible with BOOTP.

Figure 14.6 shows the structure of a DHCP message.

Figure 14.6
The DHCP message format differs from the BOOTP message format only in the 16-bit FLAGS field.

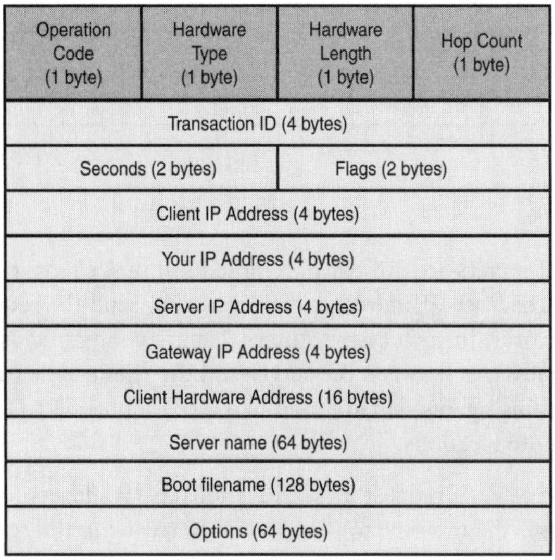

Operation Code (1 byte)	Hardware Type (1 byte)	Hardware Length (1 byte)	Hop Count (1 byte)
Transaction ID (4 bytes)			
Seconds (2 bytes)		Flags (2 bytes)	
Client IP Address (4 bytes)			
Your IP Address (4 bytes)			
Server IP Address (4 bytes)			
Gateway IP Address (4 bytes)			
Client Hardware Address (16 bytes)			
Server name (64 bytes)			
Boot filename (128 bytes)			
Options (64 bytes)			

The DHCP message format also has a 16-bit FLAGS field and extra subfields in the Options field. The FLAGS field forces the client to broadcast its reply to the client. A unicasted reply cannot be processed by the client because it does not identify its own IP address.

CH
14

The Options field has additional subfields, such as a field that specifies the type of interaction between the DHCP server and the client and a field that denotes the lease time. Figure 14.7 illustrates the format of the subfields that specify the messages exchanged between the client and the server.

Figure 14.7
Format of the subfields in the Options field.

Table 14.4 describes the DHCP message types and the type value for the messages.

TABLE 14.4 DHCP MESSAGE TYPES	
Type Number	**Description**
1	DHCPDISCOVER
2	DHCPOFFER
3	DHCPREQUEST
4	DHCPDECLINE
5	DHCPACK
6	DHCPNACK
7	DHCPRELEASE

RELAY AGENT

If DHCP or BOOTP servers are present in remote locations, clients cannot reach them because the limited broadcast IP address, which is used to send the request, is valid only within local area networks. In such cases, routers that are configured as relay agents can be used to transfer the messages between the server and the client. Relay agents, also called helpers, act as forwarding agents that are used by UDP on port 53 to forward messages to clients located in remote locations.

When a relay agent receives a request message, it adds its IP address in the Gateway IP Address field and passes the message to the server. On receiving the reply from the server, the agent forwards the message to the client.

SUMMARY

BOOTP and DHCP are two commonly used bootstrapping protocols that help a computer to obtain configuration information from servers that are designated as BOOTP or DHCP servers. The computers that request for configuration details are called the BOOTP or DHCP clients.

The main difference between BOOTP and DHCP is that BOOTP messages contain the path to the boot file whereas DHCP messages contain all the configuration details in the message. Another difference between BOOTP and DHCP is that DHCP allows dynamic allocation of IP addresses to its clients.

DHCP is backward compatible with BOOTP because both BOOTP and DHCP messages have a similar format. The difference between the message formats is the presence of a 16-bit FLAGS field, which is unused in the BOOTP message, and the presence of extra subfields in the Options field.

If a BOOTP or DHCP server is located in a different network, then routers that are configured as relay agents can receive the messages from the client and forward them to the servers.

CH

14

CHAPTER 15

SUBNETTING AND CLASSLESS ADDRESSING

In this chapter

IP ADDRESSING SCHEMES

IP addresses are used to identify computers that are connected to a network. They enable communication between computers irrespective of the type of network technology used to connect the computers. IP addresses are broadly divided into three types of address classes: Class A, Class B, and Class C. Classification is based on the number of bits allotted for the network ID and the host ID on the network.

→ For more information on address classes, **see** "The Network Interface and Link Layers," **p. 25**

The original addressing scheme that was developed for Ipv4 could not cater to the increase in the number of computers getting connected to the Internet. Let us analyze the disadvantages with the different address classes that are available in IPv4. Class A addresses can be used for very large networks, and not all organizations would require a class A network. There can be a maximum of only 126 class A networks in the IPv4 address space. In addition, class A networks that are available in the IPv4 address space have already been exhausted. Medium-sized networks can use class B networks and currently only a few class B networks have not been assigned to any organization.

The rigid classification of the addressing scheme resulted in organizations having more than 254 hosts being allotted class B networks. This led to a wastage of addresses. For example, an organization that required addresses for 500 hosts was allotted a class B address, which can support around 16,000 hosts. This also led to the rapid depletion of the class B address space. The class C addressing scheme can be used to create small networks that can comprise of 254 hosts each. An organization that needs to set up a large network needs to obtain more than one class C network and also create a mechanism that would enable routing between the different class C networks. Methods that can be used to meet the increase in demands of the organizations had to be designed. In addition, steps had to be taken to check the fast depleting number of unassigned IP addresses. These methods were created because the number of bits allotted to an IP address would remain the same for the IPv4 address space. The methods that were designed are subnetting and supernetting. Supernetting is also known as Classless Inter-Domain Routing (CIDR). InterNIC has also allocated a portion of the IPv4 address space for use only on private internets. This is also known as private address space, which is discussed later in this chapter.

Subnetting and supernetting are handled by Internet Protocol (IP) in the Internet layer of the TCP/IP reference model.

Note

The problem with the insufficient addresses in the Ipv4 address space is commonly referred to as *the three bears problem*. The number of Ipv4 addresses provided in the addressing scheme is not at an optimum. Like the fairy tale, they are either too small or too large and never "just right."

SUBNETTING

An IP address can be logically divided into two components: network ID and the host ID. The number of bits that are used to identify the network depends on the address class used. For example, if an organization has been assigned a class B address, the number of bits that can be locally administered by the organization is 16 bits. Therefore, a total of $2^{16}-2$ $(2^{16}-2)$ hosts can be connected to this network, which will be sufficient for the current requirements of the organization. However, if the organization requires multiple networks for its operations, it needs to acquire more Class B addresses based on its requirements. Instead of obtaining more class B addresses, the organization can divide the class B address that has been allocated to it into a number of smaller networks called subnets. The divisions of subnets and the addresses of the hosts in the subnets are not visible to users on other networks. For computers on other networks that need to send data to this network, the entire network is considered as a single entity. Routers perform the task of coordinating and managing network traffic from the different subnets to provide the illusion of a single network to other networks.

→ For more information on address classes, **see** "The Network Interface and Link Layers," **p. 25**

The creation and administration of the subnets is the responsibility of the network administrators in the organization. For example, if the organization has obtained a class B address numbered 156.67.0.0, the last 16 bits in the address can be locally administered by the organization to create subnets. However, as mentioned earlier, the addresses that are assigned to the computers in the subnets will not be visible to the other networks. The computers on the other networks can communicate only through public addresses and not the locally created addresses. The task of enabling communication between computers located on subnets and computers located on external networks is managed by routers.

The /16 network or the class B network can be locally administered to create two /17 networks or four /18 networks. The method by which the subnets are administered depends on the requirements of the organization and the Internet Service Provider (ISP). Other ISPs will have the option of whether to allow or listen to those subnet announcements. Irrespective of the option set by the other ISPs, the subnet announcements can be advertised to all the ISPs.

Note

Internet Corporation for the Assignment of Names and Numbers (ICANN) assigns public addresses to an organization.

Devices that are used to bridge the gap between networks are known as routers. They direct the traffic from the network to other computers (see Figure 15.1). Subnets use routing tables maintained on routers to communicate with each other.

Figure 15.1
The computers on subnets that are local to an organization communicate with computers on different networks through routers.

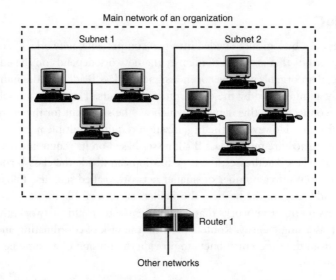

Main network of an organization

Subnet 1

Subnet 2

Router 1

Other networks

➜ For more information on IP and the Internet layer, **see** "The Internet Layer Protocol," **p. 43**
➜ For more information on routing concepts, **see** "IP Routing," **p. 259**

ADVANTAGES OF CREATING SUBNETS

Every organization has its own set of requirements for setting up networks. Subnetting manages these requirements while assigning IP addresses for local hosts on its networks. This reduces the need for organizations to obtain a large number of public addresses from ICANN. In addition to being able to divide a large network into small networks, subnetting also enables small networks to communicate with each other.

An organization can choose to implement small networks for many reasons. For example, the organization might require networks that use different network technologies to be connected to each other. In addition, network technologies also impose restrictions on the length of the cables that are used, the number of hosts connected to each network, and so on. To overcome these restrictions, smaller networks can be combined to form large networks. Dividing a large network into smaller networks also helps reduce network congestion. For example, subnets can be created based on the bandwidth requirements of users. Data that is to be sent over higher bandwidth lines can be sent through a network that supports higher bandwidths so that the network traffic does not clog the entire network.

HIERARCHICAL SYSTEM OF ASSIGNING IP ADDRESSES FOR SUBNETWORKS

To reach a host, the first step would be to identify the network number followed by the host address. The method of dividing an IP address into network ID and host ID is referred to as a two-level hierarchy in the IP addressing scheme. However, in the case of subnetting, the local part of the public address is used for creating subnets. In such a case, to reach a host on the network, the network number must be first identified followed by the subnet number.

This is referred to as a three-level hierarchy in IP addressing. In a three-level hierarchy, the host address is logically divided into three components: network number, subnet number, and host number (see Figure 15.2).

Note

The terms network number and network ID can be used interchangeably. Similarly, the terms *host number* and *host ID* and *subnet number* and *subnet ID* can be used interchangeably.

Figure 15.2
The host addresses, irrespective of whether they belong to class A, B, or C, contain three components, namely, the network ID, subnet ID, and host ID.

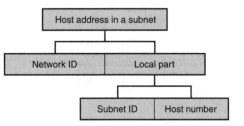

CREATING SUBNETS

Subnets need to be created after analyzing the requirements of the organization and the type of address that is obtained from ICANN. For example, if the organization has obtained a class A address, the number of bits that can be administered by the organization locally is 24 bits. A total of $2^{24}-2$ hosts can be connected to each class A network.

→ For more information on how $2^{24}-2$ hosts can be connected to a class A network, **see** "Addressing," **p. 30**

Before creating subnets, there are some important points for consideration:

- The address range must be planned, including the addresses required for routers.
- A subnet number of all 0s and all 1s cannot be assigned. These addresses are reserved for special purposes. The network broadcast address is an example of a reserved address.

Note

Today routers of various vendors such as Cisco are capable of using the zero subnets for addressing. Therefore, network administrators have started assigning zero subnets.

Let us take an example of an organization that requires 13 subnets to be created with a class B address. The following steps need to be performed for the same:

1. In a class B network, 16 bits can be administered by the organization locally. The 16 bits that have been allocated need to be used for creating the subnets and the host numbers. The number of subnets that needs to be created is 13 + 2. The number 2 represents the reserved addresses. Therefore, a total of 15 subnets need to be created.

2. After having analyzed the number of subnets, the number of bits that needs to be allocated for the subnet number needs to be determined. To create 15 subnets, 4 bits are required. Of the 32 bits that are used for representing the IP address, 16 bits will be used for the network ID, 4 bits will be used for subnets and the remaining bits will be used for assigning host addresses. This bit pattern can be used to find the value of the subnet mask of the network. The usage of a subnet mask is covered in the next section. Figure 15.3 displays the bit pattern before and after the creation of the subnets.

Figure 15.3
The number of hosts that are to be connected to a subnet along with the number of reserved addresses is used to arrive at the bit pattern for creating a subnet.

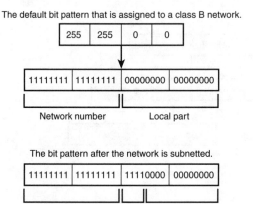

The default bit pattern that is assigned to a class B network.

| 255 | 255 | 0 | 0 |

| 11111111 | 11111111 | 00000000 | 00000000 |

Network number   Local part

The bit pattern after the network is subnetted.

| 11111111 | 11111111 | 11110000 | 00000000 |

Network number   Subnet   Local part
                   number

Four bits in the local part are allocated for the subnet number.

The same set of steps is also used for creating subnets for class A and C networks.

PRIVATE ADDRESS SPACE

Although TCP/IP was created for the Internet, it can be used for networks that are not connected to the Internet. Organizations that are using TCP/IP for setting up an intranet need to follow the same addressing schemes that are followed on a network that is connected to the Internet. However, as the number of hosts and the networks increase, the address space will be exhausted. One of the methods by which exhaustion of the address space can be prevented is to use the private address space for routing within networks in an organization and to use a NAT router to manage translation of private and public IP addresses. The networks that are not connected to the Internet are also known as *private internets*. The following range of IP addresses that are reserved for assigning IP addresses to private internets cannot be used for other purposes. Internet Assigned Numbers Authority (IANA) allocates these addresses.

- 10.0.0.0–10.255.255.255 (10/8 prefix)
- 172.16.0.0–172.31.255.255 (172.16/12 prefix)
- 192.168.0.0–192.168.255.255 (192.168/16 prefix)

CH
15

Any number of private internets can use the same address space. The usage of this address space need not be approved by IANA. The addresses that are used in the private intranet are not visible to the computers that are connected to the Internet. This prevents any duplication of IP addresses. Hosts having addresses from the private address space allocated to them can communicate with computers that are connected to the Internet through intermediate devices. These devices, also known as gateways or routers, accept information from an intranet and forward them to other computers.

The private address space is used for assigning IP addresses to hosts on a subnet. A subnet using the private address space appears as a single network to other networks and computers. Only the address of the router is visible to computers on other networks. The entire subnet appears as a single route, and this is referred to as *route aggregation*. The router maintains a table called the routing table, which contains details about the addresses of the hosts in the subnet. Only the globally valid external IP address of the router that connects the network to the Internet is visible to other networks. Local computers must translate their private IP addresses into this globally valid IP address for communicating with computers existing on external networks.

Note

> The networks that are connected to the Internet are also referred to as *public networks*.

The advantage of using the private addressing scheme is that it offers more flexibility to organizations for setting up private intranets according to varying organizational requirements. This addressing scheme also helps conserve the addresses in the Ipv4 address space. On the other hand, it is difficult to migrate from a private address space to a public addressing scheme while using a private addressing scheme.

Note

> Proxy ARP is a technique that enables a single IP address to be shared between two networks. This technique can be used only on networks that use Address Resolution Protocol (ARP) for address resolution. Apart from Proxy ARP, Network Address Translation (NAT) is another technique that uses address translation as a tool to conserve the Ipv4 address space.

USING SUBNET MASKS

Subnet mask is a value that is used to extract the network number from an IP address. This is done by performing a binary AND operation between the IP address and the subnet mask. Consider a situation in which data needs to be transmitted from computer A to computer B. The sender, in this case computer A, must identify the network to which computer B belongs. To perform this, the network ID of the sender and the receiver must be extracted and compared. If they belong to the same network, data can be transmitted directly. Otherwise, data needs to be sent to a router, which in turn can execute data transmission. To determine if the network numbers are the same, the binary AND operation is performed with the network ID of the sender and the subnet mask of the subnet. The same operation is performed with the address of the receiver and the subnet mask of the subnet. If the result of both the operations is the same, it is inferred that both the computers belong to the same network. If the result is not the same, the sender forwards the data packets to the appropriate router, which in turn forwards the data to the destination computer.

Note

The sender uses the same subnet mask when specifying the address of the sender and the receiver.

One important consideration is that all the computers on a subnet need to use the same subnet mask. Otherwise, the data packets will not reach the correct destination. When a host needs to send data packets to a destination, it will fail to find the correct network number because of the incorrect subnet mask that is used.

Note

Every host on a network contains the value of the subnet mask of the network. If the hosts on the subnet use Dynamic Host Configuration Protocol (DHCP) for obtaining IP addresses dynamically, they can obtain the subnet mask of the network from the DHCP server through the DHCP message.

→ For more information on DHCP messages and dynamic allocation of IP addresses, **see** "Bootstrapping Protocols: BOOTP and DHCP," **p. 229**

The subnet masks differ with the type of networks that are used. This is because of the variation in the number of bits allotted for the network ID and the host ID. For a class A network, the subnet mask that must be applied is 255.0.0.0 because the first byte represents the network ID on a class A network. For example, if the address of computer A is 3.20.16.1 and the address of computer B is 3.20.16.3, a binary AND operation is performed on the host address and the subnet mask. The result of the operation will be the network number of the computers. If the network numbers are different, the binary operation provides different numbers as the result. The subnet masks for class B and C networks are 255.255.0.0 and 255.255.255.0, respectively.

Assume that communication needs to happen between Computer A and Computer B, which are part of a class C network. The addresses of the computers are 196.35.50.2 and 196.35.50.3, respectively. The default subnet mask of a class C network is 255.255.255.0. If Computer A needs to send a message to Computer B, it needs to check if the destination is also a part of the same network. To do so, the network numbers of both the source and the destination computers have to be extracted and compared. To find out the network number of the source computer, the binary AND operation is performed on the source address and the subnet mask.

11000100 00100011 00110010 00000010 (Address of computer A)

11111111 11111111 11111111 00000000 (Subnet mask)

The result of the binary AND operation is 11000100 00100011 00110010 00000000, which is 196.35.50.0, when represented in the dotted decimal notation.

To extract the network ID of the destination computer, the same operation has to be performed between the destination address and the subnet mask.

To extract the network number of the destination address,

11000100 00100011 00110010 00000011 (Address of Computer B)

11111111 11111111 11111111 00000000 (Subnet mask)

The result of the binary AND operation is also 11000100 00100011 00110010 00000000, which is 196.35.50.0, when represented in the dotted decimal notation. The network numbers of both the source and the destination being the same, it is concluded that both computers belong to the same network. Computer A sends the message directly to Computer B. If the network numbers were different, Computer A must forward the message to a router, which in turn would forward the message to the appropriate destination.

Look at a situation in which Computer A, which belongs to a class C network, needs to communicate with Computer B, which belongs to a class B network. The addresses of Computers A and B are 196.35.50.2 and 130.10.50.3.

As stated earlier, to initiate the communication, the network numbers of the source and the destination computers need to be extracted and compared.

To find out the network number of the source computer, a binary AND operation is performed.

11000100 00100011 00110010 00000010 (Address of Computer A)

11111111 11111111 11111111 00000000 (Subnet mask)

The result of the binary AND operation is 11000100 00100011 00110010 00000000, which is 196.35.50.0, when represented in the dotted decimal notation.

To extract the network number of the destination computer, the same process is repeated.

11000010 00001010 00110010 00000010 (Address of Computer B)

11111111 11111111 11111111 00000000 (Subnet mask)

The result of the binary AND operation is 11000100 00100011 00110010 00000000, which is 130.10.50.0, when represented in the dotted decimal notation. The network numbers of the source and the destination computers are not the same. Therefore, Computer A forwards the message to routers, which in turn forward the message to Computer B. Also, note that the value of the subnet mask that is used for extracting the network number depends on the type of network to which the source computer belongs.

In Windows 2000, the IP address, subnet mask, and the default gateway values can be configured at the time of installation or later (see Figure 15.4). These values comprise one of the components of the properties of the TCP/IP protocol stack that is installed with the operating system.

Figure 15.4
The IP address, default gateway, and subnet mask are configured as the properties of TCP/IP installed on a computer.

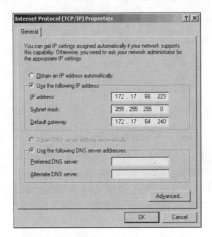

In the case of networks that are further divided into subnets, the network number that denotes the address of the physical network along with the subnet number must also be compared. The subnet mask that is created in this case will be dependent on the number of bits that are used for the subnet number. To continue with the example that was discussed in the previous section, assume that the class B address that is assigned to the network is 165.32.0.0 and this network is further divided into 15 subnets. In this case, the subnet mask for the network will be 255.255.240.0. The binary representation of the subnet mask is

11111111.11111111.11110000.00000000.

This indicates that 4 bits are allotted for creating the subnet numbers, and the remaining bits can be used to assign addresses to the hosts.

Note

Although subnet masks with noncontiguous bits are allowed, it is recommended you use subnet masks with contiguous bits to reduce the overhead on the additional operations needed to arrive at the network number.

SUPERNETTING

Supernetting is the process of combining two small networks to form one large network. It is the reverse of subnetting. In subnetting, a single public IP address is used to create multiple subnets, and the subnets communicate through routers. Supernetting enables networks with different public IP addresses to be connected to each other. The different public addresses that are used for supernetting must belong to the same class. To put it differently, multiple networks with different IP addresses use the same interface.

Supernetting was also created to solve problems caused by the decrease in the number of class A and B addresses in the IPv4 address space. Medium-sized networks prefer class B networks instead of class C networks because a single class C network can support only 254 hosts. The lack of class B addresses is a problem. Studies about the usage of IP addresses also reveal that only 3% of the assigned IP addresses are used. Methods that would enable the efficient usage of the address space had to be devised. Supernetting helps solve the problem caused by an insufficient number of class B addresses. This is done by enabling an organization to combine more than one class C network to form a supernetwork instead of obtaining a single class B network.

One important point for consideration is that the class C addresses that are assigned to the network must be contiguous.

Two problems had to be solved to implement supernetting efficiently. First, the organizations that were assigned blocks of class C networks found the implementation of supernetting to be difficult. To ease the administration overhead on the organizations, the task of assigning IP addresses is handled by organizations called Internet Service Providers (ISP). The ISPs are allotted blocks of class C addresses from ICANN. The organizations that require networks to be set up take the help of ISPs for address assignments. Second, the problem of the increase in the size of routing tables caused by an increase in the number of class C networks needed attention.

The number of entries in a routing table increases with the number of routes. Each router on an average needs to hold about a half a million routing table entries, which constitute information about the other routes. Although the storage could be managed, the overhead on renewing and replicating the entries across the routers would bring down the efficiency of the network. In addition, as the number of routes increases, the complexity of algorithms that are used to maintain the routing tables also increase. This problem is commonly referred to as the explosion of routing table entries.

As a solution to this problem, a technique called Classless Inter-Domain routing was created. This technique enables the aggregation of many routes into a single one to minimize the number of entries in a routing table. The name Classless Inter-Domain Routing (CIDR) comes from the fact that this method does not assign IP addresses based on the address classes. CIDR does not use the predefined format of assigning addresses based on the number of bits assigned to the network ID and the host ID. In other words, CIDR is not based on the old process of assigning Class A, B, and C addresses based on a predefined network prefix. Instead, the current implementation of CIDR can use network prefixes that can be 13 to 27 bits in size. Thus, CIDR can be used to create networks as small as 32 hosts or those over 500,000 hosts. This technique can be used to make efficient use of the address space and also enables optimum usage of the allotted address space.

In CIDR, the class C address space has been distributed across four regions and they are as follows:

- 194.0.0.0 to 195.255.255.255 for Europe
- 198.0.0.0 to 199.255.255.255 for North America
- 200.0.0.0 to 201.255.255.255 for Central and South America
- 202.0.0.0 to 203.255.255.255 for Asia

The division of the class C address space into four groups ensures that the address space is equally distributed across all the regions and enables an easy administration of address classes.

CIDR does not provide a complete solution to the exhaustion of the 32-bit address space. It has been designed to use the existing address space optimally.

Note

The next generation of the Internet Protocol (IP) commonly referred to as Ipv6 or IP Next Generation (IPng) provides enhancements to the current version in many aspects. One of the enhancements is a solution to the problems caused by address space exhaustion. The size of an address in the IPv6 address space is 128 bits compared with 32 bits in the IPv4 address space. Experts do not anticipate any problems caused by address space exhaustion because of the magnitude of the number of bits allocated for an IP address in the IPv6 address space scheme.

→ For more information on IPv6, **see** "IPv6," **p. 403**

Note

A router stores the routing information in the RAM. If the number of entries in the routing table increases, the system will slow down and can lead to a system crash. In some cases, routers use static RAM for storing information. Static RAM are expensive resources and cannot be upgraded frequently to accommodate the increase in the number of routing table entries.

IMPLEMENTING SUPERNETWORKS

The format in which a class C address is represented is a.b.c.0. The last byte represents the host number. If an organization requires 1,400 hosts, six contiguous class C networks are given to the organization instead of a class B address. To arrive at the number of class C networks that is required to create the supernetwork, the number of hosts required is divided by the number of hosts that can be connected to one class C network. The number of hosts that can be connected to a class C network is 254.

SUPERNET MASK

Having arrived at the number of class C networks that are required, the next step in creating the supernet is to find the supernet mask for the network. Like the subnet mask, the supernet mask along with the address of a host is used to determine whether a host belongs to the supernet or not. However, the steps followed to perform this operation are different for subnetting and supernetting. In subnetting, the local part of an address is further divided into subnet numbers. However, in the case of supernetting, depending on the number of class C networks that are connected to the supernetwork, the network ID is manipulated. For example, if a supernet needs to be created by combining nine networks, then four bits will be required from the network ID. To find the supernet mask for this network, the default subnet mask of a class C network is required. The default subnet mask for a class C network is 255.255.255.0. If the last 4 bits of the network number are reserved for the supernet, the bit pattern would be

11111111.11111111.11110000.00000000.

This bit pattern is used as the supernet mask for the network. The supernet mask when converted to the dotted-decimal notation becomes 255.255.240.0.

USING THE SUPERNET MASK

Consider a situation in which eight class C addresses have to be combined to form a supernet. The number of bits that are required would be 3 because 2^3 will generate eight combinations. Three bits from the network ID portion in the default subnet mask of a class C network must be set aside for representing the supernet. The supernet mask of the network would be 255.255.248.0, and the bit pattern for the same would be 11111111.11111111.11111000.00000000.

Now, let us analyze the use of the supernet mask to find whether a host address is a part of the supernet or not. In a supernet mask, the position of the last 1 indicates the lowest address that can be assigned to a class C network in the supernet. In continuation of the example, the lowest address that can be assigned to the class C network is a.b.8.0. Now, if the result of the binary AND operation performed on the address of the destination and the supernet mask result in the address of the lowest class C address on the network, it is inferred that both the computers belong to the same network. Otherwise, the packet is forwarded to the appropriate router.

The addresses of the other class C networks that can be created in the supernet are a.b.9.0, a.b.10.0, a.b.11.0, a.b.12.0, a.b.13.0, a.b.14.0, and a.b.15.0. Each of these networks can be connected to 254 hosts each.

Note

The values a and b referred to in the examples can be considered as any valid class C address.

Let us consider the example of a host that belongs to the supernet and one that does not to understand how the supernet mask is used to determine whether the supernet can accept the packet. If the host address is 196.100.10.1, the bit pattern of the host address would be

11000100.01100100.00001010.00000001.

This concept is illustrated in the following syntax.

```
11000100.01100100.00001010.00000001------------------------(Destination Address)
AND
11111111.11111111.11111000.00000000------------------------(Supernet mask)
```

The result of the binary AND operation is

11000100.01100100.00001000.00000000

The result of the operation specified above is 196.100.8.0, which is nothing but the value of the lowest class C address that can be specified in the range. The data packet is forwarded to the appropriate class C network.

Let us consider another example where the host address is 196.100.16.1. Now the bit pattern of the host address would be

11000100.01100100.00010000.00000001.

This concept is illustrated in the following syntax.

```
11000100.01100100.00010000.00000001------------------------(Destination Address)
AND
11111111.11111111.11111000.00000000------------------------(Supernet mask)
```

The result of the binary AND operation is

11000100.01100100.00010000.00000000

The result of the operation specified above is 196.100.16.0. The derived class C address does not belong to the supernet. Therefore, the data packet is forwarded to a router.

SUMMARY

The IP addressing scheme that was created for IPv4 comprises 32 bits that were allotted for assigning IP addresses. The exponential growth in the number of computers getting connected to the Internet resulted in problems related to address space exhaustion and management of routing tables. Methods that can be used to make optimum utilization of the existing address space had to be created. Two such commonly used methods are subnetting and supernetting. Supernetting is also referred to as Classless Inter-Domain Routing. In subnetting, a single public IP address is further divided into multiple networks called subnets. The addresses of the hosts in a subnet cannot be used to communicate with other networks directly. The hosts in a subnet communicate with other networks through routers. Supernetting enables a block of IP addresses to be combined to form a large network called a supernet or supernetwork. Supernetting was created to overcome the problem of any decrease in the number of class B addresses in the IPv4 address space.

CHAPTER **16**

IP ROUTING

In this chapter

ROUTING CONCEPTS

Routing, one of the important functions of IP, is responsible for locating the best path to a target host. In the case of a local host, the ARP is used to locate the MAC of the target host and the datagram that is transmitted. The process is much more complex in the case of a remote host. Routing functions are required to ensure that the datagrams can reach the remote host and if the next hop router in the route is accessible. The IP Routing process determines the best possible route to reach the target host. Values are assigned to different routes based on the distance between the originating and the destination computers. The shortest possible route is preferred over the other routes.

All IP-enabled networks have a routing table, which contains a mapping of the target hosts and their corresponding gateways. To send a datagram, the sending computer looks up the local routing table to check for mappings for the target host. However, if the target host is not listed in the local routing table, the request is forwarded to the default gateway specified for the computer.

ROUTING PRINCIPLES

If the target host is not located on the local network, the packet is directed to the router for transmission. The router checks the routing table for possible routes of transmission and determines how the packet can be routed. If the router finds multiple routes, the decision is based on either existing routing policies on the network or built-in algorithms implemented on the routers. If destination addresses are not matched with the entries in the routing table, a default route is adopted to route the datagram. If partial routing is not allowed, the datagram is discarded. We will cover more about this in Chapter 17, "Routing Mechanisms."

A routing mechanism is used to identify the route for the transmission. IP searches for a matching host address and network address. If a matching address is not found, the router searches for a default entry in the routing table. However, routing need not necessarily occur only through the routing table. A typical example of this fact is the Internet where there are a number of routers. If the routing were to happen only on the basis of the entries in the routing table, the number of entries in the routing table would be too high to attain any efficiency. Other methods of routing are based on certain selected algorithms, such as Next-Hop routing.

→ To learn more about Routing Algorithms, **see** "Routing Algorithms," **p. 283**

ANALYZING THE ROUTING TABLE

Having seen that routing tables play an important role in the routing process, let us take a closer look at the contents of the routing table. A sample routing table is shown in Figure 16.1.

To view the routing table on a Windows NT or a Windows 2000 machine, proceed to the command prompt and type **Route Print**. Information in the routing table is classified under various categories. Table 16.1 describes each of these categories.

Figure 16.1

A sample routing table that displays active routes available in the network.

TABLE 16.1   ROUTING TABLE CATEGORIES

Category	Explanation
Network Destination	This field contains a list of network addresses that have been mapped to a gateway or a machine.
	0.0.0.0 maps to the *default gateway*, if any.
	127.0.0.0 is a loopback address that is used for diagnostic purposes.
	172.17.68.0 refers to the local network address.
	172.17.68.223 refers to the local host.
	172.17.255.255 refers to the network broadcast address.
	244.0.0.0 is the default multicast address. If the computer is a part of any multicast group, this and other multicast entries, if any, are used to communicate on the multicast network.
	255.255.255.255 is a limited broadcast address that is used by the router to listen to broadcasts on the local network. Messages destined for this address can only be listened to and cannot be transmitted to other networks.
Netmask	This field contains the netmask value corresponding to the destination address.
Gateway	This field contains the gateway used to route the packets. In Figure 16.1, the IP address 172.17.68.223 has been used in most cases. This IP address refers to the computer from which the command was issued. The computer has been used as the gateway because the destination addresses were also on the same network.
Interface	The interface is the IP address that is configured on the local computer for the local network adapter that is used when an IP datagram is forwarded on the network. At the beginning of the routing table, a list of the interfaces available is displayed.
Metric	This field contains the number of hops between the host and target machines.

CH

16

> **Note**
>
> *Network broadcast address* refers to the IP address that is used by the router as a destination IP address if the router does not know the correct destination IP.

> **Note**
>
> *Multicast networks* are networks that allow transmission of datagrams to multiple recipients simultaneously. Multicast networks form a part of an Mbone, also known as a Multicast backbone. *Multicast addresses* are unique network addresses that are organized into a predefined group of IP addresses.

It is important to know how the routing table is structured. The computer starts from the bottom of the routing table and works upwards to find a possible transmission route. In the routing table, the most restrictive netmasks are placed at the end of the table. This enables the computer to filter the routing table to find if there are any exact route matches to the individual host.

The computer works up the routing table while attempting to find an exact match to the destination. Next, it attempts to find a match to another computer on the same network as the destination and so on until it reaches the top of the routing table. The uppermost entry in the routing table is the least restrictive subnet, 0.0.0.0, which refers to the default gateway. If the computer has two network interface cards, each on a separate network, the computer can be used as a router between the two networks. To do this, you have to enable the IP Routing capabilities on that computer.

STATIC VERSUS DYNAMIC ROUTING

Routing methods are broadly classified into static routing and dynamic routing. *Static routing* refers to the routing method where a route for a datagram is not determined based on the status of the network or availability of routers on the network. Static routing implements routes that are predetermined based on predefined values, such as the distance between the originating and destination computers and the number of routers to be traversed by a datagram before reaching the destination computer. Static routes are preconfigured by the network administrator and are used when the topology of the network remains fixed. These routes are generally used for small networks, or when you want to force routing along a certain path.

On the other hand, the *dynamic routing* method takes into account a number of factors that are currently affecting a network. These factors include changes in the availability of routers, network traffic, or load on the routers. To route a packet, the computer can pass the packet to the next hop machine instead of computing the entire path. This process is carried on to move the packet closer to the destination machine. However, for the next hop method to work, a loop should not be formed. Figure 16.2 illustrates this scenario where there are four routers connecting five network segments.

Figure 16.2
A sample network where four routers are used to connect the different segments.

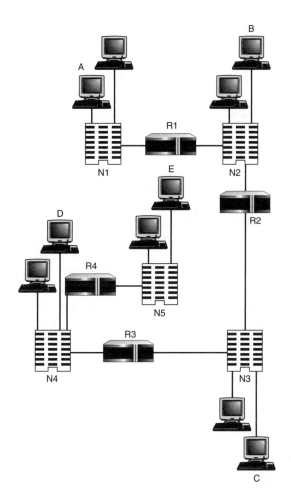

CH
16

If host A in N1 sends a packet to host D in N4, the packet must be routed through R1, R2, and R3. Host A takes the IP address of the destination computer which is host D, the AND process is performed, and the host is identified on a remote network. Therefore, the packet is passed to the next hop router, R1, in this case. R1 checks the IP of the next segment, N2. The packet is again forwarded to the next hop because the destination network does not match the N2 segment. This process is carried on until the packet finally reaches host D. However, on a big network with a large number of routers, the packets might be trapped in a routing loop. For example, in the above scenario, the packets could be routed back to R1 from R2 if the IP address specified in the packet does not match any of the segments on the network.

To avoid this problem, it is necessary to ensure that there is consistency in the routes to be followed. You can either manually configure consistent routes to be followed or enable a router to communicate the routing information through a special protocol. The two approaches are known as static routing and dynamic routing, respectively. We will take a brief look at both of these approaches in this chapter. However, detailed discussions of dynamic routing methods and protocols have been reserved for later chapters.

COMPARATIVE ANALYSIS OF STATIC AND DYNAMIC ROUTING

Static routing has a number of advantages over dynamic routing. Static routing is simpler to configure, reliable, imposes lower overheads, and is easier to maintain. However, static routing suffers in scalability and limited features. Let us take a closer look at these advantages.

Static routers are simpler to configure. The administrator can add specific entries to the routing table and can control exactly how packets are to be routed. A static route either works or does not work. Therefore, if a datagram is transmitted but does not reach its destination, static routing ensures that it is discarded and not routed back to the sending computer. As routes are preconfigured, there are fewer overheads on the router devices. Runtime updates of the routing information are also made redundant by static routing. Therefore, there are fewer overheads on the network bandwidth. Maintaining static routes is simple because each route is predetermined. If a packet from a particular location is not being transmitted correctly to the destination, only that particular set of routes needs to be checked. This saves valuable time in maintenance. It is also possible to monitor transmission speeds of individual routes. This helps in identifying requirements for upgrades and in the addition of routers.

Another advantage of static routing is that it can be used to enhance security. For example, in your company, the connection to the Internet could have a statically defined route to a security server. No access would be possible without having first passed the security mechanisms provided by the server. Static routers are difficult to maintain in cases where the network is large and dynamic in nature. For example, if you have eight routers on your network and want to expand the network by adding one more router, you will have to reconfigure all the routers. All the existent paths will have to be entered again into the new router. As the size of the network increases, the complexity of routing and configuring static routing information also increases. For example, take the case of a large static network comprising more than 300 network segments with each segment being serviced by four routers to connect to other segments and to external networks. You must manually configure routing information for 1,200 routes on each router. Any change to these routes would require tremendous and tedious change in routing information on each router.

Dynamic routers, on the other hand, have a number of additional features, such as re-routing, that ease the administrative load on a large network. Consider a network that has 200 network segments that need to be interconnected. In this case, if you use static routing, you will have to configure the next hop for each router to all the other routers. For example, if you have 20 routers interconnecting all the network segments, you will need more than 4,000 routes. That is too huge a number to implement with a manual configuration and maintenance process because many routes would draw considerable administrative effort. If you use dynamic routers, each of the 20 routers can manage any change in the next hop without requiring intervention from the network administrator.

Dynamic routing also ensures that routers act intelligently and re-configure the routes to bypass any inactive router or failed link, which is quite common. As a result, if a single router fails, the transmissions can occur through an alternative route.

> For the router to select an alternative route, it is important that inactive or inoperable routers exist in the current route. The router can also select an alternative route if there are failed links on the current route.

In dynamic routing, any modifications to the network topology automatically trigger a reconfiguration of the routing tables. All the routers are notified of changes to the network.

CH
16

Like all technologies, both dynamic and static routing have their share of advantages and disadvantages. The decision on choosing the method of routing depends on the requirements of a network. For example, if you have a slow link and few routers, choose static routing. However, if you have a number of segments or if the network is expected to be undergoing changes all the time, choose dynamic routing.

A MEDIAN SOLUTION

It is not necessary for you to follow any one type of routing to implement on your network. You can create a hybrid routing model to be followed for your routing needs. In the hybrid model, your network consists of both static and dynamic routers. However, the extent of activity and the number of routing options that are supported determine the different parts of the network that are to be placed on dynamic routing and static routing.

Before looking at the type of routing to be implemented, let us look at the interactions between static and dynamic routers. Static routers have a set of routes that are configured to access certain network segments and routers. Any changes in these routes would have to be manually implemented to ensure that the performance of the router is not affected. These routers cannot send any routing information to dynamic routers. Therefore, if a dynamic router has a route that accesses a static router, both routers are rendered static for that route. Although this negates the idea of using a dynamic router, the solution to this problem is that dynamic routers update routing information amongst other dynamic routers and do not exchange routing information with static routers.

To illustrate how a hybrid model of static and dynamic routers can be implemented, consider a network with a number of segments. Divide this network into two areas, the access network and the core network. The *access network* consists of all the user computers on the network. This network has no more than two routers connected to them, and these routers do not route datagrams from the sending computer to the destination computer. These routers merely point to the next hop and provide connections to the user machines located on its network. The *core network*, on the other hand, consists of an interconnection of a number of different routers.

To manage routing, a hybrid routing model is implemented where a static router manages the access network and dynamic routers manage the core network. Access networks do not have too many connections and can work on static routers. This will enable you to control the access provided to the users of these networks. Using static routers helps you avoid maintaining a certain trust relationship with the other routers to exchange routing information. This gives you administrative control over how a segment routes its packets, at least up to the default router.

The core networks, on the other hand, contain a number of routers. These routers help route the packets between the different access networks and the Internet. The number of routers and routes involved make it essential that a continuous update of the routing information occurs on the core network. In this situation, dynamic routers best serve the interests of the network. The automatic update and the re-routing facility ensure that the performance of the network is not affected.

Another example of the hybrid routing model is the routing model used to connect a network to the Internet. All the network segments are connected using static routers. The Internet gateway is controlled through a dynamic router. The static routers contain a mapping to the default gateway that routes the packets to the Internet router. In this way, any IP address that is not found on the local network and for which no route exists is forwarded to the Internet router. Apart from the routing model used for network-to-Internet connectivity, hybrid models in which remote access routers send regular routing information updates to dynamic core routers. However, the remote access router is configured as a static router that uses a default static route to the core router. In this model, core routers are implemented as dynamic routers that obtain regular route advertisements from static remote access routers that send these advertisements through a preconfigured default route.

CONFIGURING STATIC ROUTES

In this section, you will look at how to configure static routes in a Windows environment. To view the routing table, open the command prompt and type the command **ROUTE PRINT**. This will display the routing table shown in Figure 16.3.

Figure 16.3
The routing table of a computer displayed by the ROUTE PRINT command.

Alternatively, you can use the `Netstat` command to view the routing table. The `Netstat` command would enable you to view a list of active and recent connections, as shown in Figure 16.4. To view the routing table, type **Netstat -rn** in the command prompt.

Figure 16.4
The routing table and recent active connections of 172.17.199.127 displayed by the Netstat -rn command.

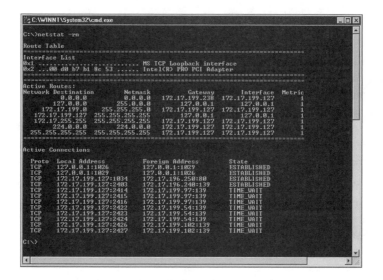

The -r option lists the contents of the routing table. The contents would be listed with the Fully Qualified Domain Name (FQDN) of the destinations. The use of the -n option enables you to view the IP address of the destination instead of the FQDN. To view the help on the `Netstat` command, type **Netstat ?** at the command prompt.

When you are using a static router, it is important that you configure certain specific routes, especially if your network consists of more than two subnets. To add a static route, use the `Route Add` command. This command takes the following parameters:

- IP address of the destination—This is a mandatory parameter. You cannot use wildcards for the destination IP address.

- Subnet mask—This parameter is used to indicate the subnet mask of the destination computer. If the mask and the destination IP address do not match, the ANDing operation to determine the validity of the subnet mask will result in an error. If no subnet mask is specified, the default value of 255.255.255.255 is assigned.

- Default gateway—The gateway, if any, to be used for the route.

- Network interface number—This parameter indicates the interface number to be used for the route. If an interface is not specified, the interface to be used for the route is determined from the gateway IP address. This option can be implemented using the IF parameter.

- Metric—This parameter is used to specify the cost for the route. Costs include the bandwidth, load, delays, path length, and stability of the routers in a route. An important point is that the metric that is adopted for a route depends on the routing protocol being implemented. For example, if the Routing Information Protocol (RIP) is used as the routing protocol, the hop count is the only metric that needs to be specified as a parameter.

The following code shows you how to configure a route:

```
ROUTE ADD 172.17.199.0 MASK 255.255.255.0  172.17.199.127 METRIC 1
```

You will receive a message if the attempt to add a route fails. This command adds a route to the routing table. Now, the computer can access the rest of the network. The command mentioned here would not work on your network because your IP addresses would be different. By default, routes are not preserved when the system is restarted. Using the -p option with the Route Add command helps you make the routes persistent, regardless of the number of times a computer is booted. However, the -p option does not work on the Windows 95 operating system.

You can use the ROUTE CHANGE command to change the gateway. The ROUTE CHANGE command can also be used to change the metric assigned to a specific route when you need to optimize the transmission of datagrams on a route. The following syntax illustrates how to change the metric value assigned to a particular route.

```
ROUTE CHANGE 172.17.199.0 172.17.199.127 METRIC 2
```

The metric value 2 is an arbitrary number that indicates the cost of the new route specified in the ROUTE CHANGE command. The metric value can be specified ranging from 1 to 9,999. Routing algorithms use this value to determine the cost metric while deciding on choosing this route. You can confirm the change by viewing the routing table. You can also add additional routes to the same destination through different gateways. To delete a route, use the ROUTE DELETE command as shown in the following syntax.

```
ROUTE DELETE 172.17.199.0 172.17.199.238
```

You would need to specify the gateway if multiple routes to the same destination address exist. If you do not mention the IP address of the gateway, all routes to that destination will be deleted. This command enables you to use wildcard entries to delete all similar routes. In addition, the -f option can be used with the ROUTE DELETE command. When used with the -f option, the ROUTE DELETE command clears the routing tables of all gateway entries. When the -f option is used in conjunction with any of the other commands, the tables are cleared before running the command.

Note

Once a persistent change is made, it cannot be reverted. Make a note of the existing configuration before proceeding to alter the routing table.

ERROR HANDLING

An IP datagram travels from one router to another until it reaches the target host. Consider the example of a scenario where a datagram is sent to a target host that does not exist on the destination network. In this case, when the final router finds that the datagram cannot be delivered, it has to notify the sending computer. In a connectionless transmission system, Internet Control Message Protocol (ICMP) is used for communicating the control and error messages of TCP/IP. These messages are encapsulated within an IP datagram before being sent. ICMP messages are used to instruct the sending computer of any problems in the transmission. Two instances where ICMP messages are generated are as follows:

- Flow control—Used to instruct the sending computer to temporarily stop transmission.
- Unreachable host notification—This message is used to notify the sending computer that the target host is currently unable to receive the datagrams. The problem could arise because the destination network or host is unreachable or does not exist.

In addition to these instances, ICMP messages are used by routing algorithms implemented on routers to initiate redirecting of the routes and for checking the availability of remote hosts.

CH

16

> **Note**
>
> ICMP is an error reporting protocol that only informs the sending computer of errors in transmission and cannot correct errors. Although it does suggest alternative routes to be taken, it does not perform any corrective action.

Take the example of the routing process over the Internet, which is based on a connectionless transmission system. The role of ICMP here is to report the error in transmission to the sending computer only. Most errors in the routing process occur only during the process of hopping from one router to another. For example, if the fourth router in a six-hop route transmits the datagrams wrongly to another router, the error cannot be reported to the fourth router. ICMP can only report the error to the sending computer, which has no control over the routers. ICMP cannot communicate the error to the erroneous router because the datagram only contains the source and destination IP addresses and not the routing map of the datagram.

→ To know more about ICMP, **see** "Introduction to ICMP," **p. 62**

ICMP ERROR MESSAGES

As mentioned in Chapter 4, "Internet Control Message Protocol," ICMP messages use a double level of encapsulation. ICMP messages are also routed back to the sending computer like a normal datagram. There are no special routing systems implemented for an ICMP message. Therefore, even ICMP packets can be lost or discarded. However, the only exception to an ICMP error message is that an error in the transmission of an ICMP packet will not trigger another ICMP message to report the error. This prevents an infinite loop of ICMP error messages.

When a router is unable to deliver an IP datagram, it sends a Destination Unreachable message to the sending computer. The structure of ICMP messages was discussed in Chapter 4. Let us briefly look at exactly how the router communicates the error. A typical ICMP packet consists of the following fields:

- Type
- Code
- Checksum
- Unused
- Data

→ To learn more about the fields in an ICMP packet, **see** Table 4.1, "Fields of an IP Datagram," **p. 65**

The Type field for a Destination Unreachable message is 3. The code value is used to describe the exact nature of the error. Table 16.2 summarizes the different error codes and their descriptions.

TABLE 16.2   DIFFERENT TYPES OF DESTINATION UNREACHABLE ERROR MESSAGES

Error Code	Description
0	Signifies that the network was unreachable.
1	Signifies that the host computer was unreachable.
2	Signifies that the protocol was unreachable, that is, there was a protocol mismatch. In addition, the protocol module or process port may not be active on the destination computer.
3	Signifies that the destination port was unreachable.
4	Signifies the requirement for fragmentation.
5	Signifies that the source route failed.
6	Signifies that the destination network was unknown.
7	Signifies that the destination host was unknown.
8	Signifies that the source host was isolated.
9	Signifies that the communication with the destination network was prohibited because of an administrative restriction.
10	Signifies that the communication with the destination host was prohibited because of an administrative restriction.
11	Signifies that the destination network was unreachable for the specific service requested.
12	Signifies that the destination host was unreachable for the specific service requested.

ICMP error messages also contain the address of the destination computer. This enables the sending computer to identify which datagram failed. The error codes also enable the computer to identify the cause of the error. If a Network Unreachable error occurs, it implies that the error was caused due to router problems. However, if a Host Unreachable error is reported, it implies that the host was either nonexistent or had some temporary connection problems.

Take the example of a datagram that is sent with the no fragmentation bit set. The router must fragment the datagram to ensure the delivery of the datagram. In such a situation, the router sends an ICMP error message of type 3 with the error code set to 4. ICMP messages do not correct errors. They only help the computer in identifying the problem route or destination.

CH

16

ICMP AND ROUTER CONTROL

ICMP messages are also used to report the status of routers to computers that are sending datagrams to the router. For example, consider a scenario in which a number of computers simultaneously send packets to the router for transmission. Routers have limited memory and cannot store the packets for transmission. If too many packets arrive at the router simultaneously, the router queues up the packets in the order in which the packets arrive at the router. If the router's buffer is full, the router has to drop the packets.

In such situations, to ease the load on the router, ICMP messages are sent to the sending computers to inform of the congestion at the router. These messages are known as *source quench* messages. The destination computers that receive this message will then reduce the transmission rate of the datagrams to enable the router to receive all the datagrams that are transmitted from the sending computer. Although source quench messages reduce the speed of transmission, they enable the router to route all datagrams. A source quench message is identified with the value 4 specified in the Type field of the ICMP message packet, as shown in Figure 16.5.

Although congestion states can be notified, there are no ICMP messages to notify the computers that the congestion is released and that the transmission can occur smoothly. The sending computer continues to operate under reduced speed until the source quench messages are not received. Then, the computer gradually increases the rate of transmission until it reaches its original transmission rate.

ICMP AND ROUTER REDIRECT ERRORS

Routers are assumed to know the best path for the transmission of a packet. Routers can also send an ICMP message to redirect the packet through a better router or gateway because that route is known to be shorter or less congested. ICMP Redirect messages are also used to notify an error in the selection of the route. However, ICMP redirect messages sent by routers are ignored by sending computers in certain scenarios to prevent security lapses. For example, when the sending computer is behind a firewall, the sending computer ignores the redirect message. Figure 16.6 illustrates a scenario where there are a number of possible routes (Route 1, Route 2, and Route 3) between the sending computer and the destination computer.

Figure 16.5
The sample packet of an ICMP Error message structure.

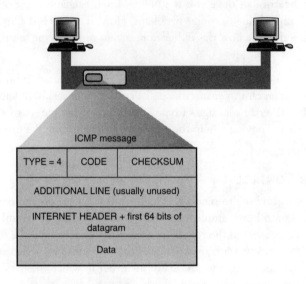

ICMP message

TYPE = 4	CODE	CHECKSUM
ADDITIONAL LINE (usually unused)		
INTERNET HEADER + first 64 bits of datagram		
Data		

Figure 16.6
A network where there are a number of possible routes between Host A and Host B.

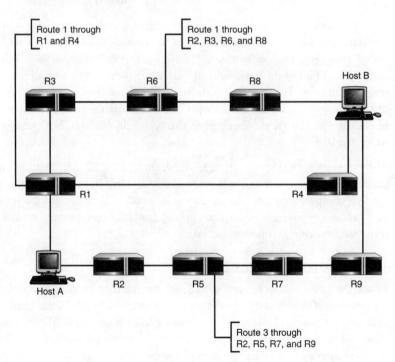

Route 1 through R1 and R4

Route 1 through R2, R3, R6, and R8

R3   R6   R8   Host B

R1   R4

Host A   R2   R5   R7   R9

Route 3 through R2, R5, R7, and R9

In the figure, only the source and destination computers and the routers are represented. In this case, the packet is sent from Host A with minimal routing information. If R1 is the default gateway, the packet reaches this router. The router then forwards this packet to R6 through R3. When the packet reaches R8, it finds that the route selected is not the most optimal route and sends an ICMP redirect error message back. However, the router, having received the packet, continues to route it to the destination computer, Host B. To update the routing table of the sending computer with information about the existence of a shorter route, the ICMP redirect error is used. The next time a packet is to be delivered to the destination, Host A will also provide this additional routing information along with the packet.

Note

The router R8 cannot send an ICMP redirect error to router R1 and instruct it to use the shorter route through R4. The ICMP message will go only to Host A because R8 does not know the address of router R1.

CH
16

The reason why ICMP performs a redirect is to enable the sending computer to build up a routing table that contains a list of optimal routes. The advantage of this approach is that the host can boot up with a minimal number of persistent routes, which could be just one route pointing to the default gateway. The host then builds up the routing table each time an ICMP redirect message comes. ICMP redirect messages contain a value of 5 in the Type field of the ICMP packet, as shown in Figure 16.7.

Figure 16.7
The packet structure of an ICMP Redirect Error message.

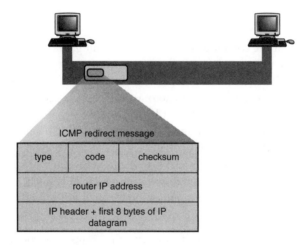

The packet contains a Router Internet Address field in place of the Unused field seen in the earlier ICMP messages. This field contains the address of the router that is to be used by the sending computer to deliver the packet to the destination. The Code field of the packet identifies the type of redirect message and can contain four possible values (0–3), as explained in Table 16.3.

TABLE 16.3   DIFFERENT TYPES OF ICMP REDIRECT ERROR MESSAGES

Error Code	Description
0	Signifies that the datagrams for a particular network needs to be redirected
1	Signifies that the datagrams for a particular host needs to be redirected
2	Signifies that the datagrams for a particular type of service on a network need to be redirected
3	Signifies that the datagrams for a particular type of service provided for the host needs to be redirected

For security reasons, the sending computer checks the IP address of the router that sends the redirect and the IP address of the new router that is specified. The redirect is accepted only if

- The IP address of the router that sends the redirect and the IP address of the new router do not match. This prevents rogue routers from designating themselves as the best path.

- The new router exists on the directly connected network, and the router that sent the redirect is on an indirect route to the destination host.

Unless both these conditions are satisfied, the host does not update its routing table with the destination routing information. In addition, the network administrator managing the host network is alerted that the routing information has not been updated.

ICMP AND ROUTER LOCATION

It is not necessary that the computer should have a default gateway configured. The computer can find out the existence of routers on the network through the ICMP Router Solicitation message. The computer broadcasts this message and listens to all the replies from the routers. This computer helps to automatically update the host of changes in router states. For example, take a scenario where a Windows 2000 host boots on to the network. The computer acquires the default configuration from the DHCP and BOOTP services. However, the configuration provided by these services is static and manually configured by the administrator. If the router crashes, the host computer would not know that the router has crashed and would continue to receive error messages. This is where router discovery routines help the host to continue communication through other routers in a multirouter environment.

The router discovery routine consists of two parts, the requisition from the host to find routers and the acknowledgement of the router's availability. The host broadcasts a Router Solicitation message, which contains a value of 10 in the Type field, as shown in Figure 16.8.

The host computer broadcasts the ICMP Router Solicitation messages in intervals of 180 seconds. It waits and listens for a router to advertise its presence. The solicitations are stopped once the host receives an acknowledgement from a router.

Figure 16.8
The packet structure of an ICMP Router Solicitation message.

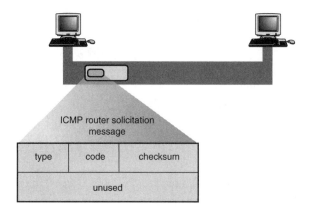

The routers respond to a solicitation message with the ICMP Router Advertisement packet. In a multirouted environment, the router not only advertises its presence, but it also advertises the presence of other routers. The Type field of this ICMP packet contains the value 9. A typical ICMP Router Advertisement packet consists of 8 bytes of header information followed by the addresses of the different routers being advertised, as shown in Figure 16.9.

Figure 16.9
The packet structure of an ICMP Router Advertisement message in a typical multirouted environment.

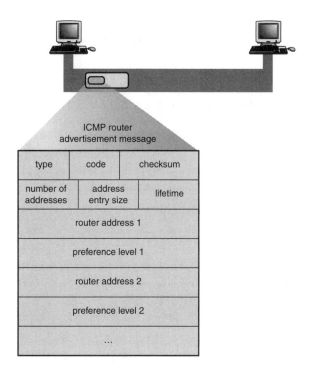

CH
16

The Number of Addresses field contains the number of routers that are being advertised in the message. The Address Entry Size field always contains the default value 2, except for Ipv4 addresses, which are represented by the value 1. The Lifetime field represents the number of seconds that the advertisement can be considered valid. The default lifetime for an advertisement is 30 minutes.

The data section of the packet contains a list of router addresses and their respective preference values. The preference value for a particular router identifies the relative preference of routers over the other routers in the list. The router with the highest preference value is selected as the default gateway.

In addition to responding to ICMP Router Solicitation messages, the routers can periodically issue ICMP Router Advertisement messages. The lifetime of an ICMP advertisement is usually about 30 minutes. Routers, by default, send the advertisement packets in intervals of 10 minutes. This ensures that even if the host misses one advertisement, it will be able to catch the next advertisement before the lifetime expires.

As with other ICMP messages, the host cannot issue an ICMP Router Advertisement message in an attempt to share its knowledge of the existence of routers with the other hosts and routers. If the sending computer does not receive any response for a solicitation message, it can transmit the ICMP Router Solicitation packet three times. If no response is received for the messages, the host has no option but to wait for an ICMP Router Advertisement message. This restriction ensures that the network is not congested with Router Solicitation messages.

> **Note**
>
> It is possible to prevent the sending computer from issuing and responding to the router discovery messages by disabling the option. You can edit the PerformRouterDiscovery Registry setting to disable the router discovery process.

SUMMARY

Routing is an important function of TCP/IP that enables different networks to communicate. The purpose of routing is to find the shortest possible route between two hosts. The host starts with minimal routing information, and the router ensures that the packet is delivered to the destination computer. There are two types of routing—static routing and dynamic routing. Static routing involves manual manipulation of the routing table to control the process of routing a packet. Dynamic routing involves the use of certain special routing protocols that communicate changes in the routing environment of the network. You also saw how to manipulate the static routing table through Route commands.

The use of ICMP messages helps the host to know when a packet id is not delivered and the reasons for the errors in a connectionless environment. In addition to using ICMP error messages for fault isolation, the ICMP messages also enable the host to learn about the routing environment of the network through redirect errors and router advertisements.

CHAPTER 17

ROUTING MECHANISMS

In this chapter

INTRODUCTION TO ROUTING MECHANISMS

Sending letters or gifts by mail is a popular method of greeting and communicating with people. At Christmas time, millions of gifts and cards are delivered across the country and all over the world. To ensure a safe and timely delivery of your greetings, a large network of postal services across the country and around the world works in the background. The postal system is managed by a collection of post offices that act as staging posts where letters and packages are first delivered and sorted before being redirected to their final destination. To ensure safe and smooth communication between computers, the Internet is built on a system of intermediate devices that act as staging posts, similar to the staging posts used in the postal system. These intermediate devices are called routers. Each router is linked to a centralized communication device called the backbone, which links a set of routers across geographic locations. You will learn about the evolution of the routing architecture and the various mechanisms used to route information between computers in the following sections.

Before delving into the routing architecture, you need to understand how data is directed to the correct destination computer. To determine the method of transmitting data over the network, the path to the destination computer must be determined. This process is similar to the sorting done by postal employees at a staging post to determine the next staging post where the mail must be delivered. To determine information about the path to be taken by a datagram to reach its destination, routing information is extracted from a table called the routing table where routes are stored. This table stores information on network destination IP addresses, netmask corresponding to the network destination addresses, gateway information, information on network interface drivers, and the number of hops or number of routers that lies between the local computer and the target computer.

→   For more information on routing tables, **see** "Analyzing the Routing Table," **p. 260**

An important fact to note is that each datagram needs to pass through a number of routers before reaching its final destination. At each router, the path to the next router must be determined using the information in the routing table. This path might change depending on the availability of the router. For example, if a new router that provides a shorter transmission path to the destination is available, the routing table is updated with the address of that router by discarding the old router address to shorten the transmission path. On startup, routers initialize the routing table by populating a blank routing table with information stored on its hard disk. The routing table contents are updated according to the conditions existing on the network. The method of initializing and updating routing tables depends on the operating system installed on the routers. Some operating systems installed on a router open existing routing tables from the hard disk or populate blank routing tables on startup by using login scripts that are specific to the operating systems.

When we send mail, we specify the destination mailing address without specifying the names of the staging posts. Similarly, when a datagram is sent from the source router of the network where the sending computer is located, the only routing information that is supplied by the sending computer to the source router is the destination address and a default route to the nearest router. The router must determine the route that must be taken by the datagram with the help of the partial routing information provided by the sending computer. This is especially difficult considering the fact that finding your way around the "network of networks" with little information is like trying to find your way out of a maze.

Source routers direct datagrams with the help of partial routing information by specifying the address of the nearest router that lies on the path to the destination. This route is termed as the default route. For example, if a datagram sent from computer A located on network N1 needs to reach a destination computer B located on network N2, (see Figure 17.1) and if the router has only partial routing information to route the datagram, it routes the datagram to the router R1 that lies on the path to network N2. In turn, router R1 directs the datagram to router R2. Subsequently, the datagram passes through a number of routers on this default route until it reaches the router connected to the destination network N2 that hosts the destination computer B. Figure 17.1 shows how a datagram is routed through the default route with the help of partial routing information.

Figure 17.1
Routers use a default route to direct datagrams to their destination if they have partial routing information.

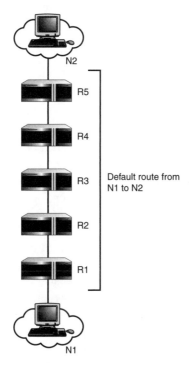

Default route from N1 to N2

EVOLUTION OF NETWORK ROUTING ARCHITECTURE

Now that you are familiar with how routing is managed, knowledge of the underlying routing architecture is essential to comprehend how routing mechanisms work. Routing architectures have evolved over the years beginning with the early ARPAnet to the Internet that we know today. Initially, the Internet was designed with a collection of core routers that stored all possible destination routes in their routing tables. Each router that linked the sending computer's network to the Internet used the default route that always pointed to any one of the core routers. By following the default route determined by local routers, datagrams that contained partial routing information ultimately reached their correct destination through the core routers.

The core router architecture provided support for modifying the structure of a local network without modifying the components of the Net connected to the local network. This feature also induces the possibility of errors occurring in the validity of a route taken by a datagram. For example, if the changes to the structure of the local network are not updated on the routing table of a core router, the destination computer located on the restructured local network becomes unreachable. This is because the route provided by the core router's routing table is an old one, which does not correspond to the restructured network architecture of the local network where the destination computer is located.

Early Internet routing architectures were organized into two groups with a collection of core routers managed by the Internet Network Operations Center (INOC) and other routers that routed datagrams from computers located on the local networks to the core routers. This was because ARPAnet was identified as the backbone on which other routers could connect to the rest of the nascent Internet. A number of local networks, such as universities and research groups that populated the early Internet, had to be connected to ARPAnet through local routers. The local routers, in turn, linked to a set of core routers, which formed the ARPAnet backbone.

Early routing architecture faced certain performance deficiencies, especially when routing datagrams with partial information. For example, consider a situation in which a sending computer named M1 sends a datagram with partial information to a destination computer located on the network linked by the core router named R12. The datagram is directed to all the core routers to verify if any of the routers have a direct route to the destination computer because the datagram has only partial routing information. Before reaching the core router R12, the datagram needs to traverse a number of other core routers. Then, R12 directs the datagram to the local router, which in turn transmits it to its final destination. On the other hand, datagrams with complete routing information are transmitted directly to the destination networks and computers. To manage routing datagrams with partial information, all local network routers must constantly update their routing tables with default route information to maintain consistency with other routers whenever the default route changes. These requirements lead to wastage of network resources and possible loss of data if default routes are not consistent among all local routers. Figure 17.2 shows you how partial routing information on datagrams can cause giant datagram transmission cycles.

To overcome such issues, a better routing architecture was devised. In the new architecture, each local network was connected to a core router and the routing information available in core routers was exchanged. Any change in routes was updated in the core router routing tables. All core routers contained routing information for all possible destinations, which removed the need for maintaining default routes. If the destination address on a datagram does not match the information in the routing table of a core router, it is discarded after sending an ICMP destination unreachable error message to the sending computer.

Figure 17.3 shows how central core routers overcome problems that occur from routing datagrams with partial routing information.

Figure 17.2
Partial routing information causes giant routing cycles resulting in wastage of resources.

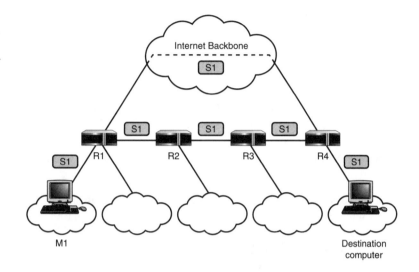

Figure 17.3
Routers that support default routes take circuitous routes to direct datagrams to their destination while central core routing architecture ensures that datagrams with reachable destination addresses are routed directly to the destination computer.

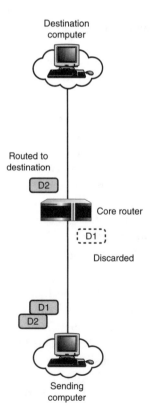

In Figure 17.3, datagrams D1 and D2 are transmitted to the receiving computer through the core router. Datagram D1 contains partial routing information and is discarded by the core router. D2 specifies a reachable destination address and is successfully routed to the correct destination computer.

Although the central core router architecture provided an efficient method for transmitting datagrams, the growth of the Net necessitated a change of design in the architecture. For example, the exponential growth of ARPAnet resulted in the need to open another backbone to manage the load. In addition, the number of new networks being added to the backbone necessitated a higher degree of consistency among the core routers to ensure consistent routing table information on all core routers. The central core routing architecture required local networks to be connected to a core router, which was not possible with the exponential growth of the Internet. These restrictions meant that the core router architecture limited the size of the network without allowing growth and expansion.

As with any system that becomes obsolete with time or change of technology, the central core router architecture had to give way to a more scalable routing architecture. To manage the expanding Internet, the National Science Foundation (NSF) launched the NSFNET backbone in addition to ARPAnet. In the early days of NSFNET, it acted more like any other local network that was linked to the ARPAnet backbone. In the course of time, NSFNET began to grow with many other local networks linking up to the backbone to form a sizably large network of networks. This eventually formed a part of the Internet that we know today. This growth necessitated multiple routers linking NSFNET and ARPAnet. Now, NSFNET was no longer a subsidiary local network connected to ARPAnet but an equivalent backbone. Such a routing architecture is called *peer backbone network architecture*.

The addition of peer backbones to the routing architecture raised many new issues in implementing routing between the peer backbones. Take a scenario where a datagram needs to be transmitted from a computer named M1 located on a local network connected to NSFNET to a destination computer named M4 located on a local network connected to the ARPAnet backbone. The datagram can be routed through any of the routers (R1, R2, or R3) connecting NSFNET and ARPAnet. Now, the choice of router to be used depends entirely on the network policies implemented by the managers of the backbones based on the performance and capabilities of the routers. For example, if the destination computer M4 is located at a geographic location close to the router R3, the datagram must be directed through R3 into ARPAnet into the local network where the destination computer M4 is located. Figure 17.4 shows how peer backbones work.

Routing algorithms that implement routing over the peer backbone architecture need to consider a number of issues. For example, consistency of routes must be maintained in the routing tables of the routers that connect the peer backbones. This eliminates the possibility of a datagram not reaching its destination because it is being routed in a circular path. Moreover, to improve efficiency in datagram transmission, the transmission route for datagrams sent by each computer must be customized taking into account the geographic location of the sending and receiving computers. For example, the shortest route for a datagram being sent from a particular computer through a particular router must be adopted instead of a longer route. To manage such issues, routing algorithms need to be implemented. You will learn more about the routing algorithms in the next section.

Figure 17.4
Routing algorithms implemented by the routers determine the choice of route. The algorithms adopt a route that provides the shortest possible route between the router and the desti-nation computer.

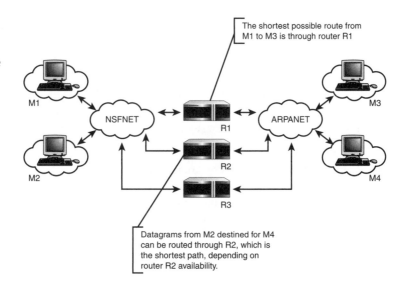

The shortest possible route from M1 to M3 is through router R1

Datagrams from M2 destined for M4 can be routed through R2, which is the shortest path, depending on router R2 availability.

CH
17

ROUTING ALGORITHMS

In the early days of networking, determining routes for transmitting datagrams to their des-tination was not an issue of concern because of the small number of computers connected to a network. These routes did not change frequently and were considered static. Therefore, routing tables contained information that was predetermined and hardly required any modification. However, as the Internet started growing at an exponential rate, the networks started exhibiting dynamic features. For example, new networks were added to the Net and necessitated changes in transmission routes because the new networks provided shorter paths to destination computers.

On the other hand, the increase in the use of the Net also resulted in overload and network failure. The need to manage a dynamic network necessitated a mechanism that determined routes automatically based on the availability of networks and the shortest possible path available to the destination computer. This mechanism is called a routing algorithm.

With the progress in the size of the Internet, a number of routing algorithms have been proposed and implemented. Today, we can classify these algorithms based on their imple-mentation in static and dynamic networks. Some of the routing algorithms include flooding, flow-based algorithms, distance-vector algorithm, link state algorithm, and hierarchical algorithms.

ROUTING ALGORITHM DESIGN PREREQUISITES

Before analyzing each algorithm, it is important to understand certain implementation goals that must be met by an algorithm. Routing algorithms must consider factors, such as optimality, simplicity, stability, and robustness, and convergence while determining routes. A routing algorithm must be designed as a piece of software that works as a simple component, which does not require huge software or hardware resources. In addition, the algorithms must work with a high rate of efficiency to maximize the utilization of available resources. For example, some corporate networks might have routers running on legacy computers that do not offer much processing power. When routing algorithms are implemented on such computers, they must not overload the OS, which might result in a crash.

Another implementation goal that must be ensured is stability and robustness. In contrast to the early Internet, networks of today are highly dynamic and can throw up unforeseen situations, such as congestion or network failures. An algorithm must be robust enough to manage such situations and re-route datagrams through the shortest path available when the normally used shortest path is unavailable.

The exponential increase in the number of users has placed a tremendous strain on routers. For example, news channels running Web sites propagate real-time information on political or sporting events. When such events occur, the load on the routers that link news channel Web sites is tremendous. Routing algorithms implemented on routers must be designed as a stable piece of software that will be able to withstand a large flow of network traffic at any time.

In addition to load management, routers must also communicate any changes in routes to other routers whenever destination routes change. All routers must come to an agreement on the best routes to be adopted to transmit datagrams. This process is called *convergence*. Consider a scenario where a router fails necessitating the recalculation of routes in the routing table of other routers. All routers must perform this recalculation, inform each other of their "opinion" on the best possible route, and come to an agreement on the optimal routes that must be adopted. If this process is not completed quickly, old routes that include the IP address of the crashed router continue to be used by routers resulting in missing datagrams or in routing loops. Convergence assumes a high importance among design goals for creating a routing algorithm. The process of converging on common routes must not cause instability on the network. Until common routes are identified, all routers will not be able to route any datagram. In the worst scenario, this state of instability must be as short in duration as possible.

While determining the best possible route, algorithms perform their calculations based on certain parameters called metrics. This capability of an algorithm, called optimality, is also a design goal that must be taken into account before designing a routing algorithm. While calculating the best possible route for a datagram, an algorithm can use a number of metrics. These metrics include the propagation delay, available bandwidth, path length, router load, and stability. Each of these metrics not only deals with the efficient transmission of datagrams but also help in calculating the cost of routing the datagrams. Table 17.1 describes each of the metrics in detail.

TABLE 17.1 ROUTING METRICS

Metric	Description
Delay	Specifies the delay in the time taken for a datagram to be transmitted from the sending computer to the destination computer. A number of factors contribute to this metric. For example, the actual physical distance between the sending and the destination computers can be vast. On the other hand, though the sending and destination computers are located on networks that are not far apart, other factors such as full buffers or congestion on the routers can cause delays while transmitting datagrams. In addition, the bandwidth of the networks that is used by a datagram to reach its destination also contributes to the delay in transmission.
Bandwidth	Indicates capability of a network to transmit a certain measure of data at any given interval of time. This metric is very important for determining which networks must lie in the transmission route of a datagram. Typically, if available, networks with large bandwidths are preferred to transmit datagrams of large sizes to ensure zero fragmentation and quick transmission. If the network has heavy traffic because of its large bandwidth capability, it is preferable to choose a network with lower bandwidth but less traffic. This is because lower bandwidth networks might be more efficient and effective in transmitting datagrams than high bandwidth but congestion-prone networks.
Path length	Specifies the total cost for transmitting a datagram. The cost, in terms of network resources used, for transmitting a datagram through a number of networks to the destination computer needs to be measured to identify the shortest path. Cost can be determined in a number of ways. For example, the total number of routers (representing each network) that needs to be traversed in a particular route can be taken as the path length for a route. This calculation for determining the path length is called *hop count* where a hop is taken to be a router that needs to be traversed in a route.
Router load	Specifies the load on a router. Each router provides a number of resources, such as processor time or memory, for receiving and redirecting datagrams to its destination. When a router manages a large number of datagrams, the load on its resources is tremendous. Routing algorithms need to identify the amount of load that exists on the routers in a particular route to determine whether a datagram can be transmitted without being discarded or queued indefinitely on a particular router. Determining this factor can be load-intensive because routers need to communicate their current capabilities with each other. Algorithms must use this metric sparingly.
Stability	Specifies the stability of the router. Although routers are designed to withstand high processing requirements, there are times when routers crash rendering the entire network unusable. Some routers are much more stable than others while some recover quickly from crashes. Routing algorithms need to estimate the stability of the routers in a particular path before transmitting datagrams through a route. To do this, a metric called stability or reliability is used by an algorithm. The metric can be determined by using a reliability rate number specified by the network administrators for each router. The number is usually calculated based on the number of errors per bit generated by a router.

CH

17

STATIC ROUTING ALGORITHMS

Some of the earliest routing algorithms were static algorithms. These algorithms were primarily concerned with transmitting datagrams efficiently without taking into account any changes in the status of networks because of the static nature of the networks in the early days. Two typical examples of routing algorithms are flooding and flow-based algorithms.

A simple method of transmitting datagrams is by using a static algorithm called flooding. Typically, the flooding algorithm is used in scenarios where it is necessary to propagate the same information to multiple destination computers. For example, this routing algorithm is most suitable when a piece of data stored on the central server of an organization must be updated on the regional servers located at the branch offices of the organization.

When a datagram is received through a particular route, it is sent through all possible routes available from the router except through the route it was received. Though this system appears to be simple, it results in an unaccountably large number of duplicate packets being transmitted all over the network from a router. To prevent duplication, a number of methods can be implemented. One method is to assign a sequence number that uniquely identifies each datagram. Each time a datagram is sent, the sequence number is incremented. If an incoming datagram is numbered less than the pervious datagram, it is identified as duplicate and is discarded.

Another method of preventing duplication is to assign a hop count number for each datagram. The hop count refers to the number of routers that must be traversed by a datagram to reach its destination. Before transmitting the datagram from the sending computer, the exact number of hops is set to a datagram. On reaching each router, the counter is decremented by 1. If the count reaches 0 without the datagram reaching its destination, it is discarded as a duplicate datagram. In addition to avoiding duplication, a technique called selective flooding is implemented to ensure an accurate transmission of datagrams. Selective flooding identifies routes that lie in the direction of the destination computer and directs datagrams towards these routes instead of propagating datagrams all over the network. Because of the excessive network traffic generated by implementing the flooding algorithm routing technique, the use of this algorithm has been discontinued. Today, routing software based on flooding algorithms is non-existent.

Network traffic has increased by leaps and bounds over the past few years. When we compare the network traffic volume that existed in the early days of the Net, it is difficult to believe that network traffic volumes have grown from a mere 50Kbps on ARPAnet to intercontinental cables that support more than 1GB of network traffic per second. However, in the early days it was possible to measure the flow of traffic and create routing protocols that determined routes based on the traffic flow on static networks. Flow-based algorithms work on the fact that given a predefined volume of traffic on a static route at any given point of time, transmission of datagrams on that route can be controlled to utilize the route to its optimum. For example, if the flow of traffic on the route between computers M1 and M2 is known in advance, routing algorithms can be designed to determine if the route is best suited for transmitting a datagram at any point of time. Flow-based algorithms take into account the average number of datagrams transmitted per second, the capacity or bandwidth of a route, and the average flow of datagrams per second on the route. In addition, the delay in transmission is taken as a fraction of the total traffic on a route. All these factors are used to calculate the total traffic on a route. The total traffic for all routes possible between the router and the destination computer is calculated, and the best route with the least traffic is used to transmit datagrams.

DYNAMIC ROUTING ALGORITHMS

Currently, all networks, from the global Internet to any corporate intranet, are dynamic in nature and require constant monitoring to resolve congestions or failures in any part of the network. To route a datagram over a constantly changing network environment, dynamic routing algorithms are required. These algorithms take into account any changes that have occurred in the status of the networks in a particular route before routing a datagram. Two of the most popular types of dynamic routing algorithms are the distance-vector algorithm and the link state algorithm.

One of the earliest dynamic routing algorithms that was implemented on the Net was the distance-vector algorithm. The algorithm, also referred to as the Bellman-Ford algorithm or Ford-Fulkerson algorithm, works on the principle of maintaining consistent routing information on the routing tables of all the routers in an internetwork. The routing table is initialized with destination addresses and distance to the destination address. This distance is measured in terms of hops, which is the number of routers that must be traversed by a datagram to reach the destination address. One of the earliest implementations of the distance-vector algorithm is the Routing Information Protocol (RIP).

CH
17

→ For more information on Routing Information Protocol, **see** "Introduction to Interior Gateway Protocols," **p. 295**

From time to time, information on the distance and the destination address is updated on the routing table whenever changes in the route are detected. For example, the addition of a router to an existing route might reduce the distance between the sending and the destination computers. This information must be updated on the routing tables of all the routers that lie on the route to enable all the routers to route a datagram in the correct path. Information on the destination of a datagram, also called a vector, and the distance between the sending and the destination computer is propagated to all the routers in a route.

Information is sent as a data pair that includes the distance and the vector, which is the reason for the naming of the algorithm as the distance-vector algorithm. If the information arriving from another router, R1, is not present in the routing table of a router, R2, or if the distance-vector pair provides a shorter route to a destination computer, the routing table on R2 is updated. When the changes in the routing table of router R2 occur, routing table information in router R3 must also be updated because R3 uses R2 for routing its datagrams.

One important requirement that must be complied by all participating routers is the need to communicate routing information quickly. In a dynamic network environment where routes are subject to constant change, if convergence of routing information does not happen quickly, the risk of routing datagrams through nonexistent routes becomes high.

For example, take a scenario where a datagram is sent through routers R1, R2, R3, R4, and R5. When the datagram reaches R3, the router R4 crashes and requires another router R6 to take its place. If this information is not updated on the routing tables of R3, it continues to route the datagram to R4, which is still recovering from a crash and is unable to transmit the datagram. The datagram can be discarded or lost. To implement distance-vector algorithms on dynamic network environments, the timely propagation of routing information is essential.

In the course of time, as the Internet started to move away from its ARPAnet origins and began including a vast number of routers, this requirement resulted in the constant failure of the distance-vector algorithm. This was primarily because it was becoming impossible to propagate routing information to all routers in a short time. Therefore, a new algorithm called the link state algorithm replaced distance-vector as the foremost routing algorithm. Today, a number of routing algorithms have been designed based on this algorithm. One example of a protocol based on the link state algorithm is the Open Shortest Path First (OSPF) protocol.

The link state algorithm deals with a network as a graph that consists of nodes and links with the nodes corresponding to a router and the links corresponding to a network. A link that connects two routers (represented as nodes) signifies that the routers are directly connected to each other and are referred to as neighbors. Each router tests the availability of its neighbors. It performs this task by sending a probe message that verifies if the neighboring router is functional. After obtaining information on the status of its neighbors, the router propagates link status information to all the other routers by sending a link status message. This message contains information on the availability of a link or a router. In this way, all routers have information on the availability of routers in a particular route. This information is used to determine the route for transmitting datagrams.

Link status messages do not provide routes for datagrams but only provide information that helps in determining routes. The job of determining routes is done by a router with the help of the short path first algorithm proposed by Dijkstra in 1959. Dijkstra's algorithm places labels on each node in the graph with the labels containing information on the distance between the node and the source node. As the algorithm proceeds through the graph, it updates the label to reflect the distance between each node from the source and helps in determining the shortest distance between the source and the destination nodes (or the source and the destination routers). Using this method, link state algorithm computes the shortest path that can be taken by a datagram to reach its destination computer.

The algorithm does not propose to communicate link status information to all routers but only to neighbors. Link status information is converged faster than the routing information in the distance-vector algorithm. Moreover, convergence times are very short because link state routing updates routing information on the occurrence of an event in contrast to timed updates implemented by distance-vector routing. Another advantage enjoyed by the link state algorithm is that the increase in the size of the network does not affect the propagation of information unlike distance-vector algorithm because link status messages are propagated to neighbors only and not to the entire internetwork.

SUMMARY

Routing mechanisms form the underlying structure for transmitting data over internetworks. Routing mechanisms are implemented on a routing architecture that originated as a set of computers connected to the ARPAnet backbone. The exponential growth of the Internet necessitated the creation of another backbone called NSFNET. This changed the routing architecture from a core routing architecture to a peer backbone routing architecture. To determine the route to be taken by a datagram, routers extracted routing information from routing tables maintained in a router. Although routing datagrams that contained partial information was supported, the inherent inefficiencies of this method resulted in the core routing architecture adopting a method by which only datagrams that contained complete routing information were transmitted.

Routing algorithms manage the actual routing of datagrams. Before designing an algorithm, factors such as optimality, simplicity, stability and robustness, and convergence must be taken into account. Algorithms are classified into static routing algorithms and dynamic routing algorithms based on the type of networks they support. Flooding and flow-based algorithms are types of static routing algorithms. Distance-vector and link state routing algorithms calculate routes on dynamic networks.

CH
17

CHAPTER **18**

ROUTING ON AUTONOMOUS SYSTEMS

In this chapter

AUTONOMOUS SYSTEM ROUTING ARCHITECTURE

A well-defined structure is one of the most important assets of any organization from a large company to a system of government. Empires such as the Roman Empire or the Mughal Empire had well-defined and efficient administrative structures in the peak of their existence. On the other hand, students of history would consider an unwieldy or grotesque administrative structure as an indication of the decline of an empire. The structure of the early Internet did exhibit such an unwieldy formation because of the routing architecture of the time. Fortunately, the architecture was changed and a new system of networks called autonomous systems was implemented to reorganize the rapidly growing Internet into well-defined autonomous groups. In addition to saving the Net, this move launched the "cyber civilization" that we live in today. You will learn about the evolution of autonomous systems and the routing mechanisms used within autonomous systems in the following sections.

Early Internet routing architectures were characterized by the need to link networks to a backbone, which was either the ARPAnet backbone or the NSFNET backbone. Routers were always designed in such a way that they linked a network to a backbone. This architecture worked well for the nascent Internet, which did not contain many networks and was not expanding at the rate in which it is today. The core routing architecture solved routing problems, such as routing loops, by implementing an exchange of routing information between all routers. In the course of time, the core routing architecture was beset with a number of new problems. One such problem was related to limiting the number of routers connected to a backbone. If a large number of routers were linked to a backbone, the volume of routing traffic required to exchange routing information would become unmanageable. Moreover, the sizes of the routing tables would become impractically large.

Another constraint imposed by the core routing architecture is that organizations cannot implement routing policies that differ from other routers. For example, an organization cannot implement a particular route based on its own cost estimates because routing on the core routing architecture involves all routers that are connected to the backbone. Moreover, an organization cannot have multiple routers servicing its network because only one router per network is allowed to access and route information to and from the backbone. These constraints resulted in routing anomalies, such as extra hops and hidden networks.

As the utility of the Net started becoming apparent, its popularity increased, resulting in the addition of new users to the Internet. Constraints on the number of routers in the core routing architecture prevented all routers from being added to the group of routers exchanging routing information. The routers that did not participate in the routing information exchange process were called *nonparticipating routers*. Datagrams that were sent to nonparticipating routers had to be routed to any of the participating routers because routing information was not directly available to nonparticipating routers. This step was required to ensure correct transmission of the datagram to the destination address specified on the datagram. However, this resulted in an extra hop each time a datagram is transmitted to a nonparticipating router. This anomaly is termed the *extra hop problem*.

Another problem caused by nonparticipating routers occurs when a datagram must be routed to a computer located on a network that is serviced by a nonparticipating router. Although nonparticipating routers link to a participating router for sending and receiving information, the backbone is not aware of any such router because routing information about nonparticipating routers is not provided to the backbone. An incoming datagram that is to be redirected to a computer linked to a nonparticipating router must pass through the participating router linked to the nonparticipating router. The participating router then redirects the datagram to the nonparticipating router on its way to the final destination. This problem is similar to the extra hop anomaly except that it occurs while the nonparticipating router receives datagrams. The basis of this problem is that the existence of the network serviced by the nonparticipating router is hidden from the backbone because the information about the nonparticipating router is unavailable. This routing anomaly is called the hidden network problem. Figure 18.1 shows how the restrictive core routing architecture causes the extra hop and hidden network anomalies.

Figure 18.1
Restriction on the number of routers results in nonparticipating routers using an additional routing stop to send and receive datagrams.

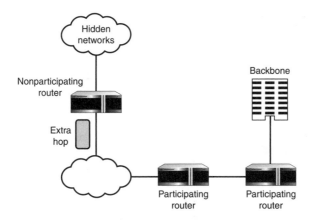

Such anomalies instilled the realization on the part of network designers that the restrictive core routing architecture might spell doom for the Internet and that the routing architecture needed a new design. Primarily, a routing architecture was required that could accommodate an arbitrary number of networks and customize network architectures and policies as per the requirements of all organizations connected to the Internet. Regardless of the local network architecture or policies followed by organizations, the routing architecture must provide a way by which information exchange can occur between all routers, an organization's routers, and external routers. Such a system was also required to organize the unwieldy structure that was becoming the Internet into well-defined administrative groups with each group linking to a backbone.

This system, named autonomous systems, was adopted as the new routing architecture. An autonomous system (AS) can be defined as a network group that has total administrative control over all routers present within the system. The problems related to nonparticipating routers diminished with the introduction of the AS architecture because each AS has complete information on all routers, including nonparticipating routers, within its group and advertises this information to other ASs. This way, all ASs have complete information about each other. Figure 18.2 shows how the Internet was restructured into AS.

Figure 18.2
All routers in an autonomous system must advertise information about any hidden network to the primary router in the autonomous system.

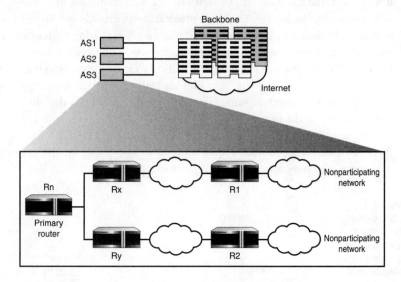

In the figure, information about the nonparticipating routers R1 and R2 are provided to the primary router Rn by the participating routers Rx and Ry. In turn, this information is supplied to other ASs. Information about all networks is available throughout the Internet, regardless of the routing architecture or policies implemented within an AS.

Note

To uniquely identify an autonomous system, each AS was given an *autonomous system number*.

To implement such an exchange of data, routing protocols were implemented. The inherent complexity and the autonomy provided to each AS resulted in a diverse implementation of network architectures and policies. On the other hand, the architecture outside the AS was simple and standard with each AS linking directly to a backbone. This difference in networking environments necessitated the implementation of two types of routing protocols within and in between the ASs. Protocols implemented within an AS came to be known as Interior Gateway Protocols (IGP), and those that were implemented for communication between different ASs were termed Exterior Gateway Protocols (EGP).

Some fundamental differences exist between IGP and EGP. For example, organizations can implement IGP routing protocols that support higher bandwidth because of the lower costs involved in implementing high bandwidth connections. IGP does not provide information about other ASs because that is the domain of EGP. Unless organizations explicitly want to control access, policies are not implemented within an AS. Another important feature supported by IGP is its ability to converge faster than EGP. This feature ensures the quick update of routing information when changes to routes occur.

EGP, which enables communication between ASs, is much more expensive to implement. It is usually implemented on low bandwidth links. Moreover, long distances between ASs make AS-to-AS links highly unreliable, which necessitates a connection-oriented link using EGP. Access policies are implemented using EGP to prevent unauthorized access into an AS. Another distinctive feature of EGP is its ability to manage large volumes of information. EGP has to route datagrams from the entire AS and exchange routing information with other ASs. In other words, a router installed with EGP must manage routing information about approximately 40,000 networks that populate the Internet.

→ For more information on EGP, **see** "EGP," **p. 312**

INTRODUCTION TO INTERIOR GATEWAY PROTOCOLS

Routing datagrams within an AS is a complex issue especially because different ASs need to route datagrams based on their individual capabilities and requirements. For example, certain ASs might need protocols that converge at a fast pace because online services, such as air reservation systems or news networks, are run on these ASs. On the other hand, certain ASs might not need fast converging routers. Moreover, networks contained within ASs might be designed with varying software and hardware configurations. The diversities inherent within an AS have necessitated multiple routing protocols that are commonly named IGP. Routing Information Protocol (RIP), Open Shortest Path First (OSPF), and Enhanced Interior Gateway Routing Protocol (EIGRP) are some of the popular IGPs. You will learn more about these protocols in the following sections.

CH
18

ROUTING INFORMATION PROTOCOL

One of the earliest IGP implementations was a protocol popularized by the Berkeley family of Unix operating systems called Routing Information Protocol (RIP). The base research on RIP was conducted at the Palo Alto Research Center (PARC) owned by the Xerox Corporation. PARC was successful in developing a routing protocol named Xerox NS RIP. Later, researchers at the Berkeley University further developed on XNS RIP and implemented their own version of RIP in BSD Unix OS as a routing daemon program called *routed*. Initially, the utility of RIP was not visible and was adopted simply because it was implemented as part of BSD Unix. In the course of time, as the popularity of BSD Unix increased, routed was accepted as a leading IGP routing protocol. However, RIP and its latest version, RIP2, suffered from certain limitations, which has led to the protocol being replaced by other effective IGPs, such as OSPF and EIGRP. Before detailing RIP's limitations, let us have a look at the RIP message format, which is the fundamental unit around which the entire RIP framework is built.

Note

Routed, the RIP implementation in BSD Unix OS, is actually pronounced *route-D* to signify that the utility is a route-Daemon program.

RIP MESSAGE FORMAT

RIP message formats can be classified into two types, request or response. *Request* messages are used to request routing information from other routers while *response* messages transmit the requested routing information. Both message types use the same format and are distinguished by the values specified in the Command field in the message header. Each message is divided into the header section and a list that contains information about destination networks in the form of network IP and distance pair values. Figure 18.3 shows the format of a RIP1 message.

Figure 18.3
The network information list in the message is optional and is not included when a request type of message is sent using RIP.

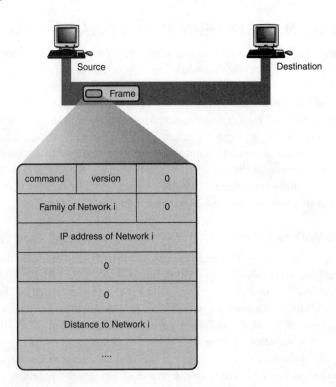

The fields displayed in the figure are detailed in Table 18.1.

TABLE 18.1   FIELDS IN AN RIP1 MESSAGE

Field	Description
Command	Contains information that describes the purpose of the message. Commands contain information in the form of a number signifying an action. For example, the number 1 signifies that the message is a request to another router for full or partial routing information. In response, routers can transmit routing information by specifying the number 2 as the Command field value. Numbers 3 and 4 are used to turn on and turn off the trace mode, respectively. This obsolete feature was earlier used to trace an RIP message. Command number 5 is a reserved number that is used only by Sun Microsystems in its applications. You can also specify commands 9, 10, or 11 to signify that the message is an update request, an update response, or an update acknowledgement. These commands are used only when dealing with demand circuits. Typically, only commands ranging from 1 to 5 are used for routing information exchange.
Version	Provides RIP with the advantage of implementing both its versions (1 and 2) on the same router. Each message is distinguished by its version number and is appropriately directed to the correct version of RIP.
Family of Network i	Indicates the family of network addresses to which the destination address belongs. This specification was used to distinguish between the various address families used on BSD Unix OS. The value 2 is specified in this field when indicating the IP addressing scheme as the network family used for RIP.
IP address of Network i	Specifies the destination network address. A maximum of 14 octets can be specified as the destination network address. However, only four octets are used in the IP addressing scheme. The remaining fields are left blank with zero value.
Distance to Network i	Specifies the distance, in terms of number of hops, from the source router to the destination router. A maximum of 15 hops can be specified for routing a message. The hop count is specified as 16 if there are no routes to the destination router.

CH
18

The 15 hop count and the need to propagate periodic updates of entire routing tables resulted in routing inadequacies in RIP1. The development of subnetting in the IP addressing scheme posed another problem for RIP1 in transmitting datagrams to networks created as subnets of another network. This is because the RIP1 message format did not contain a field to specify the subnet mask of the destination computer. If routing information containing subnet IP addresses must be updated on another router located across subnets, the subnet prefix contained in the routing information and the subnet prefix of the network used for transmitting the message must be the same. This is because in the absence of a subnet mask field in the message, routers operating in a route that spans across subnets must be able to determine if the datagram belongs to its subnet. Without the subnet mask field, this is virtually impossible. Therefore, in RIP2, a Subnet Mask field was included in the message format. Figure 18.4 shows the RIP2 message format.

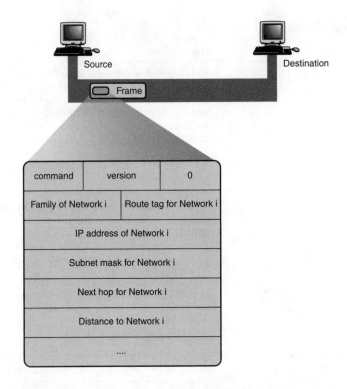

Figure 18.4
The Subnet Mask field that was added as an improvement over RIP1 is used to identify the destination subnet.

The RIP2 message format is similar to the message format of the first version but contains certain improvements. In addition to the Subnet Mask field, two new fields have been added to the message structure. They are the Next Hop field and the Route Tag field. The Next Hop field specifies the IP address of the next router in the route to the destination router. The Route Tag field acts as an information holder that can hold 16-bits of information, such as the IP address of the source router or the AS number, when the datagram is being sent from another AS.

RIP IMPLEMENTATION

RIP is an implementation of the distance vector algorithm and works on the principles proposed by the algorithm, such as the distance-vector pair. To implement RIP, computers involved in the routing transaction are classified into two types, active and passive. Active hosts are the source routers that advertise routing information containing distance and vector information every 30 seconds. The update timer is used to track the time elapsed between each advertisement. Active routers also exchange routing information with other active routers in the AS.

Passive computers are also routers that lie on the route to the destination router. The passive routers use the routing advertisements to update their routing table. They use the information while routing a datagram to its destination. The updates contain information as a list of pairs with each pair containing information on the IP address of a router (lying in the route) and the hop count used to reach that router. By transmitting this information to all the routers, the route that must be taken by the datagram is identified in advance by all the routers.

If the routing information already exists on the routers, routing tables on the routers are not updated unless the source router advertises shorter routes. One exception to this rule is the fact that if a particular route link fails and the source router sets the metric for that route to 16, the entry would be updated in the table of the neighboring passive router to invalidate that route. The routing tables are updated on the passive routers only when the routing information that is advertised by the source router provides a shorter route with less hop count.

→ For more information on distance vector algorithm, **see** "Routing Mechanisms," **p. 277**

PROBLEMS IN AN RIP IMPLEMENTATION

Although RIP's routing implementation seems to be quite straightforward, the vagaries of the Internet are not taken into account. A number of factors can affect distance vector algorithm implementation. Some of these factors can be the crash of a router lying on the route to the destination, lag in the time taken to update routing information, or occurrence of any routing loops. These disabilities are inherited by RIP as well.

Apart from the network diameter limitation of 15 hops allowed for RIP, one of the most debilitating problems that occur in an RIP implementation is the problem of slow convergence. This problem occurs when information about the loss of a link or any other changes to the route is not propagated quickly to other routers on the route. For example, take a scenario where router Ri is connected to another router Rj, which in turn is connected to the router Rn. If the connection between Rj and Rn is lost, Rj updates the hop count in its routing table with an infinity value (hop count 16) signifying that the connection to Rn is not possible. If this information is not communicated quickly to Ri, after the 30 seconds time limit, Ri advertises the old routing information containing the distance in hop counts to reach the vector Rn as being wrong information. When Rj receives this information, it computes that the distance vector value proposed by router Ri (which is wrong) is lower than its current value of 16 hops. It updates its routing table by changing the route to Rn with router Ri as the next hop because it offers a lower hop count to reach the destination.

This step causes a routing loop to develop where a datagram bounces back and forth between the routers until its time-to-live value runs out. The problem continues to exist in the next round of routing information updates between Ri and Rj where the hop count on both routers are increased by 1 with the next hop destination being specified as each other. Both routers continue to live in the routing loop and increment their next hop information towards infinity. The term *count to infinity* is used to describe this problem.

A number of solutions have been prescribed for this problem including techniques such as split horizon, hold down, triggered updates, and poison reverse. Although these techniques do not adequately solve the problem, they reduce the ill effects of the anomaly to some extent. The entire problem hinges on the fact that a router sends updates on routing

CH
18

information to the same router from where it received the information. The split horizon technique stops this from happening. To continue with our example of routers Ri and Rj, Ri is not allowed to send routing information updates to Rj because it received the information from Rj in the first place. This prevents the routing loop from occurring despite the time taken for Rj to communicate the loss of the link to Ri. Now, after Rj propagates the next round of routing information updates, all routers are informed that the link to Rn does not exist. Figure 18.5 describes how the count-to-infinity problem is resolved by the split horizon technique.

Figure 18.5
The split horizon technique restricts inaccurate hop count advertisements to resolve the count-to-infinity problem.

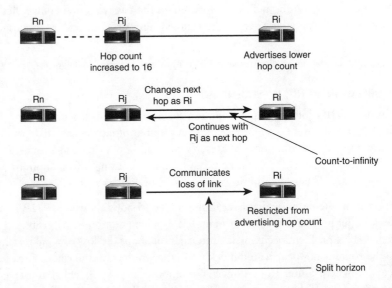

From the split horizon technique, it is quite clear that news about loss of links or any such bad news reaches all routers at a slow pace. This is because when a router identifies a shorter route to the destination, it is able to advertise the "good" news to all routers immediately. The good news takes effect when all routers receive the information and update their routing tables with the shorter route information. On the other hand, vital information, such as loss of a link caused by router failures or crashes, is not propagated fast. Instead, a router waits for a timeout period to expire before it finds another route and propagates this new routing information as a replacement for the old route. The poison reverse and the triggered update techniques are used in combination to resolve this anomaly, which is another cause for the slow convergence problem.

In the poison reverse technique, the source router that first advertises routing information sets the distance value to infinity (16 hops) when it sends the next round of routing information updates to all the participating routers. This ensures that all routers discard the route through the failed router. To ensure that this technique is fully successful, the source router must propagate routing information containing the "bad" news immediately without waiting for the timeout period to elapse. To ensure a quick propagation of routing information, the triggered update technique is implemented where changes to routes are monitored and any loss of link in the route is identified and propagated immediately without waiting for the timeout period to elapse.

The hold down technique is a reverse of the triggered update technique. In this technique, when a participating router receives information on the loss of a link from the source router, it usually waits for 60 seconds to ensure that all routers receive the "bad" news. Any wrong information on the existence of the lost link is ignored during the hold down period. In addition, the hold down period ensures that wrong information is not propagated to other routers. After all routers have received the "bad" news, alternate routes are converged by all routers.

Note

One disadvantage of the hold down technique is that if all participating routers do not implement the same hold down period, routing loops can occur. Another disadvantage is that although alternate routes are available, these routes are not implemented until the hold down period elapses.

Open Shortest Path First

The problems faced by distance vector routing algorithm implementations necessitated the development of a better algorithm that could converge faster in an increasingly dynamic network environment. This need translated into the creation of the link state algorithm with the shortest path first technique used to converge and compute distances at fast speeds to match the dynamic conditions existing on the network. The Internet Engineering Task Force (IETF) decided to develop an implementation of this algorithm to provide an alternative for distance vector implementations. The result of an IETF workshop was the formulation of a new IGP called Open Shortest Path First (OSPF), which is based on the link state algorithm. As the name suggests, IETF distributed the IGP as an open source for the benefit of all. This and some other advantages that resolve problems inherent in RIP have made OSPF one of the premier IGPs in use today.

OSPF Message Formats

Before going into the advantages of OSPF, let us look at the message formats used in OSPF. The protocol uses four different message types to implement routing and to propagate routing information. These message types include hello message, database description message, link status request message, and link status update message. When you learn about these message types, you will also come to know how routing is implemented using OSPF.

All message types contain a header (see Figure 18.6), which holds information on the `version`, `type`, `message length`, `source router IP address`, `area ID`, `checksum` value, `authentication type`, and `authentication` value. Table 18.2 describes each of these header fields.

TABLE 18.2 THE FIELDS OF AN OSPF HEADER

Header Field	Description
Version	Specifies the version of the OSPF protocol.
Type	Specifies the message type and the action it is meant to perform. A value of 1 in the `type` field indicates that the message is a hello message. The value 2 in the field indicates that the message is a database description message. The value 3 indicates that the message is used as a link status request message. Specifying the value 4 indicates that the message is a link status update message. Link status acknowledgement messages are indicated by specifying the value 5 in the field.
Message Length	Specifies the length of the message.
Source Router IP address	Specifies the IP address of the router that sends the message.
Area ID	Specifies a 32-bit number that is used to identify the area.
Checksum	Specifies a `checksum` value that is used for authenticating the validity of the message on receipt of the message. The sending router runs a mathematical algorithm against the message and stores the result in the `checksum` field. The receiving router runs an identical algorithm on the message received and matches the result with that stored in the `checksum` field. A mismatch indicates that the OSPF packet was damaged in transit.
Authentication type	Specifies an authentication type to authenticate the message in addition to the `checksum` value. If the value 0 is specified, authentication is not implemented. If the value 1 is specified, a password is provided in the `authentication` field.
Authentication	Specifies a password as an authentication measure. The maximum length of the password field is 7 octets, which can be split across two fields with a size of 3 and 4 octets, respectively.

The first step in the routing process implemented by OSPF is to verify the availability of all the participating routers. To do so, OSPF sends a hello message (see Figure 18.6) to all routers. This message contains fields, such as `network mask`, `dead timer`, `hello interval`, `GWAY PRIO`, `designated router`, `backup designated router`, and a list of neighbor IP addresses. Table 18.3 describes each of these fields in detail.

TABLE 18.3 THE FIELDS OF AN OSPF HELLO MESSAGE

Field	Description
Network mask	Specifies the subnet mask of the network used to transmit the datagram.
Dead timer	Specifies the timeout value for receiving a confirmation of existence from a neighboring router. If the router does not respond within the specified time limit, it is considered nonexistent.

TABLE 18.3   CONTINUED

Field	Description
Hello interval	Specifies a time in seconds that can elapse between two hello messages.
Designated router	Specifies the IP address of the router that is acting as the primary router of the network over which the hello message must traverse.
Backup Designated router	Specifies the IP address of the router that is acting as the backup router of the network over which the hello message must traverse.
GWAY PRIO	Specifies a priority number that is used in determining a router as the designated router or a backup designated router.
Neighbor i IP address	Specifies a list of IP addresses indicating the addresses of all routers that sent hello messages to the sending router.

OSPF DATABASE DESCRIPTION MESSAGE

After receiving responses from routers for the hello messages sent, the sending router is able to determine the availability of all neighboring routers on a network. This information is used to update a database maintained by a master router called the *topology database*. The master router determines the composition of all routes existing on the network. A topology database is a road map that contains information on the distance that needs to be traversed from each router to reach a particular destination. The graph containing links and nodes implemented by the shortest path first algorithm is represented as the topology database on the master router. The information contained in the topology database must be propagated to all participating routers to ensure that correct routing information is maintained on all routers. For this purpose, the master router propagates a message called the database description message to all participating routers (slaves). Database description packets are used to describe the contents of an OSPF router's link-state database. All routers on the network will function, at different times, as both master and slave during the database description exchange process. Figure 18.6 describes the database description message format in addition to the message header and the hello message formats.

The database description message contains fields such as the OSPF header, database sequence number, and a list containing individual fields for each network. Information related to networks is specified in fields, such as link type, link ID, advertising router, link sequence number, link checksum, and the link age. In addition, the list contains I, M, and S bits. Table 18.4 describes each of these fields in detail.

CH

18

Figure 18.6
The database description message is used to propagate routing information computed on the master router based on the Dijkstra's SPF algorithm. The hello message acts as an information gathering tool to contribute to the creation of the database description message.

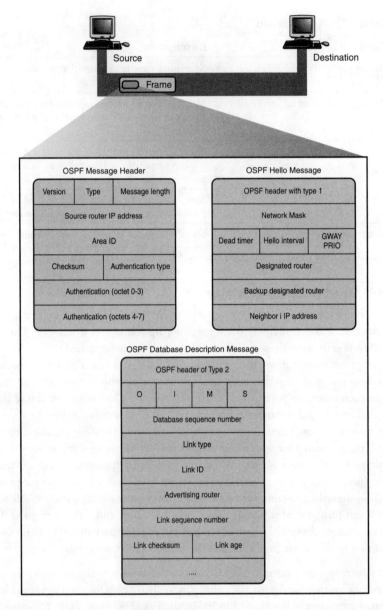

TABLE 18.4   THE FIELDS OF AN OSPF DATABASE DESCRIPTION MESSAGE

Field	Description
Database sequence number	Specifies a sequence number to uniquely identify each message if multiple description messages are sent to the participating routers.

TABLE 18.4   CONTINUED

Field	Description
IMS bits	Specifies information on the multiple description messages sent by a router. The I bit specifies the sequence number of each message. For example, the I bit for the first message is set to 1. The M bit is used to indicate if additional messages are to follow. This is done by setting the M bit to 1. The S bit is used to indicate if the sending router is a master router or a slave router. The value 1 set for the S bit indicates that the sending router is a master router. The value 0 indicates that the sending router is a slave router.
Link type	Specifies the type of the link by using a number code. For example, if the number 1 is specified in the link type field, it indicates that the link is a router link. The value 2 indicates that the link is a network link. Values 3 and 4 indicate that the link is a summary link to an IP network or a border router, respectively. External links that connect a router to an external site are indicated using the value 5.
Link ID	Specifies an IP address or a network mask that provides a unique identity for a link.
Advertising router	Specifies the IP address of the router that has advertised this particular link.
Link sequence number	Specifies a sequence number that uniquely identifies the message. This field is used to discard duplicate messages or to identify messages received at random to reorder them later.
Link checksum	Specifies a binary value that is used as an authentication value. The checksum value sent from the sending router must remain the same on the receiving router to signify that the message has not been tampered.
Link age	Specifies the time when the link to a router was achieved. The time is specified in seconds.

CH

18

OSPF LINK STATE ADVERTISEMENT MESSAGE

After receiving a database description message, each router compares the information contained in the message with the information in its topology database. If it identifies that information on certain links are missing, it sends a link status request message requesting for the missing link information from a neighboring router. The message contains fields (see Figure 18.7) such as the link type, link ID, and the IP address of the advertising router. In response, the neighbor sends a link status update message that contains fields such as the number of link status advertisements and a list of link status advertisements. Each link status advertisement contains fields such as link age, link type, link ID, advertising router, link sequence number, link checksum, and the length of the message. Figure 18.7 shows the format of the link status request and update message formats along with the contents of an advertisement contained in a message.

Figure 18.7
Routers use link status messages to update link status information in their topology databases.

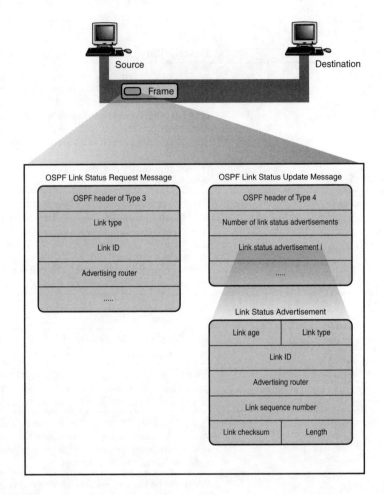

Using the updated information on the topology databases, routers determine the shortest path to any destination router for routing datagrams.

ENHANCED INTERIOR GATEWAY ROUTING PROTOCOL

The latest and most powerful IGP that has become one of the most prevalent IGPs in use now is the Enhanced Interior Gateway Routing Protocol (EIGRP). The protocol derives its popularity from its ability to incorporate the features of a link state algorithm implementation into a distance vector algorithm implementation. In addition, EIGRP also contains features that enable it to avoid routing loops and to determine alternate routes at a much faster rate than any other link status algorithm implementation.

Note

Although EIGRP provides powerful routing features, it has never been adopted as a standard routing protocol by the Internet Engineering Task Force (IETF). It has remained with Cisco Inc as a proprietary routing protocol that is not implemented on popular operating systems, such as Windows or Unix. You might not be able to find many implementations of EIGRP.

Before delving into the implementation of EIGRP, let us have a look at the most basic unit of EIGRP, which is the EIGRP packet type. EIGRP uses packet types, such as hello, update, query, and reply, to communicate routing information. A hello packet is used to verify the existence of a neighboring router. Each hello packet can be acknowledged using an acknowledgement packet. Update packets are similar to the link status update packets that convey link status information. Specifically, update packets propagate any change in the availability of neighboring routers to all participating routers to enable these routers to update their topology databases. As with the hello packet, the receipt of update packets can be confirmed with an acknowledgement packet. Query packets are used to check for the availability of a neighboring router that can forward datagrams along the shortest, loop-free route. Such routers are called *feasible successors*. In response, a reply packet is sent to the querying router instructing the querying router not to change its topology database because feasible successors for a particular route already exist.

EIGRP IMPLEMENTATION

An EIGRP implementation carries all features that are characteristic of both distance vector and link state algorithms. As in a link state algorithm implementation, the first step in an EIGRP implementation is to verify the existence of neighboring routers. To achieve this, EIGRP sends hello messages to neighboring routers at periodic intervals. By verifying the acknowledgements for the hello messages received from the neighboring routers, EIGRP determines all available routers on a network. Once the availability information is procured, EIGRP sends update packets to inform participating routers about the latest routing information existing on the network.

The safe and secure delivery of update packets are ensured by a component feature of EIGRP called Reliable Transport Protocol (RTP). This feature implements acknowledgement of EIGRP packets sent over the network. Once update packets are safely transmitted and their receipt acknowledged, another component called Diffusing Update Algorithm (DUAL) processes the latest routing information to arrive at a feasible successor for each route. This process is repeated each time a change in the participating router availability is noticed. If the existence of a feasible successor for a particular route does not change, DUAL does not compute new feasible successors because of the need to avoid the increase in convergence time caused by such an unnecessary computation.

CH
18

EIGRP COMPONENTS

An EIGRP implementation runs on three important components: neighbor tables, topology tables, and route tags. A neighbor table, as the name suggests, maintains information such as neighbor IP addresses and interfaces. The neighbor table also holds a host of information relating to the transmission of packets to a neighbor. For example, sequence numbers specified in a packet sent to a neighbor is recorded in the table to verify the sequence number with the acknowledgement received from a neighbor. This enables the authentication of a packet sent to a neighbor. In addition, information on round trip times taken for retransmission of a datagram and information on the packets queued to be transmitted is maintained in the neighbor table.

Topology tables are used to maintain information on the destination IP addresses propagated by neighbors. This information provided by the topology table is used by DUAL to determine the feasible successor for a particular route. Entries maintained in the topology table are made by the IP software running on the router. The IP software extracts hello messages or advertisements received from neighbors and enters relevant information into the topology table.

Route tags are used to provide additional information in any packet. The tags are primarily used to specify information in a packet being transmitted beyond the AS. Such packets are affixed with route tags that contain information on the router ID of the source EIGRP router, the AS number where the destination router is located, and the identity of the protocol used in the EGP. In addition, information on the bit flags indicating the default route taken by the EGP, the cost of transmission for the EGP, and certain information that can be included by the administrator of the router are also included in the route tags.

SUMMARY

Several anomalies existed on the early Internet because of prohibitive restrictions posed by the core routing architecture. These anomalies, namely extra hop and hidden network anomalies, necessitated a design change in the prevailing routing architecture and resulted in the creation of ASs. Each AS provided the freedom to design and manage networks internally while maintaining a standard routing mechanism for communication between ASs. Such diverse routing requirements resulted in the creation of separate routing protocols for communication within and outside the AS. Interior Gateway Protocols were used to route datagrams within an AS while Exterior Gateway Protocols were used for inter-AS communication.

Three types of IGP implementations were used for intra autonomous routing: Routing Information Protocol, Open Shortest Path First, and Enhanced Interior Gateway Routing Protocol. RIP, which is based on the distance vector algorithm, inherits all problems faced by the distance vector algorithm, such as count to infinity problem or the slow convergence problem. A number of heuristics, such as split horizon, poison reverse, triggered updates, and hold down, have been implemented to reduce the problems caused by slow convergence. As an improvement, a link state algorithm implementation called OSPF was developed by IETF. However, EIGRP, which combines the prowess of link state and distance vector algorithms in addition to new features such as DUAL and RTP, can be described as the most powerful and effective IGP in the market at present.

CH
18

CHAPTER 19

INTER-AUTONOMOUS SYSTEM ROUTING PROTOCOL—EGP AND BGP

In this chapter

EGP

So far, you have seen different ways in which routers communicate routing information across the other routers in a group. However, in the case of the Internet, a number of groups are connected through different routers. If all the routers start exchanging routing information, the magnitude of routing traffic itself would almost clog the entire bandwidth. Therefore, internetworks were reorganized into autonomous systems and routing protocols that enable routing within an autonomous system and between different autonomous systems. An Exterior Gateway Protocol (EGP) distributes routing information to routers that connect autonomous systems. An obsolete exterior routing protocol of the same name was proposed by RFC 904. This protocol was improved upon by Border Gateway Protocol (BGP). You will learn about EGP and BGP in the following sections.

The dynamic and static routing protocols are best-suited for a system that is connected over a single backbone. However, the current Internet has multiple backbones and is administered separately by different companies. In the systems studied so far, all the routers are connected directly to the backbone and could communicate the necessary routing information to the other routers. However, the system is not infinitely scalable to accommodate any number of routers.

There are two rules in communicating routing information that require a special arrangement. First, only the routers connected directly can communicate routing information directly. Second, not all networks and routers are managed by a single entity, which implies that there could be different policies followed.

AUTONOMOUS SYSTEMS—AN OVERVIEW

The Internet now comprises a number of autonomous systems that are connected. An *autonomous system* (AS) is comprised of a set of routers under a single technical administration using an interior gateway protocol (IGP), common metrics to route packets within the AS, and an exterior gateway protocol (EGP) to route packets to other ASs. A typical autonomous system connected to the Internet is shown in Figure 19.1.

Figure 19.1
A typical routing configuration where a number of autonomous systems are connected to the Internet.

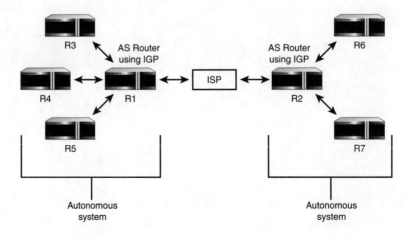

In the system depicted, two autonomous systems are connected to the ISP's network. The routers R1 and R2 are known as the participating routers. These routers forward all the traffic to the Internet. The advantage with this setup is that the other routers do not have to advertise directly to the ISP about their networks. The R1 router advertises all networks that can be addressed through it. The routers in each autonomous system can use any protocol to communicate routing information and need not be the same as the protocol used to communicate with the ISP.

Note

> The term Exterior Gateway Protocol (EGP) is used to refer to an obsolete protocol that was used for exterior routing. In addition, the same term is used for referring to protocols that are used for exterior routing. Border Gateway Protocol (BGP) is the most commonly used exterior gateway protocol. BGP is especially useful in detecting routing loops. BGP uses a path vector concept, which prevents loops in complex topologies.

BASICS OF EXTERIOR GATEWAY PROTOCOL

Exterior Gateway Protocol (EGP) is a gateway-to-gateway communication protocol that is used to exchange routing information between gateways both within an autonomous system and across autonomous systems. This protocol was released through RFC 904 in April 1984. This protocol is associated with the routers that connect different autonomous systems to the Internet. These routers are called *stub gateways*. The purpose of these routers is to act as an interface between the local networks in the autonomous system and the Internet. The stub routers respond to traffic that either originates from or is destined to the particular autonomous system.

EGP uses polling to monitor the reachability of neighboring gateways. A neighbor gateway refers to one that is either hard connected to the router or is connected through the Internet that is transparent to the routers. The network could be considered transparent to the routers if the routers use no knowledge of the internal structure of the network.

CH
19

The neighbors can be classified as *Interior Neighbors*, which refer to neighbor routers that are contained within a single autonomous system and *Exterior Neighbors*, which refer to neighbor routers that are not a part of the same autonomous system. EGP is used to advertise the networks that can be reached through a particular neighbor. However, the communication of routing information within an autonomous system has to be implemented through the system's own algorithm.

EGP is comprised of three primary components: Neighbor Acquisition Protocol, Neighbor Reachability Protocol, and Neighbor Reachability Determination. As EGP is based on polling, it is able to control the amount of network traffic being generated. In addition, EGP messages cannot be routed through another router because EGP is based on a single hop. If a router receives an EGP message that is not intended for it, it can drop the packet.

Neighbor Acquisition Protocol is used to get information about the existence of neighbor routers. This protocol uses a simple three-way handshake to acquire information about a neighbor router. The router issues a Neighbor Acquisition request. This request is broadcast repeatedly until it receives a Neighbor Acquisition reply from another router. Each Neighbor Acquisition request will contain an identification number of the request. This number is sent back to the router in the Neighbor Acquisition reply. The responding router also sends a Neighbor Acquisition request back to the first router. If a router that receives the request does not want to become a direct neighbor, it can either drop the packet or send a Neighbor Acquisition Refusal message back to the originating router.

The different EGP messages that can be sent or received by a router are mentioned in Table 19.1.

TABLE 19.1   THE DIFFERENT EGP MESSAGE TYPES THAT ARE EXCHANGED BETWEEN TWO NEIGHBORING ROUTERS

Name	Explanation
Request	Sent for either acquiring neighbors or for initializing polling variables.
Confirm	Sent for either confirming neighbors or for initializing polling variables.
Refuse	Sent to refuse permission to acquire the router as a neighbor.
Cease	Sent to sever the neighbor relationship with another router. This is also known as the process of de-acquisition.
Cease-ack	Sent to confirm the severance of the acquisition.
Hello	Sent to find out neighbor reachability.
I-H-U	Sent to confirm neighbor reachability.
Poll	Sent to request an update of reachability information from the other router.
Update	Sent to update the reachability information of a particular router. This message need not be only in terms of a response to the Poll message.
Error	Sent to report any errors in the message or the transmission.

EGP HEADER

The EGP header is a 10-octet header that contains six fields. The additional fields for each message depend on the message type. The EGP Version number contains the version number of EGP used. The Type and Code fields are used to categorize the message. The Type field contains the message type, and the Code field contains the subtype or specific code for the message. For example, the Neighbor Acquisition message contains the value 3 in the Type field and a zero if the message is a request.

The basic EGP header structure is given in Figure 19.2.

Figure 19.2
The basic EGP header structure.

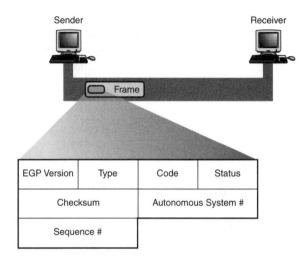

The Status field contains any message-dependant status information, such as the active mode or passive mode. The Checksum field contains a 16-bit one's complement of the EGP message. The Checksum field contains zero while computing the checksum. The Autonomous System # field contains the number of the autonomous system to which the router belongs. This will help the other routers to identify whether the router is an internal neighbor or an external neighbor. The Sequence # field contains the state variables or commands and responses.

Look at the Neighbor Acquisition message format. This message contains the Hello and Poll interval fields in addition to the normal EGP header. A Neighbor Acquisition Request message will contain 14 octets as shown in Figure 19.3.

Figure 19.3
The structure of an EGP Neighbor Acquisition Request message.

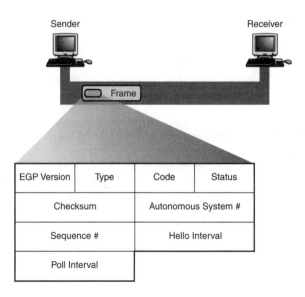

The value in the Type field is 3. The Code field could have a value in the range 0 to 4 depending on the type of command being sent. The Hello interval contains the minimum number of seconds for repeating the Hello command. Similarly, the Poll interval contains the minimum number of seconds for repeating the Poll command.

Table 19.2 describes the different values that can be contained in the Code field.

TABLE 19.2   THE DIFFERENT VALUES THAT CAN BE CONTAINED IN THE CodE FIELD OF AN EGP NEIGHBOR ACQUISITION MESSAGE

Code	Explanation
0	Used to send a Request command. The Request command is used to acquire a response from neighboring routers.
1	Used to send a Confirm message. This message is used to acknowledge the Request message and identify the router as a neighbor.
2	Used to send a Refuse message. This is an optional message and is used by the router to deny permission to be added as a neighbor router.
3	Used to send a Cease command. This is used to sever the neighbor relationship with the recipient router.
4	Used to send a Cease_Ack response. This is used to acknowledge the request to cease the neighbor relationship with the router.

EGP UPDATE STATEMENT

After a neighbor is acquired, it is important to ensure that the router maintains only those neighbors that are active. The Poll command is used to invoke a response from the neighbors. The neighbors send an Update command with a list of routers that are active and can be reached through the neighbor router. The packet structure of the Update command is shown in Figure 19.4.

The EGP Update message contains 18–20 octets including the header section and an additional 4–8 octets for every distance metric sent. The Type field contains the value 1, and the Code field contains 0. Table 19.3 gives you a description of the other fields contained in the EGP Update message.

TABLE 19.3   A DESCRIPTION OF THE DIFFERENT FIELDS IN THE EGP UPDATE MESSAGE

Field	Contains
# of Int Gateways	A number of internal gateways that are represented in this message.
# of Ext Gateways	A number of external gateways that are represented in this message.
IP Source Network	The IP Network address of the destination network for which the reachability information is being transmitted.
Gateway IP Address	The IP address of the gateway block. This IP address is presented without the network address part and is specified in one, two, or three octet format.

Field	Contains
# of Distances	The number of distances for the specific gateway block.
Distances	The number of autonomous systems.
# of Nets	The number of networks that are a part of the autonomous system and can be reached through the gateway.
Nets	The network numbers of each network that can be reached through the gateway.

TABLE 19.3 CONTINUED

The fields given in Table 19.3 are replicated for each gateway that is being acquired in the update message.

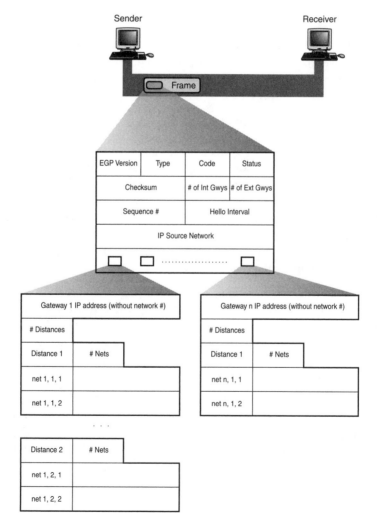

Figure 19.4
The structure of an EGP Update message.

BGP

Border Gateway Protocol (BGP) was developed as a replacement for the EGP described previously. BGP is used to exchange routing information for the Internet and is the protocol used between Internet service providers (ISP). In contrast to the obsolete EGP, which was used for interior as well as exterior routing, BGP is used only for exterior routing and has additional features compared to EGP. BGP has now become a commonly used exterior routing protocol. The latest version of BGP is BGP Version 4. BGP exchanges network reachability information amongst autonomous systems. The information exchanged also includes a list of autonomous systems that receive the information. This enables the routers to build a graph of the structure of the connectivity of the different autonomous systems. The other advantage of using BGP is that certain policy restrictions and decisions can be made to facilitate inter-autonomous routing.

The significant additions to BGP are the support for Classless Inter-Domain Routing (CIDR) through the elimination of the network class in the protocol. A direct result of the support for CIDR and supernetting is a reduction in size of the Internet routing tables. The latest BGP version (BGP-4) allows aggregation of routes, which enable supernetting of routing information. BGP works by advertising only those routes that the originating BGP speaker itself uses. This is similar to the *hop-to-hop* algorithm currently used in the Internet.

THE OPERATION OF BGP

BGP performs three types of routing: inter-autonomous system routing, intra-autonomous system routing, and pass-through autonomous system routing. Inter-autonomous system routing occurs between two or more BGP routers in different autonomous systems. Peer routers in these systems use BGP to maintain a consistent view of the internetwork topology. BGP neighbors communicating between autonomous systems must reside on the same physical network. The internetwork could consist of many domains that represent various institutions and entities. In this mode, BGP is also used to help path determination to provide optimal routing within the Internet.

Intra-autonomous system routing occurs between two or more BGP routers located within the same autonomous system. This is used to determine the router that will serve as the connection point for specific external autonomous systems. The routers within the same autonomous system use BGP to maintain a consistent view of the system topology. An organization can use BGP to provide optimal routing within its own administrative domain or autonomous system.

The third type of routing provided by BGP is pass-through autonomous system routing. Here, routing occurs between two or more BGP peer routers that exchange traffic across an autonomous system that does not run BGP. In a pass-through autonomous system environment, the BGP traffic should neither originate from within the non-BGP autonomous system nor be destined for a node in that autonomous system.

Like EGP, BGP also maintains routing tables, performs routing updates, and continues to base routing decisions on routing metrics. The primary function of a BGP system is to exchange network-reachability information, including information about the list of autonomous system paths, with other BGP systems. This information can also be used to decide on certain policies. Each BGP router maintains a routing table that lists all feasible paths to a particular network. The routing information received from peer routers is retained until an incremental update is received. The router does not refresh the routing table.

When a router first connects to the network, BGP routers exchange their entire BGP routing tables. Similarly, when the routing table changes, routers send only the portion of their routing table that has changed. BGP updates advertise only the optimal path to a network. BGP uses a single routing metric to determine the best path to a given network. This metric consists of an arbitrary unit number that specifies the degree of preference of a particular link assigned by the network administrator.

BGP MESSAGES

There are four types of BGP messages, as described in Table 19.4.

TABLE 19.4   A DESCRIPTION OF THE DIFFERENT MESSAGES IN BGP

Message	Explanation
Open	Opens a BGP communication session between peer routers. It is the first message sent by each side after a TCP connection is established. Open messages are confirmed using a keepalive message. This must be confirmed before updates, notifications, and keepalives can be exchanged.
Update	Is used to provide routing updates to other BGP systems. This message allows routers to construct a consistent view of the network topology. Update messages are used for notifying changes in the routing table in addition to its ability to withdraw certain routers.
Notification	It is sent when an error condition is detected. These messages close an active session and inform the connected routers of why the session is being closed.
Keepalive	It notifies BGP peers that a device is active. These messages are sent in short intervals to prevent the sessions from expiring.

Cн

19

The packet structure of a BGP messages is given in Figure 19.5.

Each message has a fixed-size header. A message might have a data portion following the header depending on the message type. The header contains three sections: Marker, Length, and Type. The Marker is a 16-octet field that contains a value that the receiver of the message can predict by a computation specified as part of the authentication mechanism. The Marker can be used to detect loss of synchronization between a pair of BGP peers and to authenticate incoming BGP messages.

Figure 19.5
The structure of a
BGP message.

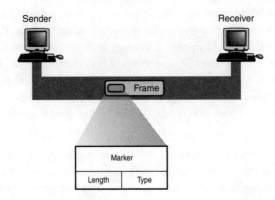

Length is a 2-octet unsigned integer that indicates the total length of the message, including the header, in octets. The value of the Length field, which must always be between 19 and 4096, can be further constrained depending on the message type.

Type is a 1-octet unsigned integer that indicates the type code of the message.

It must be noted that hosts executing BGP need not be routers. It is possible for a nonrouting host to exchange routing information with routers via EGP or even an interior routing protocol. The host can use BGP to exchange routing information with a border router in another autonomous system.

SUMMARY

To cater to the growing number of autonomous systems that are being added to the Internet, the Exterior Gateway Protocol (EGP) and the Border Gateway Protocol (BGP) were developed. Exterior Gateway Protocols are primarily used on routers that link local networks in an autonomous system to the Internet. BGP is another exterior routing protocol implemented on autonomous systems. It is primarily used to provide routing information between multiple autonomous systems and to monitor the list of autonomous systems that receive the information.

CHAPTER 20

MULTICASTING

In this chapter

FUNDAMENTALS OF MULTICASTING

You have so far learned about how a data packet is sent from a source to the destination. You also learned that data can be transmitted even if the source and the destination computer belong to two different networks. The process of transmitting data from one computer to another is referred to as *unicasting*. There are situations in which a message needs to be transferred from one computer to many computers on a network. Transferring messages from one computer to all the computers on a network is called *broadcasting*. However, if messages are sent from one computer to a specific set of computers, it is referred to as *multicasting*. Let us consider the example of sending e-mail. E-mail can be sent to one recipient or multiple recipients. Sending e-mail to one recipient can be equated with unicasting a data packet. On the other hand, sending e-mail to multiple recipients can be done in two ways. You can send messages to all e-mail addresses in your address book or to a specific group of addresses. Sending a message to all e-mail addresses can be compared to broadcasting a message. Sending an e-mail to a specific group of addresses can be compared to multicasting a message. The most common applications of multicasting include video conferencing and seminars for distance education. In video conferencing, more than one person can view the presentation at a time. From the business perspective, the cost incurred in travel can be saved by enabling the employees to view the presentation from their workplace. Video conferencing also enables an interactive mode to enable people to exchange their views. The same concept is applicable to seminars for distance education. A few other applications of multicasting include display of stock rates, streaming, and software distribution over a network. Many companies use multicasting for software upgrades and replication of data among branch offices.

> **Note**
>
> Multicasting not only transmits data in a one-to-many mode but can also provide many-to-many transmission of data. In other words, multicast messages can be sent from multiple computers simultaneously to other computers.

Having learned the fundamentals of multicasting, you need to understand how multicasting is implemented in the TCP/IP reference model. The role of the different layers in the TCP/IP reference model must be clearly understood. First, let us analyze the role of the Application layer in multicasting. The Application layer has to specify the destinations to which the message needs to be sent. However, the task of ensuring that the data reaches the correct destination is not the responsibility of the Application layer. This role, which involves the process of routing data, is the responsibility of Internet Protocol (IP) in the Internet layer. IP was designed to handle unicast datagrams initially. However, the functionality of IP had to be extended to support multicasting.

➔ For more information on the TCP/IP reference model, **see** "Introduction to Internetworking and TCP/IP," **p. 7**

ADVANTAGES OF MULTICASTING

As stated earlier, IP multicasting enables you to send a message to more that one recipient simultaneously. Unlike broadcasting in which all computers receive messages irrespective of whether they require them, in multicasting, computers can choose to receive a message. Multicasting does not affect all computers on the network. Therefore, multicasting prevents unwanted message transmission and avoids clogging of the network. Another important advantage of multicasting is that multicast messages can be forwarded through routers that are multicast-enabled. However, a broadcast message can be sent to all the computers on the local network and not across an internetwork.

Multicasting also helps conserve the bandwidth because it can transmit messages to multiple recipients simultaneously. On the other hand, when unicasting is used to send messages to multiple recipients simultaneously, a connection must be established with every recipient before message transmission. Moreover, unicasting leads to the duplication of IP datagrams and also involves the overhead of maintaining a list of unicast addresses. This will consume excess time and bandwidth leading to wastage of network resources. Multicasting helps overcome these problems.

IMPLEMENTATION OF MULTICASTING

Sending a multicast message has a few differences when compared to unicast message transmission. In unicasting, when a message needs to be sent to a destination, the source and the destination address have to be specified. However, in the case of multicasting a message, all hosts receiving the message must be represented by a single name, which is also referred to as a multicast group. Special addresses are reserved for representing broadcasting and multicasting because addresses used for unicasting a message are different from multicast group addresses. The class D addresses in the IPv4 address space are reserved for multicasting addresses.

➔ For more information on address classes, **see** "The Network Interface and Link Layers," **p. 25**

The role of the Network layer is an important aspect to be analyzed regarding the implementation of multicasting. Multicasting can be implemented either at the hardware or the software level. Although technologies such as Ethernet and token ring support multicasting, the methods implemented by them are not compatible with each other. Therefore, if multicasting is implemented at the hardware level, it can be incorporated only within the same network. Multicasting that is implemented at the hardware level is called *link layer multicasting*. However, this type of multicasting cannot be implemented across an internetwork. This is because the internetwork might be connected to networks with disparate technologies. Therefore, multicasting is usually implemented at the software level. Multicasting that is implemented by IP is also referred to as *network layer multicasting*.

CH

20

The Network layer in the OSI reference model maps to the Internet layer in the TCP/IP reference model.

Implementation of multicasting by IP is also referred to as *IP multicast*. The addressing scheme for multicasting and the rules for routing must also be defined in the Internet layer. IP coordinates with a protocol called Internet Group Management Protocol (IGMP) that has been specifically designed for handling communication of group information between the hosts and the routers.

The Transport layer protocol that is used for multicasting is User Datagram Protocol (UDP). Although Transmission Control Protocol (TCP), which also operates from the Transport layer, provides a reliable transport system unlike UDP, the end-to-end communication mechanism provided by TCP cannot be used by applications that implement multicasting. Therefore, all the applications that multicast datagrams implement UDP as the Transport layer protocol.

→ For more information on TCP, **see** "Transmission Control and Data Flow," **p. 73**
→ For more information on UDP, **see** "User Datagram Protocol," **p. 113**

THE ROLE OF NETWORK TECHNOLOGY IN MULTICASTING

The implementation of multicasting depends on the network technologies that are implemented on a network. For example, Ethernet uses a different method to implement multicasting compared to token ring and FDDI network architectures, which is why multicasting is implemented at the Internet layer instead of the Link layer. However, the involvement of the Network layer in the transmission of datagrams over the physical medium cannot be ignored. This is because a multicast address must be mapped to a hardware address or Media Access Control address (MAC). The method of mapping an IP address to the corresponding hardware address differs with the underlying network technology that is used.

If the network interface card that is installed on the computer does not support multicasting, IP uses broadcast messages to transfer the multicast messages.

Let us take an example of how a multicast address is mapped onto an Ethernet address. The size of an Ethernet address is six bytes. To differentiate between a unicast address and a multicast address, the last bit of the first byte in a MAC address is set to 1. A sample multicast Ethernet address is $01.00.00.00.00.20_{16}$. One important point to be noted is that an Ethernet card can be configured to support more than one multicast address. This can happen when a host is a part of more than one multicast group. Multicast groups are discussed in detail later in the chapter.

Two aspects differentiate the way in which token ring implements multicasting. They are as follows:

- The conventions for representing multicast addresses are different from those implemented on an Ethernet.

- The order in which the multicast addresses are stored in the memory are different from that of an Ethernet.

MULTICASTING BY USING IP

The basic function of IP is to route the data to the correct destination. IP offers a connectionless delivery system, which does not guarantee a reliable data transfer. However, it offers a best-effort delivery system for transmitting data packets. Initially, IP was created to support routing of unicast datagrams. The basic functionality of IP had to be extended to support multicasting. The following issues had to be addressed to implement multicasting support in IP:

- Special addresses to differentiate between unicast and multicast addresses are required.

- Computers that receive multicast messages are identified as a group named multicast group. Each group must be identified by a unique name as well as an IP address. The class D addresses in the IPv4 address space are used to provide this unique IP address. The structure of a class D address space is different from the other classes. Class D addresses are discussed in detail later in this chapter.

- Unlike broadcasting that is restricted to a single network, multicasting messages can be sent to multiple networks. The routers must recognize multicast messages and forward them to the appropriate destination. The functionality of the routers had to be extended to support multicasting.

- Irrespective of whether the address is a unicast address or a multicast address, the IP address of the computer must be translated to the corresponding hardware address depending on the underlying technology used.

> **Note**
>
> Routers that are configured to handle multicast datagrams are referred to as *multicast routers*. You can configure a dedicated multicast router or combine its functionality with that of a normal router.

> **Note**
>
> Routers decrement the TTL value of a multicast datagram when they forward the datagram to a different router. If the TTL value of the multicast datagram reaches the value zero before the datagram reaches the destination network, the datagram is discarded and no ICMP error message is generated about the discarded multicast datagram.

CLASS D ADDRESSES

The class D addresses in the IPv4 address space are reserved for multicasting. The number of bits that are reserved for a class D address is the same as the other address classes. Class A, B, and C addresses can be used to represent the address of the source as well as the destination addresses in unicasting. However, class D addresses in the IPv4 address space are used to specify the address of the destination only. In this case, the source can be any class A, B, or C address.

To receive a multicast message, a computer must be a part of a group called a multicast group. Unlike the format that is followed by the class A, B, and C addresses, which are divided into two components known as the network number and the host number, a class D address consists of only two components. The first part of the class D address is four bits in length and is used by the host to distinguish between a multicast message and other messages. The value of the first component must be set to 1110 to identify a multicast message. The second component represents the group number of the multicast group (see Figure 20.1).

Figure 20.1
A class D address reserves four bits to differentiate between a unicast datagram and a multicast datagram. The first four bits of the IP datagram must be set to 1110 to identify the address as a multicast address.

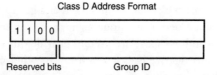

Class D Address Format

Reserved bits   Group ID

The ranges of addresses that can be used for class D are 224.0.0.0 and 239.255.255.255. Like other address classes, class D address space also consists of addresses that are reserved for special purposes. For example, 224.0.0.1 is a reserved address that is used to send messages to all systems in the same network segment. Addresses from 224.0.0.2 to 224.0.0.255 are used by routing protocols that handle multicast datagrams. Some of the reserved addresses are specified in Table 20.1.

TABLE 20.1 RESERVED ADDRESSES IN THE CLASS D ADDRESS SPACE THAT CANNOT BE ASSIGNED TO ANY MULTICAST GROUP

Address	Usage
224.0.0.2	Used to send messages to all routers in the same network segment.
224.0.0.3	Not assigned to any group.
224.0.0.4	Used by Distance Vector Multicasting Routing Protocol (DVRMP).

TABLE 20.1 CONTINUED

Address	Usage
224.0.0.5	Used to send OSPF routing information to all OSPF routers in a network segment.
224.0.0.6	Used to send OSPF routing information to OSPF designated routers in a network segment. This is also referred to as an OSPF AllDRouters address.
224.0.0.9	Refers to the RIP Version 2 group address. Used to send RIP routing information to all routers that use RIP Version 2.
224.0.1.24	Refers to a WINS server group address. Used to support auto discovery and dynamic configuration for replication between all the WINS servers.
224.0.0.10	Used by IGRP Routers.
224.0.0.12	Used by DHCP servers and Relay agents.

MULTICAST GROUPS

A multicast group refers to a group of computers to which a multicast message is sent. This is a valid class D address and is specified as the destination address in a multicast datagram. Hosts need to be a part of a multicast group to receive multicast messages. However, the reverse is not true. In other words, the sender of a multicast message need not belong to a multicast group to send a multicast message.

You can create two types of multicast groups, permanent and transient. Permanent groups are predefined by the ICANN and are reserved for special purposes. Permanent groups might contain members. However, transient groups are dynamic and are created based on the requirements of the networks. These groups are deleted when the number of members in the group reaches zero. In addition, the membership of a transient group is also dynamic. Hosts can join or leave a transient group according to their requirements. One important point to be noted is that the information on any changes that occur in the group composition must be notified to the routers on a network. To do this, the hosts and routers use a protocol called Internet Group Management Protocol (IGMP).

Note

Multicasting is also referred to as a push technology because the hosts by virtue of being a part of a group receive messages irrespective of whether they require them.

Сн

20

TRANSMISSION OF MULTICAST MESSAGES

Hosts that can participate in multicasting can be grouped into three categories. They are as follows:

- Hosts that cannot send or receive multicast datagrams. These hosts are commonly referred to as level 0 hosts.
- Hosts that can only send multicast datagrams but cannot receive any. These hosts are commonly referred to as level 1 hosts.

- Hosts that can send as well as receive multicast datagrams. These hosts that support multicasting completely are commonly referred to as level 2 hosts.

Note
RFC 1112 defines the extensions that need to be added to a host if it has to participate in multicasting. This RFC defines the functionality that is required by hosts to participate in multicasting. In addition, the extensions required by IP to support multicasting are also defined in this RFC.

FORWARDING MULTICAST DATAGRAMS OVER AN INTERNETWORK

As stated earlier, multicast datagrams can be sent to computers on the same network or on different networks. Data is delivered to computers on the same network directly from the host to the destination computers. However, if the multicast datagrams have to be sent across different networks, additional functions need to be introduced to the IP modules on the network. Let us analyze the components that are used for determining whether a datagram must be delivered to the local network or not. One component that is used in this estimation is the Time To Live field of the IP datagram. The TTL value is usually set to 1 to indicate that the datagram is to be delivered within the local network. Therefore, the routers attached to the networks ignore these datagrams. If the value in the TTL field is greater that 1, a router that is designated as a multicast router forwards the datagram to the next hop router. The TTL value for the multicast address is provided by the upper-layer protocols, namely the Transport layer and the Application layer. The upper-layer protocols also specify the destination address of the multicast datagrams. These values are placed in the IP header. After the required values are placed in the IP datagram, it is passed to the Network layer. This in turn takes care of transmitting the datagrams over the physical medium.

Note
If an upper-layer protocol does not specify the TTL value, the default value is taken as 1.

Note
When the sending computer is itself a part of the multicast group to which the message is sent, a copy of the message is sent to the sender too. However, this can be avoided if the IP module in the sender rejects such datagrams.

ROLE OF IP IN HANDLING INCOMING MULTICAST DATAGRAMS

The IP modules in any computer should be able to determine if the incoming datagrams are to be accepted. When an IP datagram is received, it is the responsibility of the IP module to check if the datagram has reached the correct group. This is done by maintaining a list of group addresses on the host. If a datagram has reached an incorrect destination, the

IP module rejects the datagram. An important point to be noted is that ICMP messages are not generated when a host rejects multicast datagrams.

> **Note**
>
> In actuality, applications that run on the hosts are assigned group numbers and not the hosts themselves. To be more precise, the processes in a host's OS that execute an application are assigned group numbers.

INTERNET GROUP MANAGEMENT PROTOCOL

In addition to the routing information propagated by hosts, information on the multicast groups on the same network or different network also needs to be transmitted to other hosts. To enable this feature, IP's functionality was extended to create a new protocol called IGMP. The specifications for communicating group membership among routers and hosts are provided by IGMP. The status of the group membership needs to be updated frequently to avoid unwanted entries from filling the list. This also prevents messages from being sent to computers that do not belong to a group.

Like Internet Control Message Protocol (ICMP) messages, IGMP messages are also encapsulated within an IP datagram and sent across the network (see Figure 20.2). The value 2 is specified in the Protocol field of the IP header to indicate that the datagram contains an IGMP message.

Figure 20.2
An IGMP message, which is eight bytes in size, is encapsulated in an IP datagram and sent over the network.

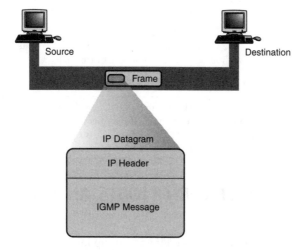

→ For more on the fields in an IP datagram, **see** "The Internet Layer Protocol," **p. 43**

The group membership information between the hosts and the routers must be exchanged in the message format that is specified by IGMP and is referred to as the IGMP message format (see Figure 20.3). The specifications to the message format are also defined in RFC 1112.

Figure 20.3
Operations such as a host joining a group or leaving the group are accomplished by exchange of IGMP messages between the hosts and the routers.

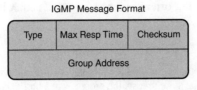

An IGMP message comprises of five fields: Version, Type, Unused, Checksum, and Group Address. The purpose of each field is described in Table 20.2.

TABLE 20.2	FIELDS IN AN IGMP MESSAGE AND THEIR PURPOSES
Field Name	**Description**
Version	Indicates the version of IGMP that is used to transfer the message. The current version of the IGMP that is used is IGMPv1. RFC 2236 defines IGMP version 2. The source and destination must ensure that the same version of IGMP is used to avoid discrepancy in the interpretation of the messages. The length of the Version field is four bits.
Type	Indicates the type of the message that is sent or received. The Type field can take two values, 1 and 2. The value 1 represents a Host Membership Query Message, and the value 2 represents a Host Membership Report. The purpose of these two messages will be discussed later in this chapter.
Unused	Indicates the eight bits that are reserved for future purpose. The length of this field is eight bits.
Checksum	Indicates the value that is used to check if the IGMP message reaches the destination without any errors. The size of this field is 16 bits. The algorithm used for computing the checksum value is the same as the one used for other protocols, such as IP and User Datagram Protocol (UDP).
Group Address	Indicates the multicast group name. The value taken by this field is dependent on the value in the Type field. If the query type is 1, the value in this field is filled with zeroes. If the query type is 2, the value in this field is filled with the group address that is sent by the host.

COMMUNICATION BETWEEN HOSTS AND ROUTERS USING IGMP

The routers and hosts use IGMP to communicate group information on the network. As stated earlier, maintaining correct group information is critical in preventing IGMP messages from clogging the network. In addition, accurate group information will help in efficient transmission of multicast datagrams. The messages that are exchanged between the hosts and the routers are Host Membership Query and Host Membership Report. The messages are commonly referred to as query and report messages, respectively.

Multicast routers use the query messages to send queries to the hosts at regular time intervals to check the status of each group. To understand how a query message is used by the multicast routers to obtain information about the groups on the network, take a scenario where a router sends an IGMP message to all the hosts on the network. The Group Address in the IGMP message sent by the router is filled with the value 224.0.0.1 to indicate that the message needs to be transmitted to all the multicast groups on the same network. The TTL value for the IP datagram is set to 1. All the hosts that are configured to accept multicast group messages receive the query messages. If the hosts that belong to a particular group do not respond to the query, the router infers that the group no longer exists and stops forwarding messages received from external networks destined for that group.

The replies sent by the hosts are referred to as reports. The value for the Type field is set to 2 to indicate that the message is a report. The host fills that value in the Group Address with the address of the group to which it belongs. After the router receives a reply from the hosts, it retains the information about the group and replicates the group information to the other routers when required. The Host Membership Report message is also generated when the host wants to join a multicast group.

Note

A host generates a Leave Group message when it wants to leave the multicast group. However, the host that generates this message must be the last member of the group.

There are a few problems that might arise when the hosts respond to the queries of a router. They are as follows:

- A network might comprise of more than one multicast group. If all the hosts respond to the router at the same time, the network traffic will become high leading to network congestion. To avoid this, every host on the network starts a timer called the delay timer. The time value is picked up as a random number. When the time elapses, the host sends the report to the router. Therefore, the difference in the timer values prevents network congestion.

- Although the problem of hosts from different multicast groups providing a simultaneous response to the router was addressed, another problem needs to be resolved. When a router addresses a query, all the hosts that belong to the same group will receive the message. If all the hosts start sending reports to the router, the network will be congested and flooded with redundant data. When a host sends a report to the router, it places the addresses of the group in the destination IP address field of the IP datagram, which holds the IGMP message. As a result, all the hosts in the multicast group receive the message. After the other hosts in the same multicast group receive the message, they stop the timer and do not generate any report for the same group and therefore prevent redundant messages from being sent over the network. This can be compared to a situation in which you mark a copy to all the members of your team to inform them about team activities. This would also help them coordinate with the team.

CH
20

> **Note**
>
> When a host does not want to be a part of a multicast group, it must not respond to the router. The membership of the group is removed automatically.

Irrespective of whether the messages need to be sent to the hosts on the same network or on a different network, the group address that is specified in the IP datagram must be mapped to the corresponding hardware address. Let us take the example where an IP address must be translated to the corresponding Ethernet address. The last 23 bits of an IP datagram, starting from 10 to 32, are mapped to the last 23 bits in the MAC address. This method has a disadvantage because more than one group address would map to the same hardware address. Let us analyze why this occurs. Bits 5 to 9 in the IP address that are not used in mapping the IP address to the hardware address can generate 32 different combinations that makes the group addresses unique. If these bits are ignored, the same hardware address will map to many group addresses. The solution is that hosts receiving unwanted datagrams must discard them.

If the underlying hardware technology does not support multicasting, the router uses the broadcast address to send the multicast datagrams.

> **Note**
>
> A group of multicast routers that enable multicasting over the Internet are referred to as the multicast backbone or the Mbone. This enables computers to exchange all types of information, such as data, audio, and video files.

After the routers map the group address to the corresponding hardware address, the messages are sent to the other network by encapsulating the message in a frame. Multicast routers across the network keep exchanging information about the groups at frequent intervals of time. This is required because hosts on a subnet can be a part of multicast groups that exist across an internetwork.

An important component of the multicast system that plays a vital role in multicasting is the multicasting protocol used by the routers to exchange information. The commonly used protocol is Distance Vector Multicast Routing Protocol (DVRMP). This protocol allows multicast routers to exchange information. The protocol is an extension of the Routing Information Protocol (RIP) that is used for routing unicast datagrams. The other standards that are used for exchanging routing information are the Multicast Open Shortest Path First (MOSPF) protocol and Protocol Independent Multicast (PIM). All these standards act as an extension to the protocols that are used for unicasting messages. PIM is more efficient than the other protocols because it can interact with all the unicasting protocols. This capability also defines its name.

SUMMARY

Multicasting is the process of transferring messages from one computer to a group of computers on a network. The most common applications of multicasting include video conferencing and software distribution. Datagrams that carry multicast messages are referred to as multicast datagrams. The name given to a group of computers that participate in multicasting is called multicast group. These datagrams can be delivered to hosts on the same networks or across different networks. However, multicast datagrams are addressed to groups of computers, unlike unicast datagrams that are routed to a single address.

To enable IP addressing for a group of hosts, the IPv4 address space includes a separate class called class D, which is dedicated for assigning multicast addresses. A class D address has to be converted to a hardware multicast address so that it can be transferred over the physical medium. Routers also play a vital role in multicasting. A router that is involved in unicasting a message can itself double up as a multicast router to transfer multicast datagrams. Routers can also act as dedicated multicast routers and exist as separate entities. To track information about groups, routers interact with the hosts at frequent time intervals. The protocol that is used by the hosts and routers to exchange group information is IGMP. This protocol is an extension to IP and operates from the Internet layer of the TCP/IP reference model. IGMP messages are encapsulated in an IP datagram and sent over the network.

CH
20

CHAPTER **21**

SECURITY CONCEPTS AND PRIVATE NETWORK CONNECTION

In this chapter

VIRTUAL PRIVATE NETWORKS

The exponential growth of the Internet has led to many changes in the way organizations do business. Organizations have launched their corporate and trading centers at different locations on the globe to expand their businesses. Organizations need to analyze the requisite cost of enabling a secure and effective communication mechanism. To establish such a communication mechanism, organizations implement a virtual private network (VPN). The concept of connecting two private networks through a public medium of communication is called *virtual private networking*. The public medium of communication that is referred to in this context can be the Internet or any public network.

A VPN helps an organization to reduce networking costs by making use of existing network infrastructure and at the same time ensures secure communication. The infrastructure that is being used belongs to a third party, mostly an ISP. The company need not invest in the infrastructure. By taking advantage of the networking infrastructure offered by the Net, VPNs enable organizations to expand their network presence.

To understand the intent behind the term virtual private networks, take the case of an organization that has launched corporate centers at two different places. The organization has two options: it can use an existing public communication channel (Internet) that is provided by a third party to make the branch offices communicate or create a new communications network that runs on costly dedicated lines owned by the organization. The cost effective choice rests with using the existing public communication infrastructure. This is because the hosts that are attached to the private networks communicate with each other because they are physically connected to each other and this infrastructure costs more.

On the other hand, hosts that are connected through a public communication channel, such as the Internet, communicate through a point-to-point connection that simulates a direct link between the hosts. Therefore, these types of networks are called virtual private networks. However, the confidential data that is communicated over a VPN is not completely secure from intrusions by other organizations that use the Net for similar communication. To ensure a secure transmission of confidential company information over a public network, one more level of security is added to the data. To put it in a different way, the data that is sent over the private network is encapsulated in a different datagram before being transmitted. This process is referred to as tunneling data. In addition, it is also encrypted using special encryption techniques that have been created for implementing VPNs.

> **Note**
>
> The number of layers of encapsulation that is added to the data depends on the tunneling protocols that are used.

The benefits that an organization can derive out of implementing a VPN are increases in sales with comparatively little investment. In addition, a VPN enables the organization to build strong business partnerships and strategic alliances that help in the overall growth of the organization. Some of the benefits of VPN are listed as follows:

- Secure fulltime access to worldwide corporate resources
- Connectivity implemented in a short period
- Minimal investment in establishing the required network infrastructure

Like any network, a VPN also consists of servers that authenticate the clients and provide services that are required by the clients. The components of a VPN include the VPN clients, VPN servers, and the special-purpose protocols that are used for communication in a VPN. A client that requires a VPN connection from a different network needs to be authenticated by a VPN server. After the VPN server authenticates the client, a connection is established between the server and the client.

DIFFERENT TYPES OF VIRTUAL PRIVATE NETWORKS

There are four broad categories of VPNs that can be implemented:

- Intranet-based VPN
- Extranet-based VPN
- Remote-access VPN
- Router-to-router VPN

To start with, consider a scenario in which an intranet-based VPN exists for an organization that has a network that connects all its branch offices. The work at one of the departments is sensitive in nature and so it is kept off the network. Although this ensures confidentiality and security of data, it isolates that particular department from the rest of the network. The solution works by establishing a VPN connection between the department's network and the organization's main network. This type of a network is called an intranet-based VPN because of its implementation within a company's intranet. This VPN implementation ensures connectivity, even as it provides security by way of the authentication mechanisms implemented on the VPN servers managing the network connections.

On the other hand, an extranet VPN connects a company's network with external networks owned by business associates, suppliers, or clients. This type of VPN can be implemented if companies enter into an agreement and require access to each other's resources. For example, universities and research centers can connect to the networks of other universities and enhance collaborative learning and research.

Based on the method of establishing communication, VPNs can also be classified into router-to-router VPNs and remote access VPNs. In the case of a router-to-router VPN, clients contact a router, which in turn communicates with the VPN servers. The connection can be established only if the client and the server authenticate each other. An extranet-based VPN can be implemented either as a router-to-router VPN or as a remote-access VPN.

In a remote-access VPN, a VPN client can directly establish a connection with the remote access VPN server without using a router. The remote access VPN server authenticates the clients. After the clients are authorized, they are allowed to access the network and the

CH
21

resources that are managed by the remote access server. Mobile users can use this method to connect to a private network.

> **Note**
>
> Remote access service is a feature that is supported by various operating systems to enable remote users to access the resources on a network. The users must use a dial-up connection to establish a connection with the remote access servers. The client can access the resources as if it were directly connected to the networks. The prerequisites for implementing remote access service, or RAS as it is commonly referred to, is that both the client and the server must have the required software installed. In addition, the client must have a telephone connection. The client might also have an indirect connection through a virtual private network. In other words, the client can have a connection to an ISP, which is connected to the remote server.

> **Note**
>
> Although a RAS server authenticates a VPN client, it will not be able to access the resources held by the RAS server unless the client has the required permissions to access the resources. The same applies for accessing all the resources on the network managed by the RAS server.

ADDRESSING IN A VPN

So far, we have been discussing the basics of a VPN and the different types of VPN implementations. Let us discuss an important requirement for implementing a VPN, the addressing scheme. The hosts on a VPN use the same addressing scheme as in any other network. However, the need for IP addresses also depends on whether the hosts must connect to the Internet. If hosts need Internet connectivity, the network would require public addresses. Addressing schemes such as subnetting, supernetting, or Network Address Translation (NAT) can be used to obtain the minimum required number of public IP addresses for optimum use. Apart from being used to save IP addresses, NAT can also be used for secure transmission of data. NAT is discussed later in this chapter.

If an organization is implementing an intranet-based VPN, addresses in the private address space would be the only required addresses. However, if a connection to the Internet is required, the address requirements must be planned accordingly. This type of network is also referred to as a hybrid network (see Figure 21.1). You also need to understand how computers that use a private IP address communicate with other computers on the Internet. This is done through a set of gateways known as application gateways. The *application gateway* accepts requests from an internal host and passes it to the destination. Every application that runs on the host will require an application gateway to forward its requests to computers on the public network.

Note

It is not a must that an intranet-based VPN must be connected to the Internet to form a hybrid network. A hybrid network can also be formed if an intranet-based VPN is connected to a network of a different organization, which is public with respect to the hosts that are connected to the intranet.

Figure 21.1
An intranet VPN can also be planned to make use of the resources on other networks by creating a hybrid network.

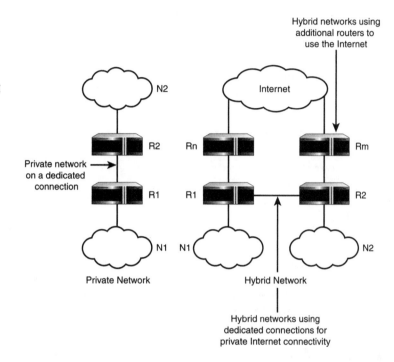

➔ For more information on the addressing schemes, **see** "The Network Interface and Link Layers," **p. 25**
➔ For more information on subnetting and supernetting, **see** "Subnetting and Classless Addressing," **p. 245**

PROTOCOLS REQUIRED TO IMPLEMENT A VPN

The protocols that are used for communication on a VPN play a vital role in implementing a VPN. These protocols can be classified into two types, LAN protocols and remote access protocols. The LAN protocols are used for transmission of data whereas remote access protocols handle security issues related to VPN. Internet Protocol (IP) is an example of LAN protocol. Point-to-Point Tunneling Protocol (PPTP) and Layer 2 Tunneling Protocol (L2TP) are the commonly used remote access protocol, which are used for tunneling data.

CH

21

> **Note**
>
> PPTP is an extension of Point-to-Point Protocol and is a product of Microsoft. Layer 2 Forwarding (L2F) was created by Cisco Systems to support VPNs. Both standards have their advantages and disadvantages. To make the efficient use of the features available in both standards, the companies got into an agreement and created a protocol called Layer 2 Tunneling Protocol (L2TP).

DATA TRANSFER BETWEEN COMPUTERS ON A VPN

Data transfer between hosts on a VPN is done as if both the sender and receiver are directly connected to each other. The data that is to be transferred is sent through a tunnel, which is a set of specifications that are used to ensure secure delivery of the data being transmitted.

Before learning about tunneled data validation, we need to understand the security mechanisms that are used with IP to implement security in the tunneling process. IP provides security features such as authentication and integrity of data, where validating the sender and the receiver of data is referred to as *authentication of data*. Ensuring that the data that is sent reaches the receiver unaltered is called *data integrity*. These features are implemented by special headers called Authentication Headers (AH) and IP Encapsulating Security Payload (ESP).

> **Note**
>
> The hosts (sending and receiving) that support AH and ESP in their IP software modules can make use of these features to provide integrity and confidentiality. The IP module on the hosts that do not recognize these headers ignore them when they are encountered in the datagrams sent and received by the host.

> **Note**
>
> An authentication header is also encapsulated in a frame along with an IP datagram and data. The information that is used for authentication is calculated based on the fields in the IP datagram that do not change. For example, the value of the TTL field in an IP datagram is not a constant. Therefore, this field cannot be taken into account when calculating AH fields for the IP datagram. RFC 1826 provides the specification for an IP authentication header.

Apart from authentication and data integrity, tunneled data needs an additional level of security called confidentiality. This security measure ensures that data is transmitted in a format that is comprehensible to the intended recipients alone. Confidentiality of data is very important because in a VPN data is transmitted through a number of public networks. Confidentiality is implemented by a protocol called Internet Protocol Security (IPSec). L2TP relies on IPSec for encryption services. PPTP utilizes Microsoft Point-to-Point Encryption (MPPE) to encrypt PPP frames.

In the process of tunneling, the contents of the IP datagram are hidden from the users of the public network by encrypting the contents of the IP datagram and then adding an additional header to it before it is sent over the network (see Figure 21.2). The routers that forward data over a VPN must decrypt the contents of the header to arrive at the information that is required for routing. If the router needs to forward the data once gain, it needs to encrypt the information in the header and then forward the datagram. However, not all routers can decrypt information that is present in the IP header. Only headers that possess a valid encryption key can decrypt the contents of the IP datagram.

Figure 21.2
The contents of an IP datagram are encrypted and an additional header is added by IPSec before it can be forwarded through a public medium.

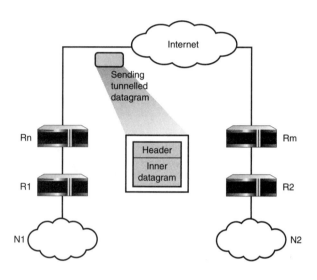

Note

IPSec can be used for implementing security on networks that use IP as the communication protocol. It cannot be used on networks that do not implement TCP/IP for communication.

→ To learn more about IPSec, **see** "IP Security," **p. 347**

NETWORK ADDRESS TRANSLATION

Although VPNs offer an effective security mechanism for private internetworks, the cost of running separate application gateways for software installed on the computers in a private intertnetwork was too high. Therefore, an alternative security mechanism, called the Network Address Translation (NAT), was developed. NAT offers an encapsulation of an arbitrary number of computers and applications running on local computers. Although security is one of the major gains, NAT primarily attempted to solve the problem of lack of addresses in the IPv4 address space. As the need for security for information stored and transacted on private internetworks gained importance, the security features provided by NAT was found useful.

Ch
21

In simple terms, NAT implements a method of maintaining network addresses of computers in a private internetwork. To transmit datagrams to and from these computers, the private internetwork is connected to the global Internet through a computer called the NAT box that has a valid public IP address. The destination address specified in each incoming datagram is translated using the addresses maintained by NAT. The source address in an outgoing datagram is also translated to indicate the single valid IP address and not the internal computer's actual network address. Outgoing packets from the intranet have their private addresses translated by the NAT into a single public address. NAT boxes can also provide a multiple public IP address conversion feature called multi-address NAT. Incoming packets from the Internet have their public addresses translated by the NAT into private addresses. By following this method, internal resources were encapsulated from the Internet. Figure 21.3 provides a conceptual overview of NAT.

Figure 21.3
In addition to encapsulation of local computers on a private internetwork, NAT also eases the problem of lack of addresses in the IPv4 address space.

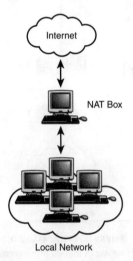

NAT implements an address table to maintain network address entries on the NAT box, much like the entries maintained in the routing table of a router. Although the contents of a routing table are dependent on inputs from other routers on the Internetwork, the contents of a NAT translation table are totally under the control of the NAT box. NAT uses a number of methods to initialize and populate the translation table.

For example, take a scenario where a local computer sends datagrams to an external server. When the datagram reaches the NAT box, before being routed to the next hop, the NAT box extracts the host address specified as the source IP address in the datagram and inserts this data as an entry into the NAT translation table. In addition, the NAT box replaces the source IP address with the NAT box IP address. In this way, the IP addresses of all outgoing datagrams are recorded and the actual source IP address is encapsulated from the destination computer.

Now take a scenario where all incoming datagrams are directed to the NAT box IP address because that is the only destination IP address available. If there are no corresponding NAT table entries, there is no possibility of routing an incoming datagram to the correct local computer because all incoming datagrams contain the same destination IP address, which is the NAT box IP address. Therefore, external servers have to run a Domain Naming Service (DNS) that tries to identify the IP address of an internal computer by using its domain name. When the external DNS requests the IP information, the DNS located on the NAT box translates the local computer name into the correct IP address and enters it into the NAT translation table before sending the NAT box IP address as a response to the external DNS query. When the incoming datagram arrives at the NAT box, its source IP is identified and linked to the DNS response sent. Now, the NAT box knows that for a particular datagram received from a particular external server, a particular local computer network address is the correct destination. By using this method, incoming datagrams are routed to the correct local address, NAT table entries are inserted, and local network addresses are encapsulated from probing DNS queries.

→ For more information on how DNS works, **see** "Transfer of DNS Messages," **p. 215**

TYPES OF NAT

Over the years, NAT implementations have been enhanced to provide more effective IP translation services primarily to meet IP address requirements and to provide security to private internetworks. However, as in the case of internetworks, NAT was also implemented as a static address translation service to cater to static networks. In this type of address translation, network addresses are not maintained in a table. Instead, each incoming or outgoing datagram was allocated a new IP address.

This simple address translation method was possible on static networks where network conditions did not change much. However, on dynamic networks of today, such simple address translation mechanisms do not work due to the constant change in the availability of routers and networks. Therefore, dynamic network address translation was implemented. Implementing dynamic NAT necessitated the creation of the translation table that can maintain information on the external source or destination address and the corresponding local computer IP address. This was because datagrams received from an external server must be directed to the correct local computer based on the information maintained in the address translation table. Dynamic NAT can be implemented by using two address translation methods: Multi-address NAT or Port-mapped NAT. Many NAT implementations, such as slirp and masquerade, use either of these techniques or a combination of both techniques to provide address translation features.

At a given point of time, computers in a private internetwork typically exchange datagrams with multiple external computers. A scenario where a local computer communicates with only one external computer is not always the case though it is possible. For example, a local computer might communicate with an external FTP server alone to ensure quick download of large files. However, considering the large volume of information available on numerous computers on an internetwork, this scenario is impractical. Another scenario where a single external destination computer might be accessed by multiple internal computers is the most practical and prevalent occurrence. Therefore, NAT boxes provide multiple valid IP addresses to enable local computers to communicate with multiple external computers. This feature is termed as multi-address NAT.

Although multi-address NAT provides a many-to-many communication mechanism between computers on a private internetwork and the external network, the number of external computers that can be accessed by a local computer at a given point of time is limited to a certain number depending on the capacity of the NAT box. To extend multi-address translation features, another NAT technique called port-mapped NAT, also called Network Address Port Translation (NAPT), can be implemented. In addition to translating external and internal addresses, port-mapped NAT translates source or destination ports into NAT ports. For this purpose, additional fields that record source, destination, and NAT ports are provided in the NAT translation table. An important point to note is that port-mapped NAT can be implemented only when computers (local and external) communicate using TCP or UDP.

Here's an example where a local computer named M1 and an external computer named M2 need to establish a TCP/IP connection over port 80. Typically, one computer needs to initiate an active open and the other needs to respond with a passive open. In our case, M1 performs the active open by instructing its OS to open a port and initiate the connection. Now, the OS opens a port with an arbitrary port number and sends the initial SYN datagram to the NAT box. The NAT box records the internal address and port number before assigning a NAT port number to the connection. Next, the NAT box sends a SYN to M2, which accepts the SYN and opens a connection with an external port number before sending the acknowledgement to M1. The NAT box receives the acknowledgement, and records the external address and port number in the row of the NAT translation table corresponding to M1. This way, M2 can receive multiple active opens from the private internetwork all initiated from what appears to be a single computer (the NAT box). Providing encapsulation to internal port numbers not only implements security for the TCP or UDP connection but also avoids any of the conflict that might occur if multiple local computers use the same port number to access an external computer.

NAT Implementation Problems

As with any networking application running on dynamic networks, NAT must implement features to manage the dynamic network conditions existing on the internetworks of today. Primarily, changing network conditions mean that the entries maintained on the NAT translation table must be constantly updated to reflect the correct availability status of external and internal computers communicating using the NAT box. The need to maintain correct availability information stems from the fact that a translation table entry related to a closed or dead connection might unnecessarily occupy NAT resources, such as port number or address.

To avoid wastage of precious NAT resources, a timer is set for each entry. The problem arises while deciding on the optimum timeout value for an entry. In the case of closed connections, low values can be set to enable quick release of NAT resources. However, timeout values for active connections depend on current requirements existing in the NAT box. For example, if the NAT box needs to service a large number of internal computers and is running short of NAT resources, a lower timeout value needs to be set for an entry related to an active connection. On the other hand, if the need for NAT resources is not high, longer timeout values can be set for each active connection entry in the NAT translation table.

Another factor that needs to be taken into account while implementing NAT is the problem of fragmentation. Although fragmentation prevention measures, such as path MTU discovery, determine the maximum segment size for each datagram, sometimes fragmentation is unavoidable. In such situations, information on translated ports and addresses are usually specified in the first fragment of a packet. The problem arises when fragments are received out of order. For example, if an incoming packet is fragmented into three parts and fragments 3 and 2 arrive before fragment 1, it is not possible to direct the fragments to the correct local computer because the information on the source address and port of the packet is stored in fragment 1. Therefore, the only way out is to wait until fragment 1 is also received and then determine the correct local computer to which the fragments are destined.

NAT implementations also have problems while dealing with Application layer protocols, such as ICMP, FTP, and DNS. Locating a DNS server as an external service outside a private internetwork negates the use of the server. This is because the external DNS always provides only one IP address, which is the NAT box address, as the resolved IP though the name of a local computer is specified to the external DNS server for being resolved. The NAT box always encapsulates an internal computer and provides its own IP as the resolved address. Moreover, no entry is made in the translation table because the NAT box does not resolve the domain lookup name with any internal computer's IP address on its own. However, if an internal DNS server was present, that DNS resolves the name and obtains the corresponding IP of the internal computer, which is then supplied to the NAT box where it is entered into the translation table. The NAT box supplies its own IP address as the resolved IP for the lookup name specified by the external DNS server. In addition, information on the external DNS is also entered in the entry. Therefore, a connection is made the next time the same external DNS server provides the same lookup name to obtain the IP address.

FTP poses a different kind of problem for NAT implementations. Some FTP commands require exchange of IP addresses as data represented in binary formats. Such binary information can be of an arbitrary size. The problem arises when IP addresses specified as the data are translated by the NAT box. When this translation occurs, the size of the resultant IP addresses might increase or decrease the original packet size. This might result in unnecessary fragmentation of the packet.

An ICMP message is another problem area faced by NAT. Each message contains information related to the sending computer, such as the local computer IP address. However, after transition, only the NAT box address is stored in the ICMP message. Therefore, it becomes impossible to identify the correct local computer to which the ICMP message must be routed.

CH

21

Summary

There has been a tremendous change in the way organizations conduct their business due to the increase in the popularity of the Internet. At this juncture, organizations need to concentrate on minimizing costs and at the same time expand their business. The solutions taken by the organization must also be secure. Virtual Private Networks (VPN) offer a good solution for creating cost-effective networks that are secure enough for the organizations to conduct their business communication.

A VPN is created by connecting two private networks through a public medium. A VPN can be intranet-based or extranet-based. VPNs can also be classified as router-to-router VPNs or remote access VPNs depending on the type of access provided by the VPN. The data that passes through a private network is tunneled by providing and encapsulating the IP datagram in a header created by IPSec. The fields in the IP header are also encrypted using special encryption techniques.

Apart from security features implemented for external users accessing internal resources through VPN, Network Address Translation (NAT) offers an encapsulation of an arbitrary number of local network computers and applications running on those computers. Although security is one of the main aspects of NAT, it was primarily created to solve the problems of the exhaustion of the IPv4 address space. As the need for security for information stored and transacted to and from private internetworks gained importance, the security features provided by NAT was found useful. The two types of NAT that are implemented are static NAT and dynamic NAT.

Organizations can use VPN and NAT to implement foolproof security features for their internetworks. VPN can be used to secure intranet communication implemented on the Internet and NAT can be used to secure internal network IPs from external intrusive access.

CHAPTER **22**

IP SECURITY

In this chapter

INTRODUCTION TO IP SECURITY

You use a variety of communication media to transfer information to another person. Today, you can use e-mail, pagers, or the postal system to communicate information. However, the simplest form of communication that still exists is direct talk between two people. In this form of communication, air is the communicating medium. If you need to communicate sensitive information, you may be concerned that others might overhear the information that you are passing on to another person. Therefore, you might try to reduce the chances of information leaks by talking in hushed tones as a "security" measure. Although the reach of the Internet as a communication medium cannot be compared with air, widespread implementation of the Net over the past decade has raised a number of security issues. A number of solutions have also been proposed and implemented.

In contrast to a word-of-mouth communication, information communicated over the Net faces a variety of risks ranging from tampering, impersonation of identity, and lack of privacy. This is because information is not transmitted over the Net as a single block but as separate units called frames, which might have to traverse large geographic distances and a number of routers owned by other organizations. Therefore, defensive mechanisms must be constructed starting with the most basic unit, which is a frame and its contents that includes the IP datagram, the TCP segment, and the raw data transferred from an application. Although individual fields in a frame offer security measures in the form of checksums, the IP datagram provides the maximum security measure in the form of a security framework that secures data from most security threats existing on the Net today. This framework, called IP Security (IPSec), provides a broad outline that includes a combination of datagram formats, protocols, and security measures, such as encryption and authentication. You will be introduced to IPSec and will analyze the components of IPSec in the following sections. Before learning about IPSec, it is important to understand the security issues that necessitate the implementation of the IPSec framework.

Note

The process of modifying data into a format that is incomprehensible to unauthorized users or computers is called encryption. The intended recipient or authorized user who wants to reconstruct the data into a comprehensible format must use special encryption keys to decrypt the data. A wide range of encryption algorithms has been used to encrypt data being transmitted over the Net. RSA (Rivest, Shamir, and Adelman) and various derivations of RSA, such as Message Digest 5 (MD5), are some of the popular encryption algorithms that are being implemented today.

SECURITY THREATS ON THE INTERNET

The last decade of the 21st century can be described as the start of the Internet Age. The Net started moving away from its military implementation areas into a number of diverse fields. Today, the Net provides the vital competitive edge to various corporate sectors. For example, companies can use the Net to transact with their bankers, branches, employees, suppliers, distributors, customers, and so on. However, the need to transmit sensitive information over networks owned by various organizations has posed various security threats. For example, decisions related to new sales strategies might be communicated to branch offices from a head office through the Net. The routers that link the head office and the branch offices might be managed by other organizations. Therefore, data transmitted through these routers is not entirely secure from being read. Communication between the branch offices of a company is not the only data that can be read from intermediate computers. This security issue, also called eavesdropping, can lead to a leak of sensitive information, such as credit card numbers, bank account numbers, passwords, and any confidential transaction that can occur on the Net.

Another security concern related to transmitting data is the possibility of data being tampered before reaching its intended destination. For example, if you are transmitting confidential information to your business associate and your competitors tamper with the information contained in datagrams before it reaches its destination, the modified information will cause miscommunication and lead to making wrong decisions or strategies and, ultimately, business losses for your organization. The identity of authorized users also falls under the category of confidential information that must be safeguarded. For example, despite the strong preventive measures that you implement to secure your house, if you lose the keys to your house, all these measures are nullified. Similarly, security measures that are implemented to prevent access to the confidential information stored on internetworks can be nullified if security keys, such as usernames, passwords, or encryption keys, are available to unauthorized personnel.

The wide reach of the Net has benefited a vast number of users who can access and use products and services in addition to the large volumes of information that is available. The very notion of the Internet has been based on its ability to afford easy accessibility to available resources. However, a mode of disruptive attack that can prevent authorized personnel from accessing the resources on an internetwork has become a major security issue called the *denial of service*. Denial of service attacks are characterized by an effort to disable access to networks and the services they provide by using a variety of communication disruption techniques. For example, if a computer sends a vast number of initial synchronization (SYN) datagrams to a server on a network without acknowledging the reply SYNs sent from the server, this could crash the server because the server allocates memory resources for creating endpoints for each dummy SYN received. Unless the connection process is completed or terminated, vital resources on the server would be unnecessarily occupied. Moreover, other connections that actually need to be accepted might be queued or rejected, causing a denial of service. Methods similar to a SYN flood attack are implemented to cause the disruption of a connection existing between hosts and between clients and servers. Denial of service attacks are also targeted at individual user accounts with the aim of denying services to a particular user. For example, take the case of a salesperson who needs to access a company Web site to provide the latest prices and schemes available for a product to a client. By denying the salesperson access to the company Web site when the sales person tries to log on to the site, competitors can inflict heavy losses on the company.

BROAD OVERVIEW OF IPSEC

At the root of the security issues lies the fact that attacks occur at the level of datagrams. Although a number of measures and precautions have been proposed for security loopholes existing on the Net, many fail to address datagram level security. By providing comprehensive security for a datagram, security lapses that occur can be stopped at the root. IPSec proposes a framework that provides comprehensive security features for each datagram transmitted over the Net. This framework is comprised of three components: additional IP headers, negotiated security features, and encrypted key management features. Take the case of a datagram that must be processed by IPSec to implement security. To begin, IPSec encrypts or scrambles the data contained in an IP datagram. To unscramble data, it provides additional headers that can be appended to the existing IP header format. These headers, Authentication Header (AH) and Encapsulated Security Payload (ESP), contain encryption information and the keys required to unscramble encrypted data.

When the AH or ESP-secured datagram reaches a router, IPSec determines whether the datagram needs to be encrypted based on the information available in AH or ESP headers. Next, it determines whether encryption features are available on the sending and destination computers. To enable this, the computers must enter into a contract, called a security association (SA), which defines the type of encryption that must be applied to the datagrams being exchanged between them and the mode of transport that must be implemented for data exchange. To manage security associations, the IPSec implementation on each computer provides a security policy database (SPD), security association database (SAD), and selectors. A number of factors need to be taken into account to determine the SA that can be applied to a connection. To determine the correct encryption strategy to be used, the SA must be created based on factors such as the source IP address, destination IP address, usernames or host names, the Transport layer protocol used, and the source and destination ports implemented. These factors are collectively called *selectors*.

To identify whether you need to apply encryption to a datagram, discard the datagram, or exempt the datagram from IPSec implementation, IPSec uses the information stored in an SPD to determine its status. Each entry in an SPD contains information regarding the SA that exists between sending and receiving computers. An SPD entry points to a SAD entry and the selectors that need to be taken into account to create the SA for the datagram being transmitted. SAD contains information on the encryption algorithms, authentication algorithms, and other information related to the IP security provided by the SA. A variety of algorithms can be implemented to provide encryption features for the datagram. For example, MD5 or Secure Hash Algorithm (SHA) algorithms can be implemented to provide authentication features for the datagram. In addition, you can use the Data Encryption Standard (DES) algorithm to implement the cryptographic encryption of data contained in the datagram. After an SA between sending and receiving computers has been established, data contained in each datagram can be encrypted.

However, before transmission, it is important to define the encryption keys that must be used on either of the computers to unscramble encrypted information. A key is a combination of numbers that is generated by a key hash algorithm. Remember that the keys to any security system must also be secured to ensure the validity of the system. To implement this vital aspect in the IPSec security framework, a set of standards called Internet Key Exchange (IKE) has been proposed. IKE also implements a security association between the sending and receiving computers to establish the procedure for transmitting key information between the computers. After the IKE SA has been established and keys have been encrypted, the IKE SA is made part of the main SA that manages secure data transmission. Now that the SA has been established, the outgoing datagram is ready to be transmitted to the receiving computer. On the receiving computer, the SA decrypts key information by using IKE and then decrypts the datagram before providing the information to higher layer protocols. Figure 22.1 provides a bird's eye view of the IPSec framework and how it implements security.

Figure 22.1
The IPSec framework provides comprehensive security for the contents encapsulated in an IP datagram. In this way, it addresses the root problem that has plagued data transmission.

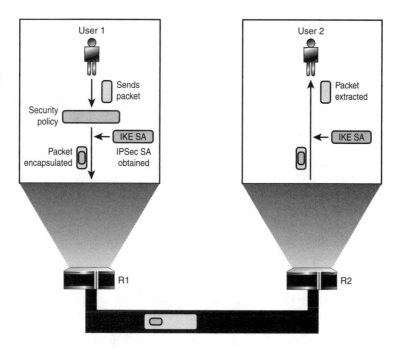

Although each datagram is provided with adequate security through encryption, the process of transmission still holds certain security threats as discussed earlier. To manage this aspect, the datagrams are further encapsulated into a tunnel that encrypts the entire IP datagram before being encapsulated into a frame. This mode of transport is called *tunnel mode*. One important advantage of the tunnel mode is that the encryption and decryption is implemented between the sending and receiving routers. Therefore, the corresponding routers manage implementation details, such as IPSec SA and IKE SA negotiations. Another mode of transmission called the *transport mode* can also be used to send secured datagrams. Unlike the tunnel mode, when datagrams are transmitted using the transport mode, only a part of the datagram is encrypted and not the entire datagram. Although the overhead of encrypting the entire IP datagram is not there, when the transport mode is used to transmit IPSec secured datagrams, sending and receiving computers must manage the negotiation of IPSec and IKE SA information. In addition, hackers can identify the source and destination of the datagram being transmitted. Therefore, the tunnel mode is the most secure and preferred mode of data transmission.

THE AUTHENTICATION HEADER

The transportation of finished products over long distances always holds the risk of damage or theft. Fragile products can be damaged in transit. Most organizations insure their goods before sending a consignment to its destination. Glass, for example, is a particularly fragile product that is difficult to transport without damages or loss. The duty of the transportation service is to package the fragile products with adequate protective material before transporting the goods. It is also imperative that the consignee at the destination verifies the status of the goods that have been delivered before accepting them. These measures have to be taken to ensure the integrity of the transported goods.

Maintaining the integrity of transported products is a measure that can be translated into the sphere of data transmission over the Net. In an environment where a datagram must traverse huge geographical distances before reaching its destination, the integrity of the data contained in the datagram is susceptible to change or damage. It is also important to verify the source of the datagram to ensure that an authentic sending computer has transmitted the datagram. IPSec provides you with a method to manage the authentication and integrity of the data contained in a datagram by adding an additional header to the IP datagram called the authentication header. There are certain fields in an IP datagram that are modified in transit. For example, the time to live field or the checksum value in an IP datagram header is recomputed at each hop. AH does not provide authentication features for such fields, which are called *mutable fields*. Although AH can be used to implement authentication and integrity of data, AH does not provide features that encapsulate the contents of a datagram. This deficiency enables users controlling the routers transmitting the datagram to view the datagram contents. It is essential to transmit an AH-secured datagram in tunnel mode to ensure comprehensive security for the data being transmitted.

Each datagram undergoes a process before being transmitted or on arrival from another computer. Before delving into the processes involved, you need to learn about the format of AH and its location in an IP datagram. AH is placed after the IP header and before the Transport layer protocol header in the IP datagram format. AH contains fields such as Next header, Payload Len, RESERVED, and so on. Figure 22.2 shows you the location of AH in the IP format and the organization of AH fields.

Figure 22.2
Information provided
in the AH fields is
used by the security
policy database to
create an SA.

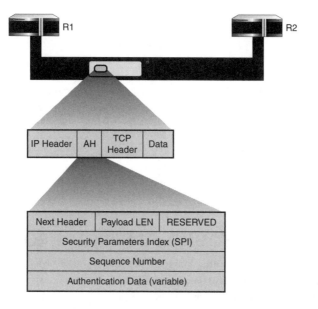

Table 22.1 describes the role of each AH field in detail.

TABLE 22.1   FIELDS IN AN AUTHENTICATION HEADER

AH Field	Description
Next header	Specifies the type of the IP datagram that is to be transmitted next. For example, IP datagrams with AH are indicated with the decimal number 51. In the Next header field, this value is specified as an 8-bit binary value.
Payload Len	Specifies an 8-bit binary value that indicates the length of AH.
RESERVED	Specifies 0 as the value for the field because the field is reserved for future use. The length of this field is 8 bits.
Security Parameters Index (SPI)	Specifies a 32-bit value that is used in combination with the destination IP address and the Authentication data field to uniquely identify the SA implemented on sending and receiving computers. Although arbitrary values can be specified, certain values are reserved and cannot be used. For example, the Internet Assigned Numbers Authority (IANA) has reserved values ranging from 1 through 255 for future use. In addition, the value 0 can be used only when authentication is implemented on the local network and not over the Net.

TABLE 22.1 CONTINUED	
AH Field	**Description**
Sequence Number	Specifies a 32-bit value that acts as a counter that provides a serial number for the datagrams transmitted using a particular SA. It is mandatory for the sending computer to specify the sequence number, regardless of the fact that the receiving computer might not process this field.
Authentication Data	Specifies an Integrity Check Value (ICV) that is used by the receiving computer to verify the authenticity of the incoming datagram.

OUTBOUND AND INBOUND AH FIELD PROCESSING

The AH specified in each outgoing datagram is subjected to a process to implement the authentication information in the datagram. This process, called the *outbound process*, is performed by the IPSec implementation on the sending computer. The outbound process must begin with the identification of an SA that is associated with a datagram. This is because the sending and receiving computers need information on the algorithms used to provide authentication and integrity features in IP datagrams. If an SA does not exist, the process of creating a new SA must be initiated. You will learn about how an SA is created in the later sections of the chapter.

After an SA is established, the Sequence number field of the IP datagram AH is initialized to 0. When subsequent datagrams are transmitted, the number will be incremented monotonically. However, sequence numbers can be incremented to a certain maximum value beyond which their value is reset to 0 and then incremented thereon. Now, the AH Sequence number field in each datagram is assigned a value that has already been assigned to another datagram that was transmitted before the sequence number reset occurred. This anomaly, called *replay*, could lead to a duplication of AHs. To prevent the occurrence of replay, an anti-replay setting must be enabled on the sending computer. Anti-replay ensures that the sequence number does not replay before the SA for the datagram is terminated. If such a situation occurs, the SA is terminated and a new SA is created.

The final step in the outbound process is ICV (Integrity Check Value) calculation. Many products, such as a software package or a can of soda, come in a protective seal that can be used to verify if the product has been tampered with or duplicated. ICV acts as a protective seal for a datagram. If the contents of a datagram are tampered with during transit, when ICV is calculated at the receiving computer, the same ICV is not derived. In this way, AH provides authenticity and integrity to a transmitted datagram. ICV is similar to the checksum field implemented on TCP or UDP datagram headers and is calculated in a similar manner. Primarily, ICV is derived based on the values of all the immutable fields in an IP datagram, AH, and encapsulated upper-layer protocol data. On deriving ICV, the IKE SA is established and the outgoing datagram is transmitted to its destination.

On receipt of the datagram, a process similar to the outbound process is performed on the datagram. This process, called the *inbound process*, verifies the authenticity and integrity of the datagram received from the sending computer. As the first step in inbound processing, the SA associated with the datagram is verified. The SA includes information on the authentication algorithms that must be used to compute ICV for the datagram. In addition, information on whether the sequence number specified in the incoming datagram must be checked for replays is also provided in the SA. The SA also specifies information on the keys that must be employed to work with the algorithms.

After obtaining the information specified in the SA, the sequence number indicated in the AH of the datagram must be verified for replay. This measure is implemented to discard duplicate IP datagrams. If the sequence number of a datagram is found identical to that of a previously received datagram, which is also associated to the same SA as the incoming datagram, the incoming datagram is discarded. The last step in inbound processing is the computation of ICV for a datagram. Information on the ICV computed at the sending computer is specified in the `Authentication data` field of AH. Information on how to compute the ICV based on the fields in the incoming IP datagram is specified in the authentication algorithms of the associated SA. Using the authentication algorithms, an ICV is computed and compared with the ICV computed at the sender computer as specified in the `Authentication data` field. If the ICVs match, the authenticity and integrity of the datagram is validated and the datagram is passed to higher-layer protocols for further processing. If the ICVs do not match, the authenticity or integrity of the datagram is suspect. Therefore, the datagram is discarded.

ENCAPSULATED SECURITY PAYLOAD

In an environment where datagrams need to traverse multiple routers managed by other organizations, it is not enough if you verify the authenticity and integrity of a datagram transmitted over the Net. This is because the content of a datagram is visible to the intermediate devices through which it is transmitted. When you transmit software setup files or other nonclassified information, there is no problem if datagram content is visible. However, when sensitive information, such as bank account numbers or passwords, is transmitted, it needs to be hidden from the view of users who control the intermediate devices. This need calls for the implementation of another type of IP security header called *Encapsulated Security Payload* (*ESP*). Although ESP provides security features that are similar to AH, an important feature provided by ESP that differentiates it from AH is *confidentiality*. This feature enables a sending computer to modify the contents of a datagram into a format that is incomprehensible to intermediate devices.

To implement confidentiality, ESP scrambles the contents of a datagram by encrypting them before transmitting the datagram. The receiving computer must decrypt the contents before transferring the decrypted content to upper-layer protocols. As in the case of AH, outbound and inbound processing occurs at the sending and receiving computers, respectively. Before delving into the details of the processes, it is important to understand how ESP is structured. Three additional components are added to an IP datagram when ESP is implemented. These include the ESP header, ESP trailer, and ESP Auth. In an IP datagram, the ESP header is located immediately after the IP header. The ESP trailer and ESP Auth components are located following the Data component. Figure 22.3 shows you the location of ESP in the IP datagram format and the organization of ESP fields.

Figure 22.3
The information provided in the ESP fields is used by IPSec to provide confidentiality in addition to authenticity and integrity for the contents of a datagram.

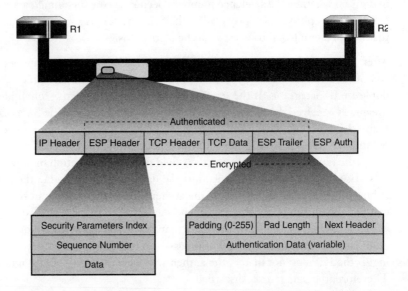

Table 22.2 describes each ESP field in detail.

TABLE 22.2   FIELDS IN THE ESP HEADER, ESP TRAILER, AND ESP AUTH COMPONENTS OF AN IP DATAGRAM

Fields	Description
Security Parameters Index (SPI)	Specifies a 32-bit value that is used in combination with a destination IP address and authentication data to uniquely identify the SA implemented on the sending and receiving computers. Although arbitrary values can be specified, certain values are reserved and cannot be used. For example, the Internet Assigned Numbers Authority (IANA) has reserved values ranging between 1 and 255 for future use. In addition, the value 0 can be used only when authentication is implemented on the local network and not over the Net.
Sequence number	Specifies a 32-bit value that acts as a serial number counter for the datagrams transmitted using a particular SA. It is mandatory for the sending computer to specify the sequence number regardless of the fact that the receiving computer might not process this field. The receiving computer can

TABLE 22.2 CONTINUED

Fields	Description
	enable the anti-replay feature to avoid the recycling of sequence numbers for a connection using a particular SA. Therefore, before the sequence number reaches the value 2^{32}, the SA that is used to transmit the datagrams is terminated and a new SA is initiated.
Payload Data	Specifies synchronization information related to the encryption algorithm used for encrypting a datagram. This information, called an initialization vector (IV), synchronizes the encryption implemented on a datagram with the encryption performed on other datagrams in an SA.
Padding	Specifies the additional bytes that need to be added to a field that might be short of four bytes, which is the minimum required size of a field. In addition, some encryption algorithms include plaintext as part of encrypted data. In such cases, padding is used to specify dummy binary units for the plaintext.
Pad Length	Specifies the length of the Padding field that indicates the number of bytes that are specified in the Padding field.
Next header	Specifies the type of data contained in the Payload Data field. The contents of the Payload Data field can be indicated using IP Protocol numbers defined by IANA.
Authentication Data	Specifies an Integrity Check Value (ICV) that is used by a receiving computer to verify the authenticity of a datagram.

OUTBOUND AND INBOUND ESP FIELD PROCESSING

As with an AH, ESP fields are also processed before being transmitted from the sending computer and on receipt at the receiving computer. The processes implemented for inbound and outbound ESP fields are similar to the processes implemented for AH. However, certain steps have been added to the inbound and outbound processes because of the feature of confidentiality provided by ESP. To start with, when a datagram is sent to the IPSec module in the sending computer, the existence of an SA associated with the datagram is verified. If an SA is not available, a new SA is initialized.

After associating an SA to the datagram, the contents of the datagram are encrypted through a process called packet encryption. First, the contents of the IP datagram are encapsulated into the Payload Data field. If the transport mode is to be implemented for transmitting the datagram, only the upper-layer protocol data contained in the datagram is encapsulated. If the tunnel mode is to be used, the entire datagram is encapsulated. Now, additional bytes must be added as padding if any extra space is left in the Payload Data field. This is to ensure that the size of the Payload Data field does not fall short of the minimum size of four bytes. Now, using the encryption algorithm specified by the SA associated to the datagram ESP fields, such as Payload Data, Padding, Padding length, and Next header, are encrypted. If authentication is also implemented, the packet encryption process is performed before the authentication process. When inbound processing is performed on the receiver's computer, ICV computation and authentication takes place before decryption. In this way, damaged or tampered datagrams are discarded before decrypting the datagram. Therefore, the Authentication Data field is not encrypted during the packet encryption phase of outbound processing.

The next step in the outbound process is sequence number generation. This phase is similar to the sequence number generation process implemented for AH. The Sequence number field is initialized with the value 0 for the first ESP-secured datagram that is transmitted. Sequence numbers for subsequent datagrams are incremented by one until the number reaches a maximum value of 2^{32}. IPSec on the sending computer assumes that the anti-replay feature is enabled on the receiving computer. Therefore, if a sequence number is incremented to its maximum limit, a new SA is created and associated with the datagram.

After the sequence number is generated, an ICV is computed based on all the fields in ESP except the Authentication data field where the ICV value is stored. As the last step in the outbound process, if required, the IP datagram might be fragmented before its transmission. However, if the datagram is to be transmitted using the transport mode, this step is implemented only after the outbound process is completed. However, in tunnel mode, IP datagrams can be fragmented before outbound processing is performed. Now, the datagram is ready for transmission.

The inbound processing of ESP-secured IP datagrams is also similar to the process implemented on an AH-secured datagram, the only difference being an additional step for decrypting the scrambled contents of an incoming datagram. Before beginning with the inbound process, fragmented IP datagrams are reassembled at the receiving computer. As the first step in the inbound process, the SA associated with the incoming datagram is identified. Next, the sequence number specified in ESP is verified for replay. If replay is identified, the datagram is discarded. However, if authentication is not implemented for the datagram, the anti-replay feature is not enabled on the receiver's computer. Destination computers that do not enable anti-replay services do not perform sequence number verification.

After verifying the sequence number of a datagram, ICV for the datagram is computed and the resultant ICV is compared with the value stored in the Authentication Data field. If the datagram's contents have been tampered with, the ICVs do not match and the datagram is discarded. If the integrity of the datagram content has been maintained, the next phase of inbound processing, which is packet decryption, is initiated. The steps that are performed in the packet decryption phase are the reverse of the steps implemented for the packet encryption phase. You can compare this to performing the steps for unpacking a gift, which are the reverse of packing a gift.

The encrypted ESP fields, such as `Payload Data`, `Padding`, `Pad length`, and `Next header`, are decrypted as the first step in the packet decryption phase. The SA associated with the incoming datagram indicates decryption algorithms that need to be used for this step. Any additional padding that is present in the `Payload` data field is also decrypted. Finally, the contents of the datagram are reconstructed after decryption. In the case of datagrams transmitted through the transport mode, IP header and upper-layer protocol data is reconstructed. Datagrams that are transmitted through the tunnel mode are completely encrypted along with the IP header. Therefore, the entire datagram must be decrypted. Now, the reconstructed data is ready for upper-layer protocol processing.

SECURITY ASSOCIATION AND INTERNET KEY EXCHANGE

For a novice learning to cook a meal, it is not enough if all the ingredients and cooking appliances are ready. In fact, all these objects are of no use if the novice does not have a cookbook. A cookbook contains vital instructions on how much of the ingredients must be used and in what order. Security associations are similar to cookbooks from the point of view of an IPSec implementation. Additional headers, such as ESP or AH, only contain the "ingredients" for implementing security. If the SA "cookbook" does not provide instructions on how security can be implemented, the ESP or AH ingredient will be of no use in securing a datagram. The instructions provided by an SA must be present on sending and receiving computers. Therefore, the sending computer must indicate the SA that must be implemented on the receiving computer.

As you learned earlier, SA is comprised of three components: Security Policy Database (SPD), Security Associations Database (SAD), and Selectors. SPD performs the role of coordinating the SA information stored on SAD. As one of the earliest steps in the outbound or inbound process, an SA lookup is performed. When this step occurs, the existence of an entry in SPD is verified. Each entry contains information on transport modes and algorithms. Most importantly, it contains a reference to the corresponding SAD entry. The entries in SAD are created based on the information extracted from the IP datagram being processed. This information, called Selectors, is instrumental in determining the appropriate SA specification for a datagram. Some of the commonly used Selectors are discussed in Table 22.3.

TABLE 22.3   SELECTORS USED FOR CREATING AN SPD ENTRY

Selector	Description
Destination IP address	Specifies the destination IP address that matches with the IP address provided in the IP datagram encapsulated in a tunnel. The Selector is specified as an entry in SPD to determine the SA specifications that must be implemented for the datagram.
Source IP address	Specifies the IP address of the sending computer.

TABLE 22.3 CONTINUED	
Selector	**Description**
Name	Specifies the username, login account, or the DNS name of the sending computer.
Transport layer protocol	Specifies the Transport layer protocol that is used to encapsulate data in the datagram. This information is obtained from the Next header field in AH or ESP or the Protocol field in the IP datagram.
Source and destination ports	Specifies the ports used on sending and receiving computers. Information on the ports can be obtained from the Transport layer segments encapsulated in the datagram.

Each of these Selectors plays a vital role in the creation of a SAD entry. SAD can be described as the core component of an SA where SA specifications are found. A SAD entry contains a wide range of information that is used by IPSec to encrypt, decrypt, authenticate, and verify the integrity of an IP datagram when inbound and outbound processes are implemented. The fields present in SAD are described in Table 22.4.

TABLE 22.4 FIELDS IN A SECURITY ASSOCIATION DATABASE	
Field	**Description**
Sequence Number Counter	Specifies a value that is used by IPSec to generate the sequence number in an AH or ESP header of a datagram. The counter can be 32 bits in size.
Sequence Number Overflow	Specifies whether the replay of a sequence number is allowed.
Anti-Replay Window	Specifies a counter that is used by IPSec to determine if the sequence number specified in a datagram is a duplicate. The counter can be 32 bits in size.
AH Authentication	Specifies the algorithm or key that must be used to implement authentication in the AH of a datagram.
ESP Encryption	Specifies the algorithm or key that must be used by IPSec to implement encryption on the contents of a datagram.
ESP Authentication	Specifies the algorithm or key that must be used by IPSec to implement authentication features in an ESP-secured datagram.
Lifetime	Specifies the time that indicates the lifetime of an SA after which the SA must be terminated or replaced with a new SA. The Lifetime field must also contain information on whether the SA must be terminated or replaced. The field might contain information in the form of time units or bytes.

TABLE 22.4   CONTINUED

Field	Description
IPSec protocol mode	Specifies the transmission mode that must be adopted for the datagram. The transmission mode can be transport or tunnel.
Path MTU	Specifies the Path MTU that is estimated for the datagram.

In addition to defining an SA for a datagram, a mechanism to encrypt, decrypt, or authenticate datagrams must exist to implement the security features proposed by the IPSec framework. To implement this mechanism, a combination of numbers called *keys* must be created and shared between sending and receiving computers. This process is managed by a protocol called the Internet Key Exchange (IKE). The key management process is implemented by IKE in a two-step format. The first step deals with authenticating the computers to each other.

A number of methods can be implemented by IKE to authenticate sending and receiving computers to one another. The computers can exchange pre-shared keys as part of the authentication phase in the key management process. Next, a combination of numbers called a *keyed hash* is created on the sending computer and sent to the receiving computer. The receiving computer uses a pre-shared key to derive a keyed hash of its own. If this keyed hash matches with the keyed hash received from the sending computer, the computers are authenticated to each other.

Another method of authenticating computers to each other is by using public key cryptography where computers generate a random number called a *nonce*, encrypt the nonce using each other's public keys, and then exchange the encrypted nonce. If the computers are able to reconstruct the nonce by using their public key or keys, the computers are authenticated to each other. In contrast, if this reconstruction is not achieved, the computer that has sent the encrypted nonce is trying to impersonate the actual sending computer. This way, computers are reliably authenticated to each other.

Digital signatures can also be used by IKE to authenticate computers to each other. This method is similar to the one implemented by reconstructing encrypted nonces. In digital signature authentication, nonces are encrypted using pre-exchanged digital signatures, exchanged, and then reconstructed to obtain the identical nonces.

Sending and the receiving computers can use any of these methods to authenticate each other. Next, they exchange information on the keys that must be used on either computer in combination with algorithms to encrypt, decrypt, and compute ICVs for datagrams. The completion of this process signifies that an SA is completely established on both computers and that the exchange of secured data can begin.

SUMMARY

The vast reach and versatility of the Net has exposed it to a variety of security attacks. These security issues can affect the confidentiality and integrity of the information that is exchanged. In addition, the identity of computers is also impersonated to cause immense damage to organizations. To address the root cause of these security issues, a security framework that implements comprehensive security features for an IP datagram was proposed. This framework, called IPSec, provided security by proposing the addition of new headers, such as AH and ESP, to the existing IP datagram format, establishing security associations between communicating computers, and managing the exchange of encryption or authentication keys between the computers. These measures, when implemented, provided authentication, encryption, and integrity features for each datagram transmitted over the Net.

CHAPTER 23

IP Over Asynchronous Transfer Mode (ATM)

In this chapter

INTRODUCTION TO ASYNCHRONOUS TRANSFER MODE

It is estimated that planet Earth has been in existence for more than 4.5 billion years. When we consider such a vast time span, humankind seems to have inhabited this planet for only a microscopic instant of time. However, within this microscopic instant, humankind has made tremendous advances in the quality of its existence. The technological advances made by humankind is unparalleled to any other inhabitant of this planet, right from the primitive cellular organisms to dinosaurs, when seen from the perspective of the origin of humankind as primitive food gathering communities. When we look at these advancements, we realize that need, want, the desire for achievement, and a constant urge for improvement has played a vital role and continues to drive humankind into higher excellence. For example, although internetworking solutions have enabled organizations to exchange data over long geographical distances, organizations have felt the need for increasing bandwidth capabilities for long distance data transmission.

With increasing business dealings and transactions involving branch offices spread over long distances, organizations realized that their local networks had to be connected with each other over high-speed WAN links. Primarily, organizations aimed at increasing bandwidth capabilities of existing WAN implementations to levels that would match the bandwidths prevalent on the local networks. This need translated into the development of an intermediate mechanism that enabled the integration of WAN's long distance data transmission capabilities and LAN's huge bandwidth capacity. This mechanism, called Asynchronous Transfer Mode (ATM), has its origins in the development of synchronous data transmission mechanisms implemented on telephone networks.

Data units transmitted over telephone networks were dispatched between telephones based on a constant time interval, for example, 10 milliseconds. A typical example of synchronous data transmission is the transfer of data between computer hardware components through a computer bus. In contrast, data units transmitted asynchronously are not related to any time constant, a typical example being data transmission between computers on a local network. One disadvantage exhibited by synchronous data transmission is that data transmission over long distances results in gross under-utilization of expensive network resources.

This is because when computer data is transmitted synchronously over long distances, the transmission exhibits *bursty traffic* behavior. Bursty traffic is a condition where connections could be overloaded with packets at any given point in time and remain idle for an arbitrary period. Apart from the ability to manage bursty traffic conditions, the need for higher WAN bandwidth, and implementing such a bandwidth for inter-computer data transmission contributed to adopting ATM as a common wide area data transmission mechanism.

ATM can be defined as a connection-oriented network that allows multiple computers to access each other simultaneously. However, ATM does not allow a simultaneous broadcast of data from one computer to multiple computers existing on its network. To exemplify an ATM's implementation, compare ATMs to the telephone network that links millions of people all over the world. When you make a call over a landline to another telephone, the connection between the phones is not directly established but is routed through an automated telephone exchange that acts as a connection-oriented linking mechanism between the telephones. In addition, the exchange does not allow you to make simultaneous calls to multiple telephones. Telephone networks and ATMs are classified under a category of networks called Non-Broadcast Multiple Access (NBMA) networks.

In an attempt to integrate the prowess of LANs and WANs, ATM designers have translated the network architecture of a LAN into a WAN implementation. This is evident from the fact that switches form the primary building blocks of an ATM network. ATM switches provide a routing service that is similar to the services provided by routers linking disparate networks. ATM switches are far more powerful than their LAN implementations because of their capability to support data transmission services for an arbitrary number of computers. In addition, fiber optic cables are implemented as the physical communication medium that links computers and ATM switches in addition to providing a switch-to-switch link. To analyze the physical connection existing between a computer and its switch in detail, data is exchanged between the network interface card of a computer and the switch in the form of light. The network interface card is equipped with optical components that convert light to electrical signals and vice versa. At any given point in time, light on an optical fiber can travel in one direction only. Therefore, each connection between computers and a switch provides a pair of optical fibers to enable the simultaneous transmission of light in both directions. Connections existing between computers and a switch can be described as a *User to Network Interface (UNI)*.

CH
23

UNI connections enable communication on a local ATM network. However, if a computer needs to access another computer located on a different ATM network, it must route its connection through its ATM switch, which in turn connects to other switches that lie in the path to the destination ATM network. Such a physical connection existing between switches is called *Network-to-Network Interface (NNI)*. Although multiple switches are involved in a link between computers on remote ATM networks, the actual hardware implementation is abstracted from the computers and an illusionary effect of connecting to a single ATM network is projected to the connection computers. Figure 23.1 shows you the ATM network architecture and its logical projection.

Before delving into the implementation details of an ATM network, let us have a brief look at the benefits and application areas of ATM. One of the primary advantages afforded by an ATM network is its ability to manage bursty traffic where volatile network traffic conditions exist, regardless of the type of data being transmitted. The implementation of a standardized communication mechanism for LANs and WANs is another benefit provided by ATMs.

ATM networks can be implemented on high-speed intercontinental links, such as a T1 link that can transmit data at a bandwidth of 1Gbps. In addition, ATMs are targeted to support bandwidths of much higher capabilities running up to several Gbps. Such high-speed networking environments also need to implement adequate security measures. The inherently simple connection-oriented architecture provided by ATMs help simplify data transmission security apart from other network management services, such as network traffic management and cost estimation.

Figure 23.1
Although computer-to-switch connections can be implemented as UNI connections alone, switch-to-switch connections can be implemented as a UNI or NNI connection.

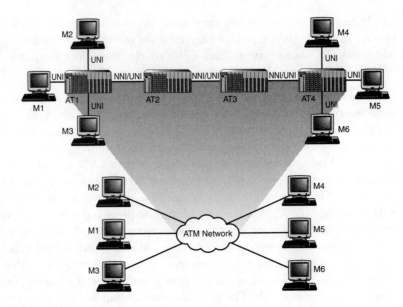

Such benefits propagate ATMs as the prime networking implementation in a variety of application areas. For example, to improve the quality of service offered to clients, Internet service providers have adopted ATMs as the primary networking technology. ATMs are implemented on LANs and virtual private networks that demand a high quality of service for multimedia services, such as video Web casting or voice transmission. In addition, a new type of ATM switch product called Enterprise Network Switch (ENS) has been developed. ATM ENS provides a wide range of services catering to LANs and WANs in addition to its transmission support for a multitude of datatypes.

With the increasing popularity of the Net and the resultant increase in network traffic, a number of backbone service providers, such as frame relays and Internet backbones, are moving away from their ISDN origins and adopting ATMs as their data transmission mechanism. In fact, ATMs are being adopted by its base technology, the telephone networks. This will enhance the transmission efficiency of the existing telephone signal carrier implementations, such as synchronous optical network (SONET). Today ATMs are being implemented by

- Internet service providers
- Corporate intranets
- Universities
- Telephone companies

ATM DATA TRANSMISSION BASICS

Connection-oriented data transmission mechanisms exhibit certain common characteristics. For example, there is always a method of establishing a connection between the communicating computers. In addition, each connection is uniquely identified to prevent the transmission of data through a wrong connection. Typically, data that is transmitted over connection-oriented mechanisms are loaded into a datagram that contains a header, which holds information about the identity of the connection and integrity check measures. The data packet is further encapsulated into its final transmission unit before being sent over the network. On the receiving end, data is unpacked from its encapsulations before being supplied to higher layer protocols or the application involved in the data exchange. Transmission Control Protocol (TCP) is a typical example of such a connection-oriented data transmission mechanism. ATM exhibits similar behavior as well. However, TCP and ATM differ in the way connection-oriented data transmission is implemented. Moreover, TCP and ATM operate from different layers in the TCP/IP reference model. TCP operates from the Transport layer whereas ATM operates from the Network layer.

Сн
23

In contrast to TCP, ATMs do not establish connections through handshake operations. Instead, a connection that is also called a virtual circuit is established between computers by using a telephony technique called *signaling*. In signaling, the switches connecting the computers exchange information to negotiate the process of establishing, maintaining, and terminating a circuit. This signaling mechanism can be manually implemented or managed by software installed on the participating switches.

Note

A *virtual circuit*, also called a *virtual channel connection*, is the basic unit that carries a single stream of cells, in a particular sequence, from user to user. ATMs use virtual circuits with fixed length cells for transporting data. This enables the use of fast hardware switching.

Certain circuits are created to exist over long periods. For example, network links between government agencies need to be established as a permanent circuit that can last for long periods, say over many months or years. ATM provides for implementing such permanent circuits in the form of Permanent Virtual Circuit (PVC). Each PVC contains a set of switches that physically connect the source and the destination computers. Administrators managing the switches need to manually configure information related to the source and the destination endpoints. In addition, information on the next hop switch in the path to the destination computer also needs to be configured. PVCs hold the advantage of incorporating multivendor switches into the circuit because switches involved in the circuit are preconfigured with standard signaling information that overcomes multivendor hardware boundaries. However, PVCs are not suitable for connecting computers that do not exchange datagrams at a certain minimum volume of traffic over long periods. To avoid the under-utilization of ATM network resources, PVCs might need to be terminated or reconfigured, which is an enormous task.

Circuits that can be easily established and reconfigured are best suited for scenarios where the source and the destination computers need to communicate as and when required. Consider the case of an air reservation system that can be used by commuters to book air tickets for traveling to and from a place named A. Although the information on the availability of return tickets from A needs to be determined quickly, it is not necessary to maintain a permanent connection to the computers at A. This is because the airliner might have services located at several destinations. Therefore, a circuit that can be easily established and terminated as and when the need arises is essential for cost-effective ATM networking. Such a circuit can be implemented using Switched Virtual Circuit (SVC) offered by ATM. SVCs use the ATM signaling mechanism to establish and negotiate a connection between the switches involved in the connection.

To better illustrate how SVC works, let us continue with the example of airline reservation. When you need to reserve return tickets from location A at location B, the computer at B establishes an SVC with the computer at A by sending ATM signals to the switches that lie in the path between the communicating computers. ATM signals contain information on the destination computer address and the bandwidth requirements that must be implemented for the efficient transmission of data to the destination computer. First, the ATM switch at location B negotiates with its next hop switch S1, configures S1 with the required communication information, and then makes it a part of the circuit. S1 negotiates with S2 and so on until all switches including the switch at the destination ATM network are added to the switched virtual circuit. After the SVC is established, the computer at location B can communicate with the computer at location A to determine the availability of return tickets from location A. Although the process seems to be time-consuming, all transactions related to establishing and terminating SVCs happen in milliseconds. Figure 23.2 shows you how an SVC is established on an ATM.

Figure 23.2
ATM signaling is used to configure switches that lie in the path between communicating computers when establishing an SVC.

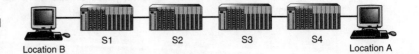

Location B   S1   S2   S3   S4   Location A

Establishing a circuit only completes half of the actual data transmission between ATM-linked computers. Data must go through a process of segmentation and reassembly before being presented to the higher layer protocols. Before going further into the actual process of data transmission, it is important to understand the environment that aids in this process. The data transmission environment implemented on each computer is comprised of three elements: the adaptation layer, cell transport, and optical components. These three elements make up the ATM implementation in the Network interface layer of the TCP/IP reference model. To start with, the encapsulated data supplied by the Internet layer is processed by an adaptation layer for errors and necessary corrections. The ATM Adaptation Layer 5 (AAL5) protocol implements this task.

After processing a datagram supplied by the Internet layer, AAL5 encapsulates the datagram into its packet before transferring the packet to the cell transport element in the ATM implementation. An AAL5 packet provides 65,536 octets of space for the data that is to be encapsulated. In addition, an 8-octet trailer is added to the AAL5 packet. The trailer contains information about the length of the packet and a checksum that provides integrity features for the packet. An 8-bit field called UU and another field of an identical size called CPI are also present in the trailer. Both of these fields do not implement any features and have been preserved for future use. Figure 23.3 shows you how the Adaptation layer is implemented in an ATM.

CH
23

Figure 23.3
Regardless of the size of the final transmission unit in an ATM, AAL5 packets can encapsulate large volumes of data by providing a maximum size of 65,536 octets for its data field.

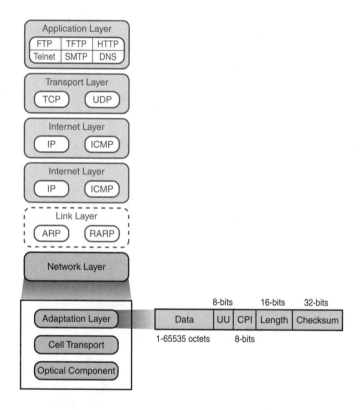

The next element in an ATM data transmission implementation is cell transport. In this phase, AAL5 packets are encapsulated into its final data transmission unit called a *cell*, which is an equivalent of a frame used in TCP/IP data transmission implementations. Each cell is a frame of a fixed sized that is converted into light by the optical component before being transmitted over optic cables. Before moving into the details of a cell format, it is essential to understand that a pair of identity values called Virtual Path Identifier (VPI) and Virtual Circuit Identifier (VCI) uniquely identifies each circuit. This is because each circuit is assigned an identity at this phase of data transmission by specifying the VPI/VCI pair as part of the cell format.

TCP uses endpoints existing at the sending and the receiving computers to uniquely identify a connection where an endpoint is comprised of the IP address/port number pair. In contrast, ATMs do not need to work with IP addresses or ports. Instead, after establishing a circuit, a 24-bit circuit identifier is assigned to the circuit and the destination for each packet is identified based on the 24-bit value. The 24 bits in the circuit identifier are divided into 8 and 16 bits for the VPI and for the VCI, respectively. Multiple computers might need to access different computers on the same ATM network. The VPI value is used to provide a common path to the target ATM network. The VCI value provides a unique identity to the individual computer existing on the same ATM network that is identified by a VPI.

In addition to the VPI and VCI values, a cell header contains fields that help manage flow control, priority, and integrity of the data contained in a cell. Each cell contains only a portion of the actual data packet that must be delivered to the destination. To denote that the last portion of the data is being transmitted from the source, the lower order bit value in the PAYLOAD TYPE cell header field is used as an end marker. Figure 23.4 shows you how a cell header is organized.

Figure 23.4
The fixed size of an ATM cell enables switches to transmit data at a speed that is much higher than routers.

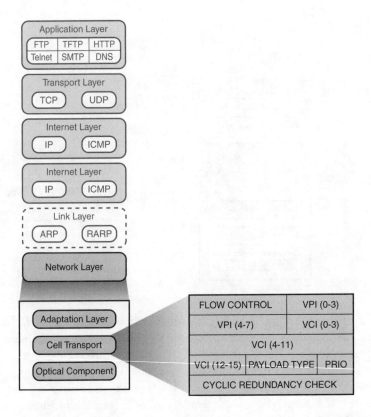

In the final phase of data transmission, cells are converted into light by the optical component and transmitted over the fiber optic cables. AAL5 packets provide capabilities for transmitting large sized packets. However, the fixed size of a cell necessitates data to be divided into multiple units. Each unit is encapsulated into a cell before being transmitted over the ATM network. The PAYLOAD TYPE field in the cell header is used to identify the last unit in the sequence of segmented packets sent over the network. This process, implemented in the Cell Transport element, is called *segmentation*. At the receiving end, the cells containing encapsulated data are cumulated until the last cell arrives from the sending computer, indicated by the PAYLOAD TYPE cell header field. When all cells have been received, the encapsulated content in the cells is unpacked and reconstructed before being supplied to the higher-layer protocols. This reconstruction process is called *reassembly*. The superior rate of data transmission achieved by ATM is possible because of its capability to segment data into fixed sized cells of 53 bytes each, and reassemble the data contained in the cells at the destination computer. The use of fixed sized cells enable the use of hardware switching, which is very fast when compared to software packet switching.

CH
23

IP DATA TRANSMISSION MODELS FOR ATM

With the advent of ATM networking, network designers realized that an integration of existing IP data transmission frameworks with the power of ATMs could provide an answer to the ever-increasing bandwidth and speed requirements of organizations. In an attempt to integrate IP and ATM, data transmission models such as Next Hop Routing Protocol (NHRP) and Private Network to Network Interface (PNNI) have been proposed. In the initial steps towards integrating IP and ATM, RFC 1577 proposed a data transmission model that helps overcome hurdles in integrating the two data transmission models. Although the proposed solutions in RFC 1577 have now been improved and deprecated, the solutions signify the fundamental framework based on which other integration models have been developed. Therefore, RFC 1577 is termed as the Classical IP over ATM model.

CLASSICAL IP OVER ATM

IP-ATM integration posed a number of problems primarily concerned with mapping source and destination computer IP addresses to the physical addresses of the computers. Typically, when a circuit is established between the sending and receiving computer, a physical address is assigned to each computer. It is impossible to generate IP addresses based on these physical addresses because of the prohibitive size of an ATM-assigned physical address. In addition, Address Resolution Protocol (ARP) used by TCP/IP to bind physical and IP addresses cannot be used on ATM networks because broadcasting is not allowed on ATMs.

PVCs and SVCs pose additional address-related problems in the process of IP-ATM integration. The possibility of identifying the destination IP address or the physical address does not exist when PVC is implemented. This is because the PVCs are manually configured and do not require destination IP addresses for data transmission. On SVCs, you need to map the destination IP address with the destination ATM physical address before establishing the SVC. In addition, you need to map the destination IP address to the SVC circuit identifiers. The network component of the destination IP address must be mapped to the VPI and the host ID must be mapped to the VCI for the circuit.

As the first step in overcoming addressing problems, Classical IP over ATM proposed a new networking architecture where the entire logical ATM network has been reorganized into smaller subnets called Logical IP Subnets (LIS). Remember that the logical ATM network is actually a collection of multiple ATM switches with each switch servicing a group of computers. An LIS might contain many such switches and groups of computers. However, from the point of view of IP addressing, each LIS exhibits the behavior of a LAN with a separate IP address prefix for the computers in the LIS. If a computer needs to communicate with another computer located in a different LIS, it needs to use a router servicing its LIS to route datagrams to its target computer.

Now that the computers have been logically organized into separate IP address groups, address resolution can be implemented within the LIS. However, it is important to note that the computers still exist on an NBMA network and cannot use broadcasting to resolve IP or physical addresses. Alternatively, a type of ARP implementation is used on ATM to obtain IP and physical addresses of computers located in the LIS. This type of ARP, known as ATMARP, provides request and response messages to query for IP or physical addresses and to obtain the necessary address in response. To manage address resolution queries, an ATMARP server that holds the IP addresses and physical addresses of all the computers in the LIS is configured. Computers in the LIS can use this server to obtain the IP or physical addresses of other computers located in the LIS.

Before establishing circuits to other computers in the LIS, each computer must establish a circuit with the ATMARP server. When the circuit with the server is established, the server sends an Inverse ATMARP request to the computer. In response, the computer must send an Inverse ATMARP reply containing its IP address and physical address. In this way, the ATMARP server collects address information of all the computers existing on the network and maintains this information in a database. After responding to the ATMARP server, computers can begin the process of establishing circuits with other computers existing in the LIS.

Consider the example of a computer named M1 that must send data to computer M2 through an SVC. M1 uses ATM signaling to establish an SVC with M2. After establishing the SVC, M1 needs to identify the physical address of M2 to map the M2 IP address to its corresponding physical address before transmitting datagrams to M2. M1 obtains the required physical address by sending an ATMARP request containing the IP address of M2 to the ATMARP server. The server performs a lookup in its database. If the server has the physical address corresponding to the target IP address supplied by M1, the server responds with an ATMARP reply containing the required physical address. On the other hand, if the requested physical address is not available, the server responds with a negative ATMARP response.

Consider another address binding scenario where computers X and Y are circuited over PVC. On PVC links, the ATMARP server is of no use because circuited computers do not have any address information about each other. Therefore, X needs to send an Inverse ATMARP request to Y with its own IP and physical address specified in the request. Now, Y responds with its address information by sending an Inverse ATMARP reply to X by using the information supplied to X in its request. In this way, X and Y exchange address information by using Inverse ATMARP messages. Figure 23.5 shows you how a communication mechanism is established on an LIS before implementing the actual datagram transmission.

CH
23

Figure 23.5
Sending computers need to use an ATMARP server to obtain destination physical addresses when communicating over an SVC. When PVC is used for communication, the communicating computers exchange Inverse ATMARP messages to obtain the required addressing information.

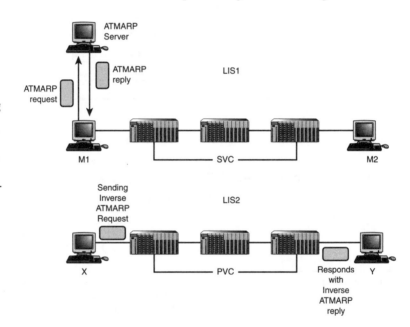

The entire ATMARP address binding feature hinges on the request reply messages. Each message contains information on the length of the addresses in addition to the fields for the IP or physical address. Figure 23.6 shows you how an ATMARP message is organized in addition to the contents of a Length field.

Figure 23.6
In addition to the length of addresses and the actual physical or protocol address, information on the type of the ATMARP message is also specified as part of the message.

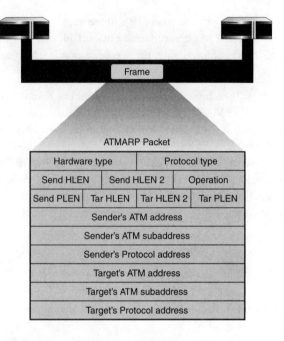

Table 23.1 describes each ATMARP message field in detail.

TABLE 23.1 FIELDS IN AN ATMARP MESSAGE

Field	Description
Hardware Type	Specifies the type of interface that indicates if the message is being sent from an ATM or an Ethernet interface. For example, the decimal value 1 indicates that the message is being sent from an Ethernet interface.
Protocol Type	Specifies the Internet protocol being used for providing the computer address. For example, to specify IP addresses in the message, the hexadecimal value 0x0800 must be specified in this field.
Send Hlen	Specifies the length of the sender's physical address provided in the message.
Send Hlen 2	Specifies the length of the sender's physical subaddress that is indicated in the message.
Operation	Specifies a value that indicates the type of message. For example, the value 1 indicates that the message is an ATMARP request. The value 2 is used to denote an ATMARP reply. The values 8 and 9 are used to indicate Inverse ATMARP request and reply, respectively. An ATMARP negative ACK is indicated by the value 10.
Send Plen	Specifies the length of the sending computer's protocol address provided in the Sender's Protocol address field.

Field	Description
Tar Hlen	Specifies the length of the target computer's physical address provided in the Target's ATM address field.
Tar Hlen 2	Specifies the length of the target computer's physical subaddress provided in the Target ATM subaddress field.
Tar Plen	Specifies the length of the target computer's protocol address provided in the Target's Protocol address field.
Sender's ATM address	Specifies the sending computer's physical address.
Sender's ATM subaddress	Specifies the sending computer's physical subaddress.
Sender's Protocol address	Specifies the sending computer's protocol address. For example, if IP is the protocol indicated in the Protocol type field, this field contains the sender's IP address.
Target's ATM address	Specifies the target computer's physical address.
Target's ATM subaddress	Specifies the target computer's physical subaddress.
Target's Protocol address	Specifies the target computer's protocol address. If IP is the protocol indicated in the Protocol type field, this field contains the target computer's IP address.

TABLE 23.1 CONTINUED

CH
23

ENHANCEMENTS TO THE CLASSICAL IP OVER ATM MODEL

Although Classical IP over ATM initiated the IP-ATM integration process, some issues were left unaddressed by the model. For example, the restriction on direct communication between computers located on different logical IP subnets introduced the problem of an extra hop. This extra hop occurs when a datagram destined for a computer located on an external LIS needs to be routed through the LIS router that links the logical IP subnets. Moreover, the IP routers linking logical IP subnets might implement inefficient route determination decisions. This is because when IP routers are used to route datagrams on an ATM network, the router does not determine routes based on the availability of switches. Instead, routes are determined based on common IP routing algorithms, such as RIP or OSPF. To resolve such issues, Next Hop Routing Protocol (NHRP) and Private Network to Network Interface (PNNI) have been proposed as enhancements to the Classical IP over ATM integration model.

In the NHRP integration model, an important enhancement is introduced in the logical IP subnet architecture by implementing Local Address Groups (LAGs) instead of logical IP subnets. The LAG architecture does not restrict communication between computers located on different LAGs. In fact, LAGs enable computers located on non-NBMA (non-broadcast, multiple access) networks to communicate with computers located in an LAG. Primarily, the difference between LIS and LAG is in the method of forwarding datagrams between computers located on different address groups.

An LIS router is required to act as an intermediary forwarding mechanism for computers located in different logical IP subnets to communicate with each other. In contrast, computers located on different LAGs can establish direct communication with each other. To implement this feature, Next Hop Server (NHS) must be configured on each LAG. When a computer needs to resolve the IP address of its target computer, it sends an NHRP resolution request packet to obtain the resolved IP address of the destination computer. The server responds with an NHRP resolution reply packet containing information about the requested resolved destination IP address that is used by the computer to send the datagram. Although this does not make the extra hop required for transmitting a datagram redundant, it is important to note that the only extra hop required in this model is when a resolved IP address is requested and replied. The datagram is transmitted directly to the destination computer and does not undergo an extra hop through a linking router.

Routing decisions play a vital role in the efficient transmission of datagrams. A typical IP router implementing routing protocols does not consider the quality of service to be extracted from a path while determining the best possible route for a datagram. To overcome this deficiency, a routing protocol that combines the features of link state protocols and ATM signaling features can be implemented for the efficient routing of datagrams. This protocol, called Private Network to Network Interface (PNNI), segments an ATM network into peer groups with a computer in each group acting as the peer group leader (PGL).

In addition to the information on the availability of computers in a peer group, the quality of service information, such as cell rate and cell delay, is exchanged as PNNI (Private Network to Network Interface) Topology State Packets (PTSP) between peer group leaders. PTSPs are analogous to link state advertisements implemented by OSPF protocols. Peer group leaders use PTSPs to generate a map of the best possible routes to be used by a datagram from any source to a destination. This information is also propagated by PGLs to the computers existing in its peer group. In this way, all computers have the optimum route map estimated by the PGL.

It is important to note that in addition to computers, each peer group also contains switches, which receive the optimum route map propagated by its PGL. When a computer needs to establish an SVC to another computer on the ATM network, it signals its switch to establish the SVC to the destination computer. The switch uses the optimum route map to devise a summary of the route map in the form of Designated Transit List (DTL). Based on the optimum routing information provided in the DTL, the switch determines the best possible next hop switch that must be signaled. In this way, each switch signals its next hop based on its DTL and establishes the best possible SVC between the sending and receiving computers.

As an extension to PNNI, Integrated Private Network to Network Interface (IPNNI) was developed to further the efficient routing mechanisms for routing datagrams across non-NBMA networks from an NBMA network. IPNNI proposes to transmit the optimum route map devised by a PNNI-enabled router to non-NBMA network routers. In this way, a non-NBMA router can determine the best possible route for datagrams that are forwarded from its network to an NBMA network. Similarly, when routing information is obtained from the non-NBMA router, an IPNNI router can determine the best possible route for datagrams being transmitted from its network over the non-NBMA network.

SUMMARY

The need for higher bandwidths in long distance data transmission resulted in integrating the capabilities of LANs and WANs by creating a powerful data transmission mechanism called ATM. ATM networks are comprised of a number of switches that link computers to each other. However, a collection of ATM switches projects the illusion of one big ATM network in operation. ATM data transmission is similar to any other connection-oriented data transmission mechanism where a uniquely identifiable link needs to be established between communicating computers and each data unit is encapsulated into a final transmission unit. ATMs link computers by implementing PVCs or SVCs. Each PVC or SVC is uniquely identified by means of a VPI/VCI pair. This information is present in the final ATM data transmission unit called a cell.

To integrate the power of ATMs with the existing IP data transmission infrastructure, a number of IP over ATM models were proposed. The integration process started with the Classical IP over ATM model. The NHRP and PNNI models further enhance this model.

CH
23

CHAPTER 24

VOICE OVER IP

In this chapter

THE NEED FOR VOICE OVER IP

To understand the importance of Internet Protocol (IP), you must first consider two essential aspects of telephony. For the more than one-hundred years since Alexander Graham Bell called out to his assistant and discovered his invention worked, people have become accustomed to communicating locally and globally through traditional means. The *de facto* technology that enables people to "reach out and touch someone" through a standard telephone is a circuit-switched system called Public Switched Telephone Network (PSTN). As happens easily with inventions of convenience, our culture pretty much thought that this was the only means of getting the job done. Along came the age of computers and the advancements that created intranets and the Internet technologies. Here, again, came a communications revolution.

Improvements and advances in the field revealed that the existing internetworks and intranets could be used as a substitute for the telephone system. The technology that applies the existing networks to work as a telephone network is called Internet Protocol (IP). An IP-based network—IP telephony—encompasses the hardware, software, and standards that are required for transferring voice over an internetwork.

The benefits have been realized at once. Organizations can reduce the costs on long distance calls because voice can be routed through the existing framework of routers in an internetwork. IP telephony was immediately popular with home PC users, who could now make use of a simple Internet connection to communicate with others at any place on the globe. IP telephony has been enhanced to transfer fax messages and video files and also enable the transmission of multimedia messages. One subset of IP telephony that deals with the transmission of voice over an IP-based network is known as Voice Over IP (VoIP). Other subsets of IP telephony include the transfer of video files, called Video Over IP and, a similar subset for sending faxes, called Fax over IP (FoIP).

Note

Other technologies used for transmitting voice include Integrated Services Digital Network (ISDN) and cellular services.

Because VoIP is a packet-switched network, it offers a few advantages compared to the earlier, circuit-switched connections used in the PSTN. In a packet-switched network, data packets can be transferred across different routes. However, in the case of a circuit-switched network, data packets can be transferred only through a predetermined path. Different applications can share the available bandwidth in packet-switched networks. Sharing the resources also helps to reduce the operation costs. In a circuit-switched network, once a connection is established, the resources in the connection cannot be used for other calls until the connection is released.

A few advantages of implementing VoIP are as follows:

- VoIP helps an organization to reduce the costs that are incurred for long distance calls.

- VoIP makes network management easier. Administering a separate infrastructure for voice transmission and transferring data files involves excess administrative overhead. By implementing VoIP, the infrastructure for the transmission of data and voice are combined. Studies reveal that 70% of incurred costs are used for administering the network. The integration of the infrastructure helps standardize the procedure for communication and also helps reduce the expense of the equipment that needs to be purchased.

- VoIP supports multimedia applications, which cannot be implemented by the conventional telephone system.

- Businesses can also implement videoconferences to reduce travel costs.

- VoIP can also be used to provide trunking facilities to establish a path between the switches in a head office and the branch offices of an organization. The trunk can be used to establish a voice intranet comprising of networks in the branch offices and the head office.

- Businesses can also improve the way their call centers are functioning by integrating voice into the applications that are being used.

Note

Voice can also be transmitted over a frame-relay network and is referred to as Voice Over Frame Relay Networks. Frame relay is a protocol that is based on the packet-switching technology like an IP-based network. The protocol can be described as one of the early attempts in improving wide area data transmission quality. Developed as an improvement to an earlier packet-switching technology called X.25, frame relays resolved problems that occurred in copper wire–based analog transmission by adopting optical communication over fiber optic cables. Today, Asynchronous Transfer Mode (ATM) has replaced frame relays as the premier WAN transmission mechanism.

Any organizational decision to implement VoIP also depends on the requirements that are specific to the organization. Implementing VoIP may not prove to be cost-effective to all the organizations. There are a few limitations that need to be considered before implementing VoIP. The limitations are as follows:

- The services that are provided by VoIP do not guarantee Quality of Service (QoS) to the users on the network. Therefore, the quality of output that is provided by VoIP is not as good as the services provided by the PSTN. Until the VoIP service quality matches the quality provided by the PSTN, the new system and the old system continue to exist.

- Both VoIP and PSTN are dissimilar in terms of signaling and the media translation used. To bridge the differences between the two networks, devices called gatekeepers and gateways must be used.

CH
24

- VoIP is still an emerging technology. Standards required for implementing VoIP are continuously evolving. The interpretation of standards among the different vendors of VoIP products has problems that lead to differences in the implementation of standards.

Note

Quality of Service (QoS) defines a few parameters by which the quality of a network can be measured. In the case of a network that implements VoIP, a technique that minimizes delay and maximizes throughput can be used to measure the quality of service provided by the network. If a network does not control the delay in voice transmission, the quality of voice will be affected and lead to customer dissatisfaction.

ROLE OF IP IN TRANSMISSION OF VOICE FILES

Audio files can be transmitted over an IP network just as a simple data file can. The audio file can be divided into many fragments and routed across the network. However, before an audio file can be transmitted over a network, it needs to be converted to digital signals. In other words, the audio that needs to be transferred must be digitized. The receiver must perform the reverse process at its end. The process of converting analog signals to digital signals and vice versa is performed by a device called codec (coder/decoder).

Note

The conventional telephone system uses Pulse Code Modulation (PCM) for conversion between analog and digital signals.

The quality of the voice that is transmitted over a network depends on three factors: delay, jitter, and data loss. The length of the route that is taken by the data packet affects delay. The delay in data transmission depends on the number of routers that need to be traversed by the data packet before reaching its destination. Each router that must be traversed is called a *hop*. The greater the number of hops, the longer the delay. Delay in data transmission is also dependent on the bandwidth available on the network. For example, if the route to be taken by the audio supports a low bandwidth, the audio file needs to be divided into smaller groups of information and transmitted. The low availability of bandwidth in the route may introduce a delay in the process.

There are situations in which audio files need to be transferred with minimal delay. Data that needs to be transferred without any delay is called real-time data. If the data that needs to be transferred is real-time data, the normal process of transferring a data file by using an IP-based network will not suffice. In any normal data transfer process that uses IP, the components of a file can take different routes and reach the destination in any odd order. However, the order of the real-time data packets must not be disturbed when an audio file is transferred.

The second important factor that can affect the quality of voice transmitted over a network is called jitter. Jitter is caused by differences in the data transmission timing or amplitude that is caused during data transmission. The data packets might follow different routes across the network to reach the destination. The variation in delay experienced by the packets leads to delay jitters. The receiver of the data packets plays a vital role in handling delay jitters during data transmission.

Finally, loss of data packets is also an important factor that affects data transmission. Because fragments of a datagram can reach the destination in a different order from how it began, the data can travel across different routes to the destination. During this process, there are chances of a fragment getting lost due to problems in a specific route. In addition, if the bandwidth available on the network is low, the audio file might have to be divided into more packets and sent across the network. A route with a low bandwidth has a greater risk of data loss compared to networks with a higher bandwidth.

THE ROLE OF THE RECEIVER IN MINIMIZING DELAY AND JITTER

CH
24

The receiving computer might receive the data packets in any order, and the data packets might not reach the destination on time. Therefore, if the receiver starts playing back the signals as soon as they arrive, the quality of voice will be affected. To control this problem, the receiver does not play back the signals as soon as they arrive. Instead, the signals are stored in a buffer called the *playback buffer*. The signals are stored in the buffer until a threshold value is reached.

After the threshold value is reached, the receiver starts playing back the signals. At any point in time, a constant time difference is maintained between the signals to minimize the difference in the delay caused during data transmission. Although this method can be used for compensating for jitter, it cannot be used to handle the loss of datagrams. Moreover, lost datagrams if retransmitted would arrive too late. A solution to this problem is to retransmit the redundant information. However, retransmission of redundant information would increase the bandwidth requirements. An important point to be remembered is that the threshold value must be set such that the jitter is very negligible. The threshold value must be decided based on the speed and bandwidth of the network.

Note

The way in which the delay is minimized is dependent on the application that is used for data transmission.

STANDARDS AND PROTOCOLS USED TO IMPLEMENT VoIP

In spite of providing a cost-effective solution to transfer voice over a network, the quality of output that is provided by VoIP is not as good as that provided by the PSTN. Until the quality of output provided by VoIP is as good as that provided by the conventional system, VoIP must coexist with the old system. PSTN and the network that uses VoIP have a few differences in the way voice data is transmitted over the network. Devices such as voice gateways and gatekeepers are used to bridge the variations in standards in VoIP and the system that uses the PSTN.

The first set of standards that was introduced for transmitting voice were the H.323 specifications. In November 1997, H.323 standards were introduced by the International Telecommunication Union (ITU) for transmission of voice over a local area network. The H.323 specifications are a group of protocols and standards that are used for transferring voice traffic over a network. The H.323 standards are commonly referred to as an umbrella recommendation for the transmission of multimedia files over a network. The specifications that are included in H.323 are applicable for voice transmission over packet-switched networks, such as an IP-based network and a frame-relay network. Enhancements have been made to the specifications to enable the transmission of voice over an internetwork.

The H.323 specifications define a few components that play an active role in voice data transmission. They are terminals, gateways, gatekeepers, and multipoint control units.

A terminal can be a computer that can send or receive audio messages. These components are described as the client endpoints on the LAN, which provides real-time, two-way communications with different hosts. H.323 terminal can be either implemented as software that executes on a Personal Computer (PC) or on a workstation. It can also exist as a hardware device, such as IP-phones.

Gateways are used to bridge the gap in the difference in standards that exists between the Internet and the PSTN. Gatekeepers are used to control the transmission of the message to the terminals. Before transmitting the data packets, the gatekeepers check the load on the network and then enable the transmission of data. They act as the central point of communication for all calls within a zone and provide call control services to all the registered end points. The collection of all terminals, gateways, and multipoint control units that are managed by a single gatekeeper is known as an *H.323 zone*. Several IP subnets that are connected by routers can be a part of an IP zone. Gatekeepers perform two functions, address translation and bandwidth management. Address translation refers to the process of translating the LAN aliases or phone numbers of the terminals and gateways to IP addresses. Multipoint Control Units provide support for conferences between three or more H.323 terminals.

REAL-TIME TRANSPORT PROTOCOL

As stated earlier, you cannot use IP to transfer real-time audio files over a network. Although a playback buffer could be used to minimize delay, this method cannot be used to compensate for data loss. Moreover, IP cannot transfer and sequence audio from multiple sources and then play them back to the destination. Real-time Transport Protocol (RTP), along with a few other standards, is used for transmitting real-time voice over on an IP-based network. RTP provides an end-to-end delivery system for transferring voice messages across computers. RTP is mainly implemented for multimedia applications, such as audio-conferencing and video conferencing.

RTP is considered an application service that relies on User Datagram Protocol (UDP) in the Transport layer to transfer messages (see Figure 24.1). RTP Control Protocol (RTCP) is used for monitoring the quality of service that is offered by RTP. RTCP also controls the transmission of RTP messages. Like RTP messages, these RTCP messages are also encapsulated in a UDP datagram and then routed over the network.

Note

RTP can be used to unicast as well as multicast voice messages. However, RTP is most commonly used for multicasting messages over a network.

Note

The UDP checksum is used for ensuring the integrity of RTP messages that are transferred over a network.

Figure 24.1
RTP messages are encapsulated in an UDP datagram and sent across a network.

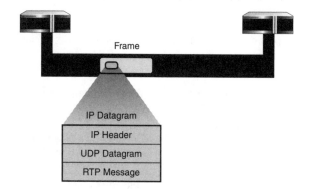

CH
24

Before understanding the fields in an RTP message, you first need to understand a few components that are required in the transmission of voice messages. Because an RTP message can be used for audio conferencing as well as video conferencing, the data that can be transmitted in an RTP message can be an audio or video file. The type of data that is transmitted by an RTP message is called the *payload type*. For example, the Joint Photographers Expert Group (JPEG) format is one of the standard payload types that is supported by RTP.

In the case of audio conferencing, users work from networks with dissimilar architectures. Dissimilarities could be caused by varying network speeds, different bandwidth, and so on. In this case, there needs to be a component, which will ensure that the quality of the audio that is transmitted is not affected by the differences. For example, if the sender of the audio file is on a low-speed network and the receiver is on a high-speed network, a component called the mixer reconstructs the audio packets to transfer them over the high-speed network. Mixers take streams of data, mix them appropriately, and output the combined stream to the network. The stream that is created by the mixer will be compatible with the network through which it needs to pass.

In the case of networks that do not accept multicast messages because of security measures on the network, components called translators can be used to change multicast addresses to addresses that are understandable by the computers on the local network. Apart from address translation, these components also take care of handling streams of data from networks with dissimilar bandwidths. Translators take streams of data and change their format according to the required bandwidth, and then transmit the data. Like other protocols, RTP messages have a fixed format in which they are transmitted over a network. Figure 24.2 shows you how the fields in an RTP message are organized.

Figure 24.2
The RTP message contains fields that help in the transmission of real-time voice messages.

RTP Message Format

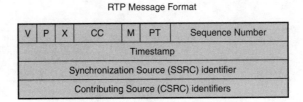

The fields that are a part of the RTP message and a description of each one of them is provided in Table 24.1.

TABLE 24.1   FIELDS IN AN RTP HEADER AND THEIR DESCRIPTIONS

Field Name	Size	Description
Version (V)	2 bits	Identifies the version of the Real-time Transfer Protocol that is used. The current version that is used is version 2.
Padding (P)	1 bit	Identifies whether the payload that is being transmitted contains padding in it. Padding is introduced in the payload because the encryption algorithms that are applied to the messages work on fixed blocks of data. For example, if the encryption can work only on blocks of 4 bytes and if the payload contains a block of data that is less than 4 bytes in size, extra spaces are appended to the block to make the size of the block 4 bytes.
Extension (X)	1 bit	Identifies whether additional header information is present in the RTP message. This field is used when the RTP message is used to carry a payload type that is not a part of the standard payload types supported by RTP.
CSRC Count (CC)	4 bits	Identifies the number of CSRC identifiers that follow in the RTP message.
M	1 bit	Identifies the end of a video frame if the payload is a video file. The interpretation of this field is dependent on the payload type that is carried by the message type.

TABLE 24.1   CONTINUED

Field Name	Size	Description
Payload Type (PT)	7 bits	Identifies the type of data that is being transported by the RTP message. Audio and video files are common payload types that can be transmitted through an RTP message.
Sequence Number	16 bits	Every data packet that is sent is uniquely identified by a 16-bit number called the sequence number. The sequence number that is generated for the first packet is a random number that is incremented by 1 for the subsequent packets.
Timestamp	32 bits	Identifies the time at which the data packet was generated. This field is used to calculate the values for the jitter and time delay. Data packets that were generated simultaneously would have the same timestamp value.
Synchronization Source Identifier (SSRC)	32 bits	Identifies the source of the data packets. The SSRC identifier is used by the receiver to reassemble the data packets that originate from the same source. All data packets that originate from the same source for a particular session must have the same value for the SSRC field.
Contributing Source (CSRC) identifiers	Variable	Identifies a list of sources from which audio and video are received. For example, if a videoconference is to be multicasted, voice can be received from more than one source. The list of CSRC identifiers along with the sequence number can be used by the receiver to synchronize data transmission.

CH
24

SUMMARY

IP telephony is a technology that enables the existing intranets and internetworks to be used as a substitute for a traditional telephone system such as the Public Switched Telephone System (PSTN). One of the subsets of IP telephony that is used for transferring voice over an IP-based network is called Voice Over Internet Protocol (VoIP). Sending and receiving voice communications over an IP-based network is less expensive in many ways compared to the costs incurred on the same in PSTN. Audio files can be transmitted over an IP-based network just like any other data file.

The first set of standards that were introduced for transmitting voice were the H.323 specifications. The H.323 specifications are a group of protocols and standards that are used for transferring voice traffic over a network. The specifications define a few components such as terminals and gatekeepers to play active roles in voice data transmission.

IP cannot be used to transfer real-time voice files, however, because IP is an unreliable and best-effort delivery system. To enable the transport of real-time voice messages over an IP-based network, Real-time Transport Protocol (RTP) is used. RTP along with Real-time Control Protocol streamlines the transmission of real-time messages over an IP-based network.

CHAPTER 25

MOBILE IP

In this chapter

AN INTRODUCTION TO IP MOBILITY

The Information Age has redefined the way we live and work in many ways. The proliferation of computers, internetworks, and computer-enabled services offered over internetworks has provided an unprecedented level of flexibility and ease in many facets of our lives. For example, you need not leave home for a long period by using the Net to work, communicate with friends, pay bills, or order food. An inverse of this scenario is also possible when you need to access e-mail or other services available on the Net when you are on a short business trip. In such scenarios, it is essential to use mobile devices, such as notebooks, laptops, or personal digital assistants (PDAs) such as palmtops to connect to your mailbox or obtain information from the PC at home or the office network.

The widespread reach of internetworks has enabled global connectivity. However, to use its reach optimally, mobile computer devices must reconfigure their IP addresses constantly. The impossibility of this requirement has resulted in the development of an extension to the existing IP implementation that can enable mobile devices to communicate from a temporary location at any point in time. This extension, called mobile IP, has added "mobility" to the existing connectivity features provided by TCP/IP in general and IP in particular. One important fact to remember is that in mobile networking, computing activities are not disrupted when the user changes the computer's point of attachment to the Internet. Instead, the required reconnection occurs automatically and noninteractively. Therefore, existing applications can resume data exchange when the user reconnects.

There are instances when your favorite bookstore or department store shifts to a new location and posts a signboard at the old location with the address of the new location. Sometimes, while visiting your favorite Web site, there might be a message redirecting you to a new URL. Mobile IP uses a concept that is similar to these redirection methods to provide mobility to IP addresses used on mobile devices.

Take a scenario in which a business consultant needs to work onsite with the client and service different clients on a project-to-project basis. The consultant might need to relocate to a different client site every couple of months or so and need a laptop to communicate with the company head office and other external networks from the current client location. To enable IP mobility, the head office, client, and external networks are classified into home network, foreign, and destination networks, respectively. However, the IP address assigned to the office PC is a permanent IP address that does not relocate when the consultant works with different clients. On the other hand, temporary IP addresses need to be allocated to the consultant's mobile device each time the consultant is relocated to different client locations. This technique forms the crux in implementing mobility to the existing IP address scheme. The higher level TCP protocol provided only the permanent IP address, and hence transparent mobility is ensured.

Each home network provides a router called a *home agent*, which acts as a "signboard" for all datagrams addressed to the permanent IP address. Correspondingly, a mobility-enabled foreign network provides a foreign agent to obtain incoming datagrams meant for the mobile device from the home agent. In addition, the foreign agent communicates the new

IP address of the mobile device to the home agent. Each time a destination computer needs to send datagrams to the mobile device, the datagrams are directed to the home agent, which redirects the datagram to the foreign agent, which in turn delivers the datagram to the correct mobile device. When the mobile device needs to send datagrams to the destination computer, the foreign agent acts like any normal router and routes the datagrams directly to the destination computer. Figure 25.1 shows you how mobile IP provides data exchange features for a mobile device.

Figure 25.1
The mobile device can communicate directly with any destination computer through the foreign agent but needs to wait for replies to be routed through the home agent and then through the foreign agent.

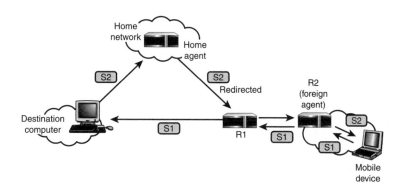

If you observe the figure, you can see that the exchange of communication between a mobile device and a destination computer forms a triangular path. This formation, called *triangular forwarding*, causes excessive overheads while implementing mobile communication. This is because destination computers that are located close to the foreign networks also need to take a circuitous path to send replies to the mobile device. Although solutions to this problem are not available in the IPv4 implementation of Mobile IP, Mobile IPv6 provides answers in the form of a technique called *route optimization*. You will learn more about later in the chapter.

CH
25

Although triangle forwarding adds to data transmission overheads, it is essential to implement the communication framework offered by mobile IP when you need to relocate and stay in a new location for a considerable period. Before moving into the intricacies of how this framework can be established, it is important to understand how the IP addresses acquire mobility. To continue with our "mobile" consultant scenario, remember that the mobile device used by the consultant must be assigned a temporary IP address called the care-of address. When the consultant is relocated to a new location, the first step in enabling mobility is to acquire an identity for the mobile device in the form of a care-of address. Mobile devices can communicate directly with their home agent if the appropriate mobility software is installed on the device. In such cases, the mobile device obtains the care-of address from a DHCP server located on the foreign network. Next, the mobile device registers its new identity by informing its home agent that it has acquired a new care-of address and instructs the home agent to redirect the incoming datagrams to this address. Addresses registered in this way are called *co-located care-of addresses*.

Typically, mobile devices use the foreign agent provided by the foreign network to communicate with its home agent. Consider a scenario where the mobile device used by the consultant does not run mobility software and the client site provides a foreign agent. As a first step, the mobile device needs to identify the foreign agent that services the client network through a process called *agent discovery*. Next, the mobile device needs to obtain a care-of address from its foreign agent. Finally, the mobile device needs to register this care-of address with the home agent by forwarding the registration request through the foreign agent. Care-of addresses registered in this manner are called *foreign agent care-of addresses*. When the agent discovery and care-of address registration process is complete, the consultant can start using the mobile IP communication framework to communicate with any destination computer.

When the mobile device returns to its home network or moves to a different foreign network, the device must communicate with its home agent to deregister its care-of address. Agent discovery and care-of address registration and deregistration processes form an important component in the entire mobile IP communication framework. You will learn more about these processes in the following sections. Before moving on, let us have a brief overview on the advantages offered by mobile IP.

One of the most important advantages offered by mobile IP is its ability to implement IP mobility without modifying the existing IP addressing scheme. In addition, mobile IP can support mobile computing between an arbitrary number of computers existing on internetworks in general and the Internet in particular. The redirection mechanism implemented by a home agent and the foreign agent encapsulates any relocation of the mobile device from connections existing between your computer in the home network and the destination computers. In addition to the circuitous routing involved in mobile IP, mobility-enabling software can be described as the only overhead that might be required for implementing IP mobility. If the foreign network offers mobile IP computing services, mobility software is not required. Today, a number of business organizations, libraries, hospitals, airports, and hotels provide mobile networking support for clients who need to access e-mail or files stored on their home networks.

In addition to mobile data transmission services, mobile IP also implements datagram authentication to ensure integrity and authenticity of data contained in the datagrams. The home agent must be certain that the registration originated from the mobile device and not from other malicious mobile devices impersonating the mobile device. A malicious mobile device can alter the routing table in the home agent with erroneous care-of address information. If the routing table is modified, all incoming datagrams destined to the mobile device will never reach the device.

To implement authentication, each mobile device and the home agent must share a security association. In addition, the computers must be able to use the Message Digest 5 (MD5) algorithm with 128-bit encryption keys to create unforgeable digital signatures for registration requests. The signature is computed by performing MD5's one-way hash algorithm over the data contained in the registration message header and the extensions that precede the signature. When a home agent receives datagrams from a mobile device, it must be able to reconstruct the signature from the authentication information present in the registration message header. If the home agent is not able to reconstruct the signature, the datagram might have originated from an unauthorized mobile device. Therefore, the datagram will be discarded. In this way, authentication security features are implemented on the mobile IP communication framework.

AGENT DISCOVERY PROCESS

One of the very first steps that must be undertaken by a mobile device is to determine its home or foreign agent through the process of agent discovery. The home or foreign agent, collectively called mobility agents, actually initiates the process by broadcasting advertisement messages. The mobile device uses these advertisements to determine its current location and identify the mobility agents. The mobile device can also inform mobility agents about its presence by transmitting solicitation messages. To achieve these presence propagation scenarios, mobile IP uses the ICMP router advertisement and solicitation messages by adding extension fields, collectively called *mobility agent advertisement extension*, to the existing advertisement or the solicitation message format.

Before delving into the details of the advertisement extension format, it is important to know that the values specified in a typical ICMP router advertisement or solicitation message are modified. Table 25.1 describes the modifications implemented in the IP and ICMP segments in an ICMP router advertisement or solicitation message.

CH
25

TABLE 25.1   MODIFIED IP AND ICMP FIELDS IN AN ICMP ROUTER DISCOVERY MESSAGE WHEN USED FOR AGENT ADVERTISEMENTS

Field	Description
TTL	Specified with the value 1. This field is specified in the IP datagram of an advertisement message.
Destination Addresses	Specifies the target addresses to which the message must be transmitted. This IP field must be specified with the value 224.0.0.1 to indicate that all computers on the network are targeted. The value 255.255.255.255 indicates that a very limited number of computers are targeted for advertisement or solicitation.
Code	Specifies a value to indicate the routing preferences of a router. This ICMP field can be specified with the value 0 to indicate that the agent advertising the message can provide routing services as well for its network. The value 16 specified in this field indicates that the agent does not act as a router for its network. Foreign agents cannot specify this value in an Advertisement message because the agent must act as the primary router for mobile nodes.
Lifetime	Specifies a time value that indicates the validity time for the advertisement if any other advertisement is not transmitted. This field is an ICMP message field.

TABLE 25.1   CONTINUED

Field	Description
Router Address(es)	Specifies an address or multiple addresses that indicate the identity of the routers present on the mobility agent's network. This field is an ICMP message field.
Num Addresses	Specifies the number of router addresses that are specified in the Router Address ICMP field. This field is an ICMP message field.

In addition to these vital changes in the contents of a typical ICMP router advertisement message, the mobility agent extension is specified as part of an agent discovery message. Figure 25.2 shows you the format of a mobility agent advertisement extension in the advertisement message sent by a foreign agent.

Figure 25.2
A home agent and a foreign agent can simultaneously transmit the router advertisement message with the mobility agent advertisement extension because mobile devices might choose a co-located care-of address or foreign agent care-of address.

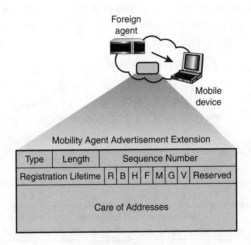

Table 25.2 describes the fields in the mobility agent advertisement extensions.

TABLE 25.2   FIELDS IN A MOBILITY AGENT ADVERTISEMENT EXTENSION

Fields	Description
Type	Specifies the type of the ICMP message. To indicate that the message is an agent advertisement message, the value 16 is specified in this field.
Length	Specifies the length of the extension in terms of octets. The Type and the Length fields are excluded from the length value calculation.
Sequence Number	Specifies a number that acts as an incremental counter referring to the number of messages that were sent to the agent. This field enables mobile devices to identify if any advertisement message was lost.

TABLE 25.2   CONTINUED

Fields	Description
Registration Lifetime	Specifies a time value in seconds that indicates the time limit within which a mobile device can send registration requests.
Code bits	Specifies code bits that are used by the advertisement to indicate various agent preferences. For example, R indicates that the agent does not allow the implementation of co-located care-of addresses on a mobile device. Typically, the code bit R is implemented on advertisements sent from a foreign agent. Code bit B indicates that the agent is currently busy and is unable to accept registration requests. Code bit H indicates that a home agent has transmitted the advertisement. Foreign agents are indicated by specifying the code bit F. Code bit M indicates that the agent implements a minimum level of tunneling security. Code bit G indicates that a type of encapsulation called GRE encapsulation is being implemented by the agent. Code bit V is specified to indicate that the agent implements the Van Jacobson header compression technique for data transmission with a mobile device.
Reserved	Specifies the value 0 and is a field reserved for future use.
Care-of addresses	Specifies care-of addresses that can be used by the mobile device. If the F code bit is set, a minimum of one care-of address must be specified in the advertisement.

The agent discovery messages also contain a prefix-length extension in addition to the mobility agent advertisement extension. Prefix-length extensions are used to indicate the network prefix of the network where the agent is located. Mobile devices use this extension to identify whether it is located on the home network or on a foreign network. The extension contains fields such as Type, Length, and Prefix Length. The following list describes each prefix-length extension field.

- Type—Specifies the type of the extension. The value 19 is used to indicate that the extension is a prefix-length extension.

- Length—Specifies the length of the prefix-length extension. A value identical to the one specified in the Num Address field of the ICMP Router Advertisement field is specified in this field.

- Prefix-Length—Specifies a number that represents the leading bits of an agent's network prefix.

An additional one-byte padding is also provided as an extension for increasing the size of the advertisement to an even size. A typical example for implementing this extension is to maintain the specified MTU size for all datagrams sent over a network.

CH

25

Registering Care-of Addresses

One of the vital steps that complete the mobile IP framework implementation is the registration process where the mobile device must register its new care-of address with the home agent. This step is analogous to specifying the new address on the "signboard." When a mobile device returns to its home network, the device must deregister its care-of address by instructing its home agent to implement the deregistration process. There are different methods that must be implemented to register a mobile device's care-of address. For example, if the mobile device needs to register a co-located care-of address, it can directly communicate with its home agent to register the address. However, there is an exception to this registration process. After registering a co-located care-of address, if the mobile device receives an agent advertisement with the R bit set on, the mobile device must repeat the registration process through the foreign agent. Mobile devices that need to register a foreign agent care-of address can implement the process through its foreign agent.

The registration process is implemented by exchanging registration request and reply messages. A mobile device that needs to register its care-of address must send a registration request to its home agent directly or through its foreign agent. After the home agent records the new care-of address for the mobile device, the agent responds with a reply message. The mode of reply can be direct or through a foreign agent based on the type of care-of address registered by the mobile device. A registration request message contains fields, such as Type, Code bits, Lifetime, and so on. Figure 25.3 shows you how the registration request message is organized.

Figure 25.3
Registration requests can be communicated directly to the home agent or can be transmitted through the foreign agent based on the type of care-of address being implemented on the mobile device.

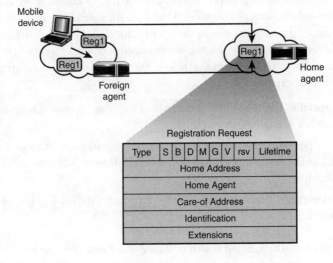

Table 25.3 describes each registration request field in detail.

TABLE 25.3   FIELDS IN A REGISTRATION REQUEST MESSAGE

Fields	Description
Type	Specifies the type of the registration message. The value 1 indicates that the message is a registration request message.
Code bit	Specifies a code bit that defines the purpose or the characteristic of the request message. For example, the code bit S indicates that the request is an instruction to the home agent to use the existing care-of address for its new location. The code bit B indicates that the mobile agent needs to receive all messages that are broadcast on the home network. Mobile devices that use co-located care-of addresses need to set the D bit to indicate that the device will handle encapsulation and decapsulation of datagram on its own. To indicate that the home agent must implement a minimum level of encapsulation, the mobile device sets the M bit in the request message. The G bit is set in the Code bit field if the mobile device needs to request the agent to implement the GRE encapsulation technique while transmitting datagrams. The Van Jacobson header compression technique can be activated on the home agent when the mobile device sets the V bit. The rsv bit is reserved for future use and is typically assigned the value 0.
Lifetime	Specifies the validity period for the registration. To deregister a care-of address, this field value is set to 0.
Home Address	Specifies the IP address of the mobile device.
Home Agent	Specifies the IP address of the targeted home agent.
Care-of Address	Specifies the care-of address being registered by the mobile device.
Identification	Specifies a 64-bit number that is used to uniquely identify a registration request and match the request with the corresponding reply to the request.
Extensions	Specifies extensions to the request message. Extensions include authentication fields for authenticating mobile device-home agent, mobile device-foreign agent, and foreign agent-home agent data transmission. All authentication extension headers typically contain fields such as Type, Length, Security Parameters Index (SPI), and Authenticator. The Authenticator field holds an Integrity Checksum Value (ICV) that is used to authenticate the request message.

CH
25

A registration reply contains fields that are identical to the request message except for the fact that the Care-of Address field is not present and the functionality of the Code and Lifetime fields are different in the reply message. The value specified in the Lifetime field depends on the value of the Code field. The Code field indicates the acceptance or rejection of the registration request. If the request is accepted, the Lifetime field can be specified a time value that indicates the validity time of the registration. The value 0 can be specified by the home agent to indicate that the requested care-of address deregistration has been implemented. If the Code field indicates that the registration request has been denied, no value is set in the Lifetime field. The home agent can specify more than 20 different types of registration request results in the Code field. Before delving into the details of the different codes that can be specified in the Code field, observe Figure 25.4 to understand how the fields in the registration reply message are organized.

Figure 25.4
A home agent can transmit a registration reply message directly to the mobile device or to the foreign agent based on the type of care-of address specified by the mobile device.

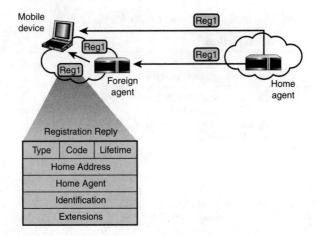

Table 25.4 describes each of the possible code values that can be set in the Code field.

TABLE 25.4	VALUES THAT CAN BE SET IN THE Code FIELD
Value	**Description**
0	Indicates that the home agent has accepted the registration request.
1	Indicates that although the home agent has accepted the registration request, it is unable to bind the care-of address with the mobile device hardware address.
64	Indicates that the reason for denying registration is not provided by the foreign agent.
65	Indicates that the registration of care-of addresses has been denied because of permission constraints imposed by the foreign network administrator.
66	Indicates that the foreign agent was unable to register the care-of address requested by the mobile device because of the lack of system resources in the foreign agent.
67	Indicates that the authentication process implemented by the foreign agent on the request message failed to authenticate the message.
68	Indicates that the foreign agent was unable to reconstruct ICV for the reply message.
69	Indicates that the Lifetime field value specified in the request message is too long a time limit. For example, if the value 0xffff is specified in the Lifetime field, the time limit indicated is infinity. Therefore, the foreign agent might deny the request.
70	Indicates that the content of the request message sent by the mobile device to the foreign agent is poorly formed.
71	Indicates that the content of the reply message sent by the foreign agent to the mobile device is poorly formed.
72	Indicates that the foreign agent was not able to implement the encapsulation features requested by the mobile device.

TABLE 25.4   CONTINUED

Value	Description
73	Indicates that the foreign agent was not able to implement the Van Jacobson header compression features requested by the mobile device.
80	Indicates that the home network to which the request was destined is unreachable.
81	Indicates that the home computer serviced by the home agent for which the request was destined is unreachable.
82	Indicates that the port provided by the home agent to receive requests was unreachable.
88	Indicates that the home agent for which the request was destined is unreachable.
128	Indicates that the reasons for denying the request were not specified by the home agent.
129	Indicates that the home network administrator has prohibited the acceptance of registration requests.
130	Indicates that the request message could not be processed because of lack of system resources in the home agent.
131	Indicates that the authentication process implemented by the home agent on the request failed to authenticate the mobile device.
132	Indicates that the authentication process implemented by the home agent failed to authenticate the foreign agent.
133	Indicates that the values specified in the request and reply Identification fields did not match.
134	Indicates that the request forwarded from the foreign agent or the mobile device has been poorly formed.
135	Indicates that the home agent was unable to manage multiple simultaneous hardware-IP address bindings.
136	Indicates that the home agent address specified in the request does not match with the IP addresses of home agents available on the home network.

After the mobile device has successfully registered the care-of address with the home agent, the home agent uses this process to forward data packets meant for the mobile device. The forwarding process uses IP-within-IP to tunnel datagrams being transmitted to the mobile device. The home agent, which is the *tunnel source*, inserts a new IP header, or *tunnel header*, before the IP header of a datagram addressed to the mobile device home agent address. The new tunnel header uses the mobile device's care-of address as the destination IP address, or *tunnel destination*. The home agent's IP address is specified as the tunnel source IP address. The tunnel header specifies the value 4 in its Next header field to indicate that the next protocol header belongs to a higher level protocol, which is another IP header.

→ For more information on IP tunneling, **see** "Data Transfer Between Computers on a VPN," **p. 340**

CH

25

After completing these tunneling specifications, the datagram is transmitted to the mobile device directly or through the foreign agent. In the IP-within-IP tunneled datagram, the entire original IP header is preserved as the first part of the payload of the tunnel header. Therefore, to recover the original packet, the foreign agent must eliminate the tunnel header of an incoming datagram and deliver the rest of the datagram to the mobile device.

MOBILE IPv6

One of the biggest disadvantages in implementing mobile IP has been its undue overhead because of the fact that datagrams need to travel in a triangular circuitous path during the exchange of datagrams between the mobile device and the destination computer. This problem, called the *triangular forwarding problem*, worsens when the destination computer is located on the foreign network. In this case, the datagrams sent by the destination computer must travel all the way back to the home agent and must be transmitted back to the foreign network. This means that the datagram must cross the foreign network boundaries two times, giving the anomaly its name, the *Two-crossing problem*. Figure 25.5 shows you how the Two-crossing problem can cost heavy network resources requirements.

Figure 25.5
If the destination computer is located on the foreign network, datagrams destined to the mobile device need to cross the foreign network boundaries two times to reach the targeted destination.

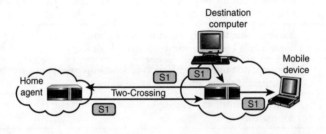

The IPv4 implementation of IP mobility was unable to provide a complete solution to the Two-crossing problem. However, Mobile IPv6 proposed to improve on the route optimization technique provided by Mobile IPv4 to minimize the effects of the Two-crossing anomaly. This technique enables mobile devices to communicate directly with the destination computer and vice versa without the additional hop through the home agent. The route optimization technique is a part of the mobile IPv6 framework in contrast to the mobile IPv4 where the technique was implemented as an extension. In contrast to the way in which route optimization is specified in IPv4, in IPv6, destination computers do not tunnel packets to mobile devices. Instead, the destination computers use IPv6 routing headers, which implement a variation of IPv4's *source routing* option.

To achieve direct communication between the destination computer and the mobile device, the mobile device IP address is specified as the IP address value in the Source address field of the IP datagram transmitted from a mobile device. Now, all datagrams destined to the mobile device are directly routed to the current network location instead of following the home agent-foreign agent path. The mobile IPv6 framework does not contain any foreign agent because IPv6 provides automated network location discovery and IP address reconfiguration features. These features are used by a mobile device to automatically identify its current network location and to reconfigure its address without the aid of the foreign agent. In addition, mobile IPv6 implements better security features by incorporating IPSec into the IP datagram framework. Now, authentication features do not exist as extensions to the mobile IP message format but are a part of the message format. Moreover, the confidentiality features provided by IPSec increments the security blanket provided to the datagrams transmitted over the mobile IPv6 framework.

SUMMARY

To provide mobility for IP addresses implemented on mobile devices, a new data transmission framework called mobile IP was developed. The framework implements a home agent and a foreign agent to redirect datagrams destined for mobile devices. Changes to the IP addressing scheme was avoided by providing a temporary IP address called the care-of IP address to the mobile device. However, care-of addresses were not revealed to higher-level protocols such as TCP. These devices can communicate directly with the home agent or need to use a foreign agent to manage communication with the home agent. To establish this framework, the mobile device needs to identify its current location, obtain a care-of address, and determine the home and foreign agents it needs to work with. The mobile device uses mobility agent advertisement extensions, which are appended to the ICMP router advertisement messages, to identify its mobility agents.

As a final step in establishing the mobile IP framework, the mobile device registers its care-of address with the home agent by transmitting a registration request to the home agent. The home agent confirms the status of the registration by responding with a registration reply message. Although many advantages can be derived from mobile IP, the overhead of implementing data transmission through a circuitous path severely affects a mobile IP implementation. Mobile IPv6 offers to minimize these resource draining overheads by providing features such as automated reconfiguration and network location discovery. In addition, a higher degree of security is implemented by incorporating IPSec into the mobile IPv6 framework.

CH
25

CHAPTER **26**

IPv6

In this chapter

IPv6: AN OVERVIEW

You have learned about the IP hourglass model in Chapter 3, "The Internet Layer Protocol." The IP hourglass model illustrates the fact that irrespective of the Application layer protocol and the Transport layer protocol that is used in data transmission, the only protocol that can be used for routing is the Internet Protocol (IP). Internet Protocol operates from the Network layer of the TCP/IP reference model. The version of IP that is referred to here is called IPv4 and has been in use since the evolution of the Internet. Although IPv4 has been widely accepted and implemented, there a few limitations that need to be addressed. This has led to the creation of a new version of the Internet Protocol called Internet Protocol Version 6 or IPv6. This protocol is also referred to as IP Next Generation (IPng).

The limitations of Internet Protocol Version 4 (IPv4) that led to the creation of IPv6 are as follows:

- The IPv4 address space would be insufficient to cater to the exponential growth in the number of hosts being connected to the Internet. Although techniques such as Network Address Translation (NAT) and private address space are being used to make the optimum use of addresses, they have limitations and cannot be implemented as long-term solutions. An IP address is not only required for desktop computers that are connected to a network. Devices such as smart cell phones, home alarm systems, and other handheld devices also require unique IP addresses for performing their respective functions. To meet these requirements, additional addresses would be required.

→ For more information on the organization of the IPv4 address space, **see** "The IP Address," **p. 31**

- IPv4 cannot be used for the efficient transmission of real-time data because it provides a best-effort delivery system. Real-time data, such as audio files in teleconference, must be transmitted without any delay or very negligible delay.

- Security of data is very important when it is transported over the Internet. However, IPv4 does not provide any authentication and encryption features by itself. Authentication and encryption have been added as an extension to IP called IPSec.

→ To learn more about IPv4, **see** "Internet Protocol," **p. 45**

After having discussed the limitations of IPv4, let us discuss how IPv6 can be implemented to overcome these disadvantages:

- IPv6 overcomes the limitation in address space by providing a 128-bit address space, which is four times as much as the address space provided by IPv4. Experts have predicted that the IPV6 address space would be able to cater to the increase in the number of users.

- The IP datagram format has been changed in IPv6 to make the header format more flexible. In addition, more options have been introduced in the IPv6 header format.

- More authentication and encryption options have been included in IPv6. This has been implemented by making the Authentication Header and the Encapsulation Security Payload (ESP) headers a part of the IP header. These headers have been included as extension headers that can be attached to the IP datagram, if required.

- The Type of Service (TOS) field that is a part of an IPv4 datagram has been replaced with the Flow Label field in an IPv6 datagram. The hosts for requesting the datagrams to be handled in a special manner can use this field. A common situation in which the Flow Label field is used would be the transmission of real-time data. In this case, a source can request for handling video and audio files from the same source computer in a similar manner.

Although there are quite a few new features that have been introduced in IPv6, its acceptance amongst users and the experts has not been as swift as was expected. This is because certain standards defining IPv6 are still evolving. Moreover, organizations have made huge investments on implementing IPv4 for their existing networks. Therefore, they are hesitant in adopting IPv6. Another factor that has resulted in a lukewarm reception for IPv6 is the general confusion and disagreement between experts on the need for IPv6 as a replacement for IPv4. RFC 2460 provides the specifications for IPv6.

→ For more information on Request for Comments and RFC 2460, **see** "RFCs," **p. 425**

Migrating from an IPv4 network to an IPv6 network must be planned properly to prevent any inconvenience to network users. Migrating from an IPv4 network to an IPv6 is done using different methods, namely dual stack, tunneling, and header translation. Each method is used under different situations. For example, when an IPv6 datagram needs to traverse an IPv4 network, the tunnel method is implemented where the datagram is encapsulated into another IPv4 datagram. When the datagram is routed out of the IPv4 network, the IPv4 shell is discarded. The header translation method has been envisaged for a scenario where IPv6 is widely implemented and when networks need to provide backward compatibility for IPv4. In this case, the receiving computer might be using IPv4 whereas the sending computer implements IPv6. The header in the IPv6 datagram needs to be translated into an IPv4 format. To enable support for both versions of IP, the dual stack method must be implemented. In this method, two different Internet layers with each layer using IPv4 or IPv6 must be implemented.

The introduction of IPv6 has also affected other protocols in the Network layer, such as Internet Control Management Protocol (ICMP) and Internet Group Management Protocol (IGMP). The functionality of Address Resolution Protocol (ARP) has been integrated with the new version of ICMP called ICMPv6.

THE IPv6 MESSAGE FORMAT

Similar to other protocols, IPv6 messages are also sent in a message format commonly referred to as the IPv6 message format. The IPv6 message format has been defined to make the datagram processing more efficient compared to that of the IPv4 message formats.

CH
26

An IPv6 data packet that is transmitted over a network is also referred to as a datagram. An IPv6 datagram is encapsulated in a frame to be transmitted over the physical medium.

An IPv6 message format consists of three parts: the basic header, payload, and the extension headers. The basic header consists of the fields that are required to transmit the datagram from the source to the destination. The payload part of the datagram represents the actual data that is received from the upper-layer protocols. Like the IP options field that is a part of the IPv4, IPv6 provides additional functionalities to the processing of the IP datagram by using special headers called extension headers. These headers are optional. The extension headers, if any, must be placed between the basic header and the payload. The maximum size of the payload that can be placed in an IPv6 datagram is 65,535 bytes.

The components of the basic header in an IPv6 datagram are

- Version: Indicates the version of IP that is used. The length of this field is 4 bits. The value of this field is 6 for IPv6.

- Traffic Class: This field can be used by the sender or a router to request additional priority for routing a datagram. The size of this field is 8 bits. The Traffic Class field is a replacement of the Type of Service field in an IPv4 datagram. The value for the Traffic Class field must be provided by the upper-layer protocols, which can be either the Application layer protocols or the Transport layer protocols.

- Flow Label: This field can be used to request special treatment for datagrams that are transmitted from a source to the destination. This field is used for transmitting real-time data in which audio and video files from a specific destination would require the same type of treatment. The field corresponds to the Type of Service (TOS) field in IPv4.

- Payload Length: This field indicates the length of the payload that follows the basic header in the IPv6 datagram. The size of this field is 16 bits, and the value that is stored in this field is an unsigned integer. Unlike the Total Length of the IPv4 header that includes the length of the IP header, the Payload Length field does not include the length of the basic header of the IPv6 datagram.

Note

The Payload Length field also includes the length of the extension headers that follow the Payload in an IPv6 datagram. The value in this field is specified in terms of octets.

- Next Header: This field is used to specify the type of extension header that follows the current header in an IPv6 datagram. The size of this field is 8 bits.

- Hop Limit: The role played by this field is the same as that of the Time To Live (TTL) field in an IPv4 datagram. The Hop Limit can be used to improve the performance of a network because it is used to prevent the data packets from remaining indefinitely on the network. Every router through which the IP datagram passes by decrements the value of this field by 1. If the value of this field becomes 0 before the datagram reaches the ultimate destination, an Internet Control Message Protocol (ICMP) error message is sent to the originator of the datagram.

- `Source Address`: This field is used to specify the address of the originator of the message. The size of this field is 16 bytes.

→ To learn more about the IPv4 message format, **see** "Format of an IP Datagram," **p. 47**

- `Destination Address`: This field is used to specify the address in the final destination of the message. Similar to the `Source Address` field, this field is also 16 bytes in size.

Note

An important point to be noted is that the `Destination Address` field need not hold the address of the ultimate recipient if an extension header called the Routing header is present in the IP datagram.

IPv6 EXTENSION HEADERS

As stated earlier, an extension header enables additional functionalities to be implemented while transmitting a datagram. These extension headers are placed between the basic header and the payload data in the datagram. There are six different types of headers that can be placed in an IP datagram. They are as follows:

- Hop-by-Hop Options
- Routing
- Fragment header
- Destination Options
- Authentication
- Encapsulation Security Payload

An IP datagram can contain more than one extension header. Two important points that need to be considered about the processing of extension headers are as follows:

- The extension headers are processed only at the final destination of the datagram with the exception of the Hop-by-Hop Options and Routing extension headers. These extension headers need to be processed by the intermediate routers to transmit the datagram to the correct destination. The final destination is identified after comparing the address of the host with the value in the `Destination Address` field of the IP datagram.
- Extension headers must be processed only in a predefined order. A host cannot circumvent an extension header and proceed to the next header. The order in which the extension headers need to be placed is specified in RFC 2460 and is as follows:

CH
26

1. The IPv6 header or the basic header

2. Hop-by-Hop Options header

3. Destination Options header

4. Routing header

5. Fragment header

6. Authentication header

7. Encapsulating Security Payload header

8. Destination Options header

9. Upper-layer header

The Upper-layer header identifies the header that has been sent by the upper-layer protocols, such as Transmission Control Protocol (TCP) or User Datagram Protocol (UDP). An upper-layer protocol can also be a protocol that operated from the Application layer, such as Simple Mail Transfer Protocol (SMTP) or Hypertext Transfer Protocol.

Every extension header is identified by a unique value for a host to identify it. This value is specified using the Next Header field, which is a part of the basic header or any extension header. If the value that is provided is invalid, an ICMP parameter problem error message is generated and sent to the originator of the message. Table 26.1 displays the values that can be assigned to the Next Header field and the corresponding extension header types.

TABLE 26.1   THE VALUES THAT CAN BE ASSIGNED TO THE Next Header FIELD

Code	Extension Header Type
0	Hop-by-Hop Extension header
2	Internet Control Message Protocol (ICMP)
6	Transmission Control Protocol (TCP)
17	User Datagram Protocol (UDP)
43	Routing header
44	Fragmentation header
50	Encrypted Security Payload (ESP)
51	Authentication header
59	Null, which implies that the current extension header is the last header in the IPv6 datagram
60	Destination Options Header

Figure 26.1 displays the structure of a sample IPv6 datagram with extension headers.

Figure 26.1
The IP modules identify the extension headers by using the value of the `Next Header` field of the previous header.

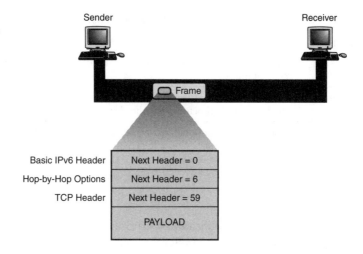

Basic IPv6 Header	Next Header = 0
Hop-by-Hop Options	Next Header = 6
TCP Header	Next Header = 59
	PAYLOAD

The extension headers like the IP options field in an IPv4 datagram are optional. Therefore, the transmission of a datagram is not completely dependent in the extension headers that follow the datagram.

> **Note**
>
> If the Hop-by-Hop Options Headers is present in the datagram, it should be placed immediately after the basic header.

> **Note**
>
> In certain cases where an IP datagram is tunneled and sent over a secure connection, the upper-layer header can be an IP header. In other words, an IP datagram will be encapsulated within an IP datagram. The IP datagram that is encapsulated can also contain its own set of extension headers.

CH

26

HOP-BY-HOP OPTIONS

The Hop-by-Hop options header, if present, must immediately follow the basic header in an IPv6 datagram. This header is used to specify the information required by intermediate routers on the path of the datagram to the ultimate destination. This extension header is used when the source needs to pass certain information to all the intermediate routers in the route. The information that can be passed by the source can be any control message or a message that can be used for debugging. The Next Header field of the basic IPv6 header must hold the value 0 to indicate that the extension header that follows is a Hop-by-Hop extension header. Using the Jumbo Payload option, you can use the Hop-by-Hop options header to accept a payload of a size greater than 65,525 bytes. Table 26.2 displays the components of a Hop-by-Hop extension header.

TABLE 26.2   COMPONENTS OF THE HOP-BY-HOP EXTENSION HEADER

Field Name	Description
Next Header	An 8-bit field that indicates the type of the extension header that follows the current one.
Hdr Ext Len	An 8-bit field that is used to store the length of the extension header excluding the first eight octets in the header.
Options	Is a variable-length field that is used to specify the options in a type-length-value (TLV) format. The three components are Option Type, Option Data Len, and Option Data.

ROUTING

The Routing header is used to specify a route that is to be taken by a datagram. A Routing header is also commonly referred to as a Source Routing header. The information that is provided by the Routing header is similar to the Strict Source Route and the Loose Source Route options that are provided by the IP Options field in IPv4. To identify a Routing header, the value in the Next Header field of the header preceding the current one must be 43.

→ To learn more about IP Options in IPv4, **see** "IP Options," **p. 58**

The components of the Routing header are discussed in Table 26.3.

TABLE 26.3   COMPONENTS OF THE HOP-BY-HOP EXTENSION HEADER

Field Name	Description
Next Header	An 8-bit field that indicates the type of the extension header that follows the current one.
Hdr Ext Len	An 8-bit field that is used to store the length of the extension header excluding the first eight octets in the header.
Routing Type	An 8-bit field that is used to indicate the type of routing that is required. Currently, only one type of routing can be implemented and is referred to as loose source routing. The value that is stored in this field for loose source routing is 0.
Segments Left	An 8-bit field that is used to specify the number of routers yet to be visited to reach the ultimate destination.
Type-specific data	A variable length that is used to list the addresses of the routes en route before the final destination is reached. An important point to be noted is that this field provides the addresses unlike the Segments Left field, which specifies the number of segments en route to the final destination.

FRAGMENTATION

Unlike IPv4, which enables intermediate routers to fragment a datagram depending on the Maximum Transfer Unit (MTU) of the network through which the datagram needs to pass, IPv6 supports only an end-to-end fragmentation. In other words, only the source of the fragments can perform the fragmentation. The intermediate routers cannot perform fragmentation. The reassembly of the fragments is performed only by the final destination of the datagrams like the implementation in IPv4.

To implement end-to-end fragmentation, the sender needs to find the optimum value of the MTU, so that the intermediate routers need not fragment the datagrams. To find the optimum size of the MTU, the source uses path MTU discovery. However, if the size of the datagram is too large to be occupied in a single frame, the datagram is fragmented and sent over a network. To enable the fragments to be reassembled at the destination properly, a fragmentation header is also attached to the datagram that is transmitted over the network. The fragmentation header contains fields that can be used by the receiver to reassemble the packets.

Note

The fragmentation header must be present in all the fragments of a datagram.

If end-to-end fragmentation is implemented, a question arises as to what would happen if there is a problem with the route and the datagram needs to be sent through a different route, which requires fragmentation. If a datagram needs to be sent through an alternative route because the original route has a problem, the transmission of the datagram will be smooth as long as fragmentation is not required to transmit the datagram. However, if the route through which the datagram must be transmitted requires fragmentation, an error message is sent to the source. After the source receives the error message, the path MTU discovery process needs to be repeated to find the optimum size of the MTU for the new route.

CH
26

→ To learn more about path MTU discovery, **see** "Discovering Path MTU," **p. 105**
→ To learn more about how fragmentation is implemented in IPv4, **see** "Transmission of Datagrams," **p. 54**

Table 26.4 displays the components of a fragmentation header.

TABLE 26.4 COMPONENTS OF THE FRAGMENTATION HEADER

Field Name	Description
Next Header	An 8-bit field that indicates the type of the extension header that follows the current one.
Reserved	An 8-bit reserved field that is reserved for future use. Currently, the value of this field is set to 0 when a datagram is transmitted. The receiver ignores the value in this field while processing the datagram.

TABLE 26.4 CONTINUED

Field Name	Description
Fragment Offset	A 13-bit unsigned integer that is used to specify the position of a fragment relative to the original datagram. This field is used by the receiver to reassemble all the fragments in the datagram. The use of this field is the same as the Fragmentation field of an IPv4 datagram.
Res	A 2-bit field that is reserved for future use. Currently, the value of this field is set to 0 when a datagram is transmitted. The receiver ignores the value in this field while processing the datagram.
M flag	Is a 1-bit field that can be set to 0 or 1. Setting it to 1 indicates that there are more fragments following the current one. A value of 0 in this field indicates that the current fragment is the last one. The role of the M field in an IPv6 datagram is the same as the More Fragment field in an IPv4 datagram.
Identification	A 32-bit field that is used to identify all the fragments that belong to a datagram. This field plays a vital role in reassembling all the datagrams together by the receiver.

The IP datagram that needs to be transported over the network is comprised of two parts, the unfragmentable part, and the fragmentable part. The unfragmentable part consists of the basic IPv6 header and an extension header that can be processed by the intermediate routers. Therefore, the extension header that is a part of the unfragmented part can be a routing header or a Hop-by-Hop option header.

All the fields in the basic header are copied to the fragments of the datagram. However, the Payload Length field of the fragment is changed to reflect the size of the fragment. When the fragments are reassembled at the receiver's end, the Payload Length field is once again changed to reflect the size of the datagram.

If the originator of the datagrams does not implement path MTU discovery, the optimum size of the MTU is assumed to be 1280 by default. Therefore, hardware technologies that are used for networks implementing IPv6 must support a minimum of 1280 bytes of MTU.

Note

For networks in which the size of the MTU is less than 1280 bytes, the Physical or the Data Link layer must handle fragmentation separately.

Similar to the process of reassembling IPv4 datagrams, in the case of IPv6 datagrams, if all the fragments of a datagram do not arrive within 60 seconds of the arrival of the first fragment, the entire datagram is discarded. In addition, an error message is sent to the originator of the message.

Destination Options

The Destination Options header has the same format as that of the Hop-by-Hop options header. Unlike the Hop-by-Hop options header that is used to send information to all the intermediate hosts on the network, the Destination Options header is used by the source to send information to the ultimate destination of the datagram. The intermediate devices cannot process the contents of the Destination Options header.

Authentication

The Authentication header is used to authenticate the sender of the message and ensure that the message has not been changed in transit. Authentication is required to check if the originator of the message is an authorized user on the network. Data Authentication can be done using different algorithms.

→ For more information on the Authentication Header, **see** "The Authentication Header," **p. 352**

Encapsulated Security Payload

The Encapsulated Security Payload (ESP) header is used to ensure confidentiality of data. Although ESP provides security features that are similar to AH, confidentiality is an important feature provided by ESP that differentiates it from AH. This feature enables a sending computer to modify the contents of a datagram into a format that is incomprehensible to intermediate devices. This feature of IP is very useful when the data from a private network needs to be transferred over a Virtual Private Network.

→ For more information on ESP, **see** "Encapsulated Security Payload," **p. 355**

IPv6 Addressing

As already stated, one of the main advantages of IPv6 is the availability of a large address space that is comprised of 128-bits. Every host on a network that implements IPv6 is represented with an IP address of 16 bytes. These addresses are represented in a notation called the hexadecimal colon notation. In this notation, the IP address is divided into eight groups of four bytes. The value in each group is provided in the hexadecimal notation.

Ch

26

An example of an IPv6 address is ABC3:56AC:7845:9078:6757:5645:6787:8900

IPv6 also supports a notation called the abbreviated notation in which leading zeros in groups can be truncated and displayed in a concise form.

For example, if the IP address of a host is ABC3:56AC:7845:0078:6757:5645:0087:ABC4, the leading zeros in the groups can be represented as ABC3:56AC:7845:78:6757:5645:87: ABC4.

Lastly, if a group is comprised of zeros, the value of the group can be replaced with a colon.

For example, if the IP address of a host is ABC3:0000:7845:0078:0000:5645:0000:ABC4, it can be abbreviated as ABC3::7845:0078::5645::ABC4.

IPv6 supports three types of address: unicast, anycast, and multicast IP. A unicast address is used to send messages to a single computer on a network. An anycast address is used to represent a group of addresses that are represented as a single address. When a message is sent to an anycast address, the message is sent to any computer of the group. The third category of addresses that is defined by IPv6 is called the multicast addresses. These addresses are used to represent a group of computers to which a message needs to be sent. Unlike an anycast message, a multicast message will be transmitted to all the computers in the multicast group.

SUMMARY

Although IPv4 has been the most successful data transmission protocol, certain limitations in its implementation have necessitated the development of a newer IP version called IPv6. One of the main limitations of IPv4 is the insufficient address space. The exponential growth of the number of users connecting to the Internet and the number of networks cannot be accommodated in the IPv4 address space. Techniques such as NAT and subnetting that are used for conserving IP addresses are not permanent solutions to the address space problem. The number of bits in the IPv6 address space has been increased to 128 bits. Apart from the change in the number of bits for the address space, certain other enhancements have also been introduced in IPv6.

The IPv6 message format has been changed to make the datagram processing more efficient. There are six types of extension headers that are defined in IPv6. The extension headers are placed between the basic header and the payload. IPv6 also defines three types of addresses: unicast, anycast, and multicast addresses. For ease of use, an IPv6 address is represented in the hexadecimal colon notation.

CHAPTER 27

QUALITY OF SERVICE

In this chapter

INTRODUCING QUALITY OF SERVICE

One of the most important factors that contribute to the success of any business organization is quality. In addition to a reasonable cost, clients expect quality in the products or services they purchase. For example, on special occasions, you prefer to dine in a particular restaurant due to a number of factors, ranging from the ambience, service, and choice of food available in the restaurant. To achieve these factors, the restaurant needs to implement quality while preparing food, maintaining the ambience, and providing table service to its clients. With the transformation of the Net into a profitable business area, implementing quality has become one of the prime factors in ensuring success. For example, users might subscribe to a Web site that offers real-time information on stock prices or other vital business information. The Web site must ensure that the latest information is provided to its users by implementing quality in its speed of data transmission.

The Net has come a long way from its initial textual information exchange capabilities and has redefined the nature of information exchange. Today, in addition to text and software files, multimedia data files, such as graphic files, voice, and video are exchanged on the Net. The multimedia files constitute a considerable volume of the information exchanged on the Net. Future data transmission environments can use these data formats to combine telephony, television, and the Net. To implement such a data transmission environment, real-time transmission of voice, video, and graphics files need to be implemented.

However, attempts to implement the real-time exchange of such data formats have posed an interesting challenge to the existing data transmission infrastructure. For example, consider a scenario where a videoconference needs to be conducted between the operational heads of different branch offices of an organization. Usually, the videoconference is implemented over a satellite link with the branch offices being connected to the head office over the satellite link. To minimize the cost, the organization decides to conduct this conference over the Net. However, when the conference is conducted, a number of difficulties in the implementation of a simultaneous video transmission are noticed. Finally, the conference is abandoned because of link failures and slow transmission of video images.

A number of factors, such as network traffic or low bandwidth, on the network transmitting the images can be attributed as the cause of poor transmission quality. However, the primary reason for the failed videoconference is the fact that the multimedia data transmission for the conference was implemented on a traditional IP networking infrastructure. IP provides the *best-effort data transmission* performance, which is primarily concerned with the reliable transmission of data, regardless of the time taken to transmit data. Therefore, when real-time transmission of voice or video files was required for the conference, the best-effort data transmission model was unable to provide such a transmission service.

Besides video conferences, real-time transmission of multimedia data files needs to be implemented in a variety of other scenarios, such as voice streaming, video streaming, or telephony implemented over the Net, called *IP telephony*. In each of these scenarios, the existing best-effort data transmission model implemented by IP is not enough to provide real-time transmission of data. Adding the required bandwidth to the transmitting networks is one of the solutions. However, this is not always feasible or cost-effective.

The root cause of the problem in IP's best-effort data transmission model is that this model does not focus on the constraint on transmission time. In addition to the increase in bandwidth, a mechanism that enables the real-time transmission of data must be implemented. To establish such a mechanism, some amount of automated real-time traffic management capability must be incorporated into the networks that implement data transfer. Real-time traffic management includes features that can ensure a networking environment that facilitates real-time data transmission without much data loss, jitter, or other transmission hitches (for example, latency) that are encountered in a traditional IP best effort transmission model. Such a mechanism is proposed by a concept called Quality of Service (QoS).

To revisit the existing business scenario existing on the Net, it is important to note that although dot com businesses provide Web-based services to their clients, the quality of services provided by a Web site is not under its control. In turn, Web sites need to depend on their Internet Service Providers (ISPs) to manage the networking environment they require. For example, on an average, about 20% of Web page retrievals fail. Moreover, 15% of HTTP GET requests take greater than 10 seconds. Therefore, ISPs should provide the Web sites they service with quality in networking environment, or QoS. In simple terms, QoS can be defined as an assurance provided by an ISP to its subscribers. This is necessary to maintain a certain predefined status in the networking environment that enables the smooth transmission of data, especially multimedia data. Predefined network environment status can include parameters such as bandwidth, latency, and any other parameter that ensures the required networking environment for the smooth transmission of data. ISPs and their subscribers need to define the required parameters clearly and the capability of an ISP to provide QoS based on the parameters. Therefore, ISPs and subscribers enter into an agreement called Service Level Agreement (SLA) that defines the required QoS. In addition to defining the required QoS parameters, the SLA also defines the remedial measures or penalties that must be incurred by the ISP for failing to provide the QoS assured by the SLA.

A simple method to implement QoS on existing IP networks is to reserve networking resources on the participating routers that enable connectivity between sending and receiving computers. A Web server can be a sending computer, and user computers can be the receiving computers. IP provides a Transport layer protocol called Resource Reservation Protocol (RSVP). Another method of implementing QoS is to provide priority and the required QoS for a particular class of datagrams. This method, called differentiated service, enables participating routers to differentiate between datagrams marked for QoS implementation and other datagrams that need to be transmitted without QoS facilities. You will learn more about these QoS implementation models in the following sections.

CH
27

RESOURCE RESERVATION PROTOCOL

In an attempt to implement QoS on IP networks, a collaborative research on a mechanism that implements resource reservation was conducted at the Palo Alto Research Center

(PARC) and at the University of Southern California's (USC) Information Sciences Institute (ISI). The research resulted in the development of Reservation Protocol, also called Resource Reservation Protocol (RSVP). By 1995, RSVP had been demonstrated to provide QoS features and was standardized by the Internet Engineering Task Force (IETF) into an RFC. Today, RFC 2205 provides the standards for implementing RSVP. Primarily, RSVP can be described as a Transport layer protocol that reserves network resources on the participating routers to implement QoS while transmitting datagrams. RSVP provides guaranteed service, where network resources for a specified volume of traffic is guaranteed to an ISP's client.

Although RSVP plays a vital role during data transmission, the protocol does not route datagrams. Instead, RSVP runs as a background process implementing QoS on the participating routers. Another important distinction between routing protocols and RSVP is the fact that RSVP implements QoS for a group of datagrams that have identical sending and receiving computers in addition to the similar port numbers used for transmission. The process of managing the flow of datagrams in groups is called a *session*. In contrast, routing protocols process and determine routes for every individual datagram arriving at a router. It is important to note that in each session, groups of datagrams are transmitted in a single direction following the simplex mode of data transmission.

RSVP implements a simple process for reserving resources on participating routers. As a first step, the sending computer must transmit a message to the receiver to provide information on the route to be taken by subsequent datagrams in the session. In addition, this initial message, called a path message, also provides information on the state of the network existing in a particular path or route. After receiving the path message, the RSVP implementation on the receiver transmits a resource request message requesting each router in the path to reserve the required resources. It is important to note that RSVP is a receiver-based model, where each receiver is responsible for choosing its own level of reserved resources, initiating the reservation and keeping it active as long as it wants to. In a way, RSVP is a distributed solution for the resource reservation problem, and enables heterogeneous receivers to make reservations specifically tailored to their own needs. Also, the receiver-based model prevents excessive overhead at the sender, especially if large multicast groups are involved.

On receiving the request, the RSVP implementation on each router processes the request. During this process, RSVP uses its policy control component to determine whether the router has the capability to reserve the requested resources. In addition, RSVP uses another component called *administration control* to determine whether the receiver has the permission to request such a reservation. If permissions and the capacity for resource reservation are verified, the request is confirmed with a positive acknowledgement to the receiver. If all routers confirm the resource reservation with acknowledgement, the resource reservation process is complete and data transmission can commence. When a datagram arrives at a router, RSVP processes the datagram to identify QoS parameters, called QoS class, which must be implemented on the datagram. The packet classifier component implements this task. Next, resources are allocated and QoS is implemented on the datagram by transmitting the datagram according to its QoS requirements. The packet scheduler RSVP component manages this task. Figure 27.1 provides a bird's-eye view of the RSVP QoS implementation process.

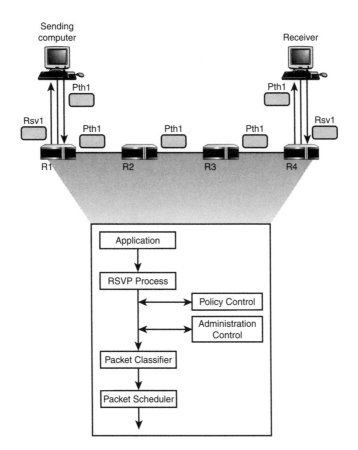

Figure 27.1
The packet classifier determines the QoS class for each packet and the scheduler orders packet transmission to achieve the promised QoS for each stream.

In Figure 27.1, observe that a reservation message, Rsv1, is sent from the receiving computer to the sending computer. The reservation message follows the path taken by the path message, Pth1. In addition to the path and request messages, RSVP error, acknowledgement, and teardown messages play an important role in RSVP's QoS implementation. Typically, RSVP error messages are transmitted when errors occur in the processing of path messages or request reservation messages. Path error messages are transmitted back to the computer that sent the unsuccessful path message. The reverse is true of the reservation request error message where the error message is transmitted back to the receiving computer that sent the unsuccessful request. A participating router can reject a request based on a number of factors. For example, if a router is unable to allocate resources for QoS parameters, such as bandwidth or other factors, the router will reject the request. If vital information, such as path or flow, is incorrectly specified, the router can reject the request. Routers also reject requests if the receiver does not have the permission to make a resource allocation request. In contrast, if the request meets all the required parameters, a confirmation message is sent to the receiver from all the participating routers in the form of a request acknowledgement message.

To manage dynamic network environments, a timeout value for the resource allocated and the path is maintained on sending and receiving computers. If the timeout value expires without any change in the reservation or path state, terminal messages that destroy the existing path or reservation state can be transmitted from either end point. The messages, called teardown messages, are classified into path teardown messages and the reservation request teardown messages. As the name suggests, path teardown messages terminate the existing path information on all participating routers at the expiry of a timeout value. Correspondingly, the reservation request teardown message terminates resource reservations. This feature avoids setting hard-coded reservation and path settings on participating routers. Therefore, it is termed as the RSVP soft state feature.

To move into the crux of the RSVP implementation, it is essential to understand the RSVP message format. All RSVP messages are organized with a message header and multiple object fields. The RSVP message header contains fields such as Flag, Type, Send TTL, and so on. Table 27.1 describes each header field in detail.

TABLE 27.1   FIELDS IN AN RSVP HEADER

Field	Description
Version	Specifies the version of RSVP being used for QoS. Currently, RSVP version 1 is prevalent.
Flags	Specifies flags for a message. The intent of the flags has been defined. The flags are reserved for future implementation.
Type	Specifies a number code that indicates the type of the RSVP message. Reservation requests are indicated by the number 2. Specifying the number 1 indicates that the message is a path message. To indicate that the message is a reservation request error message, the number 4 must be specified in this field. The number 3 indicates path error messages. Successful reservations are confirmed by specifying the number 7 to indicate the reservation request acknowledgement message. Specifying the numbers 6 and 5 indicates reservation teardown and path teardown messages, respectively.
Checksum	Specifies a checksum value that is computed based on the contents of the message. The value is used to verify the integrity of the transmitted message.
More Fragments (MF)	Indicates whether there is another fragment to follow. MF is set on for all but the last fragment of a message.
Fragment offset	Specifies the offset value of the fragmented message.
Length	Specifies the length of the RSVP message. If the MF field and the fragment offset field are set, this field value indicates the size of the fragment.

TABLE 27.1   CONTINUED

Field	Description
Message ID	Specifies a common name that identifies all the fragments of a message. This field is used when reassembling the message on the next hop router.
Send TTL	Specifies a time value that indicates the IP TTL value set on a previous router.

RSVP messages contain object fields, such as Length, Class-num, Class-type, and Object content. The Length field specifies the length of the message object. The Class-type field and the Class-num field provide unique identities to the various object classes that comprise an object. The Object content field contains objects that provide vital QoS information based on the type of the message. Table 27.2 describes the classes that can be specified in an object.

TABLE 27.2   CLASSES IN AN Object Content FIELD

Class	Description
Session	Specifies information on the IP address and the port of the receiving computer to identify the session.
Time Values	Specifies the TTL value that provides a lifetime value for path and reservation states.
Flow	Specifies the QoS parameters that are used for reserving resources.
Filter	Specifies conditions that must be implemented by the sending computer while transmitting datagrams. If the specified conditions are not met in a datagram, QoS is not implemented for the datagram.
Sender Template	Specifies information that enables routers to identify the sending computer.
Adspec	Specifies window advertisement information as part of an RSVP message.
Policy Data	Specifies policy information that is used by RSVP implementation on participating routers to allow further RSVP processing or to discard the request.
Error	Specifies error information. This field is used to specify error information on path error or reservation request error messages.
Integrity	Specifies authentication information to authenticate the sending computer and to verify the integrity of the RSVP message content.
Reservation Confirmation	Specifies the IP address of the receiver, which is used to send reservation acknowledgement information.

CH
27

TABLE 27.2 CONTINUED

Class	Description
RSVP Hop	Specifies the IP address of the previous hop router that forwarded the message.
Null	Specifies a Null value that is to be ignored during the RSVP QoS implementation process.

Although RSVP provides the means to implement QoS on IP networks, QoS implemented on Asynchronous Transfer Mode (ATM) networks is much more efficient and effective. This is because IP implements packet-switching during the QoS implementation whereas ATM implements circuit-switching with a fixed cell size of 53 bytes. This makes ATM QoS implementations much quicker compared to RSVP QoS implementations. To incorporate ATM's QoS features into IP networks, a number of IP over ATM models have been proposed.

→ To learn more about IP over ATM, **see** "IP Data Transmission Models for ATM," **p. 371**

DIFFERENTIATED SERVICES

Although RSVP was an effective QoS implementation protocol, it was difficult to implement RSVP sessions on a large scale. RSVP implementations were router-intensive, which implied that the routers had to maintain state information, resource allocation, packet classification, packet scheduling, and policy control in addition to their usual datagram-routing services. Therefore, another method that used the existing IP network infrastructure to provide a simpler implementation of QoS was essential. This need necessitated the development of differentiated services as an alternative QoS implementation model.

Differentiated services use the Type of Service (ToS) field in the existing IP datagram framework to classify datagrams into various service classes. These service classes provide the required QoS functionality as specified in the SLA between an ISP and its clients. For example, certain clients prefer service classes that implement quick and jitter-free data transmission. ISPs and their clients can enter into a static or dynamic SLA. Dynamic SLAs take into account the varying networking conditions and the data transmission requirements that might arise dynamically. Therefore, dynamic SLAs are treated as an on-demand service agreement. In contrast, static SLAs do not change during the period of time for which they have been created. Based on the service class indicated as a requirement by the SLA, QoS is implemented on each datagram to be transmitted from a router. It is important to note that QoS is implemented at each hop between sending and receiving computers. This Hop-by-Hop QoS implementation is called Per-Hop Behavior (PHB).

Typically, clients are offered a premium differentiated service or an assured service based on certain specific QoS requirements. For example, an assured service is best suited for clients who need reliability in data transmission. On the other hand, clients who need data transmission at a fast pace and with low jitter might need to choose the premium service. Clients who choose the premium service need to specify a fixed peak bit rate that defines the volume of traffic that will be transmitted from the client at any specified point in time. The clients must not overshoot this specification because ISP routers can provide QoS only for the volume of traffic specified in the SLA. If a client transmits datagrams at a peak bit rate higher than the SLA-specified limit, the ISP's router discards the excess datagrams.

To implement premium services, the sending computer (the ISP's client) needs to set the bit rate in the IP ToS field to indicate that the datagram needs premium QoS service. Upon arrival at the ISP's router, the datagram might be reassembled if it has been fragmented to comply with peak bit rate specifications. After reassembly, the ISP's router, which manages incoming datagrams from clients, processes the datagram and identifies it as a premium class datagram. Next, the datagram is sent to a Premium Queue (PQ) where the datagram is transmitted to its destination. The transmission is effected with a QoS based on the QoS parameters specified in the SLA.

Assured services are also implemented in a manner that is similar to premium services. When the datagrams transmitted by a client arrive at the ISP's router, the router first verifies whether the datagram has exceeded the traffic limit indicated by the SLA. However, unlike premium services, the excess datagrams are not dropped immediately. Instead, excess datagrams are marked as "out" datagrams and datagrams that are within the bit rate specified by the SLA are marked as "in." All datagrams are sent into an Assured Queue (AQ) where the decision of dropping excess datagrams is implemented by a mechanism called *RED with In or Out (RIO)*. This mechanism is based on the *Random Early Detection (RED)* queue management mechanism.

Note

In the absence of queue management mechanisms such as RED, a condition called *tail drop* occurs on routers that have overflowing buffers. When a tail drop condition occurs, all datagrams that arrive at a router are arbitrarily discarded because of the full buffer condition existing at the router. To avoid this situation, the RED queue management mechanism sets a threshold limit for the router's buffer and starts dropping an arbitrary number of datagrams when the threshold buffer limit is reached. In this way, buffer congestion and tail drop are avoided.

CH
27

RIO does not discard datagrams in a random manner. Instead, RIO maintains separate threshold limits for in and out datagrams. If the threshold for out datagrams is exceeded, only out datagrams are discarded randomly. Only when both out and in threshold values are exceeded, both in and out datagrams are randomly discarded. However, out datagrams are discarded at a higher number than in datagrams when both thresholds are exceeded. In this way, the data loss is not perceived much by the end user. Moreover, RIO also checks the transmission of data from clients in excess of the agreed specification in the SLA. Figure 27.2 shows you how an assured service is implemented.

Figure 27.2
Implementing RIO on routers ensures the minimum loss of datagrams. It also checks the transmission of datagrams from ISP clients in excess of SLA specifications.

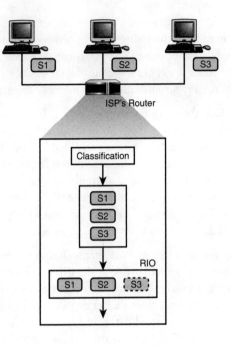

SUMMARY

With the advent of the Net as a profitable business area, the need to provide quality of service to clients has become an essential component to run successful Web-based businesses. However, the existing IP data transmission model was unable to cope with the changing nature of data that needs to be transmitted. Therefore, a new transmission model called Quality of Service was proposed. QoS assures the required data transmission environment to provide reliable, real-time transmission of data.

QoS can be implemented using the RSVP or differentiated services transmission mode. RSVP implements QoS by reserving network resources on participating routers. Differentiated services provide an assured service or a premium service based on the IP ToS field setting. Assured differentiated service implements a reliable transmission of data even under network congestion conditions. Premium service implements jitter-free and quick transmission of data for clients subscribing to such a service.

RFCs

In the quest for standardizing the implementation areas that make the Internet, the Internet Engineering Task Force devised a documentation mechanism called Request for Comments (RFCs). Any implementation, be it protocols or a new method of communication, can be proposed to IETF in the form of a document. IETF analyzes the document and publishes it as an RFC with a unique RFC number. The RFC is subject to additions or modifications, which in turn could be published as RFCs. Finally, when all changes and modifications on an RFC are completed, the proposed implementation can be termed as an Internet Standard. For example, RFC 793, which provides specification for the Transmission Control Protocol (TCP), is an Internet standards document. Today, 3,238 RFCs have been published by IETF covering a multitude of subjects that affect the Internet. To obtain a complete list of all RFCs, you can access the RFC Index maintained by IETF at

http://www.ietf.org/iesg/1rfc_index.txt.

Table A.1 provides a list of RFCs that are related to the chapters in this book along with a brief description of each RFC.

TABLE A.1   A BRIEF DESCRIPTION OF RFCs

RFC Number	Description
768	Defines specifications for implementing an unreliable transmission of datagrams by using the User Datagram Protocol (UDP). The RFC provides specifications for the message formats used in a UDP datagram.
791	Defines specifications to implement a packet-switching technology by transmitting data in blocks called datagrams using the Internet Protocol (IP). The RFC also defines methods to identify the source and destination computers, fragmentation of datagrams, and reassembly of datagrams.
792	Defines specifications to implement a mechanism of communicating messages from a computer or a router using the Internet Control Message Protocol (ICMP). The RFC defines the various types of ICMP messages and their formats.
793	Defines specifications to reliable connection-oriented transmission of datagrams between computers using the Transmission Control Protocol (TCP). The RFC provides information on the TCP datagram format apart from information on establishing and terminating connections and implementing reliable datagram exchange.
821	Defines specifications for implementing reliable and efficient mail transfer. The RFC proposes Simple Mail Transfer Protocol (SMTP) to provide such a service. Specifications related to SMTP commands and the mail transfer process implemented by SMTP is provided in the RFC.
826	Defines specifications to convert IP addresses used by the global Internet to LAN addresses or Ethernet addresses by using the Address Resolution Protocol (ARP).
854	Defines specifications to implement a terminal emulation program that enables computers to work on remote processes using a terminal provided by the Telnet protocol.

TABLE A.1   CONTINUED

RFC Number	Description
896	Defines specifications to overcome the Silly Window Syndrome by using congestion control methods. This RFC standardized the Nagle's Algorithm.
903	Defines specifications to enable diskless workstations to identify their IP addresses by using their hardware address. To implement this address resolution, the Reverse Address Resolution Protocol (RARP) is proposed in this RFC.
904	Defines specifications for implementing a routing protocol, called Exterior Gateway Protocol (EGP), which enables exchange of routing information between autonomous systems.
950	Defines specifications for implementing subnets within a network for allocating subnet IP addresses to the computers in the subnet instead of acquiring individual IP addresses for each computer.
959	Defines specifications to implement sharing and transfer of files from remote computers using the File Transfer Protocol (FTP). The RFC proposes specifications for implementing file transfer, access, and user authentication to provide security during file transfer.
1058	Defines specification for implementing a routing protocol called Routing Information Protocol-Version 1 (RIP 1), which routes datagrams based on the distance-vector algorithm.
1094	Defines specifications for accessing files from remote computers using a protocol developed by Sun Microsystems called Network File System (NFS). The RFC provides specifications for porting NFS by using Remote Procedure Call (RPC) built on External Data Representation (XDR).
1112	Defines specifications for implementing transmission of datagrams from a computer to multiple computers identified by a multicast group.
1157	Defines specifications that enable network management using Simple Network Management Protocol (SNMP). The RFC provides information on the SNMP architecture and the elements of the protocol that are used to implement network management.
1282	Defines specifications to implement remote login facilities by using the Rlogin protocol. The RFC provides information on the remote login process implemented by Rlogin.
1338	Defines specification for using the existing IP addressing scheme to enable IP address conservation. The RFC proposes a new addressing methodology called supernetting.
1542	Defines specifications for implementing an automated bootstrap process by using the Bootstrap Protocol (BOOTP).
1577	Defines specifications for implementing IP and ARP over an Asynchronous Transfer Mode (ATM) environment.
1583	Defines specifications for routing datagrams using the Open Shortest Path First (OSPF) protocol.

APP

A

TABLE A.1 CONTINUED

RFC Number	Description
1644	Defines specifications that propose a transaction-oriented service that improves efficiency in the process of establishing and terminating TCP connections. To implement this feature, the RFC proposes an extension to TCP in the form of TCP Extensions for Transactions (T/TCP).
1732	Defines specifications for RIP Version 2 that provides additional security features for RIP.
1771	Defines specifications for implementing an inter-autonomous system-routing protocol called Border Gateway Protocol (BGP).
1784	Defines the standards to implement a simple file transfer mechanism that implements file transfer without advanced features such as user authentication implemented by FTP. To implement such a mechanism, the RFC proposed the implementation of Trivial File Transfer Protocol (TFTP).
1889	Defines specifications for implementing a real-time data transmission protocol called Real-Time Protocol (RTP) that enables real-time transmission of multimedia files.
1932	Defines specifications for implementing IP over the ATM framework.
1939	Defines specifications to enable computers to access and retrieve mail from a mail server by using the Post Office Protocol-Version 3 (POP3). Apart from POP3 commands, the RFC defines the process that must be implemented to achieve mail retrieval.
2002	Defines specifications for implementing mobility to IP addresses by using the Mobile IP framework.
2060	Defines specifications that enable computers to access and modify e-mail from a mail server by using the Internet Message Access Protocol (IMAP). The RFC provides information on IMAP commands, process, and mailbox-related information.
2131	Defines specification for enabling computers to obtain configuration information from a server by using Dynamic Host Configuration Protocol (DHCP). The RFC provides information on how DHCP implements server-based workstation configuration.
2205	Defines specifications for implementing a resource reservation mechanism called Resource Reservation Protocol (RSVP) to provide Quality of Service (QoS) for an Internet Service Provider's (ISPs) client.
2332	Defines specifications for implementing a mechanism for detecting network addresses provided on Non Broadcast Multi Access (NBMA) networks by using the Next Hop Resolution Protocol (NHRP).
2401	Defines specifications for implementing IP Security on the Internet by providing a security framework called IPSec. The RFC provides information on how IPSec can be implemented.
2402	Defines specifications for implementing authentication on IP datagrams transmitted using IPSec. The RFC provides information on the Authentication Header (AH) extension to an IP datagram.

TABLE A.1   CONTINUED

RFC Number	Description
2406	Defines specifications for implementing confidentiality on IP datagrams transmitted using IPSec. The RFC provides information on the message format of Encapsulated Security Payload (ESP).
2409	Defines specifications for implementing encryption key management by using the Internet Key Exchange (IKE).
2460	Defines specifications that propose the implementation of the next version of IP called IPv6.
2616	Defines specifications that enable transmission of data in a hypertext format by using the Hypertext Transmission Protocol (HTTP). The RFC provides information on the process enabling hypertext transmission and the options for headers and status code messages.
3022	Defines specifications for implementing a Network Address Translator (NAT) that enables translation of external and internal network IP addresses.

APP

A

APPENDIX

LOCAL AREA NETWORKING BASICS

LOCAL AREA NETWORKS

Networking technologies have made a profound change in the way we live. With the aid of computers, you can run businesses without ever leaving home. To make such a scenario possible, a number of interdependent technologies, such as transmission control, messaging, file transfer, and so on, come into play. However, all these technologies work within a networking framework defined for transmitting data over a limited network. This networking framework is called a Local Area Network (LAN). Networks that implement connectivity between computers located within short distances are termed LANs.

In simple terms, LANs can be described as a network of computers located in close proximity sharing common resources, such as printers or scanners. Networks implemented in most business organizations follow this model where a LAN connects the computers used on the office network and share printers and other common network resources. LANs are known to provide highly reliable and quick data transmission features that enable file transfers or messaging facilities between the connected computers. LANs can be physically organized in accordance with the requirements of the organization implementing the LAN. However, based on the method of transmitting data between the computers in a LAN, four LAN architectures or topologies have been proposed: ring, star, tree, and bus.

On ring topologies, data is transmitted starting from the sending computer to all the computers in the network one after the other forming a closed loop or ring (see Figure B.1). For example, if there are computers C1 to C4 in a ring topology, data is transmitted starting from C1 to C2, C3, C4 and back to C1. On a star topology, computers communicate by transmitting data to an intermediate device, such as switch, hub, or any computer. In this way, computers are logically arranged in a star formation (see Figure B.1). Tree topologies are similar to star topologies except for the fact that each computer linked to a hub or a switch can also control other computers like nodes and branches on a tree (see Figure B.2). The bus topology defines the simplest logical LAN architecture among all topologies. In a bus topology, data can be transmitted to all computers on the network one after the other. A bus topology can be described as an open-ended ring topology that does not loop into a ring (see Figure B.2). Figures B.1 and B.2 show the different topologies that can be implemented on LANs.

To implement data transmission on various topologies, two prominent networking protocols have been developed. These include Ethernet and Fiber Distributed Data Interface (FDDI).

ETHERNET

Robert Metcalfe and his colleagues at the Xerox Corporation's Palo Alto Research Center (PARC) conducted research on enabling all computers located in the Center to connect to the laser printers developed by Xerox. The outcome of this research resulted in a networking protocol that provides connectivity to computers located in close proximity. After leaving Xerox Corporation, Metcalfe continued his research and was able to obtain corporate support from Digital Inc, Intel, and Xerox to develop Ethernets as one of the most effective and efficient local area network technologies.

Figure B.1
The ring and star topologies.

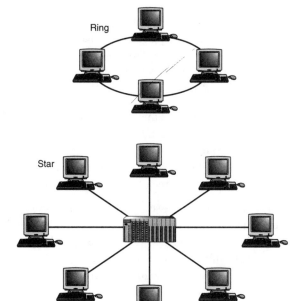

Figure B.2
The tree and bus topologies.

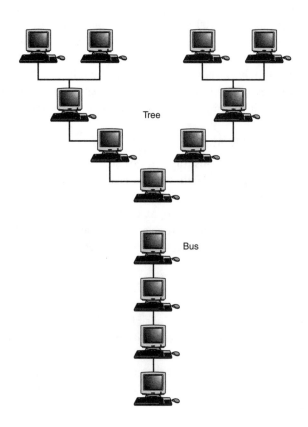

> **Note**
>
> The word *ether* in the term Ethernet was coined by Metcalfe to convey the fact that Ethernet can act as a communication medium that can transmit data to connected computers in a manner similar to ether existing in space that enables the propagation of electromagnetic waves through space.

To transmit data on Ethernets, a protocol named Carrier Sense Multiple Access Collision Detect (CSMACD) is implemented on Ethernet LANs. As the name suggests, CSMACD provides connectivity from one computer to all the computers in the network. In addition, CSMACD enables the detection of a condition called collision detect where data transmitted from two or more computers on the same physical medium collide.

To understand how collisions happen it is essential to know that on LANs, computers connect to a single cable that runs through the entire network. In this way, all computers are interconnected to one another. Therefore, computers must use this primary cable as the only physical medium through which they can communicate, which might result in a collision. This condition can be described as analogous to train accidents where trains traveling in opposite directions on the same rail track might collide if they do not change tracks.

To avoid collisions, the carrier sense feature provided by CSMACD enables computers to detect if other computers on the LAN are using the primary cable. However, if the cable runs over a distance of more than 200 feet, it is impossible for computers to detect if the cable is in use by other computers. This is because data travels at the rate of 100 feet per nanosecond. Therefore, when transmitting the second bit, two computers located more than 200 feet apart might still transmit potentially colliding data simultaneously. When collisions occur, CSMACD provides a backoff feature that enables computers to restrict data transmission for a predetermined time limit. In this way, collision conditions can be remedied.

FIBER DISTRIBUTED DATA INTERFACE

The American National Standards Institute (ANSI) developed the Fiber Distributed Data Interface (FDDI) as a LAN protocol with the first proposals for FDDI being submitted in June 1983. FDDI implements data transfer by converting electrical pulses from computers into light and transmitting light over fiber optic cables. In FDDI terminology, a single ray of light entering a fiber optic cable at a certain angle is called a mode. FDDI provides two fiber optic cable types for transmitting light over the cables, namely, single mode and multi-mode fiber optic cables.

As the name suggests, multi-mode cables transmit multiple rays of light simultaneously. In contrast, single mode cables can support the transmission of only one ray of light at a given point. However, when multiple modes are transmitted, the ray arrives at its destination at different instances causing a condition called modal dispersion. This condition requires receiving computers to manage the receipt of data at different time instances, although data had been sent at the same time from the sending computer. In contrast, modal dispersion is non-existent in single mode fibers because of the fact that only one ray of light is transmitted at a given time.

In addition to the modal fibers, FDDI defines specifications that act as an interface between the higher layer protocols and the physical medium. For example, the specification on Media Access Control (MAC), first proposed in February 1986, proposes specifications for managing algorithms, frame formats, frame checksums, and so on. The Physical layer protocol (PHY) defines specifications for translating electrical pulses into light and vice versa. PHY was first proposed in August 1985. Specifications related to the physical medium components, such as optical component, fiber cables, and so on are defined in the Physical-Medium Dependent (PMD) specification that was first proposed in June 1988. FDDI also provides Station Management (SMT) specifications that provide rules for configuring FDDI workstations, identifying faults, and recovering from faults.

To learn more about the basics of networking, access
`http://www.cisco.com/univercd/cc/td/doc/cisintwk/ito_doc/`.

TROUBLESHOOTING TCP/IP

So far, you have learned about the functions and the working of protocols in the TCP/IP reference model. You know how the protocols interact with one another to transfer data. Although the protocols have been designed to address problems that might occur during data transmission, errors can occur for various reasons. These can include a faulty cable, improper functioning of a component, and incorrect configuration settings. The root cause of the problem needs to be identified and an appropriate solution needs to be applied to it.

The process of isolating a problem and applying corrective measures is known as *troubleshooting*. The problems must be solved so that network users experience minimum inconvenience. The following sections provide generic information on troubleshooting and preventive measures you can implement to avoid problems apart from a few utilities that can be used for troubleshooting.

To apply a corrective measure, one needs to have a good understanding of the steps involved in data transfer. Data transfer could be done across computers on the same network or across different networks. All the operating systems come with different tools and utilities that can be used by the network administrators and technicians to trace a problem.

The first step in the troubleshooting process is to identify the hosts between which the problem occurs. After the hosts are identified, the next step is to determine the layer in which the problem occurs. For example, a faulty cable might be the cause of the problem in the Network layer, whereas an improper IP address might be the problem in the Internet layer. Another problem is that a layer cannot bypass the layer directly above or below it and communicate with the other layers directly. For example, the protocols in the Application layer of the TCP/IP reference model cannot bypass the Transport layer to communicate with the Internet layer. Such disruptions in the sequential order of TCP/IP interlayer communication is possible if Application layer protocols are programmed without following the specifications proposed by IETF.

Communication between two computers is not necessary for transferring files alone. If a client computer needs to access resources on a Web server, the client must establish a link to the Web server. This type of communication involves all five layers of the TCP/IP reference model. The next step is to identify the various tasks to establish a connection between the client and server, and also identify the protocols that are used.

Consider a situation in which a user wants to access the Web site www.xyz.com. The following list discusses the process involved in establishing communication between a user working from a client computer and a server hosting the Web site:

- Processing by the higher layer protocols—The first step is to provide the address of the Web server in the browser, which directs this information to the Application layer protocol. The Application layer protocol that is used in this case is Hypertext Transfer Protocol (HTTP). This protocol uses the Transmission Control Protocol (TCP) in the Transport layer. The default port number that is assigned to the server is 80. For the next level of transmission, the Internet layer needs to be contacted. For this, the

IP address of the Web server is required. Converting a host name to the IP requires the Domain Naming Service (DNS) that operates from the Application layer. The DNS service is invoked to get the IP address.

- Processing in the Internet layer—Internet Protocol adds the required header information for transmitting data and passes it onto the Network layer.

- Processing in the Link layer—The Network layer can transfer data only if the hardware address of the hosts is available. Now, the Address Resolution Protocol (ARP) that operates from the Link layer will be required to map the hardware address with the corresponding IP address and is invoked to perform the process.

- Processing in the Network layer—After the hardware address is found, the connection request is passed from the client to the server through frames.

These steps are implemented to send requests to the server. After the server accepts the request, a port number is assigned to the client and all the transactions with the client must happen using the same port number. The client can start communicating with the server only if the server validates and acknowledges the connection.

Before considering the potential problem areas, it is important to note that if the connection is not established with the server, it must be due to the malfunctioning of the protocols in the layers or it could be due to improper configuration of the settings. A network administrator has to narrow down the problem to one layer and then a protocol. The complexity of the problem will also depend on whether data is sent to a computer on the same network or in a different network.

The steps that are followed to establish a connection with a different host are also dependent on the type of transaction that is involved. For example, the steps that are involved in sending mail by using SMTP differ from the process that is discussed above. The problems that might occur at various TCP/IP reference model levels are as follows:

- Problems related to the Network layer—At the Network interface layer, the problems could be due to faulty cables, improper soldering, or mismatch in the frame headers if different network technologies are used.

- Problems related to the Internet layer—At the Internet layer, the problem could be due to an incorrect IP address, wrong subnet mask, or an incorrect default gateway. The `ipconfig` command can be used to check the configuration settings and to resolve incorrect IP addresses. Connectivity problems must be checked depending on whether the data packets are sent to a host on the same network or on a different network. If there is a problem in transmitting messages to a host on the same network, connectivity to the host can be checked using the `ping <host address>`. If data packets need to be transferred across networks, problems could be due to the default gateway or the destination computer. As a first step in isolating the problem, connectivity between the host and the default gateway needs to be checked. If the connection between the host and the default gateway does not pose problems, the next step would be to check for the connectivity between the host and the destination computers. To resolve this problem, the Ping utility can be used. To start with, check if TCP/IP is installed properly on the local host. If there is no problem with the local host, check whether the connection between the default gateway and the destination computer is problem free.

- Problems relating to DHCP—Administrators need to ensure that every host on the network has a unique IP address. Otherwise, the transmission of data will be hindered. Administrators need to ensure that each client is connected to a single DHCP server only. In certain situations where connectivity problems could cause improper connections to the hub, two DHCP servers might be connected to the same network. To understand the need to avoid two DHCP servers from servicing a network, consider the process that occurs when a host is added to a network. The host requires an IP address to communicate with other computers. Therefore, it sends a broadcast to all computers on the network. The DHCP server answers the client with the IP address of the client. In cases where two DHCP servers are present on the network, the client receives a response from both servers. The client accepts the response that arrives first and ignores the second response. However, if the first response contains an IP address that does not belong to the correct subnet, the host will not be able to communicate with other computers on the network. Apart from ensuring the existence of a single DHCP server for each network, the network administrator can also implement an additional check to overcome this problem. The administrator needs to check the IP address determined by the DHCP server with the corresponding subnet mask before sending the response to the client.

- Other connectivity problems—Connectivity problems might also occur because of improper DNS settings. In Windows 2000 Server, the mapping between the host names and the corresponding IP address is stored on the Windows 2000 Server that is configured as the DNS server. If the Ping command succeeds when used with an IP address but fails when used with the name, the mapping between the name and the addresses must be checked in the DNS database. In addition, you might need to check if the name server settings for the hosts are configured properly.

TROUBLESHOOTING UTILITIES

The Ping utility is used for checking connectivity between two hosts. The Ping command uses ICMP error messages to check for connectivity problems. It can be used only for checking the connectivity at the Internet layer of the TCP/IP reference model. In other words, this command can be used only for checking IP level connectivity. To check if the TCP/IP protocol suite is installed properly on the local computer, use the Ping command followed by the loopback address.

The syntax of the Ping command is ping *IP address* or ping *Host name*. Both commands are used for checking the connectivity to the host. When the second format is used and if the command fails, the name resolution problem must also be checked. This involves troubleshooting the DNS server configuration. In addition to the Ping utility, network administrators can also use the tracert utility to obtain information on DNS resolution and route hops.

→ To learn more about tracert, **see** "Tracert," **p. 71**

The ipconfig command is used to check the configuration settings of a computer. When used with the ipconfig/all option, it displays all the configuration settings of the computer. When you specify the ipconfig/release option in the command prompt, it terminates the DHCP configuration information present on the computer. To enable DHCP configurations, you need to specify the ipconfig/renew option.

Note

App

C

Some networks might need to configure the IP addresses of each computer manually. Such IP address configurations are called static IP addresses. On networks where computers are assigned static IP addresses, the ipconfig release and ipconfig renew commands will fail. The commands are to be used only on networks that implement dynamic addressing using DHCP.

This pathping utility has been introduced in Win 2000 and combines the functionality of both the Ping and the tracert utilities. This command checks for connectivity and also displays the number of hops and the addresses of each one. (See Figure C.1.) In addition, it sends packets to each hop and displays statistics on the packet loss at every hop. Packet loss is displayed in terms of the number of packets sent and received. A network administrator can use these statistics to find problems with each hop and respond appropriately.

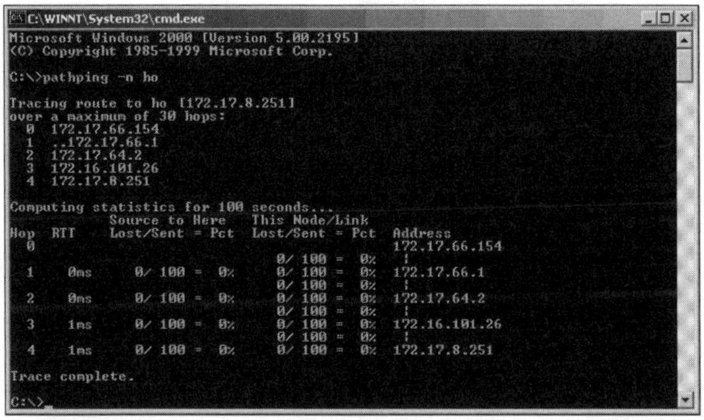

Figure C.1
Network administrators can use the pathping command to identify hops where packet loss is higher.

The arp command is used to check for problems with the hardware address settings on a host. A number of options can be specified with the arp command. To use the arp command, you need to specify arp in the command prompt followed by an option and the IP address of the target computer. Table C.1 describes each of these options in brief.

TABLE C.1 ARP COMMAND OPTIONS	
Option	**Description**
-a *in_addr*	Used to display the IP address and the corresponding hardware address of the target computer. The type of the hardware address is also displayed.
-d *in_addr*	Used to delete the IP address specified by the *in_addr* option from the ARP cache.
-s *in_addr* *eth_addr*	Used to add an IP address indicated by the *in_addr* option to the ARP cache and bind the IP address with the corresponding physical address specified by the *eth_addr* option.
-N *if_addr*	Used to display the ARP entries stored in the ARP cache related to the IP address indicated by the *if_addr* option.

HTTP Status Codes and Header Fields

More than 40 status code messages and 50 header fields have been defined for the Hypertext Transfer Protocol. Table D.1 and Table D.2 list some of these status codes and HTTP header fields. To obtain information on the status codes and HTTP header fields, access RFC 2616 from `http://www.ietf.org/rfc/rfc2616.txt?number=2616`.

Table D.1 describes some of the HTTP status codes.

TABLE D.1   HTTP STATUS CODES

Status Code	Description
200	Indicates that the HTTP server has successfully processed the request.
201	Indicates that the request has been successfully processed and that the request has resulted in the creation of a new resource specified as a URI provided in the Entity field of the HTTP response message.
202	Indicates that the request has been accepted for processing but the processing on the HTTP server has not been completed. The actual result of the process is not indicated by another status message.
204	Indicates that the request has been successfully processed. However, the HTTP server does not specify any resource in the Entity field of the response message. However, the response might include updated metadata information.
300	Indicates that the response includes multiple resources located in different locations on the HTTP server. The client can choose the resource based on its requirements.
302	Indicates that the requested resource has been found on a temporary location on the HTTP server. However, the location might be changed in the future. The client needs to send Request URI messages to ascertain the correct location of the requested resource.
303	Indicates that the requested resource is present in another URI and that the client needs to use the GET method to obtain the resource indicated by the URI.
305	Indicates that the required resource can be accessed through a proxy server specified by the Location field of the HTTP message.
400	Indicates that the request contains a malformed URI and is termed as a bad request, which should not be repeated by the client without modification to the URI.
401	Indicates that the request message sent by the client requires the client to go through a user authentication process. The HTTP server responds with a WWW-Authenticate field in the response message that contains a challenge querying the user account.
403	Indicates that the server is able to process the request but does not intend to continue with the process.
404	Indicates that the HTTP server is unable to locate the required resource indicated by the URI specified in the request.
405	Indicates that the HTTP server does not allow processing for the method indicated in the Request-Line field for that specified resource URI.

TABLE D.1   CONTINUED

Status Code	Description
406	Indicates that the HTTP server can provide the requested resource, which might not be acceptable to the client because of the specifications indicated in the Accept field of the request message.
407	Indicates that the client must authenticate itself by providing information about its proxy server.
500	Indicates that the HTTP server is unable to proceed with processing the request because of an unexpected internal error.
502	Indicates that the HTTP server was not able to obtain the requested resource that is located on another server.
503	Indicates that the HTTP server is not available for processing the request because of overload or maintenance.

Table D.2 describes some of the HTTP header fields.

APP

D

TABLE D.2   HTTP HEADER FIELDS

Fields	Description
Accept	Specifies data formats that can be accepted as a response by the client.
Accept-Charset	Specifies a character set that can be accepted in the response to the request made by the client.
Accept-Encoding	Specifies an encoding that specifies restrictions on the content that can be provided in the response.
Accept-Language	Specifies the human readable language that must be used to provide the response for the request.
Accept-Ranges	Specifies a range of units that can be provided to obtain a range of requests required by the client.
Age	Specifies the time value that indicates the time that has elapsed since the HTTP server generated the response.
Allow	Specifies the methods that are supported by the resource requested by the client.
Authorization	Specifies the authentication information provided by the user agent in response to a 401 status message from the HTTP server.
Connection	Specifies information on the connection settings required by the client for a specific connection.
Content-Length	Specifies the length of the body field in a request or a response message.
Content-Language	Specifies the human readable language in which the content provided in the body of the message is specified.

TABLE D.2   CONTINUED

Fields	Description
Content-Location	Specifies the location of the resource, indicated by a URI, requested by client if the resource is not located on the HTTP server but can be accessed from another location indicated by the URI.
Etag	Specifies an entity tag value for the variant data requested by the client.
Expect	Specifies the server behavior that is expected by the client.
Expires	Specifies a date and time value after which the response message is considered to have expired. This feature is used by the proxy or a user agent to determine whether the cache of response messages maintained by the proxy or the user agent needs to be updated.
From	Specifies the e-mail address of the user who has made the request through the user agent.
If-Match	Specifies a match condition that can be used by the method specified in the request message to verify the existence of the entities previously supplied by the HTTP server.
If-Modified-Since	Specifies a match condition that is used to identify and retrieve resources from the HTTP server that have been modified since the time value indicated by the header field.
If-None-Match	Specifies a match condition that indicates that the HTTP server must supply resources that do not match the list of resources specified in the header field.
If-Range	Specifies a condition that enables the client to obtain a resource that is specified by the range of units provided in the header field.
If-Unmodified-Since	Specifies a condition that instructs the HTTP server to return the resource that has not been modified since a particular date provided in the header field.
Server	Specifies information on the software being implemented on the HTTP server.
User-Agent	Specifies information on the user agent that sends requests on behalf of the user. The field is used for providing appropriate responses that are compatible with the user agent, also called a Web browser.

PROGRAMMING STRUCTURES FOR DATA FORMATS

The following syntax descriptions provide sample C or C++ data structures that represent various protocol message formats. To implement Internet Protocol (IP), you can use the following data structure:

```
struct ipdtgrm
    {
    unsigned char ipver;
    unsigned char tos;
    short iplen;
    short id;
    short fragofst;
    unsigned char ttl;
    unsigned char protoc;
    short checksm;
    char *srcaddrs;
    char *destaddrs;
    unsigned char data;
    };
```

The Internet Control Message Protocol messages can be represented as data structures, displayed in the following syntax:

```
struct icmpmsg
    {
    char type;
    char code;
    short checksum;
    short msgid;
    short sqncenum;
    char *gtwaddr;
    char *param;
    char *padlen;
    int rsv=0;
    char *data;
    };
```

The following data structure can be used to represent the contents of a Transmission Control Protocol (TCP) segment:

```
struct tcpseg
    {
    short srcprt;
    short destprt;
    long seqnum;
    long acknum;
    char offst;
    char flag;
    short advtwindow;
    short checksum;
    short urgentptr;
    char data[1];
    };
```

Address Resolution Protocol (ARP) and Reverse Address Resolution Protocol (RARP) datagrams have similar structures that can be represented as follows:

```
struct arpmsg
    {
    short hdwtyp;
    short protoctyp;
    char hdwaddrlen;
    char protocaddrlen;
    short op;
    char *sendhdwaddr;
    char *trghdwaddr;
    char *sendprotocaddr;
    char *trgprotocaddr;
    };
```

TCP Application Ports

The International Assigned Number Authority (IANA) maintains port numbers by organizing them into well-known port numbers, registered port numbers, and dynamic port numbers. The following list provides a brief description of each port number type:

- Well-known port numbers—Assigned to processes or programs developed by a limited number of privileged users. Well-known port numbers range from 0 to 1023.

- Registered port numbers—Must be obtained from IANA for programs or processes developed by any user. Registered ports range from 1024 to 49151.

- Dynamic ports—Used by programs as temporary or ephemeral ports that can be used to send or receive data as and when required. Numbers ranging from 49152 through 65535 can be used as dynamic ports.

Table F.1 provides a list of some of the well-known port numbers.

TABLE F.1 SOME WELL-KNOWN PORT NUMBERS

Port Number	Protocol
18	Message Send Protocol (MSP)
20	File Transfer Protocol (FTP Data port)
21	File Transfer Protocol (FTP Control Port)
22	SSH Remote Login Protocol
23	Telnet
25	Simple Mail Transfer Protocol (SMTP)
33	Display Support Protocol (DSP)
38	Route Access Protocol (RAP)
39	Resource Location Protocol (RLP)
49	Login Host Protocol
50	Remote Mail Checking Protocol
53	Domain Name Server
67	Bootstrap Protocol (Server)
68	Bootstrap Protocol (Client)
69	Trivial File Transfer Protocol (TFTP)
70	Gopher
79	Finger
80	Hypertext Transmission Protocol (HTTP)
92	Network Printing Protocol (NPP)
93	Device Control Protocol (DCP)
97	Swift Remote Virtual File Protocol (SRVFP)

TABLE F.1   CONTINUED

Port Number	Protocol
109	Post Office Protocol Version 2 (POP2)
110	Post Office Protocol Version 3 (POP3)
111	SUN Remote Procedure Call (RPC)
115	Simple File Transfer Protocol (SFTP)
119	Network News Transfer Protocol (NNTP)
123	Network Time Protocol (NTP)
143	Internet Message Access Protocol (IMAP)
152	Background File Transfer Program (BFTP)
161	Simple Network Management Protocol (SNMP)
179	Border Gateway Protocol
194	Internet Relay Chat Protocol (IRC)
209	Quick Mail Transfer Protocol (QMTP)
213	Internet Packet Exchange (IPX)
220	Interactive Mail Access Protocol v3(IMAP3)
264	Border Gateway Multicast Protocol (BGMP)
359	Network Security Risk Management Protocol (NSRMP)
363	Resource Reservation Protocol (RSVP) Tunnel
389	Lightweight Directory Access Protocol (LDAP)
413	Storage Management Services Protocol (SMSP)
434	Mobile IP–Agent
443	HTTP over TLS/SSL
444	Simple Network Paging Protocol (SNPP)
469	Radio Control Protocol (RCP)
537	Networked Media Streaming Protocol (NMSP)
546	Dynamic Host Configuration Protocol v6 Client (DHCP6 – Client)
547	Dynamic Host Configuration Protocol v6 Server (DHCP6 – Server)
554	Real Time Stream Control Protocol (RTSCP)
563	Network News Transmission Protocol over TLS/SSL (NNTPS)
574	FTP Software Agent System
631	Internet Printing Protocol (IPP)

APP

F

For a complete list of registered, well-known, and dynamic/private port numbers, access
http://www.iana.org/assignments/port-numbers.

GLOSSARY

Absolute Uniform Resource Locator (URL)   A partial URL containing information on the file path starting from the root directory on the server.

Accelerated open   A connection establishment technique used by T/TCP that reduces SYN and ACK segment exchanges in a typical TCP connection.

Access network   A network consisting of all the user computers and not more than two routers. The routers on an access network do not manage datagram routing from the sending to the destination computers but only route datagrams to the next hop router.

Accessing messages   The process of reading and manipulating messages from the mail server.

Acknowledgement frames   A special frame type that is used to confirm the receipt of data.

Acknowledgement packets   A packet type that acknowledges the receipt of other packets.

Active close   The process of initiating the connection terminating action.

Active open   The process of initiating the establishment of a connection.

Adaptive bridge   A kind of bridge that is capable of determining the kind of frames that must be forwarded.

Adaptive retransmission algorithm   A weighted average method used for determining the timeout value.

Address resolution   The process of mapping a software address to the corresponding hardware address and vice versa.

Agent-driven negotiation   A process that requires the user agent (which is the browser) to send a request to the server, which verifies its capabilities and sends a response indicating all the possible features it can support.

Alias expansion   The process of identifying the correct mail address in the electronic mailing list.

Anonymous File Transfer Protocol (FTP)   A type of FTP operation that enables anonymous users to log on to FTP sites.

ARP cache   The location on the local hard disk of a host that contains a list of IP addresses and the corresponding physical addresses.

ARPAnet   The predecessor of the Internet, which was initially established with four computers located in the University of Utah, the Stanford Research Institute, University of California, Los Angeles, and the University of California, Santa Barbara.

American Standard Code for Information Interchange (ASCII)   A method of representing the letters of the English alphabet with numbers ranging from 0 to 127.

Asynchronous Transfer Mode (ATM)   A connection-oriented network that allows multiple computers to access each other simultaneously without allowing broadcast of data from one computer to multiple computers existing on its network.

Atomic data types   See *Simple data types*.

Automatic configuration   A method of dynamic allocation of IP addresses implemented by DHCP to allocate IP addresses for the clients on the network.

Autonomous system (AS)   A set of routers under a single technical administration using an interior gateway protocol (IGP), common metrics to route packets within the AS, and an exterior gateway protocol (EGP) to route packets to other autonomous systems.

Autonomous system number   A number that uniquely identifies an autonomous system.

Bandwidth delay product   An equation which specifies that the Round-Trip Time (RTT) value must be multiplied by the minimum bandwidth available on the receiving computer.

Bandwidth   The capacity of a network to transmit data, which is measured by recording the total size of data that is transmitted over a network within a fixed time limit.

Basic Encoding Rules (BER)   An encoding scheme used for representing the managed objects.

Best-effort data transmission   A data transmission model that is primarily concerned with the reliable transmission of data, regardless of the time taken to transmit data.

Best-effort delivery system   A data transmission system that ensures minimal data loss. Data loss occurs only in exceptional situations, such as problems in the network due to a hardware failure.

Bootstrap Protocol (BOOTP)   A protocol described in RFCs 951 and 1084 and used for booting diskless workstations.

BOOTP client   The computer that requests bootstrap information.

BOOTP server   The computer that provides the bootstrap information.

Bootstrapping protocols   Protocols that are used to obtain the configuration information.

Broadcasting   The process of transferring messages from one computer to all the computers on a network.

Buffered transfer   A process of transferring data in blocks and cumulating the blocks received from the sender before providing it to the higher level protocols.

Buffers   Memory resources allocated by the operating system for cumulating data before using the buffered data. Buffers act as temporary storage memory spaces.

Bursty traffic   A condition where network traffic on connections do not remain constant and exhibit sudden increases in packet volumes transmitted or long idle times where no data transmission occurs.

Character mode   A transmission mode that echoes characters sent to the server.

Classful Internet Protocol (IP) addressing   A method of classifying IP addresses into address classes, such as class A, B, C, D, and E.

Client Message Transfer Agent (MTA)   The MTA at the sender's end that tries to establish a connection with the receiver to transfer mail.

Co-located care-of addresses   Addresses that are registered by a mobile device that directly communicates with the home agent.

Computer name   See *host name*.

Confidentiality   Data transmission mechanism where data is transmitted in a state of secrecy with the contents of the datagrams not visible to intermediate devices. This security feature enables a sending computer to modify the contents of a datagram into a format that is incomprehensible to intermediate devices.

Configurable cards   NICs that enable users to change physical addresses. Examples of configurable cards include pronet and ARCNET.

Congestion avoidance   A congestion prevention technique that stipulates that the congestion window size be increased by one segment on the receipt of an acknowledgement or acknowledgements for all the segments in the window.

Congestion   A condition in which data transmission is severely delayed because of an overload of datagrams on intermediate devices such as routers.

Connection count   An additional header field that uniquely identifies a connection established from a particular computer.

Connection   A communication channel used for data exchange.

Connectionless service   A type of data transmission where a connection is not established with the destination computer during data transmission.

Connection-oriented service   A type of data transmission where a connection is established with the destination computer before commencing data transmission.

Continuous polling   A polling method where the host continues sending messages to the router at specific intervals of time to check whether the router is functioning properly.

Control connection   A connection that is used by the FTP client to provide commands to the server for transferring files.

Convergence   A process of arriving at a consensus among all routers on the routes to be taken by datagrams.

Core network   A network consisting of an interconnection of a number of different routers.

Cyclic Redundancy Check   A mechanism that is used to verify the integrity of the data received by a computer.

Data connection   A connection established between an FTP client and server to execute the file transfer commands exchanged using the control connection. An FTP server uses port 20 to open a data connection. Clients use ephemeral ports to establish a data connection with the server.

Data packet   A packet type that holds the actual data that is required by the client computer or device.

Data packets   See *packets and data packet*.

Datagram   The basic unit of data that can be sent to the Network Interface layer.

Default route   The default path that is taken by a data packet if there are no entries in the routing table.

Delayed acknowledgements   A concept of restricting the instant transmission of acknowledgements and when a segment is received from the sender.

Destination Unreachable   A message type sent by an intermediate device due to network problems.

Dynamic Host Configuration Protocol (DHCP) client   The computer that requests bootstrap information.

DHCP server   The computer that provides the bootstrap information.

DNS caching   The process of storing DNS resolution tables into memory, which enables faster name resolution from the client side.

DNS server   See *name server*.

Domain Name System (DNS)   A technique by which the name of a computer, called the host name, can be mapped to the corresponding IP address by maintaining the mapping between the host names and the IP addresses on a distributed database called the Domain Name System database. In the context of providing a standardized service for resolving computer names, DNS is also referred to as Domain Naming Service.

Domain Naming Service   See *DNS*.

Dotted decimal notation   See *dotted-quad*.

Dotted-quad   A format of representing IP addresses as 4 byte values.

Dynamic binding   The process of mapping an Ethernet address to the corresponding software address.

Dynamic configuration   A method of dynamic allocation of IP addresses.

Electronic mailing list   A list of mail addresses that identifies a group of mail IDs with a single name.

Encoding scheme   The way in which the managed objects are to be encoded during transmission.

End of mail data indicator   The end of the mail message is indicated by a period.

Entity   An object exiting on a Web page.

Entity values   HTTP message values that point to a resource existing in a Web page.

Envelope   The address of the sender and the receiver.

Ephemeral ports   Ports created for a temporary need as and when required by an FTP client.

Error packet   A packet type that indicates the occurrence of an error.

Errors   A method of reporting problems in the network.

Exit codes   A number value to indicate the reason or meaning of the output provided by the Telnet server.

Extra hop problem   A routing anomaly that required a datagram to undertake an extra hop.

Fast retransmit and fast recovery   A technique of recovering from large data losses on Long Fat Pipes.

Fault isolation   The process of finding out the problem in the network due to which data transmission is hindered.

Fault recovery   The process of finding a solution to the problem and solving the same.

Fault tolerance   The ability of an OS to handle exceptional situations such as a hard disk failure.

Feasible successors   Neighboring routers that can forward datagrams along the shortest, loop-free route.

File handle   An opaque software object that represents the file system on the server.

Foreign agent care-of addresses   Addresses that are registered by a mobile device that communicates with the home agent through a foreign agent.

Forward address   The address of the receiver instead of the complete path to be taken by the mail.

Forward path   The route to be taken to reach the recipient to which the messages must be sent.

Fragment zero   The first fragment of a datagram.

Fragmentation   The process of dividing a datagram into multiple groups called fragments.

Fragments   Logical groups of data that are created if the size of the datagram is more than the value that can be accommodated in a frame.

Frame   The basic unit of data transfer defined by the Network Interface layer.

FTP reply code   A response is sent to the client by the server specifying a number code and a human readable message.

Full-duplex communication   Communication that happens in both directions, simultaneously.

H.323 zone   A collection of all terminals, gateways, and multipoint control units that are managed by a single gatekeeper.

Half-duplex communication   Communication that happens in both directions, but not simultaneously.

Header   A component of a datagram that typically provides information on the source and destination of the datagram along with information on the size, time to live, or encryption features that is implemented to secure the datagram.

Hop count   A process of performing a calculation for determining the path length.

Hop-to-Hop   A routing algorithm that routes datagrams based on the subnetting information available hop-to-hop.

Host   A computer that is connected to a network.

Host name   Descriptive name provided for a computer.

Hypertext markup language (HTML)   The structure and layout of the contents in a Web page instructed to the browser.

Hyperlink   A linking object, either from one site to another or within a multipage site, that appears as an underlined text or button in a Web page or document.

Hypertext   A method of linking objects, such as Web pages, software executables, graphics, and documents.

Internet Control Message Protocol (ICMP) redirect message   A message type that informs the host that the data packet can be transmitted through a different route efficiently.

Intermediate devices   Hardware components that can be used to connect networks using dissimilar network technologies, protocols, and media types.

Internet   The largest internetwork in operation that is also termed the Net.

Internet Address   A commonly used query class which is also referred to as IN.

Internetting   See *internetworking*.

Internetwork   A network of networks that can be established by connecting two or more networks.

Internetworking   A process of constructing and managing communication among different networks.

IP (Internet Protocol) addressing scheme   A common addressing scheme that is independent of the underlying hardware or software technology, and includes rules that are used to assign addresses to the hosts and networks.

IP datagram   A type of message sent by the Application layer containing encapsulated data.

IP hourglass model   The TCP/IP reference model represented in the form of an hour glass.

IP multicast   See *network layer multicasting*.

Ipv4 address space   The total number of networks and hosts that can be created by using Ipv4, a version of Internet Protocol.

Iteration   A name identification process where the name server sends a reply back to the client if it is not able to resolve the query and refers the name of other name servers to be contacted by the client to get the query resolved.

Iterative resolution   See *iteration*.

Kludge line mode   A transmission mode that enables line-by-line transmission of data without waiting for the GO AHEAD command from the server.

Layered architecture   A communication system in which the communication process is managed by a group of layers.

Link Control Protocol   A protocol that is used for establishing and testing connections over a telephone line. Both the sender and the receiver must agree upon the format of the LCP packets.

Link layer multicasting   Multicasting that is implemented at the hardware level.

Local area network (LAN)   Groups of connected computers that are located in close proximity. For example, networked computers in a corporate environment that are housed in one building constitute a LAN.

Local delivery   A method of data transmission where the sender transmits the data directly to the destination.

Local flow control   A feature of controlling the display of characters on the client monitor by using control keyboard keys.

Local part   The user ID specified in a message.

Logical mapping   A technique of relating an IP address to the corresponding physical address.

Loopback address   An IP address used to test the TCP/IP software on the local computer.

Mail address   A unique address identifying a user.

Mail gateways   Devices that are used to send mail across systems that do not use the same protocol or connection mechanism.

Mail queue   The location on the mail server in which incoming and outgoing mail is temporarily stored.

Mailboxes   A specific location on the hard disk where mail is stored.

Mailing   The process of sending mail to a user's mailbox.

Manual configuration   The process of statically binding a hardware address to an IP address of a DHCP client by assigning permanent addresses based on a configuration table maintained by the DHCP server.

Maximum Transfer Unit (MTU)   The amount of data that can be transmitted in a single frame.

Media Access Control   The hardware address of an Ethernet card.

Message   Data sent by the Application layer to the lower layer protocols.

Metropolitan area network (MAN)   Network of computers that span different locations in a city and use high-speed connections, such as fiber-optic cables.

Mount protocol   A file management mechanism that uses the port mapper and the file handle to access a remote computer's file system.

Multicast routers   Routers that are configured to handle multicast datagrams.

Multicasting   The process of sending messages from one computer to a specific set of computers.

Multihomed computer   A computer that has more than one NIC, each representing an interface to the network to which the computer is connected.

Multiplicative decrease   Remedial steps used to recover from congestion.

Name server   The server that contains the details for a zone.

Network Interface Card (NIC)   A hardware component that must be attached to every computer for it to connect to a network. The IP address that is assigned to the NIC is the one that uniquely identifies the computer on the network.

Network layer multicasting   Multicasting that is implemented by IP.

Network Management Workstation (NMS)   See *SNMP Manager.*

Network Virtual Terminal American Standard Code for Information Interchange ASCII (NVT ASCII)   An ASCII data format defined in the Telnet specification that is used to format data transferred in the files exchanged between the FTP client and server.

Nonparticipating routers   The routers that did not participate in the routing information exchange process.

Option negotiation   The process of establishing a mutually acceptable mode of transmission between the client and the server.

Packets   Data which is to be transmitted divided into manageable units of data.

Passive close   The process of waiting for another computer to terminate a connection.

Passive open   The process of waiting for another computer to establish a connection.

Path MTU (Maximum Transmission Unit) discovery   A mechanism used to determine the optimum size for avoiding fragmentation during the transmission of data.

Peer-level communication   A method of communication in which the reference model protocols that operate in a layer communicate only with the protocols in the same layer of the other computer.

Persistent connection   A continuously maintained TCP connection.

Phase   A group of transactions that take place between the source computer and the destination computer.

Piggybacking   A method of utilizing segments traveling to a particular computer for transmitting miscellaneous data, such as acknowledgments, which are sent to the same computer.

Pipeline   A feature that enables clients to transmit a sequence of messages without waiting for a response from the server for each request.

Port   A unique number assigned by the OS to the calling application.

Precedence   The component of the Service Type field that is used to set priorities.

Primary name servers   The name servers that contain zone files.

Private internets   Networks that are not connected to the Internet.

Probe timers   Specialized set of timers used to define a time limit for transmitting probe segments.

Protocol stack   A group of related protocols through which a data packet passes in the OSI and TCP/IP reference models.

Proxy agents   An agent that stores information about other agents.

Pseudo header   A conceptual prefix to the UDP datagram header containing the source address, the destination address, the protocol, and the UDP length.

Pseudoterminal driver   A virtual terminal driver that emulates the terminal driver software on the Telnet server.

Quality of Service (QoS)   A contractual agreement between an ISP and its client to provide a networking environment that facilitates real-time data transmission without data loss, jitter, or other transmission hitches.

Queries   A method of troubleshooting networks.

R* commands   See *Remote shell*.

RARP (Reverse Address Resolution Protocol) server   A computer that stores the configuration details of all the computers on the network. RARP servers can respond only to RARP requests.

Read request packet   A message indicating that the client needs to download files from the server.

Read-only community   A community that signifies that the manager can access the MIB (Management Information Base) but cannot modify the values in it.

Read-write community   A community that signifies that the manager can change the values in the MIB, in addition to being able to read the content.

Reassembling   The process of combining all the fragments at the destination.

Recursive resolution   A name identification process where the name server is not authoritative of the host name requested; it passes the request to other name servers, which can resolve the query.

Reference model   A set of specifications that designate how communication should take place on a network. The reference model covers all aspects of communication on a network.

Relative URL   The complete URL for a Web site.

Relaying   The process of transferring mail through more than one destination.

Remote delivery   The process of routing a data packet to a computer on a remote network.

Remote flow control   A server-based data transmission control used to restrict the server from sending data.

Remote shell   Remote Unix-style command primarily used on Unix systems for interaction between trusted hosts. The shell is also called R* commands.

Repeaters   Devices used to regenerate electrical signals that represent data being transmitted.

Request messages   Messages that are used to request routing information.

Request-reply   A type of data transmission where a client computer might request data from a server. In response, the server transmits the requested data.

Resource records (RR)   Special types of records that provide answers to the queries of a client.

Response codes   The response to the messages can be in the form of commands or numbers.

Response messages   Messages that are used to respond to routing information requests.

Reverse address   The reverse path that includes just the address of the sender.

Request for Comments (RFC)   A documentation forum that proposes standards in the form of a numbered document, elicits discussion on the proposed standard, and releases the finalized standards as a Request for Comment. Once published, an RFC cannot be changed but it can be deprecated by another RFC.

Root node   The topmost level in the hierarchical structure of assigning domain names to hosts. The hierarchical structure is defined by Network Information Center (NIC).

Round trip sample time   One complete cycle of a send and acknowledgement receipt for a segment.

Round-Trip Time   A weighted average of round-trip sample times.

Route aggregation   A method of creating subnets within a network and presenting an entire subnet as a single route.

Route   The path that is taken by data to reach its destination.

Routed   A routing daemon program provided by BSD Unix OS that implemented the Routing Information Protocol.

Routing   The process of delivering data from one computer to another.

Routing table   A table stored on every host on the network to maintain a list of routes through which a data packet can be sent.

Remote Procedure Call (RPC) packet   The data unit provided by an NFS application to the Transport layer protocols.

Resource Reservation Protocol (RSVP)   A Transport layer protocol that implements QoS by reserving resources on routers that lie in the path between the sending and receiving computers.

Search engine   An information querying mechanism used to retrieve information based on keywords provided by the user.

Second-level domains   The level of domains that come next to top-level domains in the domain naming convention used by DNS.

Segment header   The first part of a segment that stores important information and instructions.

Segments   Smallest unit of data that can be represented by TCP.

Sending   The process of delivering mail to the computer in which the user works.

Sequence   A structured data type used in a Management Information Base that is created using a combination of different data types.

Sequence of   A structured data type used in a Management Information Base that is created using the same sequence of simple data types.

Server-driven negotiation   The process of determining the best possible response for a request received from the client, which will cater to the client's preferences.

Server MTA   The MTA at the receiver's end that accepts the request from the client MTA.

Signaling   A connection established over a virtual circuit between computers.

Simple data types   Data types that are used to represent the smallest unit of data in the MIB.

Simplex communication   Communication that can happen in only one direction.

Simple Network Management Protocol (SNMP)   An Application layer protocol that enables network administrators to monitor and manage networks.

SNMP agent   A component of the network management system that is used to obtain information about the functioning of the managed device as requested by the SNMP manager.

SNMP manager   A computer that controls the functioning of SNMP agents.

Software address   A 32 bit numeric address represented as four numbers separated by periods. The address provides a unique identity to a computer on a network. The addresses are also called IP addresses.

Sorcerer's Apprentice   An implementation bug that occurs when packets and acknowledgements are transmitted twice.

Source quench   Messages that inform the sending computer of a congestion existing at the router.

Spooling   The process of storing undelivered messages in a mail queue.

Stream mode   A transmission mode where a file is transferred in the form of contiguous bytes.

Structured data types   Data types built using simple data types.

Subzones   A subdivision of zones.

Synch signal   The Data Mark command that indicates that the server must ignore all the packets containing characters received by the server before receiving the packet containing this command.

T/TCP A transaction-oriented extension protocol to TCP that provides quicker connection establishment and termination processes than TCP.

Telnet commands A set of instructions exchanged between the client and the server to manipulate options.

Terminal driver Software that manages the keyboard and hardware device drivers that control monitor display.

Thread A unit of program code in an application that is independent of the program code in the rest of the application. An application can implement any number of threads to manage multiple independent requirements.

Three bears problem The problem of insufficient addresses in the Ipv4 address space.

Throughput The capacity of a network to transmit data measured by recording the total size of data that is transmitted over a network within a fixed time limit.

Time to Live (TTL) A time period set by the name server for cache entries that are held.

Timeout Timer settings set on the sending and receiving computer to record the send and receive time for a datagram.

Timer A mechanism that defines the time limit for retransmitting segments and receiving acknowledgements.

Time-sharing environment A centralized computing environment that provides time sliced processing features for clients.

Token ring Technique of data communication where data transmission is controlled by a token that is passed on the network.

Token A special data packet that moves on the network. If a computer needs to transmit data, it obtains the token and starts transmitting the data.

Top-level domains The domains that are organized under the root node in the domain naming hierarchical structure conventions used by DNS.

Transaction Data exchange between two machines that follow the format of a request and a reply.

Transferring mails The process of sending messages to the mailbox of the user.

Transparent negotiation A negotiation model where the server sends a list of all possible features it can support to the cache maintained on a proxy server.

Trap community A community that enables the SNMP manager to receive trap messages, which are alert signals sent to indicate that an error has occurred.

Triggered polling A polling method where the host sends a request to the router to check the functioning of the router.

Tunnel destination The IP address of the mobile device at the end of the tunnel.

Tunnel header The IP header added to a tunneled datagram.

Tunnel source The source of the IP-within-IP tunnel which is the home agent.

User Datagram Protocol (UDP) datagram A type of message sent by the Application layer containing encapsulated data.

Unicasting The process of transmitting data from one computer to another.

User agent (UA) The component of the mailing system that is used to compose messages and send them to the MTA.

Validation A process where the cache needs to use certain header fields to verify with the server the validity of the cached response.

Virtual private networking The concept of securely connecting two private networks through a public medium of communication.

Wide area network (WAN) Network of computers that operate across different countries and use underwater cable, terrestrial, or satellite connections for communication.

Window size advertisements The process of instructing the receiver about the window size that can be accommodated by the sender.

Wrapped sequence numbers A condition where two datagrams have identical sequence numbers.

Write request packet A message indicating that the client needs to transfer files to the server.

Zone files Databases containing naming information.

Zone transfer The process of replicating a zone file's data from the primary name servers in the secondary name servers.

INDEX

SNMP (Simple Network Management Protocols), SMI (Structure of Management Information), 198-200
SNMP (Simple Network Management Protocols), trap command, 204
SNMP (Simple Network Management Protocols), trap communities, 202
telnet protocols, 150
telnet protocols, commands, 153-157
telnet protocols, modes, 157-158
telnet protocols, NVT ASCII (Network Virtual Terminal ASCII), 153
telnet protocols, options, 157-159
telnet protocols, pseudoterminal drivers, 153
telnet protocols, remote logins, 151
telnet protocols, suboptions, 157
telnet protocols, terminal drivers, 152
telnet protocols, threads, 151
telnet protocols, timesharing environments, 150

application port numbers (TCP), 452-453

application protocols
FTP (File Transfer Protocols), 80-82
HTTP (Hypertext Transfer Protocols), 80
SMTP (Simple Mail Transfer Protocols), 80
telnet, 80

architectures
AS (Autonomous System) routing architectures, 292-293
BGP (Border Gateway Protocols), 318-319

EGP (Exterior Gateway Protocols), 294, 312-314
IGP (Interior Gateway Protocols), 294-308
layered, 16
network
OSI (Open Systems Interconnection) reference models, 16-21
TCP/IP (Transmission Control Protocol/Internet Protocol) reference models, 21-29, 44
TCP/IP (Transmission Control Protocol/Internet Protocol) specifications, 21
peer backbone network, 282
routing architectures, 279
ARPAnet, 280-282
NSFNET, 282
peer backbone network architectures, 282

ARCNET (Attached Resource Computer Network), 30

ARP (Address Resolution Protocol), 28, 35. *See also* **ATMARP**
ARP cache, 36-37
message format, 38-39
programming structures, 449

ARPAnet, 280-282

AS (Autonomous System) routing architectures, 292-293
BGP (Border Gateway Protocols), 318-319
EGP (Exterior Gateway Protocols), 294, 312-314
IGP (Interior Gateway Protocols), 294-308

assigning addresses, 30
CIDR (Classless Interdomain Routing), 32
Class A addressing scheme, 32-33
Class B addressing scheme, 33

Class C addressing scheme, 34
Class D addressing scheme, 34
Class E addressing scheme, 35
classful IP (Internet Protocol) addressing scheme, 32
IP (Internet Protocol) addressing scheme, 30-31

ATM (Asynchronous Transfer Mode), 364, 367-368
AAL5 (ATM Adaptation Layer 5) protocol, 369
ATM ENS (Enterprise Network Switch), 366
cells, transporting, 369-370
IP (Internet Protocol)
ATMARP (Asynchronous Transfer Mode Address Resolution Protocol), 371-374
LAG (Local Address Groups), 375
LIS (Logical IP Subnets), 372, 376
PNNI (Private Network-to-Network Interface) protocols, 376
NNI (Network-to-Network Interface), 365
signaling, 367-368
switches, 365-366
UNI (User-to-Network Interface), 365
virtual circuits
PVC (Permanent Virtual Circuits), 367
SVC (Switched Virtual Circuits), 368
VCI (Virtual Circuit Identifiers), 369

ATM ENS (Asynchronous Transfer Mode Enterprise Network Switch), 366

ATMARP (Asynchronous Transfer Mode Address Resolution Protocol), 371-375

Z

Hey, you've got enough worries.

Don't let IT training be one of them.

Get on the fast track to IT training at InformIT,
your total Information Technology training network.

 | **www.informit.com** |

■ Hundreds of timely articles on dozens of topics ■ Discounts on IT books from all our publishing partners, including Que Publishing ■ Free, unabridged books from the InformIT Free Library ■ "Expert Q&A"—our live, online chat with IT experts ■ Faster, easier certification and training from our Web- or classroom-based training programs ■ Current IT news ■ Software downloads ■ Career-enhancing resources